Off the
Beaten Path®

NINTH EDITION

missouri

A GUIDE TO UNIQUE PLACES

PATTI DeLANO

gpp
travel
Guilford, Connecticut

The prices, rates, and hours listed in this guidebook were confirmed at press time. We recommend, however, that you call establishments to obtain current information before traveling.

To buy books in quantity for corporate use or incentives, call **(800) 962-0973** or e-mail **premiums@GlobePequot.com**.

Copyright © 1990, 1993, 1996, 1998, 2000, 2007, 2009 by Patti A. DeLano
Revised text copyright © 2002, 2005 by Morris Book Publishing, LLC

Off the Beaten Path is a registered trademark of Morris Book Publishing, LLC.

Text design by Linda R. Loiewski
Illustrations on pages 35, 134, and 171 by Carole Drong
All other illustrations by Cathy Johnson
Maps by Equator Graphics © Morris Book Publishing, LLC
Spot photography throughout © Patrick Rolands/Shutterstock

ISSN 1539-8129
ISBN 978-0-7627-4874-7

Printed in the United States of America
10 9 8 7 6 5 4 3 2 1

In memory of my daddy, John Randazzo,
and his ninety years of life with me in Missouri.
With love.

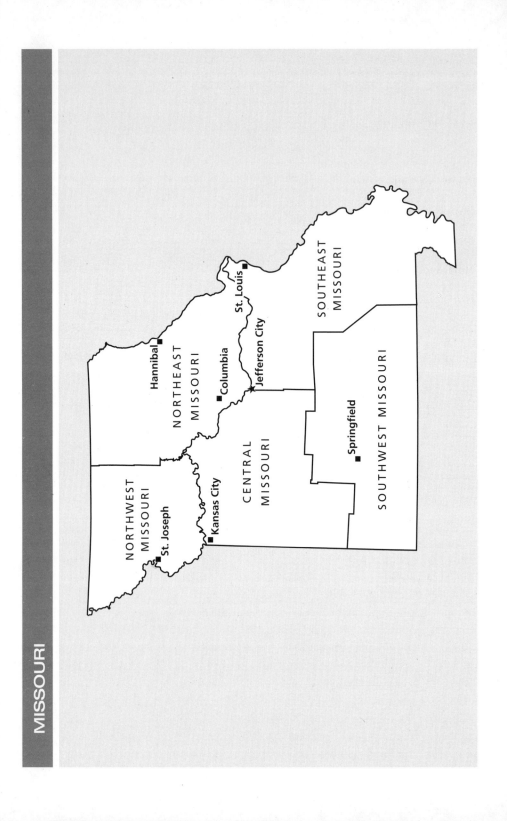

NORTHWEST
MISSOURI

St. Joseph

Kansas City

CENTRAL
MISSOURI

NORTHEAST
MISSOURI

Hannibal

Columbia

St. Louis

Jefferson City

SOUTHEAST
MISSOURI

SOUTHWEST MISSOURI

Springfield

Contents

Acknowledgments vi

Introduction vii

Southeast Missouri 1

Southwest Missouri 57

Central Missouri 99

Northwest Missouri 161

Northeast Missouri 201

Index 240

About the Author 251

Acknowledgments

No book comes easily, but a sense of humor helps. It's especially true of a book of this sort, which requires so many hours of research and fine-tuning. And so, the sense of humor and the camaraderie of my Missouri friends were essential to this ninth edition.

Thank you to William Jewell College in Liberty, Missouri, where, as a "reentry student" scholar with some, shall we say, maturity, I learned the art and craft of writing.

The Missouri Tourism Bureau and the Missouri Departments of Conservation and Natural Resources, not to mention all the visitors' bureaus and chambers of commerce I contacted in hundreds of little towns, made it easier. I want to offer special thanks to the hundreds of people around the state who sent me new information and helped make the ninth edition even more fun. Special thanks also to my friend Ginny Galyean for her work on this update.

It's impossible to include all the wonderful, quirky places I discovered in the course of researching this book—it would weigh five pounds. Others I simply did not know about; still others have recently appeared or, sadly, have gone out of business. If you know of a special place, or a change in an existing listing, please write me or the publisher so that I can add this information when I next update the book. We would love to hear from you concerning your experiences with this guide and how you feel it could be improved and be kept up to date. Please send your comments and suggestions to the following addresses: pattidelano@verizon.net or The Globe Pequot Press, Reader Response/Editorial Department, P.O. Box 480, Guilford, CT 06437. Or e-mail them at: editorial@GlobePequot.com.

Introduction

Think of Missouri and a hundred images tumble forward like candy from a piñata. The Pony Express. The Santa Fe Trail. Lewis and Clark. The Civil War. Frank and Jesse James. Mark Twain (who once said that he was born here because "Missouri was an unknown new state and needed attractions"; we certainly got one in Samuel Clemens).

But all of the images are not from the distant past, flickering like a silent movie through the veil of time. There's Branson, now threatening Nashville as the country music capital of the country, with countless entertainment palaces boasting big-name stars of everything from music to magic. There's even a rodeo restaurant! (I'll tell you how to beat the crowds and traffic and help you find a quiet bed-and-breakfast instead of a computer-located motel.) There's also Kansas City's Country Club Plaza, the world's first shopping center. Kansas City steaks. Charlie Parker and jazz. General John J. Pershing. The Gateway Arch. Barbecue. Writers Calvin Trillin and Richard Rhodes. The founder of Hallmark Cards, Joyce Hall, built an empire, with the international headquarters in Kansas City. Actors Brad Pitt, Kathleen Turner, Bob Cummings, John Goodman, and Don Johnson, as well as Walt Disney, all have ties to Missouri. And, of course, our own Harry S Truman. Now you're on a roll.

What you may not think of immediately are the things I will show you in *Missouri: Off the Beaten Path*. Did you know that J. C. Penney got his start here? There's a museum to honor his modest beginnings in Hamilton. And Jacques Cousteau—when you think of the man, you imagine oceanic dives in faraway places, right? Not always. Cousteau filmed a "deep-earth dive" right here in Bonne Terre and explored his way up the Mississippi and Missouri Rivers as well. Then there's the Kingdom of Callaway, with its postwar ties to none other than Winston Churchill. There are wineries and breweries and distilleries, and there are elegant restaurants and comfort-food cafes that range from fine French to fire-breathing Cajun, with home-style cooking settled somewhere in between.

What we are not is flat farmland, empty prairie, or wall-to-wall cows (or cowboys and Indians, for that matter). There's a rich diversity of landscape here.

Missouri is covered with forests and rolling hills. It boasts more than 5,000 caves, and those are only the ones I know about. The rugged white bluffs along the rivers (the rocky remains of a prehistoric inland sea) and the volcanic formations and underground streams and caverns in the Lake of the Ozarks area are among the most beautiful in the country. The rivers that sculpted all this spectacular scenery are magnets for exploration; the Jacks Fork, Eleven Point, and Current Rivers are designated National Scenic Riverways. Remnant prairies still beckon—patchwork bits and pieces left over from presettlement days, when the big bluestem and gayfeather grasses were tall enough to hide a man on horseback, and the wind-driven waves imitated a sea of grass.

In 1673 Marquette and Joliet came down the Mississippi River and saw the land that is now called Missouri. The Jesuit missionaries (the Mission of St. Francis Xavier) established the first white settlement in Missouri near the present site of St. Louis around 1700. The Mississippi River, which forms the eastern boundary of the state, is still one of the busiest shipping lanes in the world and has been flowing here since before the dawn of time. The upstart Missouri River, on the other hand, was the gift of a departing glacier a short half million years ago; it simply wasn't there before that time. The division between the glaciated plains to the north (rolling and covered with a generous layer of topsoil, also a legacy of the wall of ice, which stole the soil from points north) and the bony Ozark region to the south (rough and hilly with valleys cut deep into rock) is the river that bisects the state from Kansas City to St. Louis. Missouri is where old prairie runs up against the oldest mountain range in the country—a fitting symbol for one of the most historically divided states in the Union.

It was in Missouri that the Civil War was most brutal, issuing as it did from tension that had been building for decades. This pre–Civil War strife between free-state Kansas and the Southern-leaning Missouri was bloody, especially because many Missourians believed that slavery was wrong and worked with the Underground Railroad to help slaves to freedom.

After the Civil War Quantrill's Raiders and such legendary outlaws as Cole Younger and the James brothers continued the bloodshed. The state bears the reminders to this day. Civil War battlefields and tiny cemeteries, with their solemn testimony of the losses of the war, embody the lingering dichotomy between Northern and Southern sensibilities.

Before the Civil War and for some years afterward, the two rivers—the Missouri and the Mississippi—were main arteries of commerce. All of Missouri's large cities began as river ports, with a lively competition between them for business and settlers. Kansas City and its popular hot spot, Westport (formerly Westport Landing); St. Joseph, Lexington, Boonville, and Jefferson City, the capital; and Hermann, Washington, and St. Charles, the first capital, all began as ports on the Missouri. Hannibal, St. Louis, Ste. Genevieve, Cape Girardeau, and New Madrid were ports of call on the Mississippi.

In 1870 national attention focused on the great steamship race from New Orleans to St. Louis. Two boats, the *Natchez* and the *Robert E. Lee,* chugged up the Mississippi and drew crowds all along the way. Today the big rivers and their connecting waterway system make a 22,000-mile navigable network. Almost all year the tugs and barges can be seen wherever public and private docks allow commodities to be moved inexpensively by water. Only winter's ice jams stop the flow of traffic.

Kansas City, Missouri's second-largest city (now outgrowing St. Louis, much to the pride of the western part of the state), had its beginnings as a shipping point on the Kansas (then called the Kaw) River bend of the Muddy Mo, where the river turns sharply east on its trek across the state's midriff. The region known by early explorers as the Big Blue Country was occupied by the Kanza (Kansas) Indians, whose name means "people of the south wind." The peaceful Kanza engaged in farming, fishing, and trapping; they were quickly displaced when settlers began to move in.

westwardbound supplyline

In order to supply settlers moving west, packet boats departed from St. Louis and traveled to Kansas City and westward on the wide Missouri River. More than twenty steamboats a day docked at the wharf facilities in St. Joseph, carrying all types of homesteading materials, beads to trade with the Indians, tools, staple goods, everything that the growing nation needed as the Westward Expansion continued.

Missouri was once as far off the beaten path as one could get, the jumping-off point to the trackless West; beyond was the great unknown. You can still see the tracks of the wagon wheels etched deeply into our soil on the Santa Fe, California, and Oregon Trails.

Now everything's up to date in Kansas City, as the lyrics to a song once told us. A beautifully modern metropolis, Kansas City has more fountains than any city except Rome and more miles of tree-lined boulevards than any other American city. The Nelson-Atkins Museum of Art owns one of the finest collections of Oriental art in the country.

St. Louis, on the other side of the state, has a world-class botanical garden and a rich cultural heritage that rivals any big city in the East. Not surprisingly, St. Louis is proud of its French legacy, a gift of the early explorers.

The KATY Trail (its name is derived from MKT, the Missouri-Kansas-Texas Railroad) begins nearby in Machens, just north of St. Louis. This bicycle and hiking trail follows the old MKT railroad route to Sedalia, 90 miles east of Kansas City. It covers 225 miles of river bluffs, forests, and farmlands with cafes and shops along its route to cater to trail buffs. The KATY is the longest completed rails-to-trails project in the nation. There are so many fun things to do at the recently resurrected towns of bygone days. The scenery along the trail is breathtaking.

The word *Missouri* first appeared on maps made by French explorers in the 1600s. It was the name of a group of Indians living near the mouth of a large river. *Pekketanoui,* roughly its Indian name, means "river of the big canoes," and the Missouri would have required them—it was big, swift, and tricky to navigate before the locks and dams of the U.S. Army Corps of Engineers tamed it, or attempted to.

We don't know how the Native Americans pronounced *Missouri,* and it is about a fifty-fifty split between the state's current residents. In a recent survey a little more than half the population, most in western Missouri, pronounced the name "Missour-uh." The eastern half of the state favored "Missour-ee."

The "Show Me State" carries its nickname proudly. We have a reputation as stubborn individualists, as hardheaded as our own Missouri mules—or so they say—and we won't believe something until you show us. It's not such a bad way to be. Our people, like our agrarian ancestors, want concrete proof—we'll change, all right, but only when we're fully convinced that change is synonymous with progress and that progress is indeed an improvement. The past is definitely worth preserving when it is as colorful as ours.

So I will show you parts of the Show Me State that are tucked away off the beaten path. Some are in the middle of farmland, some are in national forests, and some are in our largest cities. There will be no "Worlds of Fun" or "Six Flags over Mid-America" or Royals' Stadium plugs in this book; such places are definitely on the path, and you can find them on your own. What this book does have is something for everyone, as out of the way—and "far from the madding crowd"—as you could wish.

Restaurant cost categories refer to prices of entrees without beverages, desserts, taxes, or tips. Those listed as inexpensive are $10 or less; moderate, between $10 and $20; and expensive, $21 and over. Places to stay listed as inexpensive are up to $100 per double per night; moderate, $101 to $200 per night; and expensive, $201 and up per night.

No matter where you're from, whether you love a fine Bordeaux or a fine bourbon, whether you like to go in a sports car dressed to the nines or in a pickup truck wearing an old pair of jeans, you will feel at home in Missouri.

Trivia

What's in a symbol? From early civilizations, humans have used symbols to tell the story of what is important in their lives. Missouri has had a unique history and each of the state symbols carries a poignant message of the state and its people. As times change, groups propose symbols to represent products or causes that have evolved and that they believe should be recognized. The newest state symbol is the state grape, which was approved by Gov. Bob Holden on July 11, 2003. The wine-making industry has grown and prospered, leading to the desire for a new symbol.

Missouri Information

- **State flag:** The field is made up of three horizontal bands—red, white, and blue—of equal width. The state coat of arms appears in the center. It is encircled by a band of blue bearing twenty-four white stars.
- **Capital:** Jefferson City
- **Statehood:** August 10, 1821, the twenty-fourth state
- **State bird:** Bluebird
- **State tree:** Flowering dogwood
- **State flower:** Hawthorn
- **State insect:** Honeybee
- **State tree nut:** Black walnut
- **State animal:** Mule
- **State horse:** Missouri Foxtrotter
- **State fish:** Channel catfish
- **State aquatic animal:** Paddlefish
- **State musical instrument:** Fiddle
- **State American folk dance:** Square dance
- **State mineral:** Galena
- **State rock:** Mozarkite
- **State fossil:** Crinoid
- **State grape:** Norton/Cynthiana
- **Missouri Day:** Third Wednesday in October. The day is used to encourage students to study Missouri history and to celebrate the accomplishments of Missouri citizens.
- **Origin of name:** From Native American sounds meaning "owners of big canoes." First applied to the river, then to the land.

- **Nickname:** The Show Me State
- **State song:** "Missouri Waltz," by J. R. Shannon, music arranged by Frederick Logan from a melody by John Valentine Eppel.
- **State seal:** A coat of arms appears on the seal. The shield in the center of the seal is divided into two parts. One half shows a bear and a crescent, representing Missouri. The other half shows the eagle of the United States. The two halves are bound together, or united, by a band ending in a belt buckle. The words in the band—"United we stand; divided we fall"—reflect the need for all the states to be united. Two bears support the shield and stand on a streamer on which the state motto is inscribed. A helmet appears above the shield; the twenty-four stars above the helmet indicate that Missouri was the twenty-fourth state. The date at the bottom in Roman numerals (1820) is the date of the Missouri Compromise.

Southeast Missouri

To call southeast Missouri the most beautiful part of the state wouldn't be fair; beauty is a mysterious commodity based on personal definition, as intangible as smoke. But the region has plenty to offer. There is natural beauty—dappled shade of the national forests, cascades of clear blue springs and rivers, and white river bluffs and volcanic rock formations of the Johnson Shut-ins—that meets everyone's definition of beauty. Antebellum and Victorian homes on wide boulevards grace the oldest cities west of the Mississippi. Both beautiful and historic, southeast Missouri will appeal to all your senses with its food, wine, scenery, and rich and varied past.

When the river was the frontier to the American West, thousands crossed it in search of land, freedom, and a new life. Trappers, traders, explorers, and settlers joined Native Americans in the fertile river valleys and rich prairies.

Enter the state from the east, and you will encounter the St. Louis area, the big city/small town that spreads west on Interstate 70 and south on Interstate 55. Sneak off of these two freeways, and the many small highways branching off from them, to find some of the most charming towns in the state, towns that date from the beginning of the westward expansion of the country.

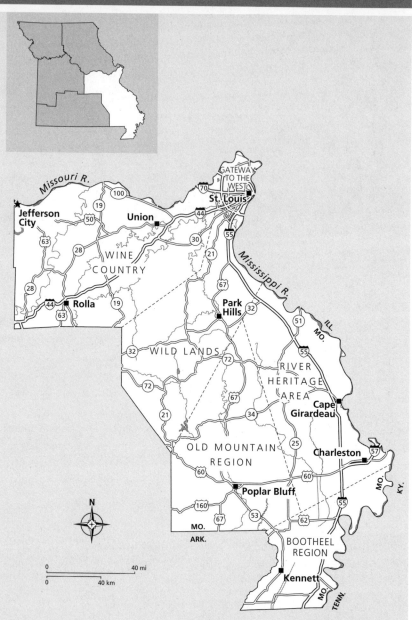

Missouri R.

GATEWAY TO THE WEST

St. Louis

Jefferson City

Union

100

19

50

44

70

30

21

55

Mississippi R.

63

28

WINE COUNTRY

67

28

44

Rolla

19

63

Park Hills

32

51

MO.

ILL.

32

WILD LANDS

72

55

RIVER HERITAGE AREA

72

67

Cape Girardeau

21

34

OLD MOUNTAIN REGION

25

Charleston

57

60

60

MO.

KY.

Poplar Bluff

55

160

67

53

62

MO.

ARK.

BOOTHEEL REGION

N

Kennett

MO.

TENN.

0 ____ 40 mi

0 ____ 40 km

Here you have a choice of crowded festivals and busy public campgrounds or the isolation and peace deep in the national forests and wildlife preserves. Missouri in winter is quietly beautiful and secluded; in summer, it is lively

graduateeducation

The oldest university west of the Mississippi River is St. Louis University, which began as an academy in 1818.

and fun. Adventures here range from scuba diving (yes! deep-earth diving in Missouri!) and white-water canoeing to wine tasting and genealogical searches in the oldest records in the American West. Whether you want to party or to get away from it all, you can wander off the beaten path into southeast Missouri.

Gateway to the West

The bustling **St. Louis** area is still the best place to begin westward exploration. Located on a shelf of riverfront under a bluff, the original city spread to the prairies surrounding it. It was the starting point for the Meriwether Lewis and William Clark expedition in 1804. The history of western expansion begins here where the Missouri and the Mississippi Rivers meet.

St. Louis, founded in 1764, boasts the oldest park west of the Mississippi (Lafayette Park), the second-oldest symphony orchestra in the nation, the world's largest collection of mosaic art at the Cathedral of St. Louis, and one of the finest botanical gardens in the world. The graceful Italianate mansion **Tower Grove House,** at the Missouri Botanical Garden, blooms with color each Christmas season. Local garden clubs, the Herb Society of St. Louis, and others bathe the house in wreaths, seasonal flowers, and greens. Candlelight tours and teas and holiday luncheons are the special events. The home and

AUTHOR'S FAVORITES IN SOUTHEAST MISSOURI

Washington

Bias Vineyards & Winery

Rock Eddy Bluff Farm

Kimmswick

Blue Owl Restaurant and Bakery

Bonne Terre Mines

Ste. Genevieve

Southern Hotel

Broussard's Cajun Restaurant

seventy-nine-acre garden are open for tours every day except Christmas from 9:00 a.m. to 5:00 p.m. For nonresidents of St. Louis County, admission is $8 for adults, $5 for seniors; children younger than age twelve free. (In the new Children's Garden, kids can climb tree houses and play in water jets.) For residents of St. Louis County, admission is $4 for adults, $2 for seniors; children younger than age twelve and members free. There is also an additional charge of $3 for a narrated tram ride; children younger than age two ride free. Write Missouri Botanical Garden, P.O. Box 299, St. Louis 63166-0299 (800-642-8842 or 314-577-5150; www.mobot.org) for more information.

Also in St. Louis are the futuristic Climatron and the country's tallest manmade monument, the **Gateway Arch,** which is also the world's third most popular tourist attraction (but we're talking beaten path here, aren't we?).

It's also a city of firsts. The first Olympiad in the United States was held here in 1904; the first hot dog, ice-cream cone, and iced tea were all introduced at the 1904 World's Fair. Remember "Meet me in St. Louie, Louie, meet me at the fair?" For more information about the city, look for the St. Louis Web site at http://stlouis.missouri.org.

The Gateway to the West (or to the East if you are traveling the other way) was fed by train travel beginning in the early 1800s. More than 100,000 passengers passed through the one-hundred-year-old **Union Station** each day. (Actually, it sounds more like a revolving door than a gateway.)

it'selementary

The first public kindergarten in the country was opened in St. Louis in 1873.

This is a two-block-long gray limestone fortress with a red-tiled roof that features a clock tower that looms 230 feet in the air. When the last train left the station in 1978, the city had a white elephant of gargantuan proportions on its hands. Union Station was too historic to tear down, too expensive to keep up. So, it received a new identity: It is a retail, restaurant, and entertainment complex whose one hundred shops, cinema, restaurants, and nightclubs are drawing tourists downtown again and sparking a revival of the area. There's even a virtual-reality miniarcade, called Virtuality, where you can slip on a helmet and join the cyber world of Zone Hunter.

The Grand Hall, once the waiting room, is now the lobby of the 546-room Hyatt Regency Hotel (800-233-1234). Room rate $119 to $210. Look up at the 65-foot barrel-vaulted ceilings and finely decorated walls. Arches and columns abound. The famous "whispering arch" allows you to whisper to a friend 40 feet away. Sculpted maidens holding gilded torches, floral flourishes, and scrollwork entice the eye. Most impressive is the glowing stained-glass window depicting three women representing New York, San Francisco, and—the one in the middle—St. Louis, the crossroads of America.

Downstairs is the Midway and cavernous Train Shed. More than eighty shops, cafes, and restaurants surrounded by walkways, bridges, fountains, and flowers fill the space. On most weekends strolling mimes and jugglers entertain shoppers. Boats cruise on a man-made lake next to an open-air *biergarten*. And although the trains don't stop here anymore, you can grab the MetroLink public rail system (314-421-6655) right outside for a ride to the Gateway Arch or Busch Stadium. The station can be reached from the airport, so if you are stuck at Lambert Field, you can get on the train and spend a couple of hours enjoying a good meal or just doodling around at Union Station. Stop at the sculpture fountain across the street from the station. It's called *Meeting of the Waters* and it symbolizes the confluence of the Missouri and Mississippi Rivers.

First, though, get a map of St. Louis. Although its many interesting little neighborhoods make the city charming, it also makes it difficult for visitors to find their way.

bowling, anyone?

The history of bowling goes back to the ancient Egyptians and Vikings and, according to the *International Bowling Museum* and *St. Louis Cardinals Hall of Fame* (111 Stadium Plaza Drive, next to Busch Stadium, in St. Louis), maybe even Fred Flintsone. The 5,000-year history of this game is only part of the fun. Your admission includes four free frames of bowling on old-time or modern lanes and two movies. Admission is $7.50 for adults, $6.00 for children age six to twelve, and free for children younger than age five. The museum is open daily from 11:00 a.m. to 5:00 p.m. and until 6:30 p.m. on Cardinals' home game nights. Stadium/museum combo tickets are $7.50 for adults, $6:00 for children. Call (314) 231-6340 or (800) 966-BOWL for information, or visit www.bowlingmueum.com.

The Gateway Arch may not be exactly off the beaten path—after all, it's one of the most-visited tourist destinations in the country—but did you know there's a wonderful museum tucked away underground beneath the Arch in the Jefferson National Expansion Memorial? It's the ***Museum of Westward Expansion,*** which documents our irrepressible urge to explore and settle lands ever farther westward. We didn't stop until we reached the Pacific Ocean; the museum makes you feel you were along for the trip. You'll see artifacts and displays that relate to the Lewis and Clark expedition, which was intended not only to find a trade route to the West but also to discover the natural history of this new land encompassed by the Louisiana Purchase. You'll find Native American and pioneer artifacts as well, and when you come back out blinking into the sunshine, you'll experience a moment of disorientation as you reenter the twenty-first century.

The museum has a $2 National Park fee, and it's more than worth the cost (tram fee to the top of the Arch is a bit higher). Also under the Arch are a fine bookstore and gift shop run by the National Park Service; be prepared to take a bit of history home with you.

Just south of the Arch the *Tom Sawyer* and *Becky Thatcher* riverboats provide one-hour cruises of St. Louis Harbor. Call **Gateway Riverboat Cruises** (800-878-7411) for times and prices. Gateway descends from Streckfus Steamers, which was established in 1884. Captain John Streckfus ran steamboats from New Orleans to St. Paul, Minnesota, and stopped in towns along the way. There was live music aboard, and Streckfus would comb the clubs in New Orleans looking for good musicians. One day in 1918 he found a musician who was fresh out of reform school. His name was Louis Armstrong, and he would work the riverboats *Sidney* and *Capital* until 1922. Legend has it, believe this or not, that the musicians called the new kind of music they played on the Streckfus riverboats "J.S." (for John Streckfus) and that eventually became the word *jazz*.

trivia

If you are doing St. Louis on the cheap, you will be glad to find Forest Park (and the St. Louis Zoo) where many of the attractions are free. You can see a Broadway-type musical that is locally produced at the outdoor Muny Theater (constructed in 1917) at no charge. Just show up early and bring a picnic because 1,620 of the 9,000 seats in this urban hillside outdoor theater are set aside as free on a first-come basis. Check the schedule at (314) 361-1900; www .muny.org. You can take a boat ride around the Grand Basin and have lunch at the Boathouse, a waterside cafe (314-367-2224; www.forest parkforever.org). And if there is a free Live on the Levee concert, you can join the crowd at the riverfront (http:// celebratestlouis.org).

While you history-minded folk are in the neighborhood of the Arch, don't miss the **Old Cathedral Museum,** visible just to the west and still in the Gateway Arch park. Here you'll find some of the finest (and oldest) ecclesiastical art in the country, with works by the Old Masters not uncommon. Documents dating from the beginning of the cathedral as well as photographs on the building of the Arch are all part of the museum. If it's Sunday evening, you can attend Mass at the cathedral at 5:00 p.m. The Old Cathedral Museum (314-231-3251) at 209 Walnut in St. Louis, is open daily from 9:30 a.m. to 3:30 p.m. Donation only.

While you are down on the riverfront, you can even take a five-minute helicopter tour of downtown. Everything you want to know about the Arch is at (877) 982-1410; www.gatewayarch.com.

AUTHOR'S FAVORITE ANNUAL EVENTS IN SOUTHEAST MISSOURI

MAY
Dixon
Bluegrass Pickin Time Music Show,
(573) 579-3574

JULY
St. Louis
Soulard Bastille Day Celebration,
(314) 773-6767;
www.soulardthecity.com

Cape Girardeau
Balloons & Arts, a festival of hot-air
balloons, (573) 334-9233

Sikeston
Annual Jaycee Bootheel Rodeo and
Redneck Barbecue Cook-off, a world-
championship event with top Nashville
recording artists performing nightly,
(573) 471-2498; www.sikeston.net

Ste. Genevieve
Jour De Fete, a large craft fair,
(573) 883-7097

Vienna
Maries County Fair, with rides, music,
demolition derby, and tractor pull,
City Park, (573) 744-5607 or 744-5882

SEPTEMBER
St. James
Annual Grape and Fall Festival,
(573) 265-3899;
www.grapeandfallfestival.com

Sikeston
American Legion Cotton Carnival, (573)
471-9956; www.sikeston.net

St. Charles
MOSAICS, an upscale yet affordable
showcase of fine artisans from across
the state, (636) 946-7776;
www.historicstcharles.com

St. Charles
Annual Missouri State Square and
Round Dance, a weekend of line dancing, square dancing, round dancing,
(636) 723-4493 or (636) 947-2497;
www.historicstcharles.com

OCTOBER
Hermann
Oktoberfest, citywide. First four full
weekends in October, (573) 486-2744;
www.hermannmo.info
Cape Girardeau
Oktoberfest, second full weekend in
October, with craftspeople in traditional
dress, bluegrass music. Black Forest
Village (an 1870s replica village),
(573) 335-0899

DECEMBER
Kimmswick
Kimmswick Historical Society's Annual
Christmas Tour of historic homes, each
with a different theme, (636) 464-8687

St. Charles
Las Posadas, a lighted Christmas walk
with Mary and Joseph, the first Saturday
night in December, (636) 946-7776;
www.historicstcharles.com

The Loop Area

The **Loop** area is fun to visit—the musicians playing on the street, the stars on the sidewalk, and the ambience. Your only regret is that your time here is too short. Even in the middle of the day, the place is alive. What must it be like at night when Chuck Berry is in town?

If you visit the new **St. Louis Cathedral** on Lindell in the Central West End, look up to the heavens, or the ceiling in this case, and you will see the largest collection of mosaic art in the world.

Bailey's Chocolate Bar at 1915 Park Avenue in St. Louis is the go-to place for chocolate lovers everywhere. David Bailey not only has a full bar with more than sixty different beers, martinis, and champagne, but he also turns out desserts using chocolate from around the world. Truffles, ice-cream desserts, and luscious chocolate drinks for those cool Missouri days (Ah, yes, try "La Morte"—Death—a blend of chocolate, vanilla, and cream.). If you don't like chocolate, but your sweet tooth demands something else, there is always a changing palate of whimsical goodies from which to choose. No sweets for you? Then look at the mix-and-match cheese menu and have several types of cheese with the fresh house-made bread, fruit, and nuts. The Chocolate Bar is open seven days a week, Monday through Saturday from 4:00 p.m. to 1:00 a.m. and Sunday from 4:00 to 11:00 p.m. Visit the Web site at www.baileyschocolate bar.com, or call (314) 241-8100.

Also in the downtown area is the **St. Louis Mercantile Library Association** at 510 Locust. If you admire the works of Missouri artist George Caleb Bingham, who captured our history on canvas; if you're awed by the accomplishments of George Catlin as he traveled among the tribes of Native Americans and painted them one by one; if you've wished you could see a painting by one of the famous Peale family of nineteenth-century artists (portrait painter Sarah Peale, in this case, who supported herself for many years here in the past century); you won't want to miss this place.

This is the oldest circulating library west of the Mississippi, and in addition to art, you can find rare books: Americana, westward expansion, river transportation, and so on. Admission is free.

The name doesn't tell you the reason for searching out this place, but once you know, you will be a regular at the **Crown Candy Kitchen** just 1¼ miles north of the Arch at 1401 St. Louis Avenue, St. Louis, where wonderful chocolate candy has been made since 1913. The main attraction here, however, is the city's oldest soda fountain. The business was founded in 1913 by the current owners' grandfather. Their father, George, inherited the business and the three current owners, Andy, Mike, and Tom Karandzieff, grew up here. Nothing much has changed in their world-class milk shakes: homemade ice cream, milk, and your choice of syrups. If you want a "malted," you can have that, too. Of course, what is a milk shake without a chili dog? Andy and Mike can fix that up for you, no problem. The malted has 1,100 calories in it, so what difference will a little chili dog make in the big scheme of things, right? Oh yes, they still make fresh chocolate candy in the winter. Truth be told they make chicken salad to die for and a great B.L.T. if you want to be sensible about lunch. Summer hours are Monday through Saturday from 10:30 a.m. to 8:00 p.m. and on Sunday from 11:00 a.m. to 6:00 p.m. In the winter they close at 8:00 p.m. Call (314) 621-9650 for more information.

As long as we are talking about ice cream, it's only fair to tell you about another favorite. This is the old 1950s walk-up kind of place with a packed parking lot. See a lot of people in bright yellow T-shirts? Lucky you; you have found **Ted Drewes Frozen Custard** at 6726 Chippewa Street, St. Louis. This place has been a St. Louis favorite since 1929 when Ted's father started the business. Drewes is known for the thickest shake anywhere (you can hold it upside down and the spoon and straw stay put), so thick ("how thick is it?") he calls it a "concrete," because it just won't shake. So thick the server wears a hard hat. These thick—very thick—shakes have mysterious names such as the "Cardinal Sin," named for the baseball team (fudge sauce and red cherries), or the "All Shook Up" (Elvis's favorite snack; peanut-butter cookies and banana). But the strawberry shortcake is the best thing on the menu. Hours are from 11:00 a.m. until a little after midnight seven days a week. For information call (314) 481-2652. There's a second location at 4224 South Grand, St. Louis (314-352-7376), if one wasn't enough. This time order the "Abaco Mocha," a tropical treat, or a "Foxtreat" with fudge sauce, raspberries, and macadamia nuts.

The *Admiral* was a rusty old riverboat that had been moored in the city since 1940. When riverboat gambling was legalized in Missouri a few years ago, the *Admiral* was born again. She underwent a $40 million renovation and became **The President Casino on the Admiral.** Her art deco splendor and 1,500 slots and gaming tables are something to behold. You can get off the beaten path (Leonore Sullivan Boulevard on the north lake of the Arch) and onto the river aboard this dockside casino for a $2 entry fee. There is a deli on the B Deck for sandwiches, and the President Buffet features lunch. Dinners range from $8.99 to $11.99. The Galaxy Room features live entertainment. Call (800) 772-3647 or check out the Web site at www.presidentcasino.com for reservations.

The **Loop** area of St. Louis has been evolving during the past thirty years into one of the most exciting and entertaining neighborhoods in the metro area. There has been a renaissance in this neighborhood between the 6,000 and 6,600 blocks of Delmar Boulevard. This area is close to Washington University and is a shining example of urban revitalization. There are more than thirty International and American restaurants whose menus offer Ethiopian, Lebanese, European, Persian, Italian, Nigerian, Greek, Japanese, Thai, Mexican, Korean, and Chinese cuisine. There are also barbecue, deli, fondue, and contemporary and classic American selections. The renaissance continues in the area of entertainment with sidewalk performers and live music. Almost every genre of music can be found in the many clubs along the boulevard. Make sure that you look down at the sidewalk stars, where the nonprofit **St. Louis Walk of Fame** is a shining tribute of more than one hundred stars honoring famous St. Louisians. There are also plaques listing their many achievements, which make this pleasant stroll educational as well as enjoyable. Also impressive and inviting are the many and diverse boutiques. **Pin-Up Bowl** is located at 6191 Delmar Boulevard.

The Mother Road

Getting your kicks on Route 66 is still possible in Missouri. As the famous highway winds from Chicago to L.A., "you go through St. Louis, and Joplin, Missouri . . ." along the Mother Road. In St. Louis, Drewes Frozen Custard has been a stopping place on old Route 66 since 1929. Farther on you can still see the distinctive art deco tile front from the Coral Court Motel at the Museum of Transportation. Next is Route 66 State Park, where the state is creating a museum devoted to roadside Americana. You can walk among Missouri's wildflowers at the Shaw Arboretum of the Missouri Botanical Garden at Gray Summit and visit Meramec Caverns at Stanton as people have been doing since 1933. Spend the night at the circa 1930 Wagon Wheel Motel, which still stands in Cuba.

Perhaps the most beautiful spot on Missouri's portion of Route 66 is Devil's Elbow along the bluffs over the Big Piney River. The 1940s Munger-Moss Motel is in Lebanon, where you can rest up for the drive through Springfield. Be sure to watch for the Shrine Mosque, an Arabian Nights–style edifice that has hosted concerts since the 1950s. On to Carthage's magnificent Victorian homes and the Route 66 Drive-In Theatre. The new highway created some havoc. Spencer is a ghost town now but some of the original roadway still remains from when the town was bypassed.

Joplin, the western end of Route 66 in Missouri, is one of the dozen towns named in the famous song immortalizing the more-than-1,000-mile route that winds from Chicago to Los Angeles through the heart of Missouri.

It is St. Louis's original bowling and martini lounge. Above eight bowling lanes are four projection screens showing music videos and cartoons. If you are a "pinup connoisseur," you will love this place. Many pinups are from original calendars and *Esquire* magazine centerfolds from the 1940s. The menu features Campbell's soup, fresh pizza, and many appetizers, sandwiches, and desserts. Visit their Web site at www.pinupbowl.com. The alley is open until 3:00 a.m. and becomes a party as much as a bowling experience after midnight, with crazy drinks in unusual colors and a mostly yuppie crowd.

Seven galleries and the ***Tivoli Theatre*** are located at 6350 Delmar. The theater has three screens and shows a variety of independent films. The Tivoli has been restored to its original 1924 splendor. Memorabilia makes this a walk down movie memory lane. St. Louis is the hometown of Chuck Berry, and located at 6504 Delmar in the Loop is ***Blueberry Hill.*** Owner Joe Edwards describes this St. Louis landmark as being filled with pop culture memorabilia, including Chuck Berry's guitar and a plethora of vintage 45-rpm jukeboxes. A wide variety of items are available on the menu. There are darts, video games, pinball games, and even a photo booth. The Duck Room features live touring bands, and don't miss the Elvis Room, which features karaoke on Thursday and Friday nights. The restaurant is open from 11:00 a.m. seven days a week; call (314) 727-4444 or visit www.blueberryhill.com.

If hotels and motels are not to your taste, call Lori and Dean Murray to join them in their home at 703 North Kirkwood Road, St. Louis. ***The Eastlake Inn Bed and Breakfast*** is a 1920s colonial inn comfortably set on a wide green lawn surrounded by flowering catalpa, magnolia, and dogwood trees. As the name suggests, the home is filled with original Eastlake furnishings. After a full breakfast you can walk to antiques shops and restaurants for dinner. You'll feel like a St. Louis native. Rooms are $100 to $200. Call (314) 965-0066 for reservations or e-mail info@eastlakeinn.com. Inexpensive.

The Laumeier Sculpture Park is located about 12 miles southwest of downtown St. Louis. The artwork here is grand and huge. Artist Alexander Liberman's *The Way* is made of steel cylinders intended for use as underground storage tanks. He arranged them in bent piles and welded them together. The whole thing was painted bright red. In June and July sculptors work for weeks on detailed sand castles; in winter a fire-and-ice sculpture made of giant ice blocks glows amid roaring bonfires. The ninety-eight-acre park has more than sixty pieces. The wooded path hides human-size sheet-metal figures by Ernest Trova. Special events—symphony, dance, ballet, and theater productions—and a gallery full of indoor art are there, too. A cafe and a museum shop are inside, but outdoors is more fun. Take Interstate 44 to Lindbergh Boulevard, go south ½ mile, and turn right onto Rott Road; the park entrance is ½ mile on the left.

It is open daily from 8:00 a.m. until a half hour after sunset. Gallery hours are 10:00 a.m. to 5:00 p.m. Tuesday through Saturday and noon to 5:00 p.m. on Sunday. Admission is free. For more information: 12580 Rott Road; (314) 821-1209; www.laumeier.com.

Webster Groves is home to an unlikely looking restaurant in an old gas station painted lavender. But venture into **Zinnia,** 7491 Big Bend Boulevard (314-962-0572; www.zinniarestaurant.com), at lunchtime and have an eating experience that has created a word-of-mouth popularity for this place that fills it up daily. The food is pleasantly different, with entrees such as trout zinnia (trout encrusted in pecan, sesame, and pine nuts). Fresh seafood is always on the menu. Desserts demand attention, too. The warm toffee pudding or crème anglaise and caramel sauce are great choices. Zinnia is closed on Mondays.

You should not go to St. Louis without visiting The Hill, southwest of the city, an Italian neighborhood famous for its restaurants. There is no favorite, because it depends on the type of ambience you seek. The best bargain is probably **Cunetto's House of Pasta** at 5452 Magnolia Avenue. It's a good place to take the family, prices are moderate, and the atmosphere is Continental—tablecloths, wine, no bright lights, and a full-service bar. Owner Frank Cunetto calls it gourmet Italian with good prices. His dad and uncle opened the doors more than thirty years ago, and it has been a popular spot ever since. Hours for lunch are Monday through Friday from 11:00 a.m. to 2:00 p.m. Dinner is served Monday through Thursday from 4:45 p.m. to 10:00 p.m. and on Friday and Saturday until 11:00 p.m. Call (314) 781-1135 or visit their Web site at www.cunetto.com for information.

But more interesting is **Charlie Gitto's on The Hill** at 5226 Shaw Avenue because this is where one of the best-loved Italian dishes—toasted ravioli—was invented in 1947. It was a lucky accident that Charlie's father was the maitre d' at this very spot when it was called Angelo's. He and Angelo were messing around with different ravioli recipes and dropped the little stuffed pillows into oil instead of water. Now they are dusted with fresh Parmesan and served with marinara sauce for the perfect appetizer. If you can't decide what to order, ask for the trio of the day, smaller portions of three menu items selected by the chef. Dessert must be tiramisu, Charlie's mama's family recipe made with cocoa, mascarpone cheese, and homemade cookies soaked in sambuca and espresso. Call (314) 772-8898 for reservations, or visit www.charliegittos.com for info.

There are about twenty Italian eateries on The Hill, but if you want to take something home, run in to **Mama Toscano's** at 2201 Macklind and carry out homemade ravioli (sold by the pound), cannelloni, meatballs, and

OTHER ATTRACTIONS WORTH SEEING IN SOUTHEAST MISSOURI

MAGIC HOUSE,

516 Kirkwood Road, St. Louis

CITY MUSEUM,

701 North Fifteenth Street, downtown St. Louis

sauce to go. Nick and Virginia Toscano make thousands of ravioli by hand, rolling out the pasta with a rolling pin. This will be much more appreciated than a T-shirt when you get home. Call (314) 776-2926 for more information. Hours are Tuesday through Friday 7:00 a.m. to 4:30 p.m., Saturday 7:00 a.m. to 4:00 p.m.

Locals all wind up at *Amighetti's Bakery and Café* at 5141 Wilson for the sweet-pepper-laced subs (314-776-2855; www.amighettis.com). Then wipe the cannoli cream off your face and be sure to take the time to visit *St. Ambrose Church,* The Hill's centerpiece about 4 blocks from Cunetto's. It is Lombardy Romanesque and was the first acoustical plaster church in St. Louis. The columns of scagliola plaster look like marble and were made using plaster, ground gypsum, sponges, and polishing. The statues were donated by groups from different villages in Italy.

'Sploding Cannoli

Speaking of cannoli, that ricotta/whipped cream treat that finishes a good Italian meal, it reminds me of a funny, call it "tradition" that has been in my Italian family for years. Who knows where it started or where it will end, but whenever a newcomer joins the family for a holiday meal for the first time—this means girlfriends, boyfriends, fiancees, visiting in-laws, whatever— we all begin to snicker and giggle when the cannoli are served after dinner. The plates are arranged so that the newcomers get a cannoli with cream filling plugging both ends while the center is filled with powdered sugar. Then everyone sits around waiting for the unfortunate person to bite into it and cause an explosion of powdered sugar that covers the face of the unsuspecting victim. I really thought the "tradition" would die with my generation, until my son's mother-in-law joined us for Thanksgiving dinner one year and my little granddaughter, bless her heart, came into the kitchen to whisper in my ear "Gramma, are we going to do the "sploding cannoli trick on Grammy?" Some traditions will never die as long as sons whisper into their children's ears . . .

Across the street is **Milo's Bocce Garden,** where locals gather. When you settle in with one of the restaurant's Italian sausage sandwiches or anchovy pizzas to watch the bocce leagues play, it sounds—and feels—as though you have crossed the Atlantic.

It's not all about food here on The Hill, though. St. Louis designer Nina Ganci imports yarn from Italy among other places and makes sweaters that are most unusual. In **Skif,** at 2008 Marconi Avenue (314-773-4401; www.skifo .com), you will find sweaters that can be worn upside-down, inside-out, or held together with chopsticks. The yarns are hand-knit by freelance weavers and then stitched into works of art by a team of designers. They actually look good on anybody and every (real) body of any size, and the asymmetrical shapes can be draped to suit your moods or show off the parts of your body you like. The sweaters are not cheap, starting at $195, but they are one of a kind and will be noticed for sure. This is a working sweater factory not a storefront.

If you prefer to head south instead, you'll find St. Louis's own French Quarter in historic **Soulard,** 2 miles south of the Arch on Broadway. There's a dandy mix of period architecture and pubs, cafes, and shops for you to browse in. You can buy everything from turnips to live chickens on Saturday mornings in the busy farmers' market in this French/Irish neighborhood, and finish up at a well-stocked spice shop. Soulard is an old brewery neighborhood where rehabilitated row houses line the streets. The Anheuser-Busch brewery is nearby, and when the wind is right you can smell hops and barley cooking. Soulard also has a large collection of jazz and blues clubs.

For information on many bed-and-breakfasts in the state, you can call Ozark Mountain Country Reservation Service, P.O. Box 295, Branson 65615; (800) 933-8529 or (417) 334-4720, or e-mail them at mgcameron@aol.com. (Kay Cameron is especially helpful if you are touring the Ozarks and headed for Branson. Check her Web site at www.ozarkbedandbreakfast.com.)

Antiques stores line both sides of Cherokee Street for 4 blocks in the funky antiques district south of downtown. Prices here are very affordable, and there are dusty treasures in dark corners and beautifully restored pieces as well. You will find rare books, antique linens and lace, and glassware; shop owners will still haggle on the price of more expensive items.

If you want to stay in the St. Louis area but not in the city itself, there is a cluster of suburban cities nearby. Many of them have bed-and-breakfast inns available. Check out the charming cobblestoned street of downtown St. Charles, once Missouri's state capital and now home to specialty shops and restaurants housed in historic buildings. There are seven B&Bs in St. Charles, located off Highway 70 west of St. Louis. Call (636) 946-7776 for more information.

Now Kansas City isn't the only Missouri city with a dollhouse museum. *The Miniature Museum of Greater St. Louis,* located at 4746 Gravois, has a fine collection of dollhouses and miniatures, many of them painstakingly hand-crafted and donated by local miniaturists. The museum is a bit off the beaten path, but well worth the visit. Hours are Wednesday through Saturday 11:00 a.m. until 4:00 p.m. and Sunday 1:00 until 4:00 p.m. There is a small admission charge. Phone (314) 832-7790 or visit www.miniaturemuseum.org for info.

Okay, it's easy to make jokes about a dog museum, and everyone who writes for a living has given it a doggone good try. But man's best friend deserves to be celebrated, and this canine tribute, the *American Kennel Club Museum of the Dog,* located in the 1853 Greek Revival Jarville House in St. Louis County's Queeny Park, about 18 miles west of the St. Louis riverfront, is worth a visit if you are seeking the best art of dogdom. Begin with the oil-on-mahogany portrait of the ex-Presidential pet Millie, the English springer spaniel who called the White House home for four years. See a sculpted bronze whippet, a massive wooden mastiff (once part of a carousel ride), and many works of art commissioned by breeders of show-winning dogs. Coonhounds, retrievers, and herders join Dalmatians, bloodhounds, and Afghans. Pekingese, wolfhounds, and dogs of every variety, including those of more mixed heritage, are celebrated in paintings, woodcarvings, ceramic figurines, and photographs that show them doing what dogs do—sniffing, running, licking, sleeping, or just being. The gift shop will give you "paws" for thought with posters, stationery, and dozens of trinkets bearing likenesses of dogs and dog accessories (tie clasps made of tiny dog biscuits, for example).

trivia

People streaking along Highway 40 near the Oakland Avenue exit are likely to hit the brakes when they see massive turtles sunning themselves on the banks of the road. These huge terrapins are not waiting to cross the road but are the creations of sculptor Robert Cassilly. If you look closely, the 40-foot-long snapping turtle, slick-shelled stinkpot, red-eared slider, Mississippi map, and soft-shelled turtle have children crawling inside their cave-like mouths, swinging from their necks, and grasping their eyeballs to climb up top their heads. A path leads to a sunken playground full of turtle eggs, some with freshly hatched crawlers emerging from the shells. Stop and visit the Turtles at Forest Park, Oakland Avenue, just off Highway 40 East anytime from sunrise to sunset.

On Sunday afternoons the popular "Dog of the Week" program features a guest breeder, trainer, or veterinarian and a dog for demonstration. A book-and-videotape library allows potential dog owners to judge the merits of various breeds. In the past well-mannered dogs were welcome to tour the gallery with their owners, but because of too many "accidents" that was stopped. The museum is at 1721 South Mason Road, St. Louis, and is open from 10:00 a.m. until 4:00 p.m. Tuesday through Saturday and from 1:00 to 5:00 p.m. on Sunday. Take Interstate 64/Highway 40 west past the Interstate 270 loop, exit on Mason Road, and drive south. Watch for the signs. Admission is $5.00 for adults; $2.50 for ages sixty and older; and $1.00 for children ages five to fourteen. The program begins around 2:00 p.m. Call (314) 821-DOGS for more information.

The **Wild Canid Survival and Research Center** at Washington University's Tyson Research Center is a fifty-acre breeding area for red wolves, Mexican gray wolves, and other canids. The goal is the eventual reintroduction of these beautiful doglike creatures, which are near extinction. The keepers here avoid touching them except for veterinary visits because it is essential to their survival to fear humans. But they do give them names: Anna and Rocky are two of fewer than one hundred Mexican grays left in the world. They are big and strong and watch their puppies closely. Another pair, Alano and Frijole, prance with tails held high to show that this is, indeed, their territory. These canids are the species' last hope for survival. They are kept in fenced enclosures and can be seen from 9:00 a.m. to 5:00 p.m. daily. (Call in advance, because walk-ins are not permitted. Tours are by appointment only.) In May the center is closed for breeding. For more information: P.O. Box 760, Eureka 63025; (636) 938-5900; www.wildcanidcenter.org.

Speaking of carnivores, St. Louis tries to keep up with Kansas City in the world of barbecue. Although admitting some prejudice on the K.C. side, there are those who say that **Phil's Bar-B-Q** (314-631-7725) comes very close to great. So jump on I-55 to the Wilbur Park neighborhood, swing by 9205 Gravois Road, and look for a rustic shack decorated with bowling trophies. It started as a backyard barbecue run by the Polizzi family. Now, three generations later, it is still the place to have ribs. The sauce is sweet and tangy and very close to great on the pork shoulder sandwich.

Florissant, just north of downtown St. Louis, is so called because the first inhabitants found it a beautiful, flowering valley. It still is—but that's not all the town has to offer. Jesuit father Pierre Jean DeSmet, champion of the Indian nations, founded the **Old St. Ferdinand's Shrine.** It's now open to the public at 1 Rue St. Francois, Florissant; (314) 837-2110.

If you just want to get out of St. Louis for a bit, here's a day trip an hour southwest of the city that you might enjoy. Take I-44 and get off on U.S. Highway 50 near **Union.** A mile or so up the road is the **Union Italian Market,** 317 US 50, Union (636-583-3252), brimming with such goodies as homemade pastas, imported groceries, and bulk spices. Owners Mary Viano Kellerman and her son, Timothy, will enjoy meeting you. Next is **Rosebud** and a batch of antiques shops on either side of the highway.

Wine Country

Wine Country towns cluster along the riverbanks like hardy grapes on vines. The towns of Defiance, Augusta, Washington, Dutzow, Marthasville, New Haven, Berger, and Hermann all have wineries that produce a variety of wines, both dry and sweet. The Seyval makes a crisp medium-bodied wine similar to a Chenin Blanc. The Vidal, a full-bodied wine with fruity characteristics, is somewhat like an Italian dry white wine. The Vignole is more versatile and can range from the style of a German Riesling to a sweet, late-harvest dessert wine. The Norton (Cynthiana) grape produces rich, full-bodied red wines, the Chambourcin a medium-bodied red with a fruity aroma. The Concord and Catawba produce sweet wines.

Outside St. Louis on I-44 West is the town of *Eureka,* home to more than sixty antiques and craft shops. Pick up a complete list of shops at the first one you spot as you come off the interstate. This town could be a one-stop, shop-till-you-drop experience, but that would be crazy, because you are now heading into an antiques-hunter's heaven.

The *Eureka Antique Mall* is at 107 East Fifth Street, North Outer Road, West Eureka (636-938-5600), and is followed by *Wallach House Antiques* at 510 North West Avenue in Eureka (636-938-6633), filled with old and new finds. There are several more antiques shops in town, so just ask around. Another fascinating stop is the *Firehouse Gallery and Antiques* at 131 South Central Avenue, Eureka (636-938–3303) with limited-edition artwork.

Midwesterners seem to have a deeply rooted preference for all things smoked, probably from all those nights our ancestors spent around a campfire. Who can resist a terrific country ham, hickory-smoked bacon, or a tender slab of ribs? You won't have to if you pay a visit to the *Smoke House Market* at 16806 Chesterfield Airport Road in Chesterfield (636-532-3314). Everything is smoked the natural way, with no preservatives and real hickory smoke. Smoked pork chops, lamb chops, Cajun sausage, along with the ribs and bacon, are available in the shop. Owners Thom and Jane Sehnert planned it that way, and Jane's got the background for it; her folks had owned the business since 1952. Hours are Tuesday through Sunday 9:00 a.m. to 8:00 p.m.

The Sehnerts branched out and opened *Annie Gunn's* next door, a grill with an Irish theme, complete with Irish potato soup and a menu of unusual sandwiches and meat from the smokehouse. The most popular is the Boursin burger, which is covered with highly spiced garlic and herb cheese. And there is the Braunschweiger sandwich, the Cajun sausage sandwich, fabulous smoked lamb chops, ribs, Reubens, French dips . . . and the list goes on. To find the smokehouse, follow your nose, or if your sniffer isn't highly trained, follow Highway 40 to the Airport Road exit and double back; it's about 30 miles west of St. Louis. Put your name on the restaurant waiting list before you shop at the smokehouse. Annie Gunn's is a popular place for locals and visitors alike.

Highway 100 along the Missouri River is a beautiful drive any time of year because of the white sycamores marking the river's course; in autumn it's spectacular. The Missouri River Valley deserves plenty of time; there's a lot to see and experience.

St. Albans is an anachronism, a tiny, planned community founded in the 1930s by the Johnson Shoe Company family. Five thousand acres of gorgeous rolling hills and meadows reminded Mr. Johnson of an area in England known as St. Albans, and he made it into a working farm. It is some 30 miles west of the city limits of St. Louis on Highway 100, an easy day trip and a destination not to be missed.

Attractions in Washington and Herman

Aficionados of French cuisine may remember Le Bistro in the town of Chesterfield. Restaurateurs Gilbert and Simone Andujar closed that place when highway work made it difficult to reach, but take heart. Simone spotted the lovely gardens of St. Albans and chose the location for **Malmaison,** St. Albans (636-458-0131). (Those whose French is a bit tenuous may wonder if the name means "bad house," and it would if it were two words. Native Frenchwoman Simone says that the lovely flowers reminded her of the garden where Josephine met Napoleon in her homeland, a garden named Malmaison.) The dining experience here is superb, as is the food; it's a favorite retreat for St. Louisians. Hours are Thursday through Sunday, 6:00 to 10:00 p.m.

Hard-core bicyclists love the St. Albans region. It is full of challenging hills near the Missouri River and great views.

This is Missouri's Rhineland, the wine-growing region. Both oenophiles (wine connoisseurs) and devotees of wine coolers will enjoy tasting what the state has to offer. There are two schools of thought about Missouri wines: Some say that because a majority of the grapes grown here are European vines on wild grape or Concord root stock (and some self-rooted French hybrids), the wines will be different from California or French wines. Others, purists to be sure (and the Mt. Pleasant Winery falls into this category), say that they will hold Missouri's best wines against California wines in a blind tasting any day and challenge connoisseurs to single them out. They have done so for *Les Amis du Vin,* or Friends of Wine, a wine-tasting club. Whether you are a member of *Les Amis du Vin* or just a wine lover, you will notice that the wines of Missouri are as varied as the vintners who make them, so don't judge Missouri wines by the first place you stop.

The Frene Creek white wines rival those of the Rhine River Valley. Pop wine drinkers will love Missouri's blends of fruit wines. The peach wine made by Stone Hill and the cherry wine by Hermannhoff are a treat over ice in the hot summer months.

Washington Landing was first settled in the early 1800s. Lewis and Clark passed through the site of the future town of **Washington** in search of the Northwest Passage and pronounced it promising because of its excellent boat-landing site. Located in the curve where the great river reaches the most southern point in its course, Washington is still a good place to stop when headed west. Visit the Web site at www.washmo.org or call (888) 7-WASHMO for information.

Don't miss the **Gary R. Lucy Gallery** at Main and Elm Streets, Washington. You may recognize Gary's work if you've picked up a Southwestern Bell telephone book from recent years; his work has graced the cover.

Gary is an extremely thorough young man. To get just the right feeling in his series of Missouri River paintings, the artist took his boat as far upriver as was navigable, to Ft. Benton, Montana, and explored interesting areas from there back to Washington. No wonder his paintings ring true. Gary's paintings are like those of other famous Missouri artists such as George Caleb Bingham and Thomas Hart Benton. He paints river scenes seen only in his mind's eye. Gary mixes research and what he sees from the window of his studio to obtain historical realism. River scenes might include side-wheelers and keelboats, iron-clads running Confederate guns, or a card game on a flatboat. The price of an original is approximately $34,000, and his early works have quadrupled in value. Prints of his oils are for sale in his studio, which is open seven days a week. Call (636) 239-6337 for information, or visit www.garylucy.com.

The circa 1837 building at the corner of 3 Lafayette and 100 West Front Street in Washington first served as an inn. It has since put in its time as a general store, riverboat captain's house, fish market, speakeasy, restaurant, and apartment house. It then came full circle to become a B&B again and has now started its second round as a store. **I.B. Nuts and Fruit Too** is more than just a shop across from the train tracks with a splendid view of the Missouri River. Owners Margaret and Robert Horn have completely redone the old beauty—Robert's an architect—and won the Washington Historic Preservation Commission Award for their restoration. Inside, you can take time to unwind and enjoy gourmet coffee and chocolates while you shop. Margaret offers home decorations, nuts, dried fruits, snacks, coffees, pastas, and an excellent selection of Missouri products that can be assembled into gift baskets and tins for any occasion. Call (636) 390-4438; e-mail ibwash@fidnet.com; or visit the Web site www.ibnuts.com. Smoking is prohibited due to the historic nature of the building and its furnishings. Carolyn McGettigan offers a wonderful selection of coffees, herbs, teas, and dried bouquets at **Not Just Cut and Dried,** which has moved to 227 Elm, Washington, and is twice the size it was before. Sit down and have a steaming cup of cinnamon coffee with Carolyn (she actually roasts the beans here), and she will make scouting Washington easier. Go ahead and have a tasty dessert, too. Hours are 10:00 a.m. to 5:30 p.m. weekdays, 10:00 a.m. to 5:00 p.m. Saturday, and noon to 4:00 p.m. Sunday; (636) 239-9084.

Only fifty years or so after Meriwether Lewis, his dog Scannon, and his partner William Clark passed by this likely town site, Bernard Weise built his home and tobacco store here on Front Street. Now that location holds the **American Bounty Restaurant,** and although the magnificent view is still one of soft moonlight reflecting on the river flowing outside, inside white tablecloths await lovers of fine food and wine. Owner Dan Hacker and chef Brian Manhardt have restored this more-than-100-year-old building at 430 West Front Street, Washington, to its original splendor. The food is what they call "New Age American," or American food with a flair. Examples include encrusted chicken rolled in hash-browned potatoes, nine-way pasta, and red baby-clam sauce. The green-apple cobbler is a specialty, but it takes a half hour to prepare so order it with dinner to ensure it arrives hot when you are ready for it. Lunch is served from 11:00 a.m. to 2:00 p.m. on Saturday, and you can eat on the patio when the weather is nice. Dinner is served 5:00 to 9:00 p.m. Tuesday through Saturday and noon to 9:00 p.m. Sunday. Seating outside in the wine garden creates a romantic mood, and the wine list features both California and Missouri wines. Call (636) 390-2150 for reservations.

You are deep into wine country here, and there is no shortage of wineries along the valley. Most offer tastings; you can choose the ones most convenient for your schedule and location. Some offer unusual wines and are well worth the effort to search them out.

Bias Vineyards & Winery, 3166 Highway B, is in picture-postcard **Berger** (pronounced BER-jer, population 214) just off Highway 100. The setting sun at Berger reflects on the river and rugged limestone bluffs; it throws long shadows across the tilled bottom and along the river. Follow the signs to a wooded hillside. As you start up the hill, there is a railroad crossing at the foot of the rise to the vineyards.

Owner Jim Bias is a retired TWA captain. He and his late wife, Norma, bought the land more than twenty-five years ago when they were looking for a country spot within commuting distance to St. Louis's Lambert Field. It came with seven acres of vines. They invested in a roomful of stainless-steel tanks and went into the wine business. One thing led to another, and soon a banquet business followed.

Saturday night buffet dinners are scheduled on the vineyard grounds from March to December; reservations are a must. Gourmet meals are served along with Bias's wines. Winter is less hectic and cross-country skiing is allowed on the property when the snow comes. Bias offers vine cuttings during the January pruning season for creating wreaths or smoking meats. Call (573) 834-5475 or (800) 905-2427 for more information. Winery hours are 10:00 a.m. to 5:00 p.m. Monday through Saturday and 11:00 a.m. to 5:00 p.m. Sunday.

Bias now has a microbrewery at the vineyard. **Grublkes,** the brewery, makes many types of beer—wheat beer, porter, stout, amber, and pale ale. It is one of the only wineries to have a microbrewery. Visit the Web site at www .biaswinery.com for more information about Bias.

Country Cottage 1840 at 33 Walnut Street is open year-round. Innkeepers Susan and Terry Black offer you your own private cottage with the feel of old-world charm. Sit on the back porch overlooking the old Victorian gardens and relax. It's a great spot to stay for Oktoberfest (the first four weekends of October) or the Holiday Wine Trail in November. Susan will start your day with a fine breakfast and give you directions to everywhere you want to go. Call (573) 834-7602 or visit the Web site at www.countrycottagebb.com. Rooms are $100 to $200.

Next on the road is *Hermann.* To orient yourself, begin at the *Hermann Visitors' Information Center* at 312 Market Street (573-486-2744). Founded in 1836 by members of the German Settlement Society of Philadelphia, Hermann was intended as a self-supporting refuge for German heritage and traditions, a sort of "second fatherland." Visit the Web site at www.hermannmo.com.

George Bayer, who had immigrated in 1830, selected a site in Missouri that resembled his home in the Rhine Valley in terms of climate, soil, and richness of wild grapevines. Bayer and the other German immigrants dreamed of building one of the largest cities in the United States in the Frene Creek Valley.

The dream quickly attracted a variety of professionals, artisans, and laborers who began the task of building the city of their dreams. It never did become that giant metropolis of the immigrants' dreams; now it is a city of festivals. There is Wurstfest in March, Maifest in May, and Oktoberfest in the fall, each drawing thousands of folks from all over the state. Hermann also boasts seven area wineries. Amtrak helps to alleviate traffic on festival weekends.

In winter and on nonfestival weekends, Hermann is just what it looks like—a quaint German town, quiet, and filled with B&Bs, the largest being the huge White House Hotel. You'll find galleries, shops, and brick homes snugged right up to the street, European-style. During the festivals, though, it becomes crowded and noisy, as busy as Bayer's dream city. Portable toilets appear on street corners, and the revelry spills from wineries downtown. If you want to be off the beaten path around here, you should aim at a weekday in the off-season. Then a traveler has this sleepy hamlet all to himself.

You can shop at *Attic Treasures,* 115 Schiller Street, which features everything from old to new. Antiques are blended with new gift items; flower arrangements are available. The shop carries a line of candles too. Hours are Sunday and Monday from noon to 5:00 p.m. and Tuesday through Saturday from 10:30 a.m. to 5:00 p.m. Phone (573) 486-4400.

The *Stone Hill Winery* on Stone Hill Highway just off Twelfth Street, Hermann (800-909-WINE) is owned by Jim and Betty Held. The world-renowned cellars are carved into the hillside and are reputed to be the country's larg-est underground vaulted cellars, and there's a breathtaking view of the town. *Vintage Restaurant* shares the picturesque hilltop location; a huge window at one end of the restored carriage house looks out on Missouri's blue hills. Visit the restaurant's wine cellar to choose the evening's libation, and do scrutinize the menu carefully—there's a cheesecake to die for. Visit www.stonehillwinery .com.

Once in town be sure to see the *Hermannhoff Winery Festhalle,* 330 East First Street, the world's largest wine hall, where you can dance to live German bands every Saturday and Sunday, starting at noon. There is no entrance fee. Enjoy a festival German dinner or a *brat mit krauts* on a bun. Contact the win-ery at (800) 393-0100. Hours are Monday through Saturday from 10:00 a.m. to 5:00 p.m. and Sunday from 11:00 a.m.; www.hermannhof.com.

There are so many great little antiques and craft shops that it would be impossible to list them all and, of course, there are many bed-and-breakfasts in Hermann. Among them is *Birk's Gasthaus,* at 700 Goethe Street (573-486-2911). This Victorian mansion was built by the owner of the third-largest win-ery in the world and is furnished in period antiques, including some 6-foot-long tubs with gold eagle-claw feet, brass beds, and 10-foot-tall doors with transoms. Rooms are $85 to $105 for a king- or queen-size bed, and $65 to $75 for a room with a shared bath, tax included. Visit the Web site at www.birksgasthaus.com. Another B&B, *Montagues,* located in the heart of Hermann's Hispanic District, 301 Schiler Street, also has a coffee shop for latte lovers; (866) 237-2043 or (573) 486-2035. Hours are Wednesday through Saturday 11:00 a.m. to 8:00 p.m. and Sunday until 2:00 p.m.

River's Edge Restaurant is right there, too, at 1720 Ferry Road, Fredericksburg. Steve and Linda Simon serve Cajun food at the riverbank loca-tion Friday from 5:00 to 10:00 p.m., Saturday from noon to 10:00 p.m., and Sunday from noon to 7:30 p.m. Call (573) 294-7207 for more information. (Note: You can take the road or the ferry—off Highway J—to get to River's Edge. Ask Steve or Linda for directions.)

Take US 50 to Loose Creek. Turn onto Highway A and go north 6 miles to *Bonnots Mill.* This tiny town is so picturesque that the Jefferson City Active Sketch Club has come here to work many times. The views of the autumn foliage and the silvery river are glorious. On Iris Avenue, nestled in a valley between two bluffs, the *Dauphine Hotel* has found a new life. The hotel has been part of Bonnots Mill since 1875, but until Sandra and Scott Holder left Washington, D.C., to visit cousins here, it was just another old, two-story hotel with a for sale sign hanging on it. Now it's a bed-and-breakfast inn with seven guest rooms, each with a private bath. In the old days the hotel had one (yes, one) bathroom for all of its guests. "We had to add a lot of bathrooms," Sandra says, "and central heat and air-conditioning. But we are where we want to be, doing what we want to do now." A big breakfast is served in the eat-in kitchen or the dining room from 7:30 until 9:30 a.m. every day. The rooms have the original bead-board ceilings and wood floors and are filled with charming antiques—many of them dating from the original hotel—and handmade quilts. After breakfast guests can lounge on the double-decker front porch. Rooms range from $80 to $125. Call (573) 897-4144 or (877) 901-4144, or visit www .dauphinehotel.com.

Kroutman's Corner Café (573-897-4346), located at 101 Main Street, Bonnots Mill, features catfish fixed seven different ways. Fried chicken and rib eye steaks are also house favorites. Hours are Thursday 11:00 a.m. to 10:00 p.m., Friday 11:00 a.m. to whenever, Saturday 2:00 to 11:00 p.m., and Sunday 8:00 a.m. to 8:00 p.m. *Johnny Mack's Bar & Grill* at 106 Riverview Drive, Bonnots Mill, features smoked ribs and smoked tenderloin. Call (573) 897-2761.

The small village of *Westphalia,* south on U.S. Highway 63, perches like a lighthouse on the hill. There is only one street, with homes built right up to the sidewalk as they are in Hermann. Everything is spic-and-span and a pleasure to the eye—*das ist gut.*

Huber's Ferry Bed & Breakfast, 4 miles north of Westphalia on US 63, at County Road 501, has a magnificent view of two rivers. It sits high on a bluff overlooking both the Osage River and the Maries River. David and Barbara Plummer are the hosts in this 1881 Missouri German-style three-story, redbrick home. The house is near the intersection of US 50 and US 63, is surrounded by four acres, and boasts the original barn, built in 1894, the oldest in the county. There are four rooms, each with a private bath. Barbara's breakfasts begin with the aroma of homemade bread baking, and then there is fresh fruit, eggs, the whole nine yards. Rooms are $70 to $140. There is a new private guest cottage with a two-person hot tub, king-size bed, and fireplace—all for $165 to $195. Call (573) 455-2979 for reservations and directions, or visit www.hubersferry bedandbreakfast.com.

On the east side of US 63 at *Vienna,* the *Americana Antique, Art, and Curio Shop* is a house, garage, and several outbuildings filled to the ceiling with what owner John Viessman calls "stuff": everything you can imagine, from old army uniforms to a reassembled log house that measures almost 6 feet wide by 9 feet tall. But his real passion is books, especially books about Missouri history. There are more than 30,000 books in the house, stacked two deep on floor-to-ceiling shelves running through what was once the home's

Just a-Pickin' and a-Grinnin'

I once knew a man who played a 1932 gold-plated five-string Gibson Mastertone banjo. I took some acoustic guitar lessons at one point in my life, but . . . bluegrass music? I knew nothing about it. I was more into classical guitar and '60s folk music. That is, until he took me to a bluegrass festival near Dixon.

The festival usually begins on a Thursday, but people start showing up a week and a half before that. Usually as soon as there are three people at the site, the music begins. People show up in campers, RVs, and pickup trucks. Tents go up, instruments come out, and the music is nonstop until the last three people leave on Sunday or Monday night.

The actual festival consists of about seventeen well-known musicians and groups that perform on a stage throughout the day and evening, but most of the really good music can be heard at the campsites in the woods—and goes on twenty-four hours a day. Don't plan to sleep much.

Although you do not have to play to enjoy the music, about 70 percent of the people attending do play. That's what makes it so much fun. All instruments are acoustic. People play banjos, steel guitars, and mandolins. People more oriented toward folk music play dobros, hammer dulcimers, and dulcimers and sing the lilting melodies of bygone days. Fiddle players compete with one another. Music is accompanied by both stand-up bass and washtub bass, and even spoons—all instruments early settlers might have made and played.

While there are hundreds of festivals throughout the country celebrating bluegrass music, this is arguably the bluegrass capital of the Midwest when Dixon Park came to be. Some of the finest bluegrass bands play here. This place has a kitchen, guarded toilets and showers, parking for a thousand cars, electricity for 400 RVs, and music, music, music.

A bluegrass festival is a family affair; there's "no alcohol, no drugs, no way!" allowed in the parks. You can literally bring your children to these festivals, have a check-in spot where you meet several times a day, and let them follow their own musical wanderings. It is always a pleasure to see a youngster working with his dad or grandpa. I saw a family with a nine-year-old girl who played the stand-up bass. They dug a hole in the ground for the bass and she stood on two wooden Coke cases to play, but play she did. In that same family, three daughters sang everything the Andrews Sisters ever knew. There were eight people in this family, including grandma and grandpa and a boyfriend, and they all slept in one tent and cooked meals over a fire.

An amateur can join with a group a little above his or her ability at a campsite when they play a familiar melody. You simply turn your back to the group and play softly until you can keep up. When you get the courage to turn around and play with the group, they welcome you and you have moved up a step in your skill level.

There is an admission charge, but it's the best money you will ever spend. Maybe next year I'll take my guitar. Call Scott and Bessie Reeder at (573) 759-3544 for more information about the festivals, held annually over Memorial Day and Labor Day weekends, or visit www.bluegrasspickintime.com.

living room. Volumes on the Civil War, Jewish folklore, and the Black experience in America are crammed together in some kind of order. "It's a constant struggle," Viessman says.

Books are everywhere among the other stuff. There is a whole wall of *Life* magazines in the barn, set up by year so people can find their birthday issue. Viessman still carts stuff home from auctions and yard sales and has been since 1969.

Viessman is at home most Fridays and weekends when he isn't at an auction. Until he quits his day job, the shop is open by chance or appointment; call (573) 422-3505. A large yellow billboard with an eagle on it stands by the driveway. An open sign is posted when he's there. He advises calling first if you're making a special trip.

Antiques lovers heading south on US 63 from Americana Antiques will want to keep a sharp eye out at the first right, Ball Park Road. If the MARIES HOLLOW ANTIQUES AND HERB FARM sign is up, be sure to turn. Follow Ball Park Road across the Maries River bridge and take the first right. Follow the winding country road past an old farmhouse off to the right and through what looks like a private driveway but isn't, down another hill and to the left. What you will find for your 2-mile effort is the wonderful garden-theme shop run by Sandy Shelton that has been featured in *Country Gardens, Country Home, Decorating Garden Style,* and *Romantic Homes* magazines. The shop is usually open Friday, Saturday, and Sunday during the months of May, October, and November. Call (573) 422-3906.

You could also take a quick left on Highway 42 and stop by the **Old Jail Museum Complex,** which got its start during the town's centennial celebration in 1955, when some concerned citizens purchased the old stone jail building to prevent it from being destroyed. The jail became a museum; over time two local log cabins have been moved to the grounds and a large weatherproof shed has been built to house items donated by county residents.

The Old Jail Complex, staffed by volunteers from the Maries County Historical Society, is open Sunday afternoons from 2:00 to 4:00 p.m. from Memorial Day weekend through June and from Labor Day weekend through September and October. Admission is $3. Society members have begun renovating the Old Methodist Church just across Highway 42. They host a crafts festival there in the fall and hope to add other events as progress is made on the structure. Genealogists might enjoy perusing the Historical Society's Record Room, which is open on Wednesdays from 1:00 to 4:00 p.m. and is housed in the basement of the Maries County Courthouse. For more information contact Sharon Wolfe, (573) 422-3679 or visit them on the Web at: www

.rootsweb.ancestry.com/~momaries/maries.htm and http://viennamo.com. While you're in the courthouse, check out the paintings of historic buildings by John Viessman and other local artists.

Kathy and Tom Corey returned home to Maries (pronounced Marys) County after thirty years and built their dream home in the rock-strewn hills above the Gasconade River near Dixon. They decided to share it and a country inn was born. The name, **Rock Eddy Bluff Farm,** comes from the location of the inn. It sits atop a rugged limestone bluff overlooking the river. Here the water curves and quickens over a shoal, then calms into a deeper pool set against the bluffs. A series of large boulders rises above the water (Thox Rock is the largest), which gave this section of the river the name Rock Eddy. The inn offers private access to the Gasconade River, and canoes are available. You can see 10 miles across the river valley between Vienna and Dixon from here. It is more a country retreat than a bed-and-breakfast, with hiking and a horse-drawn Amish spring wagon. Scenic Clifty Creek has worn a natural arch through the bluff. The inn's upper story boasts a pretty view of the river; it offers an upstairs suite that gives the sensation of being snuggled into the treetops, hence the name "The Treehouse Suite." The cost per night for one or two people is $140. The handmade quilts and ceiling fans in this suite create a restful atmosphere. You can relax on the deck and eat breakfast or watch the sun set while soaking in the hot tub dubbed "The Think Tank." The price at the inn is $95.

Turkey Ridge Cottage is away from The Bluff House and has three bed-rooms and a fireplace. It is romantic and quiet. The breakfast room has a stocked fridge or you can dine nearby. One guest left a note saying, "I am convinced that time spent at Turkey Ridge does not count against life's allotted length." The cottages are $155 nightly for two adults, $820 per week.

The Line Camp Cabin is a new addition to the place. It was inspired by a herding cabin in Wyoming. Everything here is just like it was in the 1880s: heat from a wood stove, ice box (with ice), water from a pitcher pump, and light from kerosene lamps. Here you cook, sit in the porch swing, walk to the river, and relive the past. There's even a corral for your horse if you want to bring one along. The cabin is $100 a night ($10 for additional guests) or $540 per week. This is not for everyone, but if you like roughing it a bit, you will love it. It's worth every penny. You will see bald eagles that have been nest-ing there for years and a great blue heron rookery with about fifty nests in the clutch of trees.

E-mail Rock Eddy Bluff Farm at welcome@rockeddy.com or visit the Web site at www.rockeddy.com and see photos of the area. To find Rock Eddy Bluff

Farm on the map, look for a small (nonexistent) town called Hayden off US 63, between Rolla and Jefferson City. Call (573) 759-6081 or (800) 335-5921.

The **Rainey House** at 405 South Main Street, Vienna, is a historic home where you can buy gifts. Hours are Monday through Friday from 9:00 a.m. until 4:00 p.m. and Saturday from 9:00 a.m. until 2:00 p.m. Call (573) 422-6216 or 422-3331.

A favorite local place in Vichy is the **Vichy Wye Restaurant,** open seven days a week, at the intersection of US 63 and Highway 28 (573-299-4720). Tim and Vikki Moeslein offer a smorgasbord on weekends that brings crowds from other towns around here. Diners will find chicken, fish, and ribs, bounteous vegetables, and salads. The menu offers catfish dinners and steaks. The homemade pies are well known around here, too. It's a lovely, scenic drive along US 63, so travel during daylight and enjoy the view.

It's only 9 miles from Vichy to **Rolla** on US 63. Here the famous Rolla School of Mines is located. If you are interested in mines or minerals, it's worth your while to see the museum. Be sure to take the time to see **Missouri's Stonehenge,** a half-scale version of the English one built 4,000 years ago. Missouri's version was built by the school's specialists in the fields of mining engineering, rock mechanics, explosives research, civil engineering, and computer science. It was built to honor the techno-nerds of long ago who built theirs to pinpoint the solstices and changing seasons with moonlight and sunlight falling through precisely positioned stones. The new Stonehenge, however, was built of 160 tons of granite, shaped by cutting torches and high-pressure water jets, and aligned by computer. It also includes an "ana-lemma" solar calendar used by the Anasazi Indians in the American Southwest more than 1,000 years ago and a Polaris window for sighting the North Star. It was dedicated in 1984 on the summer solstice. A member of the Society of Druids offered ancient incantations over this blend of the ancient and ultramodern.

lookingforsilver, theyfoundlead

The early French miners came looking for silver that was rumored to lie along the Meramec River but found instead one of the greatest lead fields in the world. The viburnum trend in the St. Francois Mountains now supplies more than 90 percent of the lead produced in this country, and high-grade zinc is smelted from the slag left from the lead-refining process.

If you are an alumnus of University of Missouri Rolla, then the name of this B&B makes perfectly good sense to you. At least that's what Ron Kohser thought when his wife, Barbara, voiced some doubts about it. **Miner Indulgence Bed** *and Breakfast,* at 13750 Martin Spring Drive in Rolla, celebrates the Miners—Ron is on the faculty—and has plenty of alumni and parents as guests as well. It could be the peach French toast that is often part of the full country breakfast, or the hot cup of coffee on the porch before breakfast, or the swimming pool and hot tub outside the two-story redbrick colonial home that brings people back. Whatever it is you can surf on over on the Web and make up your own mind at www.bbonline.com/mo/miner/ or see it in person: Take exit 184 from I-44 and turn onto the south outer road (which is Martin Spring) and go 1½ miles west. Rates are $85 a night. Call (573) 364-0680 or e-mail the Kohsers at estrest@rollanet.org.

After that have a major indulgence at a *Slice of Pie* at 601 Kingshighway, Rolla, which was begun by a teacher and now serves the best pie you could ever want. Call (573) 364-6203. Or, if you've eaten enough, you can visit the *Museum at the Old Courthouse* at 305 West Third Street, Rolla, which dates from the Civil War. It has an art museum and a batch of little shops inside. Call (573) 364-5977. Learn more about the city of Rolla at its Web site, www.rollacity.org.

Because Missouri is world-famous for its barbecue, it would be important to point out the best of the best all over this state. Missouri has been the center of the meat industry since its beginnings and seeing the stands of hickory and oak everywhere, well, you know, the Show Me State was just made for barbecue. Here in Rolla its *Johnny's Smoke Stak,* 201 West Highway 72, the only barbecue in town at this writing that cooks ribs the way they were meant to be cooked, far from flames and in the low and slow, lazy heat of smoke. As tradition demands, the meat is unsauced and fall-off-the-bone tender right from the pit. Sauce is made here, too, to add to the meat when it is served. Call (573) 364-4838 for hours.

There's a lot happening in *St. James* on Highway 68 east of Rolla, if you are an oenophile (that's a wine lover, remember?). Stop by *St. James Winery,* at 540 Sidney Street (573-265-7912). Jim and Pat Hofherr came here in 1970 with their three children and invested everything they had to begin the winery. After Jim's death in 1994, Pat and her three sons, Andrew, John, and Peter, ran the winery, which won more than seventy-five awards in local, national, and international wine competitions in 1995. In fact, *Bon Appetit* magazine named St. James's 1993 Seyval one of the top fifty wines in the world. Hours are Monday through Saturday from 8:00 a.m. to 7:00 p.m., Sunday from 11:00 a.m. to 7:00 p.m. Winter closing at 6:00 p.m. Call (800) 280-WINE for more information, or visit www.stjameswinery.com.

Heinrichshaus Vineyards and Winery is a family-owned winery specializing in dry wines, including Vidal Blanc and Chambourcin, located at 18500 Highway U, St. James. Heinrich and Lois Grohe are the owners and wine masters. Heinrich is from southern Germany, and their daughter, Peggy, went to school in Switzerland, where she studied wine making. The winery offers fresh grapes in season, Missouri cheeses and sausages, hand-thrown pottery, and original watercolors and prints by Missouri artists. Now this is a full-service winery—wine and cheese, a clay carafe, and original art to enjoy while you picnic on the winery grounds. Spring and fall bring festivals and bike tours to the winery. Call (573) 265-5000 for a calendar of events and directions, or watch for signs; this is on a rural route. A loaf of bread, a jug of wine, and a picnic! Hours are 10:00 a.m. to 6:00 p.m. (every day but Wednesday and holidays).

Ferrigno's Winery and B&B, 17301 Highway B, St. James, is an interesting place to spend some time in the St. James area. Winemakers Dick and Susan Ferrigno grow seven varieties of French hybrid grapes such as the Chambourcin, a red grape, and the Seyval white grape. They now have fourteen acres in vines and make nine wines ranging from very dry to semisweet. Dick's favorite wines are made from the Cynthiana, which is a red grape, and Seyval grapes. Recent DNA testing proved what many winemakers had suspected for some years—that the Cynthiana and the Norton are the same grape. These wines are dry with a definite oak flavor. You may peer through glass to watch the wine-making process at the winery or wander in the surrounding vineyards. Susan serves dinner in the wine pavilion to private groups, and there is always wine, sausage, and other items available for picnics on the grounds. Winery hours are Monday through Saturday from 10:00 a.m. to 6:00 p.m. and Sunday from noon to 6:00 p.m. Call (573) 265-7742 or (573) 265-8050 during the evenings for reservations. The winery is open April through December.

Deep underground in the unchanging atmosphere beloved by spelunkers, a long underground river flows silently through *Onondaga Cave* in the *Daniel Boone State Park,* near *Leasburg* on I-44 east of St. James. This is a place of superlatives: Massive stalagmites rise like peaks from the floor of the Big Room, said to be the largest cave living room in the world. In Daniel Boone's Room the abundance of cave formations is enough to make you shake your head in amazement. Old Dan himself discovered the place in 1798—or rather, he was the first white man to do so. Native Americans had used the area as a hunting sanctuary in earlier times.

Organizers of the St. Louis World's Fair in 1904 encouraged the cave's owners to open it to the public—it was a great hit, as visitors came first by railroad and then by surrey and wagon to explore the wonders.

Bourbon, off I-44, was once a whiskey stop on the railroad—could you tell from the name? Now it's the home of *Meramec Farm Cabins and Trail Riding Vacations.* In the same family since 1811, and now into its seventh generation, this family farm has earned the Missouri Century Farm sign awarded by the University of Missouri to farms that have been in the same family for at least one hundred years.

This is a real working cattle ranch, with critters and all—kids who don't have a grandma in the country will enjoy petting the horses, feeding the ducks, or playing in a real old-fashioned hayloft.

It's great for adults, too. Just enjoy the 10-mile trail (1½ miles follow the river's edge) that adjoins the highest bluffs on the Meramec River. Take a dip in a swimming hole, picnic on a gravel bar, or enjoy canoeing on a section of the Meramec that doesn't require a Class-V rapids expert.

Prices are $80 per couple per cabin ($10 for each additional person). The farm is just an hour's drive from St. Louis. It lies on a bend in the Meramec River near the Vilander Bluffs. A conveniently located five-acre gravel bar is there for people who want to fish and swim. Tubing and canoeing are some of the favorite activities, as are hiking and horseback riding. Ask about the many special packages that let you ride the horse that is native to the area, the Missouri Fox Trotter. According to Carol, these horses really "smooth out the rugged hills." Pervian Paso and Tennessee Walking Horses have joined the scene, too. Horseback riding is $25 an hour; four-hour trips are $90. The three-day package includes two nights lodging and eight hours of riding for two people for $500.

strangeasitsounds

In the Mark Twain National Forest you will see what are called "blossom rocks," moss and lichen-speckled sandstone rocks that appear to have just "blossomed" from the ground. The massive rocks project from the gentle slope of a wooded hillside and appear where other rocks are present. One blossom rock—125 feet in diameter and 50 feet high—is covered with flowers in early spring.

You also can bring your horse with you and Meramec Farms will provide a corral for that member of your family, too.

Carol Springer asks that you call ahead for reservations and directions. This is a working farm, and drop-ins tend to arrive at just the wrong time; but Carol has been juggling it all since 1983, so she must be doing something right. For reservations write Carol Springer, 208 Thickety Ford Road, Bourbon 65441, visit the Web site at www.meramecfarm.com, or call Carol at (573) 732-4765.

Meramec State Park Lodge at **Sullivan,** east on I-44, is an excellent spot for canoeing and exploring, though it is often crowded on summer weekends. Meramec State Park on the scenic Meramec River winds through the rough, timbered hills just east of Little Bourbon.

Missouri is known as the cave state, with more known caves than any other state—5,200 counted so far. There are some twenty-two within the park. One,

Fisher Cave, is open for guided tours; others are protected as habitat for an endangered bat species. (You didn't really want to go in that badly, did you?)

The folks at **Stanton,** farther east on I-44, argue with the people of St. Joseph, who say Jesse James died there. Stanton proponents believe that the murder of Thomas Howard on April 3, 1882, was a clever plot to deceive investigators and authorities—with the backing of then governor of Missouri Thomas T. Crittendon!

Skeptical? Well, that's the true Show Me attitude. Take your pick. Believe that Jesse died in 1951, just three weeks shy of his 104th birthday, or that he was gunned down by his cousin more than a hundred years ago. Of course, DNA testing on the body buried in Kearney proves them wrong, but old legends die hard.

Jesse was a member of Quantrill's Raiders, who captured a gunpowder mill and used the caverns as hideouts; beneath Stanton's rolling hills lies a complex of caves and finely colored mineral formations, as rare as they are beautiful. The nearby Meramec Caverns has guided tours, restaurants, and lodging.

Wild Lands

South from St. Louis you have the choice of I-55 or old U.S. Highway 61. (You can also take I-270 if you want to bypass the city entirely.) However you get there, don't miss the museum and displays at **Mastodon State Park** near Imperial; the kids will love it and so will you.

The museum features life-size dioramas, reconstructed mastodon skeletons, Ice Age fossils, and artifacts more than 10,000 years old. Ancient Indians hunted mastodons with stone-tipped spears. This was the first place that archaeologists found definite evidence of them, and it was an important discovery, to say the least. There is a small admission charge for adults. Hours are 9:00 a.m. to 4:30 p.m. Monday through Saturday and noon to 4:30 p.m. Sunday. (Winter hours are in effect January 1 through February 28. The hours are 11:00 a.m. to 4:00 p.m. Monday, Thursday, Friday, and Saturday, and noon to 4:00 p.m. Sunday. The museum is closed Tuesday and Wednesday.)

This area contained mineral springs, which made for swampy conditions perfect for preservation. Large mammals became trapped in the mineral-rich mud, which preserved their remains perfectly as the mud hardened to stone. You can still see the **Kimmswick Bone Bed,** which is one of the most extensive Pleistocene beds in the country and of worldwide interest to archaeologists and paleontologists. Explore the visitor center, too. It offers a life-size replica of a mastodon skeleton, Clovis points, and other remnants of early human occupation. Mastodon State Park (636-464-2976; www.mostateparks.com/Mastodon .htm) is south on I-55. Access to the Bone Bed begins at 1050 Charles J. Becker Drive, Imperial.

Now aim just south for the town of **Kimmswick,** laid out in 1859 by a German named Theodore Kimm. In the early 1880s, Kimmswick's beautiful Montesano Park attracted people from St. Louis by excursion boat. Riverboats and railroads stopped here. But the horseless carriage changed the destiny of Kimmswick; the new highway system bypassed the town and left it to become a sleepy little backwater. Even the trains and boats no longer stopped to trade. Soon the historic steamship *Robert E. Lee* will be permanently docked in Kimmswick. Contact the visitor center in Kimmswick at (636) 464-6464 or visit them on the Web at www.discoverkimmswick.com. Kimmswick's shops and restaurants are some of the best along the riverfront.

Mary Hostetter, owner of the **Blue Owl Restaurant and Bakery** at Second and Mill Streets, says that Kimmswick refuses to be "gobbled up by St. Louis" and works to maintain its individuality as the "town that time forgot." Mary invites you to sit in front of a cheery fireplace and try a few of her specialties.

The building was erected in 1900 and was called Ma Green's Tavern until the 1950s. It was restored in the 1970s and now has warm wood floors that are charmingly out of level and lace curtains in the windows. Railroad-car siding covers the walls, and waitresses dressed in long pinafores serve lunch on delicate blue-and-white china. Mary recently added Miss Mary's Veranda, a Victorian veranda, for outdoor dining. A new dining room has opened, too, so now there are five dining options. There is live German music with Austrian Paul Knopf on the accordion. Parking is available in the restaurant's lot.

The Blue Owl (636-464-3128; www.theblueowl.com) is open year-round Tuesday through Friday from 10:00 a.m. to 3:00 p.m. and Saturday and Sunday from 10:00 a.m. to 5:00 p.m. From country breakfasts and homemade soups (the Canadian cheese soup is marvelous) on weekdays to the wonderful Sunday special of homemade chicken and dumplings, Mary will try to fill you up. If you happen to see the pastry case as you come in the door,

trivia

Built in 1927, the Old Chain of Rocks Bridge was the first bridge to span the Mississippi connecting Missouri and Illinois. The world's longest pedestrian and bicycle bridge, it is 24 feet wide and 5,353 feet long. It was once part of Route 66 and is located 12 miles north of the Arch.

you won't allow that to happen until coffee and dessert. Take a good look at the temple of temptation: Lemon dobosh has eight layers of lemon cake with filling between each and whipped cream on top. There's an Italian cream cake, Irish apple cake, red velvet cake, and the favorite, Death by Chocolate. The Levee High Apple Pie was created to celebrate the great flood of 1993, when the river crested at 39.9 feet against the 40-foot levee. There is outdoor dining May through October.

Walk around Kimmswick; there is a lot to see here, from historic homes and businesses to some fine little restaurants and shops. But keep in mind that everything is closed on Monday. For a look at a local artist in action, visit **Kimmswick Pottery,** 6109 Front Street. Chris Ferbet creates hand-thrown pieces, some from native red clay, which she digs herself. She also carries an international assortment of hand-crafted art. You can watch her working at the pottery wheel or browse around the shop. Call (636) 464-3041 for more details. Hours are Tuesday through Sunday 10:00 a.m. to 4:00 p.m.

Kimmswick Korner Gift Shoppe, at 6101 Front Street, features not only body lotions, watches, and other such neat items, but also a collection of "Lunch at the Ritz" jewelry and Rubel angels. Alongside the gift shop is **Lillie's Cupboard,** featuring a world of chocolate and fudge, coffee, and teas. Hours for both places are 10:30 a.m. until 4:00 p.m. Tuesday through Friday and until 5:00 p.m. on Saturday and Sunday, and both can be reached at (636) 464-2028.

Swing southwest on U.S. Highway 67 at Crystal City to the city of **Bonne Terre,** a year-round resort, as interesting in December in the middle of a blizzard as it is in the heat of a 100-degree summer day. There isn't all that much to see—aboveground, that is. But if you choose **Mansion Hill** as your first stop and meet owners Doug and Cathy Georgan, the town will come alive for you. In this setting it would have to; the mansion occupies the highest point in Bonne Terre, on 132 acres of timber in the Ozark foothills. Each room has its own view of the estate (which has a 45-mile view of the surrounding area). Four huge fireplaces warm the great rooms.

The 1909 mansion was built by the lead-mining baron responsible for **Bonne Terre Mines** (the world's largest man-made caverns), which honeycomb the earth under the city. Hand-dug with pick and shovel, the mines are now flooded. They are the pride of the Georgans, who also own West End Diving in St. Louis. The mines can be explored two ways in any weather: by scuba diving, as do hundreds of divers who make the trek to Bonne Terre winter and summer, or by walking along the above-water trails. The dive experience

trivia

In Algonquian, the name *Mississippi* means "big river."

The Depot at Bonne Terre

in the mine has been named one of America's Top Ten Adventures by *National Geographic* magazine. For information about this unique experience, call (314) 209-7200 or visit www.2dive.com.

Your first view of the mine is breathtaking; under the crystal-clear water, illuminated from above by electric lights, divers can see all the remnants of the mining days, including ore carts, elevator shafts, buildings—even tools and drills left when the mine was abandoned in 1961. No less a personage than Jacques Cousteau was a guest at the mansion and filmed a dive here. Rooms at the mansion are worth every penny—$275 a night—the place is gorgeous.

From the entrance to the mines, turn right onto Park Street and go to Allen Street. Follow it until you see the old St. Joe Lead Company Headquarters on the right and the 1909 depot on the left. ***The Depot*** is built in the Queen Anne and Stick architectural styles and is on the National Historic Register. The English-style phone booth outside, a caboose, boxcars, and rail lamps and posts give it a nineteenth-century flair. Inside the depot, the Whistle Stop Saloon is filled with train memorabilia and open for banquets only. The second and third floors are part of a turn-of-the-last-century bed-and-breakfast. Call (573) 358-5311 for information. Rooms are $100 to $120 a night. The mansion and depot are filled almost every weekend, year-round, by clubs who travel here to scuba dive. All rooms have twin beds to accommodate the divers. Visit the Web site at www.2dive.com for an exciting tour of everything.

Also in Bonne Terre is the **Victorian Veranda Bed and Breakfast** at 207 East School Street. Hosts Galen and Karen Forney have opened the doors of their elegant old home. Behind the wraparound veranda lies a parlor and gathering room for your relaxation. A full country breakfast is served in the dining room in the morning. Rooms are $105 to $150. Call (573) 358-1134 or (800) 343-1134, or visit www.victorianveranda.com.

Located in an area of the Eastern Ozarks known as the Old Lead Belt, **Missouri Mines State Historic Site** showcases the mining industry in a 19,000-square-foot former mine-mill powerhouse. In 1975, the St. Joseph Lead Company donated twenty-five buildings and the surrounding land to the Missouri Department of Natural Resources. There is also an excellent mineral collection at the museum, as well as a gift shop that sells very reasonably priced specimens. The Missouri Mines State Historic Site is open Monday through Saturday 10:00 a.m. until 4:00 p.m. and Sunday noon until 5:00 p.m. Summer Sunday hours are extended until 6:00 p.m. The museum is located on Highway 32 just outside Park Hills. (The P.O. Box is 492). Phone is (573) 431-6226.

History buffs shouldn't miss the Civil War battlefield at **Fort Davidson State Historic Site at Pilot Knob.** You can still see the outlines of the hexagonal fort built in 1863 by Union forces. Flanked on three sides by high hills, the fort was vulnerable to attack from above, which must have been apparent to Gen. Thomas Ewing. After losing seventy-five men in the Battle of Pilot Knob, he had his soldiers muffle their horses' hooves with burlap and evacuate during the night.

If you happen to be on Highway 32 headed westbound for Dillard Mill, canoeing in Salem, or hiking in the Indian Trail State Forest, you might enjoy shopping in **Bixby** at the **Good Ole Days Country Store** on Highway 32. You will notice the bright red 1946 Missouri Pacific caboose tucked against one side of the store. Owners Tony and Bridget Bohac have modern gas pumps and Model-A vintage pumps (also painted bright red) out front, and inside is the same blend of old and new. Twenty-five cents buys a cup of coffee (on the honor system), while above your head an O-scale model train runs on a track suspended from the ceiling, complete with flashing lights and whistles. There's more to see. Antiques fill almost every available inch of space on the hardwood floors. Out back is an old log cabin turned antiques store, which also houses a collection of minerals from surrounding hills.

Bixby's General Store has never closed since it was first opened in 1906 when the railroad put a siding right next to the store. The store sold everything from casket materials to plows to groceries; locals didn't have to go anywhere else (not that there was anyplace else to go anyway). Now the store has made

A Billion Gallons of Water

On a hill in the Johnson's Shut-Ins Park is the Taum Sauk Reservoir hydroelectric plant. On December 14, 2005, a wall of the basin was breached and one BILLION gallons of water flooded the settlement. The park administrator, Jerry Toops, and his family were swept away in the flood. Jerry's wife, Lisa, saved their small baby by holding her and floating to shallow water. The youngest boy dog-paddled next to her, and Jerry clung to a tree. They all survived. The Goggin's Mountain hiking and equestrian trail and trailhead were not affected and are still accessible to the public. A portion of the Taum Sauk Section of the Ozark Trail has been damaged between Johnson's Shut-Ins State Park and Taum Sauk Mountain State Park. To learn more call (800) 334-6946 or visit the Web site, www.mostateparks.com.

the 100-year milestone. The store still has a lot of convenience items and a good deli for lunch and ice cream (get a real malt to eat in the caboose). Hours are 4:30 a.m. to 7:30 p.m. Monday through Saturday and 12:30 to 6:30 p.m. Sunday. For more information call (573) 626-4868.

One of Missouri's best kept secrets is the ***Arcadia Valley***—and its villages of Arcadia, Pilot Knob, and Ironton—where there are quite a few antiques shops.

Lesterville may be on the map (and it is, south of Arcadia and west of Hogan on Highway 49), but it's really not a town anymore. This unincorporated village is a quiet little place nestled in wooded country that is dotted with old farms and barns. But just down the road is the ***Peola Valley Forge,*** on Peola Road, a combination blacksmith shop and pottery that looks more like a contemporary gallery from downtown St. Louis. Doug Hendrickson makes elegant ironware and, in fact, does a brisk wholesale business in several states. He welcomes visitors—and spectators!—and will accept a commission if you've something special in mind.

Take the old Peola Road at the north end of town (it's the only way you can go) for 3 miles. Watch for circular red, green, and yellow signs. When you cross Yellow Valley Creek, you've found Doug's place. For details call (573) 637-2507, or visit the Web site at www.peolavalley.com. Shop hours are 9:00 a.m. to 4:00 p.m. daily (except Sunday and Monday). Winter hours are "sporadic," according to Doug.

Just up the road from the forge is ***Wilderness Lodge,*** also on Peola Road in Lesterville; a great old-fashioned Ozarks experience that includes Black River canoe and inner-tube floats in its package. The lodge is made of logs, and the cottages are quintessential rounded Ozark-river stone, each with a fireplace. Note:

highestwaterfall inmissouri

Mina Sauk Falls is the highest waterfall in the state. During the wet season the waterfall cascades 132 feet down a series of volcanic ledges into a sparkling clear pool with a rock bottom.

The lodge is closed during the winter. Call (888) 969-9129, or visit their Web site at www.wilderness lodgeresort.com. The lodge is open the first weekend in April through Thanksgiving weekend. Rates are $74 for adults, $35 for children ages one through twelve, and free for children younger than age one. Rates include dinner and breakfast. Float trips are an additional charge.

Highway 49 leads to the town of *Annapolis* and a turn-of-the-twentieth-century home near several rivers and lakes. Innkeepers Sharon, Joe, and Rachel Cluck invite guests of *Rachel's Bed and Breakfast,* 202 Second Street, to share the large common room and the deck or veranda overlooking the attractively landscaped grounds. Rooms are $90 to $145. Call (573) 598-4656 or (888) 245-7771. Their Web site is at www.rachelsbb.com.

Rachel has opened *Black River Cottage,* a cozy three-bedroom bungalow (surrounded by rose gardens) with a fully equipped kitchen which, at $125 a night, is great for traveling families or friends (who are close enough to share a bathroom There is a TV, VCR, and laundry equipment. The cottage sleeps eight people, has a grill and fire pit, is walking distance to fishing, and is only five minutes from the float area on the Black River. It's right next door to the B&B. Call (573) 598-4656 or (888) 245-7771, or visit www.blackrivercottage.com.

Nearby *Ironton* is the home of *Bobby Powell's Jamboree* at 135 South Main Street, where bluegrass music is played. The jam sessions begin at 6:00 p.m. and the show is from 7:00 to 9:00 p.m. Sometimes there is a dinner show, and they begin at 5:30 p.m. Call (573) 546-1441 for details.

Ready for some action? *Bluff View Marina* in nearby *Piedmont* has boats and pontoons for rent. In the summertime (May 15 to September 30) they are open seven days a week from 8:00 a.m. until 6:00 p.m. Even off season you can stop by the trailer and talk to someone about renting. Visit www.bluffviewmarina.com for more information.

The nearby *Johnson's Shut-ins* (north of Lesterville on Highway N) will surprise you with their rugged beauty, which is like terrain you'd expect to find in Maine or Colorado. These worn and convoluted forms have a story behind them; would you believe Missouri once had its own Mt. St. Helens? Prehistoric volcanic eruptions spewed tons of magma, towering clouds of ash, and acid debris, flattening vegetation and covering whole areas with newly formed igneous rock. Some 250 million years passed, and shallow inland seas encroached, covering the already ancient volcanic mountains with layers of sedimentary rock. Over the course of many millions of years, these layers built up until they were hundreds of feet thick. There were more violent uplifts across the Ozarks; the seas retreated; rain, wind, and moving water eroded the softer sedimentary rock layers, cutting the river valley ever deeper. Swirling over and between the buried igneous hills, the river scoured and carved potholes, chutes, and spectacular gorges. It is amazing that something as penetrable as water can cut the hardest stone—here's proof.

The Johnson's Shut-ins are pocketed away in the scenic St. Francois Mountains; when you see them, you will understand the name. You feel isolated, hidden, shut in—but without a trace of claustrophobia. The Black River flows through the park and winds past some of the oldest exposed rock in the country. There are little waterfalls and swirling water everywhere. Adding to the unique nature of the area are the drought-adapted plants commonly found in the deserts of the Southwest. Scorpions and the rare eastern collared lizard (which rises to an upright position to run on its hind legs and is a treat to see) also find a home in the glades. (Never put on your boots in the morning without first shaking them out—scorpions love hiding places.) Call (573) 546-2450. The Web site www.mostateparks.com can give you more information about the park and other parks in the state.

East of the park, the Taum Sauk section of the Ozark Trail leads to **Mina Sauk Falls** (the highest falls in Missouri) and **Taum Sauk Mountain,** the highest point in the state at 1,772 feet above sea level. (Okay, no snickering— this is not Colorado.)

According to Indian legend, the mountain's rugged face shows the grief of Mina Sauk, daughter of Taum Sauk, chief of the Piankishaws. Because of her improper marriage, her new husband (of the Osage tribe) was thrown off the mountain. In her despair, she leapt from the peak. The spot where she landed is considered the origin of Mina Sauk Falls, which cascade 200 feet over the granite ledges.

The **Ozark Trail** winds through the heart of Missouri. Miles and miles of rocky terrain ramble from Steelville and West Plains along glades, forests, and prairies. Here you can hear the wind and feel a snowflake on your face. The more-than-300 miles of pathways are serene and quiet, with scarcely another person along the trail. The solitude can be overwhelming and the views breathtaking. Some of the best views in the Ozarks can be found at Onondaga, Taum Sauk, and Johnson's Shut-ins. (Construction has begun to expand the trail to 500 miles of Missouri wilderness and continue it into Arkansas for an additional 500 miles on the Ozark Highlands Trail.) The northernmost part of the trail—the Courtois Creek Section near Steelville—offers

vivebastilleday!

In Ste. Genevieve the annual Bastille Day celebration on July 14, which celebrates the town's proud French heritage, rivals our own Independence Day.

a blend of bottomland and hardwood trees. The area of the **Mark Twain National Forest** boasts some of the Ozarks' tallest standing pines, and, of course, there are creeks, bluffs, and small waterfalls. The Berryman Trail for mountain bikers has a trailhead 17 miles east of Steelville and intersects the Ozark Trail at Harmon Springs. A fine spot to camp waits here with a spring and small pond. Many of these trails teemed with deer, elk, and herds of bison when they were traveled by Native Americans in the 1800s. The red wolf lived here, although none has been seen in years. Guides say black bears and wild horses may be seen. The trail offers views of the current river valley, old graveyards, caves, and bluffs. Rigorous hiking as well as more moderate hiking spots near the state parks are here as well. Primitive camping (at least 100 feet from the trail, water, and scenic areas) is allowed along most sections of the trail. Some areas are open to horses and mountain bikes. Although the trail is open year-round, the best times to visit are in the spring when the dogwoods bloom or in the fall under a canopy of russet leaves. The winters are mild in the Ozarks, though, and winter hiking can be fun. Summers in Missouri are not the best for hiking—they tend to be humid and buggy. But whatever the season, be prepared. Have a map, appropriate rainwear gear, and water—and let somebody know where you are going. For Ozark Trail Section Maps and other information, contact the Ozark Trail Coordinator, Missouri Department of Natural Resources, P.O. Box 176, Jefferson City 65102; (573) 751-5359 or (800) 334-6946.

North of the Shut-ins, through some of the prettiest hills this side of the Great Smoky Mountains, are **Dillard** and the **Dillard Mill State Historic Site.** Like a Currier & Ives scene beside its mill run, it is one of the state's best-preserved water-powered gristmills. This picturesque red building sits squarely at the juncture of two of the clearest-flowing Ozark streams, Huzzah and Indian Creeks. The original mill machinery is still in operation, grinding away.

When you've finished with industrial history, check out the natural history. Dillard has a 1½-mile hiking trail through oak and hickory forests that ends at a pine-topped plateau.

Backtrack a bit on Highway 49 and turn east onto Highway 32 to **Elephant Rocks State Park** near **Graniteville.** It is the first park in the state to have a trail designed especially for the visually and physically handicapped. Signs along the trail, written in braille and in regular text, describe the origin of the elephant rocks and guide visitors along a paved 1-mile path.

Elephant Rocks is one of the oddest geological formations—more than a billion years old—you're likely to find in Missouri. Here monolithic boulders stand end-to-end like a train of circus elephants, dwarfing mere mortals who stand beside them. Made of billion-year-old granite, the rocks were formed during the Precambrian era when molten rock forced its way to the surface, pushing the earth's crust aside. The magma cooled and hardened slowly as this area became less volcanically active; it broke in vertical cracks, which weathered and rounded to form the huge "elephants." This weathering eventually breaks even the largest rocks down into pebbles and gravel, but not to worry: More stone elephants are in the making all the time. The pink patriarch of the pachyderm herd is Dumbo, at 27 feet tall and 35 feet long and weighing in at a sylphlike 680 tons. Winding trails, colorful lichen and wildflowers, cool, oak-shaded grottoes, and a picnic area in the shadow of the rocks add to the attractions here. Call (573) 546-3454.

River Heritage Area

If you didn't head off into the wilderness back on US 67 at Crystal City but stayed on I-55 or US 61, you will now enter the River Heritage area. From river bluffs and hills to lowlands, from historic towns to waterways, the River Heritage region boasts enough destinations for several vacations. The French influence is visible everywhere you look in *Ste. Genevieve,* from the name itself to the many buildings à la française. The earliest records of the Missouri Territory invariably mention Ste. Genevieve and its ball-loving inhabitants! French Colonial-era homes are tucked in all along the Great River Road from St. Louis south to Cape Girardeau on the Mississippi River's banks. Wide porches and steep roofs have cooled these homes for more than 200 years. These homes predate the Louisiana Purchase, dating from when the French were coming up the Mississippi River from New Orleans and bringing style, food, and traditions with them.

Ste. Genevieve has been clinging to the riverbank here since the 1730s, when French trappers sought valuable beaver pelts. The 5,000 people who call Sainte Gen home still celebrate Bastille Day and are justifiably proud of their French Creole–style buildings. The "Great Flood of '93" threatened the town, but it managed to stay dry with a lot of sandbagging by citizens and history-minded volunteers from across the nation.

Many visitors to Ste. Genevieve are research scholars and genealogists from around the world. The records at the library, courthouse, and churches are the oldest in the West. St. Genevieve calls itself the oldest town west of the Mississippi (more than one Missouri town makes this claim, though) and says "all history of the West begins here."

Back Garden at the Bolduc House Museum

Stop by the information center on Third Street. Many of the town's homes date from the 1700s and are preserved as historic sites and open for tours. Start with the **Ste. Genevieve Museum,** which houses one of the first bird mounts by John James Audubon himself, who did business—albeit briefly—here in the early 1800s. You'll see French-style sabots (wooden shoes), early songbooks, a flute belonging to Audubon's partner Rozier, and much more.

The **Bolduc House Museum,** 125 South Main Street, Ste. Genevieve, was built circa 1770 and moved to its current site in 1785. The two-room French colonial is one of the best examples of its type of architecture along the Mississippi. Tour guides in period costume lead visitors through the building, where the yellow glow of tallow lamps dimly light the flintlock rifles above the mantel and the bison rug on the floor. Outside an herb garden, a well, and an orchard are inside a typical French-style palisade enclosure.

Then choose among the homes, churches, shops, and country inns dotting the town. Search out places for little treats such as Sara Menard's **Sara's Ice Cream and Antiques,** at 124 Merchant Street (573-883-5890). Sara's is closed from Oktoberfest through March. Hours are 10:00 a.m. to 6:00 p.m. and until 9:00 p.m. when school is out.

You can't help but notice the **Old Brick House,** built in 1780, which faces the courthouse square, at Third and Market Streets in Ste. Genevieve. It's owned by Rosie Schwartz. The favorite entree is liver knaefly, a liver dumpling.

Before you liver-haters turn up your noses, this German cook urges you to try the dish. It wouldn't be a regularly scheduled favorite if it weren't great, right? Okay, you want something you know, how about a sizzling steak or secret-recipe fried chicken? Whatever

you eat, enjoy the surroundings while waiting. They say that the bricks that built this wealthy merchant's home in 1785 arrived as ballast on French ships, and it is thought to be the first brick building west of the Mississippi. The building spent years as a courthouse, a school, and a tavern. In 1816 a duel was fought on its steps and a man was killed. Today the polished wood floors and lace curtains offer a more peaceful environment and the most dangerous thing here is the coconut cream pie. Hours are 8:00 a.m. until 9:00 p.m. weekdays, 11:00 a.m. until 10:00 p.m. Saturday, and 11:00 a.m. until 7:00 p.m. Sunday. Call (573) 883-2724 for information.

Just a couple of doors down the street from the Old Brick House is *The Anvil*, at 46 South Third Street, Ste. Genevieve, a bar and restaurant that serves great fried chicken and other real down-home food. Call (573) 883-7323 to find out more about it. Weekday hours are 11:00 a.m. to 8:00 p.m. and until 9:00 p.m. on weekends.

Down the block at 146 South Third Street is the circa-1790 *Southern Hotel* (573-883-3493 or 800-275-1412). Barbara and Mike Hankins saw the old wreck, which had been abandoned since 1980, and fell in love with the redbrick, Federal-style three-story hotel. "It was such a mess," Barbara says just a bit wearily, "that finally everything quit working. We stripped it back to the walls and put in state-of-the-art electrical, plumbing, and furnace fixtures." Barbara insists they made it into a bed-and-breakfast to justify owning it! It is believed to be the oldest operating hotel west of the Mississippi River. The hotel is full of antiques and claw-foot tubs. Meals feature fresh herbs from the garden behind the hotel, and flowers from the garden fill the rooms. The garden itself is magical. An arbor leads to a wide cedar swing at the center; Mike has wired the whole area with thousands of tiny white lights. When he hits the switch at dusk the garden is a romantic fairyland. Tucked away in a corner of the garden is a great little shop with dried flowers, herbal soaps, and handpainted goodies—don't miss it! You can buy the Pepper and Rose Cookbook or enroll in the "Cooking Experience" class.

It has been open since 1987 with eight guest rooms, each with its own bath. Rooms cost from $93 to $175 and include such wondrous French breakfast items as strawberry soup, artichoke heart strata (a layered egg-and-bread dish), croissants, homemade lemon bread, juice, and coffee. The e-mail address is mike@southernhotelbb.com, and the hotel's Web site is www.southernhotelbb .com.

Inn St. Gemme Beauvais and *Dr. Hertich's House* are respectively at 78 and 99 North Main Street, Ste. Genevieve. Both are on the National Register. Built in 1848 and 1850, the Inn is the state's oldest continually operated bed-and-breakfast. This lovely old Victorian will spoil you. All the rooms are suites, with big easy chairs in the sitting room and canopy beds and rockers in the bedrooms. Tea time is every day at two o'clock, and wine and hors d'oeuvres are offered every day at four o'clock. A full gourmet breakfast, of course, is served in the morning at eight and coffee is ready even earlier in the second-floor lounge for you early birds.

trivia

The Mississippi River is the reason St. Louis exists. It was the original highway for every civilization that thrived in the middle of the country. But it is also the most diverse inland river in the world. More than 500 species of wildlife use the river and its flood plains.

There is also a restaurant that can seat up to twenty six people. The cuisine is French. Dinner banquets can also be arranged any time. Outside is a lovely herb and flower garden to enjoy. The hotel is on Main Street, and so it is within walking distance to everything. Suites range from $89 (for two) to $179. Visit their Web site at www .bbhost.com/innstgemme/, call innkeeper Janet Joggerst at (573) 883-5744 or (800) 818-5744, fax (573) 583-3899, or e-mail stgemme@brick.net.

The information presented here only begins to touch on what is available in Ste. Gen; there's the *Sainte Genevieve Winery* at 245 Merchant Street (open 11:00 a.m. to 5:00 p.m. daily; 573-883-2800), the *Sweet Things* confection shop at 242 Market Street (573-883-7990), all manner of antiques shops and restaurants, and a whole list of bed-and-breakfasts. The town's Web site is www .ste-genevieve.com.

At *Perryville,* off US 61, is the *St. Mary of the Barrens Church,* dating from 1827. The grounds are open to walk through; be sure to visit the church's museums. This is also the National Shrine of Our Lady of the Miraculous Medal.

For more history (and fun), detour east a bit on the Great River Road and watch for *Tower Rock* jutting up 85 feet out of the Mississippi. Don't miss the little German towns of Altenberg, Whittenberg, and Frohna.

Stay on US 61, and the next stop is *Jackson;* all aboard the old Iron Mountain Railroad. The oldest Protestant church west of the Mississippi, the Old McKendree Chapel (circa 1819), a national Methodist shrine, is here. *TLC*

Wellness Bed & Breakfast, 203 Bellevue Street, Jackson, is the family home of Trish and Gus Wischmann, and it is known here as "The Mueller Haus." There's a relaxed, congenial atmosphere (with respect for your privacy) and a home-cooked breakfast. An exquisite gazebo is a wonderful place to curl up with a good book or just kick back and enjoy the lovely surroundings. It's a delightful resting spot. Rooms rent from $65 to $90 on weekends, $60 during the week or for extended stays. The Relaxation Getaway includes an hour of massage by innkeeper Trish, a licensed therapist, and a visit to the local fitness center. Another package is the Getaway Retreat, which includes wellness education by the innkeeper, who is a licensed health practitioner. Call (573) 243-7427 or e-mail trybnb@yahoo.com.

The best attraction for you railroad fans is the ***Iron Mountain Railway,*** 505 Benton Road, Jackson. Ride a piece of history. Sights and sounds will carry you back to the late 1800s and early 1900s, when this was the preferred method of travel.

The "mother line" of nearly all the smaller rail lines that eventually became the historic Missouri Pacific, the Iron Mountain Railway is part of the St. Louis, Iron Mountain, and Southern Railway Company. Darren the Magician roams the train to entertain the child in you. There's the Dinner Train, or you might relive the 1880s train robbery by the James Gang, or experience the intrigue of murder on a Murder Mystery Train. You can send for a schedule or check them out on the Web at www.slimrr.com/sitemap.html. Take I-55 to exit 99 and go 4 miles west on US 61 to the intersection of US 61 and Highway 25. Call (573) 243-1688 or (800) 455-RAIL for schedule and prices.

If you want to experience the elegance of the 1800s, stop by the ***Oliver House,*** 224 East Adams Street, Jackson. The lady of the house is known as Missouri's Betsy Ross. Marie Oliver and a friend designed and made the first and only official state flag. The house is decorated with authentic furniture of the period, and music plays on the Edison Victrola. Visiting hours are on the first Sunday of the month from 1:00 to 4:30 p.m. May through December. For more information call (573) 243-0533.

While you're near Jackson, take a side trip to ***Burfordville*** on Highway 34 East. The ***Bollinger Mill*** has been in continuous operation for more than 180 years—these people really kept their noses to the grindstone, didn't they? Located on the Whitewater River, the four-story, stone-and-brick structure shares the setting with the ***Burfordville Covered Bridge,*** one of five covered bridges remaining in the state.

The building of the bridge began in 1858 and, like much of Missouri's everyday life, was put on hold by the Civil War. The Burfordville Bridge was completed in 1868. It is a 140-foot span of incredibly long yellow poplar timbers, which grow near the river. It's another excellent setting for artists and photographers, not to mention history and nostalgia buffs.

You're deep in southern Missouri now, and headed for "Cape." On I-55, **Cape Girardeau** is the biggest city in the area, with a population of almost 35,000. But Cape Girardeau has also preserved its heritage carefully, and it's a beautiful city in spite of—and in the midst of—phenomenal growth. Visit the Cape's Web site at www.cityofcapegirardeau.org.

Cape Girardeau is radio-and-television talk-show host Rush Limbaugh's hometown, and the city offers a self-directed (very conservative) tour (with nothing but right turns?) past the hospital where he was born, his boyhood home, high school, and the barbershop where he got his first job. Then you can have lunch at his favorite hamburger joint, Wimpy's. Pick up a brochure at the visitor bureau at 1707 Mount Auburn Road (800-777-0068), or visit the Web site at http://rosecity.net/rush/rushtour.html.

gothicsplendor

An outstanding example of Renaissance architecture in the Gothic style is the **Old St. Vincent's Church** in Cape Girardeau. It was built in 1853 and contains more than one hundred medieval-design plaster masks and intricate interior work. It is listed on the National Register of Historic Places.

Drive through the city and note the many nineteenth-century buildings. The beautiful Glenn House, circa 1880, is a good example. The old Court of Common Pleas has a lovely hilltop setting, and Cape Rock Park is a reminder of the early trading post that predated the city itself. Civil War fortifications still remain in the area. The convention and tourism bureau is at 100 Broadway; if you plan to spend some time here, it may pay to stop. You can also visit on the Web at www.capegirardeaucvb.org.

Although Cape is modern and expanding too fast, all is not lost. Proceed directly down to Water Street, which, as you may have guessed by the name, is along the mighty Mississippi. Unfortunately, a rather tall, ugly wall has been built to protect the area from flood, so the view lacks something—water, to be exact. There is an opening and a deck you can drive onto to enjoy the sights, though, if you are fond of rivers—and who isn't? There's just something about the power of that big river.

Get a feel for the history of the area with Cape's unique Great Murals Tour. It all began at the *Southeast Missourian* newspaper building where "The Art of Printing" and "The Art of Making a Newspaper" were done in 1947. Tourists enjoyed finding famous faces in the ceramic murals, which were the first of their kind in the country. They were joined by the "Jake Wells Mural," representing the people whose dreams carved the region's progress. This is one of the largest murals in the state. In the city's downtown area five more murals celebrate the Mississippi River (in Waterfront Park), the Riverfest, the Riverfront, the Bicentennial, and the Silver Coronet Band Mural about Cape's musical legacy. The "Missouri Wall of Fame Mural" is in progress and will encompass twenty-five panels featuring famous Missourians.

If you love trains, especially Lionel electric trains, hunt up **Sneathen Enterprises** at 2526 Boutin Drive, Cape Girardeau, where Bill Sneathen will sell, buy, or trade with you. Hours are variable; call (573) 335-8091.

The **Glenn House** is a circa-1883 two-story Victorian at 325 South Spanish Street, Cape Girardeau. It is open for tours and contains period furnishing, 12-foot stenciled ceilings, and some good displays devoted to the steamboat era on the Mississippi. It is open from May through October on Saturday and Sunday from 1:00 to 4:00 p.m. or by appointment. The house is also open Saturday and Sunday from 1:00 to 4:00 p.m. in December. Call (573) 334-1177 for more information, or visit the Web site at http://rosecity.net/glenn.html.

trivia

Cape Girardeau was named after Jean Baptiste Girardot, who established a trading post here in 1733. When Spain offered inexpensive, tax-exempt land, Spanish immigrants were drawn to the area. Cape Rock (2 miles northeast via Highway 177 and East Rock Drive) is the site of Jean Baptiste Girardot's trading post. Although nothing remains of the original settlement, views of the Mississippi River are wonderful from the bluff. Good spot for a picnic.

About a block away is what will probably be your favorite place if you have any Cajun instincts at all. **Broussard's Cajun Restaurant,** 120 North Main Street, even has a test on the back of the menu to see if there is a trace of Cajun blood in your veins. The "How to tell a full-blooded, dipped-in-the-bayou Cajun from someone who just wishes he was" test begins with the question "Did your grandmother regularly eat *couche* for breakfast?" and ends with "If someone stepped on your toe would you yell '*ho yii*' instead of 'ouch'?" If any of you good ol' boys are missing home, this is the place for you. Call (573) 334-7235 or visit www .broussardscajuncuisine.com.

The food here is authentic, fire-breathing Cajun. The menu has a glossary of terms and a key to spicy foods for those of you who don't like surprises. It is an inexpensive, casual place, but bring enough money to try a Cajun Combo, which includes a little bit of everything. Also, if you have room, the special includes a salad and French bread. Other entrees are the traditional red beans and rice with sausage and fried crawfish tails. Polish it off with a draft.

theevilthatmendo

During the forced removal in 1838, twelve detachments of Cherokee were ordered by Gen. Winfield Scott to move to Oklahoma. All entered Missouri in Cape Girardeau County. Rain, snow, freezing cold, hunger, and disease took their toll on the emigrants as the ice prevented both boat and horse from moving. More than 4,000 Cherokee—nearly one-fifth of the Cherokee population—died in camps by the river waiting for the journey to resume. To learn more about this march, you can visit the office of the Northern Cherokee Nation of the Old Louisiana Territory on Independence Street (Tuesday through Saturday). You can also visit Trail of Tears State Park, located approximately 10 miles north of Cape Girardeau on Highway 177.

It features a live band playing blues and dance music Fridays and Saturdays from 8:00 p.m. until closing time. Broussard's motto is *"Laissez Les Bons Temps Rouler!"*—Let the Good Times Roll.

For a lovely bed-and-breakfast, try the **Bellevue Bed and Breakfast,** 312 Bellevue, Cape Girardeau. This 1892 Queen Anne Victorian is listed on the Historical Register and has been faithfully restored—right up to the stenciled ceilings—and filled with period furniture. The parlor has a coal-burning fireplace, but queen-size beds and private baths make this a very comfortable place to stay. Innkeepers Brian Langlois and his wife Linda Delan draw guests into the dining room for breakfast with the aroma of baking bread. The home is within walking distance of the riverfront and the many nearby shops. Rooms are from $105 to $175, and all have private baths. Call (573) 335-3302 or (800) 768-6822 for reservations. You can visit their Web site at www.bellevue-bb.com or e-mail info@bellevue-bb.com.

Molly's, 11 South Spanish Street, Cape Girardeau (573-339-1661), serves "innovative pasta," seafood, and steaks. Open Monday through Thursday 5:00 to 10:00 p.m., Friday and Saturday 5:00 to 11:00 p.m. The bar is open from 5:00 to 11:00 p.m. Reservations are recommended on weekends.

River Ridge Winery, County Road 321, Commerce, is in a century-old farmhouse nestled in the hills where Crowley's Ridge meets the Mississippi River, 2 miles north of *Commerce,* south of Cape on Highway N. The hand-tended French hybrid grapes are grown on the hills behind the winery. You may sample the fine dry and semidry table wines crafted by winemaker Jerry Smith. He and his wife, Joannie, also have a showroom of unique wine-related items. You can picnic by the river or in the vineyards, or relax by a warm fire at the house and enjoy Esicar's wurst and bread. Open 11:00 a.m. to 6:00 p.m. daily. Call (573) 264-3712, or visit http://riverridgewinery.com.

Near Cape Girardeau grits begin to sneak onto the breakfast menu, and the accent begins to sound slightly more Southern than Midwestern.

On US 61 South watch the signs for **Lambert's Cafe** in Sikeston, home of "throwed rolls." Lambert's, at 2305 East Malone (573-471-4261; www.throwedrolls .com), is a most unusual place. Yes, they do throw rolls at Lambert's.

It all began on a busy day in May 1976 when passing rolls real nice-like got too slow and a customer hollered, "Just throw me the *x*#! thing!" Before you could say "thank you kindly," others cried out for service, and they have been throwing rolls at Lambert's ever since.

The folks here take control of your dinner needs—and control is the right word (got to have it when you're lobbing a long one). Want another roll? Sing out and look alive, because one will come whizzing by. To complement the rolls thrown your way, another ladleful of sorghum (Missouri's answer to Vermont maple syrup) will be slopped onto your roll, which is already dripping butter. This will require a trip to the restroom to unstick your fingers. Lambert's is fun—if you like noise, confusion, and a lot of food and attention from the waiters. If your plate begins to look empty, someone comes by with a ladle of beans, fried okra, or applesauce and plops it in the middle of your plate; when you finish dinner, you will be full. Very, very full. Then you will discover that Lambert's is famous for the size of their slices of homemade pie and cobbler. The drinks are served in gallon mason jars, and the atmosphere is a madhouse on a good day, but it's a spot you can talk about for years. Hours are 10:30 a.m. until 9:00 p.m. or so seven days a week.

Old Mountain Region

Now you have a choice—go south to the Bootheel region or loop back up toward St. Louie. West on U.S. Highway 60 toward Dexter, the flat, Kansaslike real estate will begin to curve again in the distance.

Maybe you saw geese in the air and heard their wild cries as you ate your frog's legs. A short trip will take you through **Paxico** to **Mingo National Wildlife Refuge,** a vital 21,676-acre link in the chain of refuges along the Mississippi flyway.

The hills flatten into wetlands and plant varieties change visibly. Mingo Swamp was formed some 18,000 years ago when the Mississippi abandoned its bed, leaving an oxbow that filled in with dense swamp species. Abundant artifacts point to the area's use by Native Americans, drawn here by swamp-loving wildlife. (No artifacts can be removed from Mingo, however, so arrowhead hunters, take note.)

The area offers a brand-new boardwalk nature trail with seven interpretive stations and a chance to see wildlife in its natural habitat. There is a resident waterfowl flock as well as thousands of seasonal migrants, and two active bald

e nests are located on the refuge. Be sure to stop by the refuge visitor cen-
before heading into the swamp (especially during the winter months), not
only to let someone know where you are going, but also to enjoy the interpretive displays. The trails are accessible for all, including those with disabilities.
It's pretty impressive.

Together with the adjacent Duck Creek Wildlife Area, a state wildlife man-
agement area, this is the largest hardwood swamp remaining in the state. Lake
Wappapello is also nearby; watch for signs.

If you didn't expect to find a museum of fine art in the Ozarks, you're in
for a surprise. The **Margaret Harwell Art Museum** in **Poplar Bluff** boasts
a growing collection of works by contemporary Missouri artists. Housed in a
beautiful 1883 home, the museum has mounted one-man shows by important artists such as sculptor Ernest Trova, Swedish artist Anders Zorn,
and Missourian Thomas Hart Benton. There is no charge to view the two
exhibits. The museum focuses on themes ranging from contemporary
photography to fiber art and recog-
nizes the importance of the native
arts of the Ozark region. It has held exhibits of folk art, including quilting and
basket making. It is the only art center within a 90-mile radius and the only art
museum within 150 miles of Poplar Bluff. Docents conduct regular tours of the
exhibit. The museum, at 421 North Main Street, is closed Monday. Hours are
Tuesday through Friday noon to 4:00 p.m., Saturday and Sunday 1:00 to 4:00
p.m. Call (573) 686-8002 for information. Tours are by appointment only.

trivia

The Margaret Harwell Art Museum
is housed in a home built by James
Dalton, who invented the ten-key
calculator. It was later purchased for
Poplar Bluff with money donated by
Harwell.

But that's not all this fun little city has to offer. Leigh Rataj's **Fishermans
Net,** 8815 Highway T, 2 miles south of the dam in nearby Lake Wappapello, is
a restaurant that can be recommended on a first-person basis. Not only that, but
the person in question tasted each and every thing on the menu. Well, okay,
it was a group of about fifteen people who decided that they would just try it
all. And they did. If you have never tried fried cabbage, fried corn on the cob,
or fried green tomatoes, this is the place to do it. Just appetizers of course, but
wait! Here come the fried catfish fillets, country fried steak, and frog legs. Hush
puppies begin to appear by the basketful. Oh, my, save room to try the seafood
platter (crab cake, peel- and-eat shrimp, clam strips, and the above-mentioned
frog legs and catfish). Too much fried food? Did I mention the babyback ribs?
Shrimp scampi, prime rib, steak, or crab legs should do the trick. Seriously,
the whole smoked pork loin with sweet potato smothered in brown sugar and

butter will fill the bill nicely, too. There's still room for dessert isn't there? The dessert du jour on our visit was old-fashioned strawberry shortcake with real whipped cream. Okay, it was a lie. We didn't taste everything; we didn't have room for dessert. There is lots more. The Net is open Wednesday through Sunday from 6:00 a.m. for breakfast to 9:00 p.m. All the food is cooked to order, so don't be in a hurry. Call (573) 222-8083.

The *Lake Wappapello Outdoor Theatre* next door to the Fishermans Net comes alive on Friday and Saturday nights at 6:30 p.m. from May through October with live bluegrass and gospel music. There is no admission fee but donations are appreciated. Bring your lawn chair and settle in to enjoy the music. When it rains, everyone moves to the music barn.

Stop by *Bullwinkles Lounge, Rustic Lodge, and RV Park,* 399 Highway T, in Poplar Bluff, where owner Mike Bridges will let you park your rig in the RV park, fix you a drink, and let you play pool amid the amazing collection of "curious articles" suspended from the ceiling and walls. In good weather you can enjoy barbecue at the outside beer garden or screened gazebo. The lodge has sixteen hotel rooms as well. Call (573) 778-9278 or 778-3535 or visit www .bullwinklespub.com as well.

For just a quick barbecue fix, *Myrtle's Place Backalley BBQ* at 109 North Broadway in Poplar Bluff has carryout as well as the restaurant there in town. Owners Debbie and Tommy Sliger have it all, including breakfast. If you call in advance they will cook you a ham, turkey, pork butt, ribs, or chicken for your next get-together. Hours are Monday through Friday from 5:00 a.m. (Yes, that's a.m.!) to 3:00 p.m. and on Saturday until 2:00 p.m. Call (573) 785-9203 or (573) 778-9247. Poplar Bluff isn't all fried and barbecue, though. You can *mangiare benne* at *Castello's Ristorante,* 2216 North Westwood Boulevard (573) 776-1701, which serves old country Italian food just like Nana Ginni Castello taught the family to make. Being Italian myself, I can recommend the sauce. Hours are Wednesday through Saturday from 4:00 until 10:00 p.m.

There's Mexican, too. *El Acapulco,* 2260 North Westwood Boulevard, has a huge menu (the sizzling fajitas come to the table on very hot skillets) and it is open seven days a week from 11:00 a.m. until 10:00 p.m. Call (573) 776-7000.

Bootheel Region

You are in Missouri's Bootheel now, not really the Midwest anymore, more like the South. You can get all kinds of Bootheel travel help by e-mailing bootrpc@ sheltonbbs.com.

Southeast of Sikeston you'll find hills that really roll. *Big Oak Tree State Park* tells the story of the 1811 New Madrid earthquake, which altered the

swampattacks nomore

In Missouri's early days, the lowlands around the Bootheel were known as "The Big Swamp" because they were covered with stagnant waters of marshes, swamps, and bayous. There were mosquitoes everywhere that were the deadly enemies of settlers. A series of earthquakes in 1811 and 1812 further discouraged settlers. Today "Swamp-east Missouri" has been changed—through drainage projects—to some of the most productive land in the state.

topography of the southeast lowlands. All the land from Cape Girardeau south to Helena, Arkansas, sank from 10 to 50 feet, flooding most of what is now New Madrid, Pemiscot, and Dunklin Counties. Rich Bootheel forests were converted to swampland, providing temporary protection for the giant oak that gave the park its name. You may see trees 120 to 130 feet tall. Enjoy a bayou setting for picnics or fishing. Big Oak Tree is east off Highway 102.

Nearby **Towosahgy State Historic Site** (off Highway 77) is sixty-four acres of prehistory. Archaeologists believe the site was inhabited between A.D.1000 and A.D. 1400. Although other groups had lived in this area before that time, their societies did not reach such a highly organized level as that of the Indians at Towosahgy. Experts believe their use of the Mississippi for trade and transportation contributed to this advancement. The river was the link between Towosahgy and the ceremonial center near the present site of Cahokia, Illinois.

Cotton fields join wheat fields as you approach **New Madrid** (that's pronounced MAD-rid, much more Midwestern than Spanish) on I-55. The Mississippi River Observation Deck offers a panoramic view of the New Madrid oxbow; 8 miles of river are visible from the top of the most perfect oxbow on the Mississippi.

The oldest city west of the Mississippi (see, there's that claim again) has something for everyone. Begin at 1 Main Street. This building, on the banks of the Mississippi near the observation deck, was once the First and Last Chance Saloon. There were no roads to New Madrid; all the traffic came off the mighty river. Here was the first—and last—chance to get a drink back in 1783. It is now the **New Madrid Historical Museum.**

New Madrid looks sleepy, dreaming away beside the river. It looks safe. It looks as if nothing much could happen here—indeed, as if nothing much ever had. If that's what you think when you see the place, you're wrong.

It balances precariously on one of the most active earthquake faults on the continent. In 1811, the balance shifted. The earth shrugged. The mighty

Hunter-Dawson Home, New Madrid

Mississippi was suddenly dammed and ran backward, boats broke up and sank at their moorings, homes disintegrated before their owners' horrified eyes. John James Audubon recounted a hilarious—if frightening—tale of a wedding party broken up by the quake, and the naturalist John Bradbury described it in harrowing scientific detail as he calmly watched the earth come apart. The quake was so violent that it rang church bells in Boston.

All is not peace and quiet, even now. There is a measurable tremor on the seismographs almost every day that can be felt by local folks. The Center for Earthquake Studies at Southeast Missouri State University informs us that a major quake is not just possible, but inevitable; stresses within the earth slowly mount until something has to give. When it does, the area of damage will be more than twenty times that affected by a California quake because of the underlying geologic conditions—the ground will literally liquefy.

Residents have developed a wonderful gallows humor—you'd have to! T-shirts read, with a certain quirky pride, "It's Our Fault" and "Visit New Madrid—while it's still here." So, you want real excitement? Head for New Madrid. (Of course, the author files a disclaimer here. If there's a quake while you're in town, it's "not my fault.")

trivia

The city of Kennett here in the Bootheel is proud of its daughter, singer Sheryl Crow, who attended Mizzou before launching her career.

While in New Madrid, visit the *Hunter-Dawson Home and Historic Site.* Built in 1859 by William Washington Hunter, this crisp white house with its ornate trim and contrasting shutters recalls a more genteel era. The costumed guides who answer all your questions treat you with that special Southern charm and add to the atmosphere. A small admission fee is charged.

As you continue south from Sikeston and New Madrid, the land becomes flat bottomland. Southern-style cotton, soybeans, and peaches are the important crops here. From Kennett and Malden on the west to Hayti and Caruthersville on the east, hospitality is just what you would expect in this area of Southern heritage, and Missouri begins to feel like Dixie. Welcome, y'all.

Places to Stay in Southeast Missouri

ST. LOUIS

Hyatt Regency Downtown
1 St. Louis Station
(314) 231-1234
Moderate

Radisson Downtown Hotel & Suites
200 North Fourth Street
(314) 621-8200
Moderate

Red Roof Inn
11837 Lackland Road,
Westport
(314) 991-4900 or
(800) 843-7663
Inexpensive

Ritz–Carlton, St. Louis (Clayton)
100 Carondelet Plaza
(314) 863-6300
or (800) 241-3333
Expensive

St. Union Station Drury Inn
201 South 20th Street
(314) 231-3900
Inexpensive

CUBA

Cuba Holiday Inn Express
97 Ozark Drive
(573) 885-0100
Inexpensive

Super 8 Motel
I-44 & Hwy 19
(573) 885-2087
Inexpensive

PILOT KNOB

Ft. Davidson Motel
Highway 21 &V
(573) 546-7427
Inexpensive

EUREKA

Holiday Inn at Six Flags
I-44 and
Allentown Road
(800) 782-8108
Inexpensive

ROLLA

Zeno's
1621 Martin Spring Drive
(573) 364-1301
Inexpensive

SULLIVAN

*Econo Lodge
307 North Service Road
(573) 468-3136
Inexpensive

SELECTED CHAMBERS OF COMMERCE

Lebanon, (417) 588-3256

St. Louis, (800) 916-0092

New Madrid, (314) 748-5300

VIENNA

Scenic 63 RV Park and Motel
Highway 63 South
(573) 422-3907
Inexpensive

FARMINGTON

*Days Inn
1400 Liberty Street
(314) 756-8951 or
(800) DAYS INN
Inexpensive

LESTERVILLE

Black River Family Restaurant & Motel
Highway 21
(573) 637-2600
Inexpensive

PERRYVILLE

*Travel Lodge
1500 Liberty Street
(573) 547-1091
Inexpensive

CAPE GIRARDEAU

Drury Lodge
104 South Vantage Drive
(573) 334-7151
(free hot breakfast buffet)
Inexpensive

Holiday Inn
3253 William Street
(573) 334-4261
Inexpensive

STE. GENEVIEVE

Family Budget Inn
17030 New Berman Road
(573) 543-2272
Inexpensive

Hotel Ste. Genevieve
Main and Merchant
(573) 883-3562
Inexpensive

JACKSON

Drury Inn
225 Drury Lane
(573) 243-9200
(quickstart breakfast,
free evening cocktails, cable)
Inexpensive

POPLAR BLUFF

Super 8 Motel
2831 North Westwood
Boulevard
(573) 785-0176
Inexpensive

SIKESTON

Holiday Inn
120 South Interstate Drive
(573) 481-9500
Inexpensive

NEW MADRID

Super 8 Motel
I-55, exit 40, Marston
(573) 643-9888
Inexpensive

* has restaurant

Places to Eat in Southeast Missouri

ST. LOUIS

LoRusso's Cucina
3121 Watson (on The Hill)
(314) 647-6222
www.lorussos.com
Moderate

Norton's Cafe
808 Geyer (Soulard)
(314) 436-0828
Inexpensive

WASHINGTON

Cowans Restaurant
114 Elm Street
(636) 239-3213
Inexpensive

NEAR DIXON

The Point Steakhouse
Highway 28
(573) 759-6100
Inexpensive

RICH FOUNTAIN

White Stone Inn
Highway 63 East on State
Road
(573) 744-5827
Inexpensive

SOUTH OF VIENNA

Moreland's Restaurant
Highway 63 at 1
3448 Maries Road 325
(573) 422-9918
Inexpensive

FARMINGTON

Spokes Pub & Grill
Highways 67 & W at
B Traditions Inn
(573) 756-6220
Inexpensive

CAPE GIRARDEAU

**Cedar Street Restaurant
& Bar**
I-55 and Highway K
(573) 332-7427
Inexpensive

Port Cape
19 North Water
(573) 334-0954
Inexpensive

NEW MADRID

**Rosie's Colonial
Restaurant & Tavern**
Highway 61
(573) 748-7665
Inexpensive

Tom's Grill
457 Main
(573) 748-2049
Inexpensive

ROLLA

Alex's Pizza
122 West Eighth Street
(573) 364-2669
Inexpensive

Gordoz
1212 Highway 72
(573) 364-2780
Inexpensive

Hickory Pit BBQ
201 West Highway 72
(573) 364-4838
Inexpensive

Southwest Missouri

Mark Twain National Forest covers thousands of acres of southwest Missouri. Hundreds of miles of hiking and horseback trails free you from even the small, state-maintained highways. If you wander too far off the beaten path here, you will find yourself lost in the woods (and Missouri's bright bluebirds and crimson cardinals will clean up your trail of bread crumbs).

Many of the lovely, quick-running streams are designated National Scenic Riverways, and the "Tri-Lakes" area has water, water everywhere. Resort towns are crowded in the summer and deserted in winter. Spring and fall (while school's in session) are just right for exploration. Campgrounds and canoe rentals are everywhere, and there are both gentle rivers for floating and white water for adventure.

If caves are fascinating to you, if you like spectacular rock formations, or if you collect rocks or minerals, southwest Missouri will keep you busy. Truitt's Cave at Lanagan, Ozark Wonder Cave at Noel, the Tiff Mines near Seneca, and the Carthage Marble Quarry at Carthage are a few spots you'll want to check out. Fantastic Caverns, at 4872 North Farm Road 125, Springfield, has its own Web site, www.fantastic-caverns.com, which you can explore from home before paying the $17.50 admission fee.

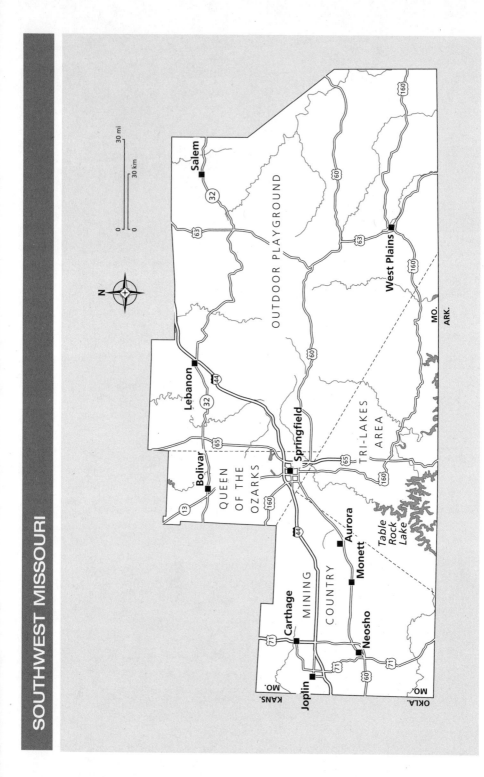

Bed-and-breakfast fans can write Kay Cameron at Ozark Mountain Country Bed & Breakfast Service, Box 295, Branson 65616. You can call her, too, at (417) 334-4720 or (800) 321-8594 for a list of B&Bs in the area. She loves match-making and finding just exactly the right place for you.

Queen of the Ozarks

The hub of southwest Missouri is *Springfield* on Interstate 44, the state's third-largest city. Its location on the spacious, grassy uplands of Grand Prairie and Kickapoo Prairie, the rural landscape of the Springfield Plain, is one of the most beautiful in Missouri.

Here's a happy combination of forests, running water, and magnificent rock outcrops dotting a farmland that resembles the bluegrass area of Kentucky. Herefords, Black Angus, Charolais, and Simmental graze in the cleared uplands. Lespedezas, orchard grass, and fescue glaze the gently rolling pastures with green. The city Web site is springfieldmissouri.org.

If you are an antiques hunter, Springfield's Commercial Street Historic District is a good place to wander around. South Campbell Street and Boonville Avenue shops just north of Park Central Square and the stores just below the square on South Street are all filled with antiques too.

battleplunges missouriintowar

Located 10 miles southwest of Springfield is the site of the Battle of Wilson's Creek, which occurred August 10, 1861, and marked the beginning of the Civil War in Missouri. The park has an interactive visitor center featuring a movie and a battle map. You can take a self-tour or a guided tour or bring your horse and ride the trails of Wilson's Creek.

AUTHOR'S FAVORITES IN SOUTHWEST MISSOURI

Bass Pro Shops Outdoor World	Jolly Mill
Japanese Stroll Garden	Omega Pottery Shop
Caveman BBQ	Candlestick Inn
Ozark National Scenic Riverways	Cathedral Church of the Prince of Peace
Coldwater Ranch	

"Whistle Stop" Trail

The **Frisco Highline Trail** is the KATY trail of Southwest Missouri. The 36-mile-long trail is now open from Springfield to Bolivar. The most beautiful part is the 18-mile stretch from Walnut Grove to Bolivar; it winds its way through pasture and forest, over sixteen trestles, and right through La Petite Gemme Prairie Natural Area. This is the second-longest hiking, biking, and equestrian trail in the state. But here's a trivia note you might enjoy: It is the route once traveled by Harry S Truman as a precursor to his "Whistle Stop Campaign" in 1948. For more information about the trail go to www.friscohighlinetrail.org.

Okay, **Bass Pro Shops Outdoor World** at 1935 South Campbell—a major intersection in Springfield—is rather on the track. It bills itself as the world's greatest sporting-goods store, then lives up to that boast. How many sports shops have a two-story log cabin right in the store? Or a sumptuous restaurant like Hemingway's, serving lobster dinner and a glass of fine wine in front of a room-size aquarium (with white-bellied sharks smiling through the glass and a 15-foot eel hiding in the filter system)?

Across the aerial walkway from Hemingway's is the old-fashioned Tall Tales Barbershop. There is original wildlife art, a museum of the outdoors, trophy animals by the hundreds, and the biggest live bass in captivity. You can buy a hand-knit sweater, get wet beside an indoor waterfall, practice with your new shotgun in the shooting range downstairs, and buy a pair of gym shoes or a fishing rod. Just plan on spending a couple of hours when you go in, and take a camera—there are photo opportunities indicated everywhere; you can pose with 10-foot black bears or tiny fawns. Call (417) 887-7334 or visit the Web site at www.basspro.com for hours.

From Bass Pro, go east on Sunshine until you come to Kentwood. Turn right onto Kentwood and you'll be at **Nearly Famous Deli & Pasta House** at 1828 South Kentwood, Springfield (417-883-3403). This family-owned restaurant turns out the most scrumptious of soups (try the chunky tomato, a daily house specialty), salads, sandwiches, dinner items, and heavenly desserts that will make you wonder why this restaurant is not called The Famous Deli. My favorite combo is the tomato soup and egg salad sandwich; both are memorable. Hours are 11:00 a.m. to 9:00 p.m. Monday through Thursday and until 10:00 p.m. on Friday and Saturday.

Ziggie's Café at 2222 South Campbell Street, Springfield (¼ mile south of Bass Pro; 417-883-0900; www.ziggiescafe.com), was voted "Best Overall Restaurant" by the local paper, the *News Leader*. Open twenty-four hours a day, it's like an old-time diner but bigger and better. The service is quick, and the menu ranges from daily omelet specials to more than seventy-five different lunch and dinner items to choose from. The large dessert case full of fresh-baked pies, cobblers, and cakes is impressive.

You will notice a Chinese restaurant on almost every corner in Springfield. This town is known as "the home of cashew chicken." This specialty is on every menu, so just pick a restaurant and try this Ozarks invention.

If you're in the mood for Italian, then you are in luck. Also just south of Bass Pro, **Digiacinto's Italian Restaurant** at 2259 South Campbell Street (417-882-5166), has really good Sicilian food. On weekends, soft piano music accompanies dinner. Hours are 11:00 a.m. to 9:00 p.m. Tuesday through Thursday and Friday and Saturday until 9:30 p.m.

Springfield is a major city, but, as in most big cities, there are hidden treasures. Gary and Paula Blankenship's **Walnut Street Inn Bed and Breakfast** at 900 East Walnut (417-864-6346 or 800-593-6346) has a quiet ambience to counter the big-city feel. Each of the twelve rooms includes a private bath, some with original porcelain antique fixtures, hardwood floors, and antique furnishings. Ozark specialties such as persimmon muffins and walnut bread are featured along with a full breakfast. The inn now offers something even more tempting: in-room massage from a certified masseuse! They also have a two-person steam bath. What a fine weekend retreat this has turned out to be. Rates are $89 to $169 per night for two persons.

The inn caters to business travelers and an additional phone line is in each suite for computers. The suites also have VCRs and CD players. In the main house and in the carriage house, Wi-Fi high-speed Internet access has been installed for business travelers. The new AA baseball stadium is located just 2 blocks north of the inn on John Q. Hammons Parkway, now the home park of the Springfield Cardinals, a minor league team affiliated with the St. Louis Cardinals. If you want a more complete view, call up the inn's Web site at www.walnutstreetinn.com or e-mail the Blankenships at stay@walnutstreetinn.com. The fax number is (417) 864-6184.

trivia

Actor Brad Pitt graduated from Kickapoo High School in Springfield. He starred in the movie, *The Assassination of Jesse James,* about Missouri's Robin Hood outlaw who, folklore has it, gave money he stole from railroad barons and Yankee banks to farmers.

The circa-1856 **Gray/Campbell Farmstead** in Nathanael Greene Park at 2400 South Scenic is the oldest house in Springfield. Guides present the history of the farmstead and conduct tours of the log kitchen, granary, two-crib barn, and family cemetery. It is open during April and October on Sundays from 1:30 to 4:30 p.m.; May through September, Saturday and Sunday from 1:30 to 4:30 p.m., or by appointment. Call (417) 862-6293.

Also in this park is the ***Japanese Stroll Garden,*** a seven-and-a-half-acre stroll around three small lakes with extensive landscaping. There is a teahouse, a moon bridge, and other features unique to a Japanese garden. It is open from April through October, Friday through Monday from 11:00 a.m. to 7:30 p.m.

civilwarstrife

Missouri gave 109,000 men to the Union cause and about 30,000 men to the Confederacy. Vicious guerrilla action terrorized the state, especially near the Kansas border. The Battle of Wilson's Creek near Springfield was one of the bloodiest of the Civil War.

An outstanding nature center, designed by the Missouri Department of Conservation, is at 4600 South Chrisman (417-888-4237). Want to know how to tell a hawk from a heron when they're far overhead? One of the volunteers will show you silhouettes suspended from the ceiling that correspond to identifying shapes on the floor. Another room invites you into the dark with displays that light up—or sing out—as you press a button or break a light beam. See a barred owl, hear a whip-poor-will, watch a flying squirrel—it's all here—3 miles of nature trails take you through Ozark woodlands—80 acres of hilly wilderness—and a small bog; cross genuine suspension bridges and learn while you take in the fresh air.

Springfield is a mecca for watercolorists. For more than forty years, the ***Springfield Art Museum*** (417-837-5700) has been the locus for Watercolor USA, one of the most prestigious shows in the nation. Every June and July the museum displays the best and the brightest; you may browse or buy at 1111 Brookside. (You'll know you're close when you see the large yellow sculpture called *Sun Target*; local kids call it the *French Fries*.) The museum owns a fine permanent collection of original works. Visit at any time of the year. Museum hours are Sunday from 1:00 to 5:00 p.m., Tuesday, Wednesday, and Saturday from 9:00 a.m. to 5:00 p.m., Thursday from 9:00 a.m. to 8:00 p.m., and Friday from 9:00 a.m. to 5:00 p.m.

The ***Landers,*** at 311 East Walnut, is the home of the Springfield Little Theatre, which features talented actors from around the Ozarks. Kathleen Turner and Brad Pitt got their starts here. In 1909 theater architect Carl Boller designed the theater to look like a jewel box and a cartouche. It has a high, curved ceiling resembling a crown. The theater has been refurbished to its original splendor. There are the original wooden armrests and floral ironwork on the seats. The ribs going up the cartouche are like a crown inset with jewels, where the lights sparkle surrounded by 14-karat gold leaf and sterling painted moldings. The baroque decor and heavy draperies give it an elegantly royal feel. The $400,000 renovation of this magnificent theater alone is worth seeing, but the fact that it also offers a six-show main season (each show running three weeks), the Springfield Opera, the Springfield Ballet, and the Mid-America Singers makes it all the more worthy of a visit. Call the box office at (417) 869-1334 for current productions, or visit www.Springfieldlittletheatre.org.

The **Virginia Rose Bed and Breakfast,** at 317 East Glenwood, Springfield, is in a 1906 farmhouse with a red barn in the middle of a subdivision—sort of a country inn in the middle of the city. Owners Virginia and Jack Buck offer guests a choice of five guest rooms, all with private baths. Well, actually there is one suite with a connecting bath that is used for families with children or couples traveling together. A big breakfast awaits guests in the morning—all for $70 to $100. Call (417) 883-0693 or (800) 345-1412, or visit www.bbonline .com/mo/virginiarose.

You will want to call Kathy Adamson and visit her shop, **Woodland Carvings,** 2269 North Farm Road 45, Bois D'Arc, while you are in the area. Kathy carves original and functional art—doors, screen doors, beds, fireplace mantels, lamps—as well as gift and art items. Her hours are irregular because of her show schedule, but it is worth the effort to contact her at (417) 672-2278 and see what she does, or visit her new Web site at www.woodlandcarvings .com. Her outdoor and western art has evolved from hand-carved deck plates and yokes that are used as

twenty-four andtwo

Missouri was the twenty-fourth state admitted into the Union, and the second state (after Louisiana) west of the Mississippi. The Missouri Compromise of 1820 allowed this state to enter the Union on August 10, 1821, as a slave state, but no other concessions were made in states formed from the Louisiana·Territory.

braces on canoes, as well as intricately carved canoe paddles. She carves river gods with long flowing beards (that resemble her husband, Sonny) for the yokes of canoes. Kathy doesn't just carve canoes however: She works "relief carving" on flat wood and creates three-dimensional scenes. Her river series showing life along the river look real enough to walk into. She carves mantels, clocks, and doors. She began by carving pieces for her own canoe, and the results were so beautiful that others asked her to personalize their crafts.

Kathy uses teak, butternut, mahogany, cedar, and walnut, relying solely on her own strength and sharp tools to create the delicate layers in the wood. She uses earth-toned artist oils and stains to add a bit of color to the carvings while allowing the grain to show through.

Outdoor Playground

Just outside Springfield on U.S. Highway 65 is another kind of mecca—tiny **Galloway** is wall-to-wall antiques. It's as if the town had been invaded by aliens selling oldies; nearly every building and home is now a shop. Find everything from a vine-and-thorn-wrapped birdhouse (to discourage cats, of course) to European china, but don't stop before you get to the flea market a half-mile or so north of the other shops. Here are two floors of great bargain flea market antiques.

West of Springfield at 528 South Highway ZZ in **Republic,** you can tour **General Sweeny's Museum of Civil War History** and see thousands of items from the bloody war fought in Missouri, Arkansas, Kansas, and Indian Territory. In this area families were split between blue and gray uniforms, and bands of killers disguised in those uniforms raided cities and farms. More than fifty exhibits will show you the progression of the war here from the 1850s in "Bleeding Kansas" to the surrender of the last regiments of Confederate Missouri troops at Fort Blakely, Alabama. There are rare photos, guns, swords, flags, uniforms, and more. The museum is open from March through October, Wednesday through Sunday 10:00 a.m. to 5:00 p.m.; November through February, Saturday and Sunday 10:00 a.m. to 5:00 p.m. Call (417) 732-1224.

Head north on I-44 to **Lebanon,** a town loaded with surprises. Flea markets and antiques shops are all over the place, more than twenty-three at last count.

Nancy Ballhagen's Puzzles, at 25211 Garden Crest Road, Lebanon, may not be for everyone, but if you are a jigsaw puzzle fan, this is a must. Nancy Ballhagen has the only jigsaw puzzle shop in the Ozarks. They have the world's largest puzzle (18,000 pieces, which measures 6 feet by 9 feet). There are double-sided puzzles, round puzzles, and puzzles within puzzles, not to mention movie poster puzzles, postage stamp puzzles, and puzzles covering any subject you can think of. Nancy says they just always liked to do puzzles, especially when the children were young, and it sort of grew into a business. They have more than 3,400 puzzles displayed in their shop and now are carving wooden puzzles. To find puzzle paradise, take exit 135 (Sleeper exit) from I-44 and follow the east outer road ¾ mile to the first mailbox on your left—you can see it from the freeway. Hours are Wednesday through Saturday 11:00 a.m. to 5:00 p.m. Call (417) 286-3837 or visit their Web site at www.missouripuzzle.com.

AUTHOR'S FAVORITE ANNUAL EVENTS IN SOUTHWEST MISSOURI

AUGUST

Springfield
Ozark Empire Fair, with live music,
(417) 833-2660

Cassville
Old Soldiers and Settlers Reunion,
(417) 847-2814

Carthage
Marion Days, annual religious events for
Vietnamese Catholics,
(417) 358-7787; www.carthage-mo.gov

SEPTEMBER

Mansfield
Laura Ingalls Wilder Festival,
(417) 924-3626

Silver Dollar City
Festival of America; Silver Dollar City
and out-of-state artisans demonstrate
and sell crafts,
(800) 952-6626;
www.silverdollarcity.com

Branson
Annual Autumn Daze Craft Festival, with
more than 150 crafters,
(888) 322-2786

DECEMBER

Silver Dollar City
Old Time Country Christmas, with lights,
music, and special Christmas attractions
for adults and children,
(800) 952-6626

Branson
Trail of Lights at Shepherd of the Hills,
a spectacular drive-through display
of lights,
(417) 334-4191;
www.explorebranson.com

Springfield
Ozark Mountain Christmas/Festival
of Lights,
(800) 214-3661

Well, maybe they don't have the only jigsaw puzzle shop in the Ozarks. Their son, Richard Ballhagen, inherited the puzzle mania from Keith and Nancy and opened **Richard's Puzzles,** 23480 Route 66, where he makes only hand-cut wooden puzzles. Although it's still all in the family, Richard's work is different. He creates heirloom puzzles or puzzles from your favorite photograph or print. Just about anything you can imagine, he can carve. The intricately cut puzzles are made of ¼-inch wood and include a variety of special effects such as silhouette pieces, sculpted borders, or a name cut right into the puzzle for a personal touch. A slide-top wooden box for storage is included with every puzzle. He keeps odd hours because he works a full-time job as well, so call ahead for an appointment, (417) 532-5355, or visit his Web site at www .rbpuzzles.com.

While you are in the Lebanon area you might want to visit **Whirlwind Ranch,** where the alpaca are part of the family. The ranch's Whirlwind Ranch Store, at 24649 Snowberry Drive, has a beautiful selection of products made from 100 percent baby alpaca fiber and blends of 70 percent alpaca and 30 percent acrylic. There are ponchos, sweaters, and blankets along with alpaca toys and teddy bears. You can even buy a pet bed stuffed with alpaca fiber for your dog or cat. In winter, there is nothing warmer than hats, scarves, ear warmers, or hiking sox made of alpaca. If you enjoy knitting, crocheting, spinning, or weaving, there is a colorful assortment of sport-weight and fingering-weight yarns, hand-dyed and made right at the ranch. Liz, Linda, and Walter Mitchko will welcome you. The Web site www.whirlwindranch.com will tell you all about the ranch. From I-44 take exit 129 and turn right to the first traffic light. Turn left onto Highway 32 East. Go about 7 miles to Snowberry Drive (the second dirt road on the left after B Highway), turn left onto Snowberry Drive, and go 2 miles—the driveway entrance is on the left at the top of the long, steep hill. Stop at the first house. Please call ahead (417-533-5280) to schedule your visit.

If you are into horses and you have your horse along, a small side trip south of I-44 on Highway J will quickly take you to **Waynesville** and the **4J Big Piney Horse Camp.** This is a chance to get off the road and into the woods, so bring your horses and ride over mountains, through beautiful valleys, along the edge of bluffs, through quiet forests, and along the famous Big Piney River. There are all types of fun activities for when you are enjoying time off the horse as well. The campsites have water and electricity, and Betty Laughlin does the cooking in a dining hall that seats up to 300 people. Modern restrooms, showers, and electricity are available, too, and horses are comfortable in their box stalls. Brothers Jimmy, Jay, Jeff, and Joey are partners in the operation. Sunday church services are held in the dining hall and on the trail. Camping arrangements must be made in advance, so call (573) 774-6879 for camping and riding dates from May through October. Enjoy the thrill of feeling the wind in your hair as you ride through this Missouri paradise.

On the square in Waynesville is the **Old Stagecoach Inn Museum,** which has been totally renovated and is exactly as it was when the stage stopped here at the courthouse. It is listed on the National Register of Historic Places and is open April through September on Saturday from 10:00 a.m. to 4:00 p.m. Guided tours are available.

Caveman BBQ might be Missouri's most unusual place to eat. Park in the gravel lot at 26880 Rochester Road just a few miles from Richland, then board the "Batmobile" to where an elevator takes you up to the restaurant, located inside a cave. It took five years of incredible labor and five years of jackhammer and shovel to remove 160 tons of rock to make enough room to seat 200 people in this former resort dance hall. Renovators tried not to change the cave's appearance too much and were quite successful. A dehumidifier keeps the restaurant dry, and small waterfalls into a goldfish pond allow natural water to drip from the ceiling. The fare is BBQ. Specialties include slabs of smoked ribs and other meats. The restaurant is a destination for river traffic, too. You can float to the bottom and walk up the bank. The dress code is casual. Call (573) 765-4554 for more information; Caveman is closed during the winter.

Fort Leonard Wood is the home of the U.S. Army Corps of Engineers. It is also the home of the Army Engineering Center and the *U.S. Army Engineer Museum.* The fort covers about 63,000 acres in the Ozarks about 130 miles southwest of St. Louis on I-44 near Waynesville. A recipe for creamed chipped beef on toast, called S.O.S. by the soldiers who had to eat it, is tacked on the wall of a restored mess hall, one of several "temporary" wooden buildings built during World War II. A field kitchen lists the fort's daily food requirements in 1943. These included 4,750 pounds of bacon, 47 gallons of vinegar, and 105 gallons of syrup.

walkingonair

Eminence is the home of astronaut Tom Akers and his family. Akers, who has had four space flights to date, holds the record for the number of hours of EVAs (extravehicular activities, or space walks), most of that time accrued while helping to repair the Hubble Space Telescope.

Colonel Akers has experienced more than 800 hours of space flight, bringing his total EVA time to 29 hours and 40 minutes. He was a member of the first three-person EVA and the longest EVA—8½ hours—in history.

The museum's oldest treasure is a signet ring that belonged to Lysimachus, an engineer general who served Alexander the Great in about 330 B.C. The museum walks people through a chronological history of the corps. There are several specialized galleries. Many of the temporary mobilization buildings, two-story wooden barracks familiar to soldiers at every post in the world and built to last about ten years, have been restored to create typical company areas. A supply room with a wood-burning stove, racks for M1 rifles and 45-caliber pistols, and entrenching tools would bring a tear to a supply sergeant's eye.

The history of the corps, however, dates from the Revolutionary War. There's a 1741 muzzle-loading cannon that the French lent to the Continental Army, and a shovel and ax dating from the 1781 Battle of Yorktown, the first engineering victory of army engineers who built fortifications and trenches into British positions. The oldest unit in the U.S. Army is the 101st Engineer Battalion of the Massachusetts National Guard, established in 1636 as the East Regiment.

Another display demonstrates low tide at Omaha Beach during the D-Day invasion of June 6, 1944, with an engineer disposing of German mines that would have been a danger to Allied ships.

Children can take the wheel of a restored pilothouse, U.S. *Snag Boat No. 13,* which kept the Mississippi River clear for more than fifty years. Other hands-on activities include a land-mine detector. Gun enthusiasts will enjoy the nineteenth-century Gatling gun, an 1819 Flintlock rifle, an 1816 Springfield 69-caliber musket, and many small arms from more recent wars.

The museum is at the corner of Nebraska and South Dakota Avenues. Hours are 10:00 a.m. to 4:00 p.m. Monday through Saturday. Admission is free but donations are accepted. Call (573) 596-0780 for more information.

St. Roberts is a popular tourist area for visiting military and families attending basic-training graduations at Fort Leonard Wood, which is the home of the Maneuver Support Center of the United States Army.

Wander down Highway VV from Licking and enjoy the rugged countryside, which contains some of the largest springs in the world. The Jacks Fork River, Alley Spring with its restored *Old Red Mill,* and the Current River near *Eminence* provide year-round canoeing. (The spring water is a consistent 58 degrees Fahrenheit year-round.)

Highway 19 is a rustic stretch of the Ozark Plateau. The hills are steep and the road curvy, so your only choice is a slow drive across narrow bridges over gleaming waterways. You can't pass anyone on Highway 19, so you may as well relax and enjoy the view. It is a scenic highway and has its share of people there just to see the towering pines that create a lush green canopy that shades the roadway. The highway snakes from near Hannibal to the Arkansas state line. You can drive from Hermann to Eminence while stopping at little shops for ice cream, sandwiches, and shopping. The views are enchanting, so take your time and slowpoke along.

Alley Spring Mill sits along the crystal-clear Jacks Fork River. It is open every day from Memorial Day through Labor Day from 9:00 a.m. until 4:00 p.m. Rangers are on hand to explain how the mill worked and the role it played in developing a community of Ozark settlers. The area still calls people together as it has for more than 10,000 years. Native Americans gathered here to hunt the abundant game and fish the rich waters. The first mill was built in 1868. A newer one replaced it in 1894. The latter was cutting edge in its technology, featuring a turbine rather than a water wheel, and rollers to replace the grist stones. Soon a blacksmith opened a shop and people began to gather here and camp with entire families while the grain was ground. Now it is a popular spot for family reunions, campouts, and fishing trips. Camping and canoe rentals are available at the mill, which is located 6 miles west of Eminence on Highway 106. For more details visit the Web site at www.eminencemo.com.

Missouri's southwestern rivers—quick-running, spring-fed, and bone-chillingly cold—are so beautiful they bring a lump to your throat. In fact, the Current, the Eleven Point, and the Jacks Fork have been designated ***Ozark National Scenic Riverways.*** It is Missouri's largest national park.

Generations of canoeists and trout fishermen know these secluded waters. You can spend the day without seeing another soul, then camp on a quiet sandbar at day's end and listen to the chuck-will's-widows and owls call while your fire lights the riffles with bronze. Pick fresh watercress from these icy waters to garnish the trout that sizzles in lemon butter on your grill, and know that life gets no better than this. There are plenty of rental outfits; pick up brochures anywhere. Ask about Bluff Hole, a hidden swimming hole where the Jacks Fork River widens. There is deep water at the base of the rock shelf and gravelly shallows near the bank. The hole is hidden away at the end of a tree-shaded path and has been a favorite of swimmers for generations.

Springs gush from beneath solid rock, slowly carving themselves a cave. Early residents built mills here to produce flour, cornmeal, and sawn lumber. There's as much natural history as history along these bright rivers.

The crystal-clear waters of the spring-fed Current River drift past rocky bluffs and shorelines thick with wildflowers. Schools of darters flash by in the cold water (water temperatures range from 53 to 57 degrees Fahrenheit year-round). This gentle wilderness is a favorite canoeing and tubing area for Midwesterners. Even beginners can navigate the waters without getting too wet except by choice. Paddle hard around the occasional rootwad, an area of ripped-up tree roots that may create some white water—or simply get out and push the canoe past it. Most stretches of the river are rated Class I, as easy as it gets. The gravel bars are fine places to pull out and have lunch or even to camp for the night. Only owls and the leaf rustle of small creatures break the silence. The tranquil moss-covered hillsides are a peaceful escape from the busy world back home. At some points along the river, the water turns a rich blue-green as it gets wider and deeper, sometimes as deep as 25 feet.

The half-day trip from Weymeyer put-in to Van Buren is an easy and beautiful route. A few miles before the Van Buren Bridge is Watercress Park, the site of a single Civil War battle—with trenches and grave sites—where the Union Army held the Confederates at bay across the river one cold night. At the pull-out spot just past the Van Buren Bridge, you can leave your canoe on the beach and let the outfitters know you are back.

Alley Spring Mill is called the most picturesque spot in the state. Some eighty million gallons of water a day flow through here, and the Red Mill has been restored to working order.

Big Spring is the largest concentration of springs in the world, which is a mystery to hydrologists, who do not understand the large volume of water. Beautiful rivers gush right out of the ground from the base of spectacular rock bluffs and create the most consistent, spring-fed, crystal-clear rivers in the country. Round Spring Cave is just off Highway 19.

If you have horses, **Cross Country Trail Rides** on Highway 19 East, Eminence, has a week planned for you. You can take the whole family on a cross-country trail ride from April through December. Jim and Jane Smith have spent more than forty years perfecting the week's adventure. You will camp for the week on Jacks Fork River. The ride returns to the base camp every night, where eighteen meals are served and entertainment is royal. Well-known country music performers entertain at a dance every night but Sunday. There are horse shows, team roping events, and other sports to show off your steed. Jane says they fill up months in advance; to ensure a spot for you and your mount, write P.O. Box 15, Eminence 65466, or call (573) 226-3492. This is a "B.Y.O.H." affair; no rental horses are available. Visit their Web site at www .crosscountrytrailride.com.

If you don't have your own horse, head for **Coldwater Ranch** on Highway 19 north of Eminence and turn right onto County Road 208. Jim and Kathy Thomas have horses at their place and will arrange anything from an hour ride to a six-day pack trip. For the overnight trips, tents, sleeping bags, food, and beverages are provided, and your steed has a saddlebag for your personal stuff. Quarter horses and a few gaited horses range from mounts for the novice to those for the experienced riders. The ranch accepts all ages; they have had four-year-olds and eighty-year-olds. Horses are $36 per hour; overnight trips range from $250 to $400 a night and include three meals and about ten hours of riding. Recent expansion on the ranch includes cabins (starting at $112 per couple; $12 per additional person) and RV/camping sites ($15 per night). You can also bring your own horse and rent a stall for $15 a night. Call (573) 226-3723 for more information, or visit www.coldwaterranch.com.

A winding drive along U.S. Highway 160 takes you to the beautiful Eleven Point River, with its many natural springs and lovely spots for picnics. You will be surprised at the excellent roads through these wooded hills. The Between the Rivers section of the Ozark Hiking Trail covers about 30 miles. The northern entry point to this section is on U.S. Highway 60, approximately 3½ miles west of Van Buren. Trailhead parking is provided for users at US 60 and at Sinking Creek Lookout Tower, about a mile west of Highway J.

The trail winds south for the first 13 miles across small tributaries that feed the Current River. Creeks with names such as Wildhorse Hollow, Devil's Run, and Big Barren flow through the area. Designed for both hikers and horses, the trail crosses a ridge that divides the Current River from the Eleven Point River along Gold Mine Hollow. The trail offers panoramic mountain views and deeply wooded areas to filter the summer sun. Deer gaze from the shadows, too. If you are a hiking enthusiast, this area is for you. Pick up a book with a listing of all the hiking trails on federal property, complete with maps, at the Federal Forest Service Office in Winona, grab your backpack, and head out.

Wooded Ozark roads stretch out before you now, with oak trees shouldering evergreens; the Doniphan Lookout Tower watches the national forest for fires here. Tune your AM radio to 1610 for Ozark Riverway information if you are headed for canoeing or camping at one of the many parks or rivers nearby.

If you have a carload of children and want a resort, the *River's Edge Resort* is also near Eminence and offers not only rooms and cabins but also hot tubs, inner tubes, firewood, and lodging on the Ozark National Scenic Riverways Jacks Fork and Current Rivers. There are rooms overlooking the river. You can visit the Web site at www.rivers-edge.com or call (573) 226-3233.

Eminence Canoes, Cottages & Camp (573-226-3500 or 800-723-1387; www.eminencecanoescottagescamp.com) has everything you need for wilderness adventure. Rent a canoe and float on the 135 miles of the spring-fed, clear waters of the Jacks Fork and Current Rivers. Unwind in the informal cottages on thirty acres. These mini-homes have one to three bedrooms and fully equipped kitchens (and gas grills, free movies, and cable TV). Or you can camp out along the Jacks Fork River Valley in the family- and pet-friendly campgrounds.

Because of the number of campers who take this route to the wilderness, the little town of *Van Buren* on US 60 is the home of several neat shops.

The *Briar Patch* at 101 Highway W is owned by Jennifer Kennedy. This charming shop has a bit of everything, including fresh flowers, candles, silk flowers, gourmet baskets, gardening tools, stained glass, and vintage jewelry. Local artists—metalwork and pottery—show their art here. Her hours are, shall we say, flexible? That translates to around 9:00 a.m. opening to about 6:00 p.m. closing, six days a week. You can call ahead at (573) 323-8560. See more of the Briar Patch, Brer Rabbit, at www.thebriarpatch.net.

The *Hidden Log Cabin Museum* is the darling of Ozark historian Wanda Newton. For many years she knew that a log cabin lay at the heart of the neat, ordinary, frame house next door. She waited for the house to go on the market and spent the time buying antiques and refurbishing them. She also studied the history of the Ozarks and dreamed. Then in 1990, it happened. The old Bowen place was for sale, and she bought it and began removing decades of "improvements" from its interior.

A one-of-a-kind "yawning" fireplace of hand-cut sandstone with a huge arch rock was professionally rebuilt and the hearth made ready for cooking with a collection of early ironware. Layers of sheetrock, insulation, and ceiling tiles were removed to expose the original construction. The furniture and household goods from the 1800s were placed in the painstakingly restored home. By the spring of 1993, her work was complete. In addition to the original log cabin room, the museum also has a dining room, bedroom, kitchen, and summer kitchen, each room filled with artifacts and furnishings. But most important is the woman who has lovingly created its homelike atmosphere. Wanda knows every jewel in this jewel box. Many of the pieces of furniture are from families who lived here. The treasures span two centuries, from tools of the early 1800s, pre–Civil War books and toys, and willow furniture made by gypsies to a 1930s Zenith radio from the Depression years. Many of the items are dated—a rope bed is from 1838, and an immigrant trunk dates from 1869. Located in downtown Van Buren, the museum is a block west of the courthouse on the south side of the Float Stream Cafe at the corner of John and Ash. Hours are Monday through Saturday 9:00 a.m. to 5:00 p.m. and Sunday 1:00 to 5:00 p.m. April through November; (573) 323-4563. Adults, $2, children, $1.

The *Float Stream Cafe* is well worth a visit. Good food is served here. There is a special every day, seven days a week. Friday is fried catfish day and Sunday has chicken and dumplings. The cafe is open from 5:00 a.m. until 9:00 p.m. Call (573) 323-9606.

The main reason for being in the area is floating the Current River. There are plenty of places to rent canoes, tubes, and rafts, but one of the nicest is the *Rosecliff on the River Lodge* at 1 Big Springs Road, Van Buren, at the Van Buren Bridge. You can spend a full day on the river with the 22-mile Log Yard trip, which leaves at 7:00 a.m. Or you can take a two-day camping trip to Eminence on the Jacks Fork River. There are short 3-mile trips or longer half-day floats. Then there is the fun of tubing along Chilton Creek, and now rafts and kayaks are featured. But whatever you do, slather a lot of sunscreen on your body because you can get a world-class sunburn in an aluminum canoe on the brilliant water of the Current. The voice of experience is telling you this.

Rosecliff Lodge has a good restaurant, the Blue Heron, which has a river view. For more information about these rooms, which all have a river view, call (573) 323-8156. Check the Web site at www.currentriverlanding.com.

Big Spring Lodge (573-323-4423) is about 4 miles from Van Buren; it is a National Park Service site on the Ozark National Scenic Riverways. Rustic log cabins with fireplaces that reflect a more relaxed pace and a dining lodge/craft shop were built by the Civilian Conservation Corps (the CCC, otherwise known as "Roosevelt's Tree Army") in the thirties. The lodge is on the National Register, and rightly so; log, timber, rocks, and cut-stone materials and unique spatial arrangements make this an excellent example of the projects that brought work to so many in Depression-era America. Dining-room hours vary with the season. For more information write Big Spring Lodge, P.O. Box 602, Van Buren 63965, or visit www.bigspringlodgeandcabins.com.

Big Spring State Park is nearby, as are the Mark Twain National Forest and the Ozark National Riverways Tourist Information Station. Call (573) 323-4236 or write for an accurate list of trails and starting points (P.O. Box 490, Van Buren 63965). Also, any Missouri tourism office can provide a list of hiking trails.

Big Spring is the largest single spring in the world, pouring out 277 million gallons of crystal-clear water each day—a breathtaking natural wonder you will want to photograph or draw.

The beginnings of *Grand Gulf State Park* (Missouri's answer to the Grand Canyon) in Thayer go back 450 million years to a time when sediment was deposited by ancient seas, forming dolomitic rock. As the area uplifted and the sea receded, water percolated down through cracks in the rock and began to dissolve passageways underneath. Streams cut their own beds on the surface of the soft rock. As air-filled caves formed and cave roofs collapsed, streams were diverted underground. The collapse of the Grand Gulf occurred within the past 10,000 years—fairly recent by a geologist's reckoning.

Today the gulf is ¾-mile wide with side walls 120 feet high. Part of the cave roof that did not collapse formed a natural bridge 75 feet high that spans 200 feet, one of the largest in the state. The park contains wheelchair-accessible overlooks with spectacular views of the chasm, a ¼-mile loop trail around the gulf, and a primitive trail across the rock bridge (don't look down). Call (573) 548-2525 for details.

West Plains is a starting point for canoeing on the North Fork River. Or you can strike off on foot into the wilderness of the Mark Twain National Forest.

Travel westbound from West Plains on US 160 to Highway 181 north to the little town of *Zanoni* if you want total peace, quiet, and privacy with nothing to disturb your sleep but the morning song of bluebirds and wrens.

Dawt Mill was established in 1897, and its water-powered buhr stone mill is still grinding grain. More than a century ago, teams of mules and horses would pull wagons filled with corn and wheat to the mill, and farmers would wait for their turn at the water-powered buhr stone mill. The cotton gin would be pumping out cleaned cotton ready to be sold or spun. While waiting for their grinding, the families would shop at the general store or use the black-smith's skills repairing farm implements and shoeing animals. People gathered on the porch of the mill to play music in the evening and would fall asleep under their wagons while the mill ground into the wee hours of the morning.

Deep in the Ozark hills near **Ava,** a bell chimes in the early morning quiet. Trappist monks in white robes and cowls move quietly into the darkness of the chapel for morning prayers and meditation. A day begins at **Assumption Abbey,** one of only eighteen monasteries of the Trappist order in the country. The abbey is surrounded by 3,400 wooded acres. The monks seldom leave the abbey, and by their simple lives of prayer, labor, study, and solitude seek a deeper personal relationship with God. So why mention a monastery in a travel guide, you might ask? Well, although man cannot live by bread alone, a visit to the Assumption Abbey bakery is in order. To be self-supporting as monasteries must, the monks discovered a market for fruitcakes. Now they produce more than 30,000 fruitcakes annually. Since the fruitcakes proved to be so popular, a new and larger bakery has been added. Fresh fruit jellies and jams are also sold in the bakery store. Call the bakery at (417) 683-2258. Each cake weighs two pounds and is generously filled with raisins, cherries, and pineapple marinated in Burgundy. Each one is bathed with an ounce of dark rum for moistness and flavor. They bear no resemblance to the ready-made kind you get from your aunt at Christmas. They are sold by direct mail to customers throughout the United States and are carried at prestigious stores such as Williams-Sonoma.

The abbey extends hospitality to men and women of all faiths. If you need a restful weekend, or counseling from the monks, you are welcome. Guests get home-cooked meals served family style by the brothers. A love offering helps defray the costs. Reservations for overnight stays are requested and donations help with the expenses. The simple quarters contain wash basins, twin beds, shared bath/shower, and a small homemade desk. Monks bring fresh soap and towels. It is a simple life. If you would like to spend a few days at this retreat, call (417) 683-5110 or write Highway 5 Box 1056, Ava 65608. For more information visit www.assumptionabbey.org. The abbey is always closed during January for the monks' retreat and reflection.

Guest ranches are fun whether you are with a vanload of children or travel alone. If the abbey is too quiet for your tastes and you still want to get some brain-clearing time, mosey over to the **Bucks and Spurs Scenic River Guest Ranch,** also in Ava, for a real Western experience. Their address is HC71, Box 163, Ava 65608. For all the details of this ranching vacation and the various

Laura Ingalls Wilder–Rose Wilder Lane Museum and Home

packages offered, visit their Web site at www.bucksandspurs.com. The most popular package is the five-night vacation, which is $1,110 for adults and $1,055 for children age twelve and younger. Weekend packages are also available for $667 for adults and $635 for children younger than age twelve (free for kids younger than age three). Family discounts are available. Call (417) 683-2381. You can get some hands-on time on this thousand-acre horse-and-cattle ranch by helping Cecil and Sonya Huff with the chores. Or you can float down Big Beaver Creek in an inner tube and study the clouds and treetops. The choice is yours. Four guest rooms sharing two baths are paneled in weathered barn wood. The dining room has a long table for chow time, or the Huffs will set up a picnic site when you ride the trails. Horses, tack, guides, and canoes are furnished. There's fishing and swimming or a turbulent game of horseshoes for excitement.

North on Highway 5 is tiny **Mansfield,** home of the **Laura Ingalls Wilder–Rose Wilder Lane Museum and Home** (417-924-3626; www.laura ingallswilderhome.com). Laura's home is just as she left it and there is a museum that contains four handwritten manuscripts. Author of the now-famous (courtesy of television) *Little House on the Prairie,* among other books, Laura was encouraged to write by her daughter, Rose Wilder Lane, a well-known author in her own right from the early 1900s. They are buried in the Mansfield cemetery. Admission: adults $8, children up to 18 years old $4, seniors $6.

Head on to **Mountain Grove** for "great steaks" at the unusual **Club 60** at 6773 US 60. The license-plate fence in front of this old 1946 tavern will catch your eye. Although drinks are served and there is a pool table, this is very much a family place. Call (417) 926-9954.

Go west on US 60 to swing back into Springfield.

In the tiny town of **Miller,** there is an exquisite Victorian home known as **Maggie Mae's Tea Room,** 206 West Fourth Street (417-452-3299). As you partake of a wide array of luncheon specials consisting of homemade soups, salads, and entrees, save room for their special desserts. There is also a gift shop adjacent to the restaurant. Shop hours are Monday through Saturday 9:00 a.m. to 5:00 p.m. Lunch is served from 11:00 a.m. to 2:00 p.m.

Mining Country

Head west on I-44 to Halltown; then slip onto Highway 96 west for **Carthage,** where the majestic 1895 Jasper County Court House stands proudly on the square, turreted like a medieval castle. Settled in the 1840s, Carthage was burned to the ground in guerrilla raids during the Civil War. The Battle of Carthage was fought July 5, 1861—sixteen days before the Battle of Manassas in Virginia—making it the first land battle of the Civil War. More than 8,000 men fought here, 1,000 of them German-American Union troops from St. Louis led by Col. Franz Siegel. The rest of the soldiers were Southern sympathizers led by Missouri governor Clayburn Jackson. Destruction of the town was total. The 1849 home named Kendrick Place, built by slaves, was one of the few homes left standing after the war. In the late nineteenth century, all new homes were built here; these are an abundance of Victorian homes and more than one hundred of them have been restored. This interesting piece of history can be researched more thoroughly at the **Civil War Museum,** 205 Grant Street, Carthage (417-237-7060), open from 10:00 a.m. until 5:00 p.m., and at the **Victorian Era Powers Museum** at 1617 West Oak Street, Carthage 64836 (417-358-2667). The Web site for both the Victorian and the Powers Museums is www.carthage-mo.gov. The curator at the Powers Museum is Michele Hansford, and she is very knowledgeable about both the Victorian era in Carthage and the Civil War battles fought near here. Lead and zinc mines were developed after the war, and wealthy owners built magnificent homes away from the mining camps. Marble quarries provided Carthage gray marble for many large state and federal buildings. The fine old homes here bespeak prosperity. It's still a beautiful city—the courthouse, high school, and many of the churches and homes are built of the stone quarried here. (The stone is not technically marble, but a limestone that takes a high polish.) Both the courthouse and high school contain murals by Lowell Davis, one of America's best-known nature artists and a native of Carthage.

Carthage has more than its share of well-known native sons and is becoming a center for artists in the area. About eighteen resident artists call it home. Internationally known zoologist and naturalist Marlin Perkins (remember *Wild Kingdom?*) was born here; you'll find a bronze sculpture of Perkins by artists Bob Tommey and Bill Snow in Central Park on Garrison Avenue.

howtomakeaspy

In her teens Myra Belle Shirley watched her town leveled by war. The Battle of Carthage was the first major Civil War battle, fought July 5, 1861. She became the infamous Confederate spy and outlaw, Belle Starr.

Follow the historic drive markers for a tour of Carthage's magnificent old mansions that have been kept so beautifully throughout the years. Innkeepers Don and Joy Sisco welcome you to their home, the imposing circa-1901 **Leggett House,** at 1106 Grand Avenue (417-358-0683). This magnificent home is in its glory again with stained glass, a mosaic-tiled solarium with a marble fountain, finely crafted woodwork, and—an elevator. Rates are $85 to $115 a night, which includes a full breakfast served in the formal dining room. Visit their Web site at www.leggetthousebb.com.

Best place to eat close by is the **Ranch House Restaurant** at 2937 South Grand Avenue in Carthage. The father/daughter team of Susan Skaggs and Dick Fanning have something for just about any appetite, including big steaks. Hours are 11:00 a.m. to 9:00 p.m. every day but Sunday. Call (417) 359-5200.

Jim and Jan O'Haro invite guests to join them at the **White Rose,** 13001 Journey Road. The house was built in 1900 of Carthage marble and was originally a thousand-acre dairy farm. The front walk is 300 feet of Carthage marble leading to this beautiful three-story home. Rose, herb, cut-flower, and vegetable gardens lead you to the old carriage house. The White Rose is not an inn in the commercial sense, but a bed-and-breakfast of the European type. It is a private home open for guests to enjoy an atmosphere of warmth and comfort. As you might have guessed from the name, the family is proud of its Irish heritage. Not only do guests receive a full Irish breakfast, but tea is served at four o'clock, and guests are given a complimentary beverage in the evening. Full-course dinners are also included in "Bed and Banquet" reservations, and ingredients used include both imported and those grown in the vegetable garden out back. The O'Haros describe it thus: "The idea is seductive and yet so simple. Who hasn't wished after a truly superb dinner . . . the kind that lingers in the memory . . . that you could just go upstairs and sink into bed instead of getting in a car and driving somewhere else? To keep the magic that surrounds the very best meals alive, you need to be able to linger, maybe to take your coffee in another room in front of a log fire, knowing that your bed is only a few steps away. . . ." Call (417) 359-9253 or e-mail joharo@4state.com for reservations. Rooms are $76 to $105. Visit the White Rose Web site at www.whiterosebed-breakfast.com.

If you fancy colonial reproduction furniture, visit the **Colonial House Historic Reproductions,** at 348 Grant Street, where every piece is authentic reproduction (is that an oxymoron?). This shop is unique to southwest Missouri. Call (417) 358-8454 or visit www.colonialhousedecor.com. Hours are Monday through Saturday 10:00 a.m. to 5:00 p.m.

trivia

The town of Noel gets popular every year at Christmas—at least its post office gets popular—as people send letters and cards here for postmarks. It's actually pronounced Nole. South of Noel is Bluff Dwellers Cave, a well-known tourist attraction that was 250 million years, give or take a million, in the making. It has drawn cave seekers since 1927.

Michael and Jeanne Goolsby have opened their 1893 Queen Anne Victorian to guests. The **Grand Avenue Bed & Breakfast,** 1615 Grand Avenue, has four original stained-glass windows. All guest rooms have private baths, cable TV, telephones, and coffee service. Two have computer hookups. The first-floor room has a king-size bed and Jacuzzi for $94 (weekdays). On the second floor, there's the Hawthorne Room ($109 weekends) with a two-person Jacuzzi, the Alcott Room ($74–$84 weekends), and the Mark Twain Room ($79–$94 weekends), which can also be made into a suite (priced from $99). The Goolsbys serve a full country breakfast (the specialty is orange nutmeg French toast) with sausage or bacon. Call (417) 358-7265 or (888) 380-6786 or e-mail reservation@grand-avenue.com. Or check their Web site at www.grand-avenue.com for a view of this stately home.

Joplin is the end of the Missouri portion of old Route 66 and has been a stopping point on cross-country travel for many decades—in fact, since 1889, when Joplin City was named for the Rev. Harris G. Joplin, a Tennessean settler. The abandoned tailing piles and mine shafts scattered about the town and the elegant homes just west of the downtown area are reminders of the mining era of Joplin. Mineral collectors are drawn to the abandoned mine dumps and chert piles and to the Tri-State Mineral Museum, one of the best museums of its kind in the state.

The Joplin Historical Society preserves much of the city's history at the **Dorothea B. Hoover Historical Museum,** located in Schifferdecker Park at the intersection of Seventh Street and Schifferdecker Park, Joplin (and adjacent to the Tri-State Mineral Museum). Hours are Tuesday 10:00 a.m. to 7:00 p.m. Wednesday through Saturday 10:00 a.m. to 5:00 p.m., and Sunday 2:00 to 5:00 p.m. Call for holiday hours, (417) 623-1180 or (417) 623-2341. To learn more about the city of Joplin, visit its Web site at www.joplinmo.org.

Outside Joplin go east on County Highway V to Diamond. From Diamond drive 2 miles on V and then south about a mile to find the **George Washington Carver National Monument,** which commemorates a man who was more than an educator, botanist, agronomist, and "cookstove chemist." He was a man who wanted "to be of the greatest good to the greatest number of people," a man who refused to accept boundaries, who drew from science, art, and religion to become a teacher and director of a department at Tuskegee Institute in Alabama. He taught botany and agriculture to the children of ex-slaves and tried to devise farming methods to improve the land exhausted by cotton. Known as the "Peanut Man," Carver led poor, one-horse farmers to grow protein-rich and soil-regenerating soybeans and peanuts. The Carver Nature Trail leads from the birthplace site through two springs and ends at the Carver family cemetery.

Joplin is also the home of the **Spiva Center for the Arts** at 222 West Third (corner of Third and Wall). Call (417) 623-0183, fax (417) 623-3805, or e-mail spiva@spivaarts.com. You can visit their Web site and see the works of the artist of the month at www.spivaarts.com. Hours are Tuesday through Saturday 10:00 a.m. to 5:00 p.m. and Sunday 1:00 to 5:00 p.m.

Just down U.S. Highway 71 is the **Real Hatfield Smokehouse,** 7329 Gate-way Drive, Neosho (417-624-3765). Owner Chad Neece has a sparkle in his blue eyes as he talks about his "home-grown" hogs. "We smoke anything you can get from a hog," he says. Bacon, hams—you name it, he smokes it. He will mail hams anywhere in the United States and even has a regular customer in London. The small smokehouse uses a special sugar cure and hickory logs to give meats a golden-brown finish and good fla-

trivia

Two major Civil War battles were fought in Newtonia—with total forces numbering in the thousands. The 1862 battle was one of very few encounters in which Native Americans fought on both sides. Southern forces had Choctaw, Cherokee, and Chickasaw soldiers, while other Cherokees fought with the Union forces. This was the first battle of Colonel J.O. (Jo) Shelby's famous Iron Brigade. The 1864 battle, also involving Shelby, was the last battle in the Civil War fought west of the Mississippi. A Civil War cemetery here houses the remains of thirteen soldiers, including the famous (or infamous to the Confederates) Robert Christian. Many slaves and their descendants are also buried here. The earliest stone is 1858.

uch salt as other smokehouses. Hours are 7:30 a.m. to 6:00
ough Saturday. The smokehouse is closed on Sunday.

most-storied and mysterious sights, visit "Spooksville," 11 miles
lin. It is here that an eerie light has been appearing in the
road most nights since 1886. This almost supernatural spook
light created panic in the small village of Hornet and is often referred to as
the Hornet Ghost Light. Early settlers actually left the area in terror because of
the giant ball of light bouncing over the hills and across the fields. Today the
light seems to concentrate on one gravel road known as Devil's Promenade or
Spook Light Road. The light has even been rumored to come right up to your
car and land on the hood, then bounce off or go out and appear later behind
you. It disappears whenever approached. If you have the nerve, take I-44 west
from Joplin to Highway 43, then drive south on Highway 43 approximately 6
miles to Highway BB. Turn right. Drive approximately 3 miles to road's end.
Turn right and drive another mile to a second dirt road to the left. If you haven't
chickened out yet, you will now be headed west on Spook Light Road. The
road is long. Park anywhere along the side of the road and wait. Try to find the
darkest spot about 2 miles down the road. You can even venture down some
of the very dark side roads. There is no charge for this thrill except the years
of therapy it will take to get over it.

   Pierce City on Highway 37 has a couple of neat little places to stop for
a rest. But this is only a rest stop because what you really want to see is the
Jolly Mill. You will be rewarded with a lovely wooded drive after you leave

Jolly Mill

Highway 97 and turn onto US 60. Go 1⁹⁄₁₀ miles to a sign on Forest Road 1010, then 1⁸⁄₁₀ miles across a creek with a bridge with no sides to Forest Road 2025, past an old white church and churchyard, then ⁷⁄₁₀ mile to the park.

This park is sort of a secret spot that the locals enjoy. Its history is fascinating. In 1848 George Isbell built a water-powered mill to serve settlers with gristmill products (and spirits). The new village that grew up around him was called Jollification, and it was a rest stop and resupply point for wagon trains headed west to Kansas and Indian Territory. When the Civil War came, the area was ravaged, and two cavalry battles raged here. Bushwackers terrorized and burned the village but, here's a surprise, the distillery was spared.

A new village rose from the ashes and the distillery resumed operation. In 1872 a railroad was built to Indian Territory, eliminating wagons. At the same time George Isbell refused to pay the new tax on spirits, stopped making whiskey (much to the regret of travelers), and turned his attention to milling flour. The village faded and by 1894 the mill stood alone with the schoolhouse. But the mill prospered; flour was milled here until the 1920s, and gristmill products were ground out here for another fifty years.

A community effort was made to have the mill placed on the National Register of Historic Places, and the mill was rehabilitated. It is once again a working mill. The water still rushes by picnic tables, the covered bridge, and another wooden bridge. It is worth the drive to see.

Webb City's claim to fame, the ***"Praying Hands,"*** is in ***King Jack Park***. This 32-foot concrete-and-steel structure is atop a 40-foot-high hill. The park is named for the ore called "jack" that made the city rich in the 1870s. There are no signs inviting the visitor to stop to see the huge sculpture, it just suddenly appears. The hands were created by Jack Dawson, an art instructor at the Webb City schools, and he intended it to be just a quiet reminder for people to turn to God. Webb City is off US 71.

When you get enough of sitting around indoors, you outdoors folks can go west on U.S. Highway 59 at Anderson to enter canoe heaven. US 59 runs along the Elk River, and the sudden appearance of the famous overhanging bluffs makes you want to duck as you drive under them.

Tri-Lakes Area

The last town on Highway 76 before you enter the Mark Twain National Forest is **Cassville.** Highway 76 is a long and winding road through the forest, so if you arrive at this point after dark, you might as well spend the night. Check out **The Rib** on Highway 112 South (417-847-3600). It's a mighty fine restaurant that lives up to its name. Darrel and Danille Norvelle and Bill and Shirley Lay offer, among other items, barbecue ribs and steak, and on Friday and Saturday nights there's a prime-rib special. Wednesday night is a personal favorite, though. That's when the pan-fried chicken, mashed potatoes and gravy, green beans, and the usual comfort food reign. Hours are Tuesday through Friday 11:30 a.m. to 1:30 p.m. and 5:00 to 9:00 p.m., and Friday and Saturday 5:00 to 10:00 p.m. Closed on Sunday and Monday.

The *Devil's Kitchen Trail* winds from the valley to the top and down again, giving a close-up look at the geology and history of the area. Eleven of the park's fourteen caves are found along the rocky bench here. Shelters like these were used by Ozark bluff-dwelling Indians who lived here about 10,000 years ago. Artifacts such as food and fragments of clothing have been found to date this culture. The Devil's Kitchen was named for the stone formation that provided a hideout for Civil War guerrillas. Heading south on Highway 112, softly winding roads, tree-lined hills, and spectacular views pop up as you crest hilltops in this lovely national forest.

Roaring River State Park is the fountainhead of the Roaring River. There is a hidden spring in a cave filled with crystal-clear aqua-blue water that stays a constant 58 degrees Fahrenheit year-round. More than twenty million gallons a day are pumped into the river. Here the state maintains a trout hatchery and stocks the river daily in season.

missouridivided

By the time the Civil War was approaching, Missouri was warring within itself. The governor and many legislators favored secession but were outvoted at the convention called to decide the matter. The governor's faction fled south to Cassville, where they signed an ordinance of secession and affiliation with the Confederate States of America.

The biggest day of the year happens on March 1, when the whistle blows early in the morning to open trout season. Anglers stand shoulder to shoulder in hopes of catching a lunker or their limit. Friendly competition abounds to catch the biggest trout. If you skip work to make opening day, try to avoid all the press who are waiting to snap pictures of the annual event. If you catch a big fish, you might just end up on the front page of the local newspaper . . . and then you will have some explaining to do when you get back to work.

The park runs the *Roaring River Inn.* The inn, made largely of wood and stone, has twenty-six rooms and a view of the river valley below. Rooms range from $90 to $115 (for suites). Cabins also are available from $93 to $110.

To reserve a cabin or room, call (417) 847-2330. Other accommodations are available outside the park and in the town of Cassville. The ***Parkcliff Cabins*** are log cabins with loft, deck, fireplace, full kitchen, and two bedrooms for $145 for the first two and additional $10 for each additional person. Call (417) 236-5902. This is the perfect romantic winter getaway if escape is what you are looking for; but then the nearness of Branson, Table Rock Lake, and Eureka Springs, Arkansas, also make it a perfect family getaway, as well. Go to the Web site at www.parkcliff.com. There are also several campgrounds in the Mark Twain National Forest, and about 20 miles east of the state park is the ***Big Bay Campgrounds.*** It has bathrooms and water and is geared mostly to tent campers. Rate is $10 a night. Call (877) 444-6777, or visit www.reserveusa.com.

Roaring River State Park is part of the White River basin. From a geologist's point of view, the basin tells a fascinating story. The White River has cut into the flat Springfield plateau, creating deep, steep-walled valleys and exposing varied layers of rock—shale, limestone, dolomite, and chert.

Pastures fringed with woods are found along Highway 76 East through the Piney Creek Wildlife Area. Mile after mile of ridge roads and startling views unfold until finally, over the crest of the last hill, beautiful Table Rock Lake appears before you. It feels like the top of a Ferris wheel from this vantage. The occasional small farm or Ozark stone cottage dots the roadside. Valleys with pastures, ponds, or a lone barn sitting starkly against the sky are the only traces of civilization.

At the town of Cape Fair you can turn right on Highway 76 to Table Rock Lake or turn left to ***Reeds Spring.*** Because of the proximity of Silver Dollar City, there are quite a few artists in residence.

Allen's Back Yard Custom Stained Glass at 17 Spring Street is where Carl and Diane Pope create huge custom windows for homes, churches, and businesses. But there is more in the 45-square-foot gallery, because the Popes display the crafts of other artists in Reeds Springs. You can purchase Potternot

trivia

Unlike Huckleberry Finn, you don't have to play hooky to go fishing in Cassville because school is officially closed on March 1 every year so residents can grab a fishing pole and open trout season. It has been a school holiday in this Ozarks town near Roaring River State Park for as long as anyone can remember. Many spend the night along the stream to secure a good spot. There can be as many as 4,000 anglers vying for spots along the stream. In 2005 Missouri Secretary of State Robin Carnahan fired a pistol at 6:30 a.m. to officially open the six-month season.

Pottery, wheel-thrown whimsical and practical creations of Tracy Adams. Moonstruck Pottery, by Lee Ann Downing, are smaller, more functional pieces. Tammy Fink's Ficklefink Pottery (don't you just love that name?) shows her raku pottery art, and another raku pottery artist, the very talented Gary McAlpin, forms unusual wall pieces that include other media such as wood, fiber, glass, and metal mixed in with the clay. Woodcarver Bill Butterfield carves beautiful detailed busts of Indians, pirates, and large animals such as moose and bear. Mike and Debbi Hackeson make wire wrap jewelry and lampwork beads. For more informarion call (417) 272-9442.

Fred and Beth Hickeman's family shows a diverse run of art at the newly opened *Gallery at the Spring,* downtown just behind the spring at 81 Spring Street. Fred does fine woodworking with oak and other woods. Beth is a painter in watercolor and acrylic. Their son Nathan and his wife, Dori, are an artistic duo who share a love of art. He does pottery and she is a photographer. Beth says they will be open "probably" daytimes six days a week. Call for hours, (417) 272-0430.

At *Omega Pottery Shop* (417-272-3369) on Highway 248 East (at the south edge of town), Mark crafts each piece of wheel-thrown stoneware and finishes it in a gas-fired kiln at 2,350 degrees—that makes it safe for oven, dishwasher, microwave, and moon missions. He travels occasionally but says it's "too much of a bother to pack everything up and move it." He would rather stay here in Reeds Spring. "Pottery is a craft that needs space to display it," he says. "That's why potters have studio-galleries." Mark enjoys doing custom work—such as lamps, sinks, and dishes. He points to other craftspeople— Tom Hess, another potter; Lory Brown, a pine-needle basket maker—all in the Reeds Spring area. Omega Pottery is open from 10:00 a.m. to 5:00 p.m. every day except Wednesday. Visit his Web site at www.omega-pottery-shop.com not only to see his wares but also to learn how pottery is made.

Hess Pottery and Baskets on Highway 413 North, a mile north of Reeds Spring, is where potter Tom Hess and basket maker Lory Brown have built a unique twelve-sided Mongolian yurt for their workshop and gallery. The natural surroundings offer the perfect atmosphere to enjoy the work these two fine artists produce. Tom's pottery is handmade, using natural red clay. Each piece is sealed with a coating of very fine clay and then fired in a kiln. It is ovenproof, dishwasher safe, and can be used in a microwave.

Lory's pine-needle baskets are made with 18-inch southern yellow pine needles and 10-inch ponderosa pine needles. These baskets must be seen to be loved. Each coil of pine needles is stitched with raffia palm leaf to the preceding coil using closely spaced stitches. The finished baskets are sturdy and durable and retain their wonderful pine scent. Call (417) 272-3283. The shop is open from 10:00 a.m. to 5:00 p.m. in the summer and "most days" in the winter. Visit their Web site at www.hesspottery.com.

Table Rock State Park is one of the most popular (meaning crowded) state parks in Missouri. Off the beaten path here means wilderness, on the path means bumper-to-bumper in summertime. As in most resort areas in the state, early spring and late fall are perfect times to roam without the huge crowds summer brings.

Author Harold Bell Wright came to these hills for his health in the early part of the twentieth century and was so taken by the beauty of the area that he settled in to write. *The Shepherd of the Hills* is his best-known and most-beloved book; it captured the imagination of generations and even became one of John Wayne's early movies (which, incidentally, borrowed only the name from the book—the script was unrecognizable!).

US 65 is an old-fashioned, uncrowded Ozark highway. You can still see the view as you crest hills here, but the *Shepherd of the Hills Inspiration Tower* offers an incredible one. The tower's first observation level is at 145 feet; the tower is 230 feet, 10 inches tall, with two elevators or 279 stairs to the top. But rest assured it is stable. It is designed to withstand 172 mph winds (gusts of 224 mph), and it cost $1.5 million to build; this is not surprising since it contains 92,064 pounds of steel and is set in forty-three truckloads of concrete. It also contains 4,400 square feet of glass, for a breathtaking view from the highest point around the Tri-Lakes area.

If you've heard of Silver Dollar City (and you will if you stay in Missouri for long), you've heard of *Branson.* Once a quiet little town pocketed in the weathered Ozark Mountains near the Arkansas border, the town has seen business pick up considerably of late.

Branson has changed in the past several years from the strip of country music "opries" and related foofaraw crowded cheek-by-jowl along Highway 76 (known as "the strip") to the country music capital of the

trivia

The Shepherd of the Hills Theater is the longest-running theater in the country. It began with a stage with its audience on blankets on the hillside, upgraded to folding chairs, and now is an outdoor amphitheater that seats around 2,500 people. The year 2007 is its forty-eighth year in nonstop operation. In 1998 there was a big fire in the dressing rooms and it was announced that there would be no show that year. People poured in with stage props (antique guns, for example) to help, and the theater was up and running in time for the annual performance.

Midwest, giving Nashville a run for its money. Twenty-seven theaters in town now feature such stars as Loretta Lynn, Andy Williams, Mel Tillis, and Elvis. No, really. Elvis is alive and well and living in Branson. Elvis (Ehlert) does an uncanny impersonation of the The King. And, possibly the most popular show in town is Japanese hillbilly fiddler Shoji Tabuchi.

Branson is trying to keep up with the demand of more than four million tourists a year, but as you would suspect, about an hour before the matinee or evening shows begin, the traffic is much like a long narrow parking lot. How bad is the traffic? Well, women have been seen leaving their husbands behind the wheel on Highway 76 while they get out and shop, buy things, and rejoin their spouses in the car a block or so up the street. We are talking gridlock here. The secret to getting around is learning the back roads. Just knowing that the quickest route from Andy Williams's Theater to Ray Stevens is Forsythe Street to Truman to Shepherd of the Hills Expressway—and not 76 Country Boulevard (a road to avoid if at all possible)—can save you enough time for dinner.

There are other little secrets, too. The chamber of commerce will give you a free, easy-to-read map showing the shortcuts from one end of the 5-mile strip to the other. The recently repaved back roads can make life a little easier, even though you can't avoid the traffic altogether. The city now has a trolley system on the strip and that helps a bit.

Do flea markets interest you? You're in the right place; downtown Branson has five of them. If you don't find something in this lineup, you aren't looking very hard, or you have a good deal more self-discipline than most of us.

Innkeepers Kay and Glen Cameron are natives of the Ozark Mountains. For several generations their families have lived in the Ozarks of Missouri and Arkansas. You met them back in the Southeast section of this book. Kay runs the Ozark Mountain Country Bed and Breakfast Reservation Service. Their home near Branson can be your home too while you visit this busy town. *Cameron's Crag Bed & Breakfast* has three beautiful rooms for your enjoyment. The Highland Rose Suite is a romantic hideaway and is a favorite for honeymoon or anniversary couples. The private spa room features a sunken hot tub for two. Sliding-glass doors open to a private deck with a fantastic view of the lake and river valley. A comfy king-size bed and reclining love seat add to the appeal. There is a private entrance, a private bath (tub/shower), refrigerator for your champagne, and microwave, coffee bar, VCR, and cable TV. That should cover everything you might want for a honeymoon shouldn't it? The suite is $125. The Around the World Suite also has a hot tub on a deck overlooking Lake Taneycomo. It also has a private entrance, king-size bed, sitting area, refrigerator, microwave, coffee bar, cable TV, and VCR as well as a large private bath (tub/shower) with a dressing room. The decor has a sort of international flavor. It is $105. You can enjoy a spectacular bird's-eye view from your suite and from the hot tub on your private deck overlooking the lake and valley in the Bird's Eye View Suite, which encompasses an entire level of the detached guesthouse. This spacious suite includes a king-size bed, living/dining area with queen-size sleeper sofa, and a full kitchen. The private bath features a shower and deluxe whirlpool bath for two. This suite also has a private entrance, cable TV, and VCR. It is $135. You can take a virtual tour of the suites at Kay's Web site, www.camerons-crag.com. Then e-mail her at kay@camerons-crag.com or call (417) 334-4720 or (800) 933-8529.

Even before you start your day, you can order a three-egg omelet at the **Hard Luck Diner** in the Grand Village Shops at 2800 76 Country Boulevard in Branson and have someone sing a country song. The singing waitstaff makes sure your day begins with a song. Call (417) 332-0150. Hours are 8:00 a.m. to 8:00 p.m. every single day.

Because Branson is in the throes of a building boom and the traffic can be a genuine pain, the best thing to do is to find a bed-and-breakfast somewhere away from Branson and then just go in when you are psyched up to do it. (Avoiding the whole place might be more to your liking.) But you've come this far, so the first order of business is to get that map (the chamber of commerce or many hotels will have them) and use all the traffic shortcuts you can. The side roads that loop off Highway 76 do reduce travel time and frustration. If you are not attending a show, stay off the streets around the 7:00 and 8:00 p.m. curtain times, when about 1,500 people per theater are all on Highway 76 and the local police are issuing tickets for driving in the center turn lane. Branson traffic lulls roughly before 8:30 a.m., between 10:00 and 10:30 a.m., and from around 2:00 to 2:30 p.m. Branson drivers are very courteous, though, and it won't be long before someone lets you pull out in front of him onto the strip.

One of the most interesting things to do when you hit Branson is to head to the old downtown area, which sits on the banks of the Taneycomo River. Here you can visualize what the town was like before it became an entertainment center. The riverfront and downtown area is going through a renaissance, and many changes are underway. To acquaint yourself with some of the improvements planned, visit www.branson.com, which is the Web site of the Downtown Branson Main Street Association (417-334-1548). To take the pulse of the town, you must visit **Branson Café,** 120 West Main Street (417-334-3021), the oldest restaurant in town. A big country breakfast with all the trimmings and friendly, charming waitresses await you when you slide into a red upholstered booth and kick back to enjoy. The waitresses are a wealth of information about where to go and what to see that is "hot" in Branson. The cafe has a daily luncheon special, which is posted in the window. All the homemade favorites appear there on a weekly basis. For dinner you might try some of the freshly caught trout from the Taneycomo River. Be sure to save room for some homemade cobbler or pie. Hours are from 6:00 a.m. to 8:00 p.m. daily; closed Sunday.

There are many gift shops on Main Street, but one of the "don't miss" ones is *Dick's 5&10 Cent Store* at 103 West Main Street. You truly do take a walk back in time to the good old days when you could have a quarter and shop to find just the right "toy" to delight your child's heart. You can find such things as those gadgets that moooo when you turn them over or paper dolls, the kind we used to play with for hours. They also have an assortment of old-time dime-store items. Call (417) 334-2410.

The ladies who like lovely things will not want to miss *Patricia's House* at 101 West Main Street, Branson. Patricia's exquisite shop is packed with French and Italian reproduction furniture, Victorian dolls, jewelry, paintings, and decorator items. All of this brings out the visitor's romantic side and makes one think of a dream bedroom. It is truly a "fantasy" shop of beautiful things. Call (417) 335-8000. Hours are 9:00 a.m. to 6:00 p.m. every day.

Keep going another block east, across the railroad tracks, and you will find the *Branson Scenic Railroad* at 206 East Main Street (417-334-6110); www .bransontrain.com). Here you can book a tour of the Ozarks countryside. The train leaves from the historic Branson Depot. You might want to call ahead for schedules and packages that are available; the train doesn't run from December to the first week in March.

If you are in a mood to do some trout fishing on Lake Taneycomo, check with *Scotty's Trout Dock,* 395 Lake Drive, Branson (417-334-4288). They can supply you with all the necessary items and good advice on how and where to catch "the big one." They rent tackle, boats, and even pontoons, and they will supply a guide if you want one. Or maybe all you need is a driver, so you can stretch out and catch some rays on the back of the pontoon— definitely a "little slice of heaven." Hours are 7:00 a.m. to 5:00 p.m.

Head west on 76 ("the strip"). You can stroll along the strip and take the trolley. Then you can leave

trivia

Children can attend several shows, such as the Osmonds and comedian Yakov Smirnoff, at no cost. If you wait until after 3:00 p.m. to visit Silver Dollar City, you get in free with the same ticket the next day.

the driving to someone else and have fun with your friends. You and the kids can "Ride the Ducks," vintage WWII amphibious vehicles that go along the strip, through an outdoor military history museum, and then splash into the lake.

The Branson/Lakes Area Chamber of Commerce will send you information packets. The one to ask for is the *Branson Roads Scholar: Mastering the Back Roads of Branson.* It contains a map of alternative routes and traffic tips. Call (800) 214-3661 or visit www.bransonchamber.com.

The most exciting part of visiting Branson is how easy it is to get up close to the stars—the music legends who are playing golf (10:00 a.m. on Wednesday at Pointe Royale Golf Course on Highway 165 often has Mel Tillis, Andy Williams, and Moe Bandy teeing off together) or shopping at the grocery store. That constellation of stars is only the beginning. Other stars are scheduled to shoot through Branson for performances, too.

So you never know whom you will see sitting in one of the many restaurants (most of which are down-home sorts of places, not exactly low-calorie eateries) in town. For the best ambience, though, drive across the lake to the **Candlestick Inn** at 127 Taney Street on Mt. Branson, where the food is more upscale. The atmosphere is romantic, the view of downtown Branson is sensational (especially during the Christmas season's Festival of Lights), and you never know who will be at one of the tables. The menu features such delicacies as crab-stuffed trout. You can see the humongous neon candle sign (it says STEAK AND SEAFOOD) from downtown, but it's tricky to find if you don't know to just follow Highway 76/68 across the bridge. Call (417) 334-3633 for reservations or visit the Web site at www.candlestickinn.com. Hours are lunch Wednesday through Friday 11:00 a.m. to 3:00 p.m., dinner Sunday through Thursday 5:00 to 8:00 p.m., Friday and Saturday 5:00 to 10:00 p.m.

Needless to say, there are many motels around Branson. You can escape the motel rut with a bed-and-breakfast if you plan ahead a little. Plus, the people in the B&Bs tend to know their way around the town and can give you the shortest, fastest routes to wherever you are planning to go. Call Ozark Mountain Country Bed & Breakfast Service at (800) 695-1546 and let Kay Cameron find you one of the more than fifty B&Bs in the Tri-Lakes area near Table Rock Lake, Lake Taneycomo, Branson, Silver Dollar City, or just across the border in Arkansas. She has about a hundred bed-and-breakfast inns to direct you to in the Ozarks, from cozy hideaways for couples to family-friendly accommodations, some with their own hot tubs or swimming pools. Kay also has the number of a show service that will deliver tickets to any bed-and-breakfast inn for you.

The easiest way to reach Branson is from US 65, which runs through the east end of town. The West Missouri 76 exit will put you on the strip, where you will watch pedestrians speed by your slowly moving car. Or you can use the back entrance and take Highway 248 to the Shepherd of the Hills Expressway to the west side of town, where things will not be much better. You can reach the Branson/Lakes Area Chamber of Commerce at (900) 884-branson for a guide that lists the shows in town and the ticket office phone numbers. There is a $1.50 per minute charge for that call (average three minutes), and you get a recording to leave your name and address. It is sometimes cheaper to call the visitor information number at (417) 334-4136, but that line is often busy and you can be put on hold for about ten minutes. They have a computerized service listing the hotels and motels with vacant rooms. For show tickets you can call BransonTix, a private company that handles about a dozen theaters, at (800) 888-8497.

The **Stone Hill Wine Company** (417-334-1897; www.stonehillwinery. com), on Highway 165, 2 blocks south of Highway 76 West, is open Wednesday through Saturday 8:30 a.m. to dusk and 10:00 a.m. to dusk on Sunday for wine sales and tastings (open until dusk in the summer). The gift shop also sells sausages, cheese, and wine-related items. Slow down 2 miles outside town and turn west onto Highway V. There's something here you won't want to miss: the **School of the Ozarks** (417-334-6411; www.cofo.edu) in **Point Lookout.**

It's a college campus, all right, but wait. What's going on here? Everybody looks so . . . busy. This is a different kind of college—a fully accredited, four-year school where each full-time boarding student works at one of sixty-five campus jobs or industries to pay in part for his or her tuition. It calls itself "the campus that works." The rest is provided through scholarships. The campus fruitcake and jelly kitchen is open during business hours weekdays. Student workers bake some 20,000 fruitcakes a year and produce delicious apple butter and many flavors of jelly.

Students built the college itself—it's a pretty one—and run the Ralph Foster Museum and the Edwards Mill (a working replica of an old-time gristmill) as part of their tuition. If you're hungry while you're here, stop at the student-run **Dobyns Restaurant** on Point Lookout. It is more than just a restaurant. The dining hall seats 275 people in an elegant and relaxed rustic lodge design with handmade furnishings and magnificent landscaping—and all the cooking is done by the students. There is even a gourmet bakery with fresh pastries and desserts. A gift shop—with student-made stained glass, jellies, fruitcakes, pottery, and freshly milled grain products—is inside. What more could you want? Well okay, there's a hotel facility as well. Prices for these luxury rooms (which have king- and queen-size beds and fireplaces with balconies overlooking the campus) range from $169 to $299 a night, but many of them sleep six, with two

On a Very Personal Note

My husband and I had driven to the Branson area to see Willie Nelson and Wayne Newton. I pointed a tattoo shop out to him and told him I wanted to go back the next day to interview the owner for the book. He went off to play golf that day, and when he came home I proudly showed him a new tattoo of a butterfly on my, uh, hip.

He was not amused. In fact, he was not pleased at all. He began to get surly about it. Then he smiled and accused me of getting a "stick-on" tattoo. He led me into the bathroom to rub it with soap and water. It did not come off. I expected him to tell his golf buddies about it the next day, but he never mentioned it to anyone. He was truly embarrassed for me. Every night when I undressed, he glared at me. Now mind you, I had just turned fifty years old and we had been married nearly twenty-five years. To say he did not like surprises is putting it mildly. He is very conservative.

Of course, so am I. The tattoo was not done by a shop but purchased in the five-and-dime downtown. But I was having so much fun I decided to carry on with the fiction. Before the butterfly began to wear off, I used alcohol to remove it and applied a new one—on the other side this time—and waited for him to figure it out. He didn't. This went on for four weeks—first on the right, then on the left—the butterflies remained on my backside, and impossibly, he did not notice their change of address. But the good news was that on the fifth week when I replaced the butterfly with a dragon, he did notice.

It was probably the best practical joke I have ever managed. My husband believed me, my best friends and my mother believed me. Only my dad (who never saw it) never believed it. He said he simply knew me too well to believe I would have a butterfly permanently placed on my derriere. Now the dragon maybe. . . .

bedrooms and pull-out couches. Smaller rooms are $65 and $69. Restaurant hours are 10:30 a.m. to 8:00 p.m. Monday through Saturday and 10:00 a.m. to 2:00 p.m. on Sunday.

The School of the Ozarks campus is beautiful, perched on its hill; don't miss the view from Point Lookout. Stand here at dusk when the bells of the carillon roll out over the mist-shrouded river below, if you want goose bumps up and down your arms. When the sun slides down the sky, that sound of bells on the crisp evening air is unforgettable. Williams Memorial Chapel is a fine place to stop for a moment; the tourist bustle slows to a halt here and there's room to breathe.

Big Cedar Lodge at 612 Devil's Pool Road in **Ridgedale,** 9 miles south of Branson, is off the beaten path literally, but is very well known by people throughout the country. You can stay in the lodge itself (winter from $79 weekdays) or in private cabins (winter from $169 weekdays), and there is a

Jack Nicklaus–designed executive golf course called **Top of the Rock.** It is an Audubon Signature Course, the first in the state and only the sixth in the country. The distinction means the course meets Audubon's environmental guidelines on natural habitat and water life. Big Cedar also has a fine trout stream and waterfalls all over the place. Devil's Pool Restaurant offers a level of dining not found easily in the Ozarks—maple-glazed quail with white bean ragout, prime rib, and a champagne brunch on Sundays. Call (800) 225-6343 or visit their Web site at www.big-cedar.com.

January is spawning season at **Shepherd of the Hills Fish Hatchery,** 6 miles southwest of Branson on Highway 165 in the White River valley, just below Table Rock Dam. The Missouri Department of Conservation produces 1.2 million fish annually, 80 percent of which go into nearby Lake Taneycomo. There is a visitor center filled with exhibits and aquariums, and four trails ranging from ³⁄₁₀ mile to about 1½ miles. Call (417) 334-4865. Hours are 9:00 a.m. to 5:00 p.m. seven days a week (except Thanksgiving, Christmas, and New Year's Day). Visit on the last Saturday in February for "Vulture Venture" (noon until 6:00 p.m.) and see hundreds of vultures enjoying their winter roosting spots. There are fun activities for the kids, too. Visit www.mdc.mo.gov and type in shepherd of the hills fish hatchery for more information.

If you want luxury in the European style, the **Chateau on the Lake,** 415 North State Highway 265, Branson, is high-dollar elegant. This ten-story hotel sits on a hill right next to Table Rock Lake and has 302 rooms and suites. A standard room with a mountain view begins at $109 and goes even higher if you want to see the lake. Now it has a world-class day spa, too. The murals that decorate the ballroom are of castles in Europe, and you can scuba dive, parasail, water-ski, fish, play tennis, or work out in a twenty-four-hour fitness center. There's a Sweet Shoppe and a deli, and even a free movie theater. The Chateau Grille offers fine dining. If you want to check it out first, visit the Chateau's Web site at www.chateauonthelakebranson.com. Call (888) 333-LAKE.

This you have to see to believe. **Cathedral Church of the Prince of Peace,** 405 Kentling Road, is the world's smallest cathedral, situated in **Highlandville.** It is the cathedral of the very, very small Christ Catholic Church, which claimed the title of "the Catholic Peace Church" in 1965. The beautiful Garden of Saints displays statues of about a dozen saints among the flower beds, with many varieties of geraniums surrounding the Ozark stone building. The garden has a shrine to Our Lady of Guadalupe with angels on either side of the opening. Red roses fill the area. A pond and fountain honoring Our Lady of Mt. Carmel floats lily pads and is home to large goldfish and blue herons.

Cathedral Church of the Prince of Peace, Highlandville

The cathedral also showcases a well-known oil painting by Tomás Fundora, *Cristo de Espaldas—The Back of Christ*—which has raised a bit of controversy wherever it is shown. Presiding Bishop Brian E. Brown OSH is the Ordinary of the Diocese of the Shepherd's Heart, a diocese of the Ecumenical Free Catholic Church. A 1,500-foot trail meanders through the woods and meadows by the 14 Stations of the Cross. But walk right up there and open the door. Inside is a cathedral—complete with pews, candles, altar, tabernacle, and prie-dieu. A rich stained-glass window catches the sunlight. If you are lucky you will hear the world's smallest cathedral pipe organ, custom built for the cathedral, with forty-two pipes and the full range of the human voice. The woodwork is old-world craftsmanship at its best. Sunday morning service is at 11:00 a.m. Built of native stone, the cathedral measures 14 feet by 17 feet and seats a congregation of fifteen; it is mentioned in the *Guinness Book of Records*. The blue onion dome suggests the church's Eastern rite affiliation. The Bishop suggests knocking on the door of the house attached to the church by a covered walkway if you want to talk about the Catholic Peace Church. Call (417) 598-0852. Exit off Highway 65 at the Highlandville exit.

Turn west onto EE Highway, drive three miles and turn right onto Kentling Road. It is 300 yards down the road on the right.

Long Creek Herb Farm is nestled deep in the woods on the Long Creek arm of Table Rock Lake. Jim Long calls it an "old-fashioned working herb farm in the heart of the Ozarks," and that describes it pretty well. Guests sip herb tea on the shady porch and listen to the tree frogs. On the twenty-seven-acre farm, skullcap, foxglove, and horehound are grown, and goats, chickens, guineas, geese, and steers are raised. Jim grows 400 cultivated and native herbs; many of them, such as sweet goldenrod and horsetail, are unique to the Ozarks.

There is a meticulously groomed demonstration garden with winding paths and a bentwood gazebo. After twenty years as a landscape architect, Jim decided that his love of plants needed a new outlet, and he wanted to share the experience of herbs with people.

He also has a gift shop where you can buy about eighty products, including seasonings, teas, and herb blends both medicinal and culinary. You can buy a Dream Pillow to induce dreams that are relaxing, romantic, or action-packed, depending on the herb blend.

The farm is open on Wednesdays in the summertime (May through October) and other days by appointment. You must call first. You will need directions or a map to find the place because you must cross two state lines and three county lines to get there. Visit their Web site at www.longcreekherbs .com. Call (417) 779-5450.

The *Golden Pioneer Museum* in *Golden* can be found between Branson and Eureka Springs on Highway 86. The owner of this museum is Winfred Prier, and the curator is Murry Carmichael. The museum is home to Arlis Coger's collections from the Trail of Tears Museum, which used to be in Huntsville. The 5,200-square-foot museum contains pots (800 clay pots, to be exact), weapons, tools, and clothing made by the Arkansas Osage Indians and found in the War Eagle (Arkansas) mounds. Here is the largest collection of Dalton points (more than 1,000), arrowheads knapped around 8000 B.C. by Native Americans living along the White River south of Huntsville. On display also is the world's largest collection of Tussinger points. The extensive mineral collection includes the world's largest quartz and crystal cluster—4,200 pounds—found in Hot Springs and displayed in its own glass case, as well as the world's largest turquoise carving, weighing in at 68 pounds. Other displays show rocks that look ordinary until ultraviolet light reveals the vibrant fluorescent color within them. There is also an incredible collection of baseball cards. The guns on display include one of only three or four derringers like the gun that killed President Abraham Lincoln. The museum also has one of the largest collections of carnival glass in the Midwest: more than seventy-two collections, and still growing. There is a gift shop, too. Call (417) 271-3300 to arrange for a tour (open April through November).

Dogwood Canyon Nature Park on Highway 86 West and Highway 13 near *Lampe* is the dream come true of Johnny Morris, founder of the Springfield's Bass Pro Shop. This 10,000-acre property preserves an Ozark wonderland that Morris now shares with the public. Three creeks flow through the canyon—Dogwood Creek, Little Indian Creek, and Hobbs Creek—creating one of the best trout streams in the Midwest. Strategically placed weirs, or dams, and a series of short spillways form terraces in the stream and aerate the water. Each dam creates a pool for the trout. Wet-season, spring-fed waterfalls from bluffs above the stream bank were made year-round attractions by the addition of pumps to recirculate water to add oxygen for the trout. Stone walkways and wrought-iron railings built by Bass Pro's staff blacksmiths guide visitors, and 6 miles of paved road pass the most interesting sights in the canyon. There are twenty-nine stream crossings on the property, and most fords are located at the base of a weir so that passengers in vehicles can view cascading water at eye level. Other crossings include stone bridges built by a local mason and a post-and-beam-covered bridge built by Amish craftsmen. The park is open to the general public year-round and for tram tours from mid-March to Christmas. Horseback trail rides are offered, and bicycle tours are also available. Try a half-day guided trophy fishing excursion on Dogwood Creek (ages 13 and older) or two hours of unguided fishing. Tour guides relate the history of the area during the two-hour tram ride, pointing out caves where workers discovered ancient burials. One site high on a bluff contained the remains of a Native American who died more than a thousand years ago—predating Missouri's Osage tribe. Remains (a child and two adults) at another site were dated to 6000 B.C by scientists—making them the oldest human remains ever found in the state. The tour crosses into Arkansas and travels among herds of bison, longhorn cattle, and elk. The visitor center has Civil War and Indian artifacts. Reservations are required for tram tours, trail rides, and fishing excursions. Call (417) 779-5983 for more information or visit www.dogwoodcanyon.com.

Just a mile east of US 65 on Highway 14, the town of *Ozark* is a haven for antiques buffs. The largest collection is housed at the *Maine Street Mall*, 1994 Evangel, a warehouse along US 65 and home to 108 antiques dealers. There are even antique cars inside. The mall is open seven days a week from 9:00 a.m. to 6:00 p.m. (5:00 p.m. in the winter). Call (417) 581-2575 for information. You will find a couple dozen more shops—filled with a gazillion items—in the town of Ozark itself. This town, 15 miles south of Springfield and near enough to Branson to draw its crowds, is a mecca for folks who love old stuff.

Dear's Rest Bed and Breakfast, 1408 Capp Hill Ranch Road, Ozark, is tucked in a beautifully natural Ozark setting where you can enjoy unexpected visits from deer, raccoons, and wild turkey, and birdsong will wake you in the morning. The rustic house was built for innkeepers Allan and Linda Schilter by local Amish builders and is filled with family antiques and old toys. The great room has a cozy fireplace, and since the home is open to only one family at a time, it becomes your fireplace, too. The all-cedar home has art-stenciled walls. The broad deck, hot tub, and covered porch are ideal places to enjoy the woodsy view or take your breakfast. You can hike on the old ranch roads and come back to steam away the cricks in a large hot tub in the woods. Birders enjoy the beautiful mountain views and the 250 varieties of birds that have been sighted in the area. There is a resident bluebird that frequents the water provided there. The pristine, spring-fed creek provides the perfect spot for "stream snorkeling" and the Schilters will provide the snorkel gear. Dear's Rest is actually 12 miles south of Ozark in the Mark Twain National Forest, so there is a world of outdoors waiting.

The bedroom contains two full-size beds and can accommodate parties of two to six. The additional people in your party will share a bath and sleep in a cozy loft for an additional $15 for each child and $20 for each adult. The room with a private bath is $145. Allan and Linda will fix you a full country breakfast in the morning and send you on your way to nearby Springfield or Branson. You can visit the B&B's Web site at www.dearsrest.com and e-mail the Schilters at info@dearsrest.com. To find the house, take Highway 14 to Highway W and then follow the road to Logan Ridge. Call (417) 581-3839 or (800) 588-2262.

What was once the largest dairy farm in this area is now home to Mark and Susan Bryant. They share it as the *Barn Again Bed and Breakfast Inn,* 904 West Church Street, Ozark. The five-acre farmstead overlooks the Finley River. The centerpiece is the two-story plank-and-stone structure, which is their home and where breakfast is served to guests. A nearby white clapboard house built in 1910 provides two guest suites. A wraparound porch leads to a deck with a hot tub. There's even a small wedding chapel near the brick pathways that wind through the shady grounds. A renovated milking parlor built in the 1920s houses three more rooms, and a swimming pool is nearby. Each room and suite has a private bath and entrance. A spring-fed creek flows just below the house, and often you will see deer, foxes, blue herons, or wild turkeys. Rooms are from $109 to $129 with full breakfast. Call (877) 462-2276 for reservations or visit www.bnbinns.com/barnagain.inn.

Places to Stay in Southwest Missouri

SPRINGFIELD

Holiday Inn
2720 North Glenstone
Avenue 3
(417) 865-8600 or
(800) HOLIDAY
Inexpensive

Lamplighter Inn
2820 North Glenstone
Avenue
(417) 869-3900
Inexpensive

Lamplighter Inn & Suites
1772 South Glenstone
Avenue
(417) 882-1113 or
(800) 749-7275
Inexpensive

Super 8 Motel
3022 North Kentwood
Avenue
(417) 833-9218
or (800) 800-8000
Inexpensive

VAN BUREN

Smalley's Motel
Business 60
(573) 323-4263 or
(800) 727-4263
(tube floats leave from motel)
Inexpensive

WEST PLAINS

Holiday Inn Express
1605 Imperial Drive
(417) 257-3000
Inexpensive

Regency Inn Suites
Highway 61 and
Highway 160
(417) 256-8191
Inexpensive

LEBANON

Best Western Wyota Inn
Business Loop 44, exit 130
(417) 532-6171
Inexpensive

Holiday Inn Express
I-44 and Highway WW
Corner
(417) 532-1111 or
(800) HOLIDAY
Inexpensive

EMINENCE

Shady Lane Cabins and Motel
509 North Main
(573) 226-3893
Inexpensive

CARTHAGE

Best Budget Inn
East Highway 96
(417) 358-6911 or
(800) 357-4953
Inexpensive

Carthage Inn
2244 Grand
(417) 358-2499 or
(800) 325-2525
Inexpensive

*Econo Lodge
1441 West Central
(417) 358-3900 or
(800) 553-ECONO
Inexpensive

*Precious Moments Best Western Hotel
2701 Hazel
(Northeast corner of
Highways HH and 71A)
(417) 359-5900 or
(800) 511-7676
Inexpensive

CASSVILLE

Super 8
Highway 37/76–86
(417) 847-4888
Inexpensive

JOPLIN

*Holiday Inn
3615 Range Line Road
(417) 782-1000
Inexpensive

REEDS SPRING

Mountain Country Motor Inn
14930 Highway 13
(417) 739-4155 or
(800) 753-2755
Inexpensive

BRANSON **

Big Cedar Lodge–Branson Area
612 Devil's's Pool Road,
Ridgedale
(417) 335-2777 or
(800) 225-6343
Inexpensive

Chateau on the Lake
415 North State
Highway 265
(417) 334-1161
Inexpensive

Econolodge
230 South Wildwood
(417) 336-4849 or
(800) 542-3326
Inexpensive

Dockers Inn
3470 Keeter
(417) 334-3600 or
(800) 324-8748
Inexpensive (breakfast
included)

Radisson Hotel
120 South Wildwood
(417) 335-5767
Inexpensive

*has restaurant
**Most hotels in the Branson
area have specials.

HELPFUL WEB SITE FOR THE QUEEN OF THE OZARKS REGION

www.springfieldmo.org

Places to Eat in Southwest Missouri

SPRINGFIELD

Bijan's
209 East Walnut
(417) 831-1480
Moderate

Nonna's Italian Cafe
306 South Avenue
(417) 831-1222
Inexpensive

Olean Zen (Pacific Rim cuisine)
20585 South Glenstone
(417) 889-9596
Moderate

Patton Alley Pub
311 South Patton
(417) 865-4255
Moderate

WINONA

Nu-Way Foods
US 60 and Highway 19 North
(Deli) (573) 325-4522
Inexpensive

WEST PLAINS

Colton Steak House & Grill
1421 Preacher Roe Boulevard
(417) 255-9090
Moderate

EMINENCE

Byerly's Family Restaurant
101 Missouri Street
(573) 226-3878
Inexpensive

KIMBERLING CITY

The Bearded Clam Lounge and Eatery
Highway 13
(417) 739-4440
Moderate

SELECTED CHAMBERS OF COMMERCE

Branson,
(417) 334-4136

Kimberling City,
(800) 595-0393

Van Buren,
(800) ozarkvb
www.semo.net/vanburen
(e-mail) vbcoc@semo.net

Central Missouri

Welcome to America's Heartland, where the Mighty Mo marks the end of the glaciated plains, and hill country begins. Remnant prairies tucked between the hills remind us that once these seas of grass covered a third of the state. In this area there are not one but three big lakes, and from Kansas City to the Lake of the Ozarks lie tiny towns built on gentle ridges, waiting to be discovered. Rough gravel roads wind through dogwood forests, along tentacled lakeshores and into towns that seem to have been protected from the rush like the wild morel hidden under a leaf. The big city here is Kansas City: the birthplace of jazz, the homeland of barbecue, and the Heart of America.

Lake of the Ozarks is not only a tourist area, it is a second homesite for people from both Kansas City and St. Louis. The eastern shore, known as the St. Louis side, has million-dollar homes in the Land of the Four Seasons resort area. Six Mile Cove (the 6-mile marker means you are 6 miles from Bagnell Dam) is called Millionaires' Cove by boaters and has some of the most opulent homes in the Midwest. A houseboat business has sprung up on that side, and visitors can now cruise the lake and see both shores without the long drive around the lake. There is also a toll bridge that connects east to west at Osage Beach.

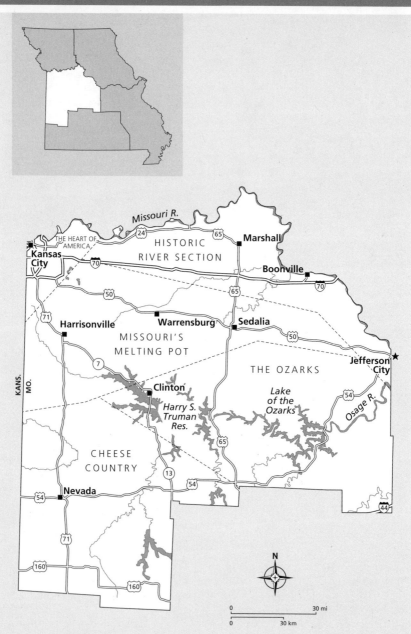

Missouri R.

THE HEART OF AMERICA

Kansas City

HISTORIC RIVER SECTION

Marshall

Boonville

Harrisonville

Warrensburg

Sedalia

MISSOURI'S MELTING POT

THE OZARKS

Jefferson City

Clinton

Harry S. Truman Res.

Lake of the Ozarks

Osage R.

KANS.

MO.

CHEESE COUNTRY

Nevada

N

0   30 mi
0   30 km

The Heart of America

Describing **Kansas City** as a city with "manure on its feet and wheat in its jeans" was a fair assessment at one time. Its two major industries were meat and wheat—all because a man named Joe McCoy convinced the local powers-that-were in 1871 that the newfangled "bobwire" (barbed wire) made it impossible to herd Texas cattle east. A central shipping point was needed, and the Kansas City stockyard was born. A fine steak house, the **Golden Ox Restaurant,** is within sniffing distance at 1600 Genessee Street (816-842-2866; www.goldenox.com). This old vintage steak house has been serving the best steaks in the world since just after World War II. It is the oldest steak house in a city famous for its beef. Owners Stephen Greer and Bill Teel are justifi-

trivia

The Kansas City strip steak was originated in Kansas City at the Golden Ox Restaurant in 1949.

ably proud. "We've spruced the old gal up," Teel says. Greer adds, "This is the real reason Kansas City is famous for steak." Now the two are pushing into another famous KC food arena by adding a state-of-the-art barbecue smoker. This is still a steak house in the best tradition, though. Prime rib, Ox club salad, and its famous bourbon pecan pie make it worth the trip. Hours are Monday and Tuesday from 11:00 a.m. to 9:00 p.m., Wednesday through Friday until 10:00 p.m., and Saturday from 4:00 to 10:30 p.m. This fine restaurant is in walking distance of Kemper Arena, where many sporting events are held. In the fall the American Royal, a longtime cattle and equine event, is held here.

Kansas City is known as the "Heart of America," not because of its location in the center of the country but because of the people who call it home. Kansas City has a symphony, a lyric opera, the Missouri State Ballet Company, baseball's Royals, and football's Kansas City Chiefs. Fountains and sculptures grace its wide avenues. Enclosed in the very heart of the city is Swope Park, the second-largest city park in the nation, with quiet, tree-shaded picnic areas and a modern zoo now upgraded to world-class. If you haven't been to KC lately, be sure to drive by the new futuristic Bartle Hall sculptures at night, beautiful in a strange, space-age way.

The Nelson-Atkins Museum owns one of the finest collections of Oriental art in the world and has a beautiful outdoor sculpture garden. The Kansas City Museum has a planetarium and an old-fashioned ice-cream parlor where you can order a phosphate or a sundae. The Kansas City studio of artist Thomas Hart Benton is now a state park.

Kansas City has more fountains than any city except Rome, and most of them are on the **Country Club Plaza.** Built in 1922 and modeled after Seville,

yardbirdatrest

Charlie "Yardbird" Parker's grave site is in Lincoln Cemetery, at 8604 Truman Road. The road to the bedraggled cemetery is narrow and unmarked. There is an entrance from Blue Ridge Boulevard.

Spain, the Plaza's Mediterranean architecture and charming fountains give this suburban shopping center something no other has. Walk around the more than one hundred designer shops, cafes, restaurants, and bars lining the wide streets. The Segway store offers guided tours during the day and at night, too. Brush Creek's wide meander through this charming area is broken by a fountain and stone pedestrian bridges right in the middle of the creek. Small boats carry visitors up and down the water. But the Plaza offers more than simply shopping—much more—especially during the winter holiday season after Thanksgiving night, when most of the fountains are turned off but the holiday lights are turned on. After dinner, there is a mass migration to see the famous Plaza lights twinkle on across the entire 15-block area, where each and every building is outlined in sparkling lights. The most popular building looks like Cinderella's enchanted pumpkin. Taking grandchildren through this wonderland has become a holiday tradition in many families. Bundle up and bring along a thermos of hot chocolate. The most romantic way to see this is in a horse-drawn carriage. Dreams are made here on snowy nights as the holiday season begins, with the flip of a switch, in Kansas City.

The first question most visitors ask when they get off a plane at Kansas City International Airport is "Where's the best barbecue?" Whether you like it to the sweet side or a bit spicy, that's for you to judge: The oldest contenders are **Arthur Bryant Barbecue** at 1727 Brooklyn (816-231-1123), and **Gates and Sons Bar-B-Q** at 1221 Brooklyn (816-483-3880). Both offer carryout, so you can do comparison tests with their different sauces until you are all "pigged out."

Gates's and Bryant's owe their fame, in part, to the fact that they used to be situated next to the old Kansas City Royals baseball stadium. Not only were they favorite places to eat before and after games, but the announcers would also be happily noshing barbecue and talking about it during the games. Then writer Calvin Trillin, a KC native and New York writer, declared KC the barbecue capital of the planet and made Bryant's even more famous. Trillin claims Bryant's is the best restaurant in the world! But no one comes here for the ambience unless you like bright lights and cafeteria-style service. The hunk of meat wrapped between two pieces of white bread is a leader in the best-barbecue-in-town-contest. Gates's has the comfy high-back booths and a tangier sauce. The only way to make a decision here is to try both. Both have Web sites: www.arthurbryantsbbq.com and www.gatesbbq.com. But there are between 100 and 150 barbecue restaurants in the Kansas City area, and most of the best are just joints tucked away somewhere, and "best" is defined by what kind of sauce you favor. ***Danny Edwards Blvd BBQ,*** at 2900 Southwest Blvd. (816-283-0880), for example, has a sign in the window that reads EAT IT AND BEAT IT, which tells you something about its size, popularity, and attitude. Open for lunch only Monday through Friday from 10:00 a.m. to 2:30 p.m., ***B.B.'s Lawnside Bar-B-Que,*** at 1205 East Eighty-fifth Street, is a fun

AUTHOR'S FAVORITE ANNUAL EVENTS IN CENTRAL MISSOURI

JULY
Osage Beach
Fireworks on the Water, Tan–Tar–A
Resort/Four Seasons Resort,
(800) 826-8272

Lexington
July Fourth Celebration, skydiving

Gravois Mills
Annual Osage Indian Heritage Days and
Crafts Festival,
(573) 378-4373

Sedalia
Annual Garden Party, Bothwell Lodge,
state historic site, roaring twenties party,
(660) 827-0510

AUGUST
Laurie
Village of Laurie Annual BBQ Cook-Off,
573) 374-8776

Sedalia
Missouri State Fair,
(660) 530-5600

SEPTEMBER
Independence
Santa-Cali-Gon Days Festival,
celebrates the Santa Fe, California, and
Oregon Trails,
(816) 252-4745

Osage Beach
Annual Fall Festival of Color
Hot Air Balloon Race,
(573) 365-6663

OCTOBER
Kansas City
American Royal Barbecue, 300 teams of
BBQers, music, dancing, and food,
(816) 221-9800

Versailles
Annual Old Tyme Apple Festival,
(573) 378-4401

Cole Camp
Low German Theatre,
(573) 668-4970

Lake Ozarks
Annual Lake of the Ozarks Dixieland
Jazz Festival, Four Seasons Lodge,
(573) 392-1731

Sunrise Beach
Annual Missouri State Buddy
Bass Championship,
(573) 374-5500

NOVEMBER
Kansas City
Plaza Lighting Ceremony,
(816) 274-8444

AUTHOR'S FAVORITES IN CENTRAL MISSOURI	
Cascone's Grill	Lyceum Repertory Theatre
Harling's Upstairs	Dutch Bakery and Bulk Food Store
Sun Ray Cafe	

spot with wooden floors that slope and old blues posters on the walls. There is a definite Louisiana influence in the food there—great gumbo as well as some of the best barbecue in town. B.B.'s is as famous for the blues jam sessions as it is for the food. The owner has a slogan: "B.B.'s restaurant is where barbecue meets the blues." Thursday nights are the best jam sessions, with John Paul's Flying Circus playing live blues music. Wednesday through Sunday nights local, regional, and national blues acts may be found. They play a two-hour set that may turn into a "jam" session with others joining in. The music is loud, the food fantastic, the crowd enthusiastic, and it is just more darn fun than you can stand. Call (816) 822-7427 to see who is playing tonight or to check the menu, or visit www.bbslawnsidebbq.com.

Fiorella's Jack Stack Barbecue, in the old train station freight house at Twenty-second and Wyandotte (816-472-7427; www.jackstackbbq.com), is definitely worth looking for. The appetizer Rack and a Half (ten huge onion rings served stacked on a stem) will start you off. Also not to be missed are the Fire Kissed Prawns. These are served slightly charred on skewers after being rubbed with the Fiorella brand of sauce, which imparts its own unique hint of garlic and cayenne pepper. The architecture in The Freight House is spectacular. A beautiful high roofline ceiling of natural wood, brick walls, and dynamic artwork set off the magnificent arched windows. There are intimate booths where you can get lost in the atmosphere. The menu is extensive, and fresh seafood is flown in every day. Although the barbecue is what many come here for, Fiorella's also offers beef, pork, and lamb ribs. The Cheesy Corn Bake is one of the sides; it consists of fresh corn kernels and a Cheddar cheese sauce that are baked to perfection. The Hickory Pit Beans are as good as they get. Portions are extremely generous, and great service tops off this dining experience. Hours are 11:00 a.m. to 10:00 p.m. Monday through Thursday, to 10:30 p.m. on Friday and Saturday, and 11:00 a.m. to 9:00 p.m. on Sunday.

Stroud's Restaurant is located north of the Missouri River, just off Interstate 35 and Brighton, at 5410 North East Oak Ridge Road, Kansas City

(816-454-9600; www.stroudsrestaurant.com). The motto stated on the waiter's T-shirts is "We choke our own chickens." Be prepared for a wait, but it is worth it. This picturesque farmstead is a walk back in time. You can stroll the garden, take a walk down to the lake to see the swans, or have a seat in an old buggy and contemplate the big family-style chicken dinner you are about to enjoy. Meals are served "family style," complete with green beans, mashed potatoes and gravy, and homemade cinnamon rolls that melt in your mouth. There are plenty of things on the menu, but the fried chicken is what keeps people coming back for more.

As long as you are north of the Missouri River, take I-35 north to Interstate 29 north to the Barry Road exit. Go right (west) and take a right into **Zona Rosa,** a new neighborhood of shops, restaurants, and condos. There are plenty of well-known names along with some homegrown ones. A favorite eatery is **Bravo! Cucina Italiana** at 7301 NW 87th St. (816-741-4114). The food is cooked right before your eyes, all fresh and made-to-order. Hours are Monday through Thursday 10:00 a.m. to 9:00 p.m., Friday and Saturday until 10:00 p.m., and Sunday noon to 6:00 p.m. Go to the Zona Rosa Web site to see what else is in store for you: www.zonarosa.com.

Here and there, drowsing on old streets, pocketed in small shopping centers, crouching behind buildings, or even tucked inside buildings, you're likely to find places that definitely qualify as out of the mainstream. After barbecue, Kansas City is famous for jazz.

Eighteenth and Vine in Kansas City was really jumping from the 1920s to the 1950s. There were smoky joints filled with baseball players from the Kansas City Negro League team, the Monarchs, and jazz musicians signing autographs for fans and talking and laughing over drinks. There were restaurants and nightclubs there—the Mardi Gras, Blue Room, and Subway Club—and baseball and jazz are forever linked in Kansas City. An untouched memory of that time can still be found at the **Mutual Musicians' Foundation,** in the old Musicians' Union Hall—a hot-pink bungalow in the historic jazz district around Eighteenth and Vine. It is, in fact, the only building inside the city limits that is on the National Register of Historic

trivia

Kansas City has more fountains than any city except Rome and all of them are turned off in the winter except one. The Northland Fountain at the intersection of North Oak Street Trafficway and Vivian Road in Kansas City North becomes a gigantic ongoing ice sculpture, never the same, as the water cascades and melts throughout the winter. Surrounding the fountain is a walk path and park, but the enormous fountain is visible from both Vivian Road and North Oak Street Trafficway.

Places. It is located at 1823 Highland Avenue. Tours are available, but the place really jumps on Friday and Saturday nights when musicians from throughout Kansas City gather here to jam after their regular gigs around the city. The traditional jazz jam starts at midnight. There is no cover charge, but donations are always welcome to keep this place open. Call (816) 471-5212 to find out more or go to www.thefoundationjamson.org.

Now the area is coming alive again, and the link is still strong. At the **American Jazz Museum,** 1616 East Eighteenth Street, Kansas City, visitors can listen to the music of such greats as Louis Armstrong, Julia Lee, Duke Ellington, Ella Fitzgerald, and Charlie "Yardbird" Parker. In fact, the museum is the final resting place of Yardbird's saxophone. The museum has an extensive exhibit honoring Ella Fitzgerald, "The First Lady of Song," with thirty of her most identifiable personal effects, including her famous cat-rim, rhinestone-covered glasses and silver pumps.

trivia

While you are downtown in Kansas City, look for the "cow on a stick." The huge bull used to be atop the American Hereford Association, but the organization has since moved. Now the giant bovine watches over the area from his perch on a pylon above Argus Health Systems. They decided to keep it so folks could find them easily.

This is one of the most interactive museums in the country. Music fills the air as the story of jazz is told through sight and sound. Visitors can listen to performances while a giant video wall projects early performances by some of these famous artists. The museum offers something for every level of jazz understanding. You can putter in a mixing station and create your own mix of sounds or enter the Wee-Bob children's activity center. Shop for a CD or tape, T-shirt, or poster in the Swing Shop.

Museum hours are Tuesday through Saturday from 9:00 a.m. to 6:00 p.m. and Sunday from noon to 6:00 p.m. Admission to the museum is $6.00 for adults, $2.50 for children, or you can buy a combination ticket to both the jazz and baseball museums for $8.00 for adults, $4.00 for children younger than age twelve; kids younger than age three, free. For more information call (816) 474-8763 or visit www.Americanjazzmuseum.com.

Kansas City's **Negro League Baseball Museum** is at 1616 East Eighteenth Street, too, and it remembers the other half of the jazz and baseball love affair—the league that played in the 1920s and 1930s before the all-white major leagues would accept black players. Black players formed their own league, and some of the best athletes ever to play the game got their start there: Satchel Paige, Ernie Banks, Josh Gibson, "Cool Papa" Bell, and Buck O'Neill. Do these names sound familiar? How about Willie Mays, Hank Aaron, Roy Campanella, or the incredible Jackie Robinson? The Kansas City Monarchs were considered the Yankees of black baseball. The Negro National League drew more than 50,000 spectators from coast to coast. Then in 1947 a guy named Jackie Robinson stepped up to bat for the Brooklyn Dodgers and smashed the color barrier right over the fence. The rest is baseball history.

The museum is more than just a collection of pictures and memorabilia: it re-creates the look, sound, and feel of the game in the heyday of the league. Its centerpiece main gallery has a three-station interactive computer module with video games, historical vignettes, and coaching tips. The museum covers the history of black baseball from its beginning after the Civil War through the end of Negro Leagues play in the 1960s, and it features a custom-designed database to search for the play-by-play of league games. There is a gift shop featuring autographed baseballs, Louisville slugger bats, T-shirts, caps, and jackets. Take a look back at Negro League baseball by visiting the Web site www.kansascity .com or www.nlbm.com. Hours are Tuesday through Saturday 9:00 a.m. until 6:00 p.m., Sunday noon to 6:00 p.m. Call (816) 221-1920 or (888) 221-NLBM for more information. Admission is $6.00 for adults and $2.50 for children younger than age twelve.

Right across the street is the historic ***Gem Theater Cultural and Performing Arts Center*** at 1616 East Eighteenth Street. As early as the 1920s,

Something Old, Something New

Although not off the beaten path by any means, there's something old and something new in Kansas City. The old Kansas City Union Station—site of an infamous gangster massacre and formerly one of the largest and busiest rail centers in the country—at 2300 Main Street, has been restored to its glorious original beauty and is now an urban plaza and entertainment center. There are several restaurants, evening entertainment at City Nights with live performance theater, motion pictures, and laser and magic shows as well as music and theater performances. There are also shopping areas and, best of all, especially for the kids, Science City, featuring more than fifty hands-on environments for all ages to explore. Science City is a city-within-a-city on multiple levels with streets and alleyways. Each exhibit is a realistic environment that offers interactive experiences with costumed citizens who live and work in the "city's" Festival Plaza, Uptown, Downtown, Southside, and Old Town. You can even explore an excavation dig site in Prehistoric Kansas City or assist a surgical team in the Operating Room. Want a chance to be on TV? You can broadcast news from the television station. You can bake a cake in the test kitchen or try your hand at being an astronaut in the space center. Or you can board a real locomotive located just outside the station. Science City's Web site is at www .sciencecity.com. Science City is open daily. Call (816) 460-9372 or (800) 556-9372 for times and shows.

OTHER ATTRACTIONS WORTH SEEING IN CENTRAL MISSOURI

Kansas City
Country Club Plaza at Christmas
Worlds of Fun/Oceans of Fun
Crown Center

Osage Beach
Outlet Mall

Camdenton
Bridal Cave

Kansas City's vibrant theatrical community was known around the world. This reconstructed theater still has the trademark neon marquee hanging outside and once again presents first-class entertainment. The latest in lighting, sound, and acoustical design have been added. The Alvin Ailey Dancers perform here along with renowned jazz groups and theater ensembles. Call the ticket office at (816) 474-6262 for a schedule filled with multimedia events.

At 2033 Vine is the **Black Archives of Mid-America,** where you can find documents, artifacts, paintings, and exhibits that explore the lives of African Americans in Kansas City, including musicians, artists, writers, and leaders in many other fields. The first-floor exhibit features the Tuskegee Airmen of World War II, and the second floor is dedicated to the Buffalo soldiers of the Civil War. Hours are Monday through Friday 9:00 a.m. to 4:30 p.m. Visit www .blackarchives.org.

Downtown (way downtown) is the **City Market,** where you can shop outdoors with a big wicker basket for just-picked produce in the wonderful atmosphere of a European marketplace. You can buy everything from morel mushrooms in early May to late-harvest turnips in October. There are always fresh eggs and chickens, and on Saturday mornings local farmers and buyers meet over the freshest produce this side of the garden. The area by the Missouri River has undergone restoration, complete with a riverboat museum.

The year was 1856 when the steamboat *Arabia* set out for the West, loaded with trade goods and passengers. As the folks at the **Steamboat Arabia Museum** say, you'll find everything from axes, awls, and augers to zillions of other treasures restored to near-mint condition. How did they manage to amass all this in one place? Well, the *Arabia* hit a cottonwood snag in the Missouri River and sank like a stone. There it rested from 1856 to 1988, a time capsule waiting to spill its treasures, both everyday and exotic, into the present. But, of course, even the everyday from more than one hundred years ago is exotic now. You'll find spurs, tinware, perfume (that retained its scent after its sojourn under 45 feet of mud and water), wine, whiskey, and champagne (still bubbly), canned goods, hair pins, inkwells, and clothing.

The Hawley family excavated the boat and spent untold hours painstakingly restoring the artifacts they found. To our good fortune, rather than selling off the bounty they opened a museum, and this treasure trove now tells casual visitors, schoolkids, scholars, living-history reenactors, and just plain history buffs volumes about what life was like on the frontier; civilization was built with the bits and pieces of trade goods carried by packets like the *Arabia*. A short film introduces you to the museum and to the excavation and restoration process. See what frontier life was like for $9.75 for adults, $9.25 for seniors, $4.75 for children ages four to twelve; free for younger kids. Hours are Monday through Saturday 10:00 a.m. to 6:00 p.m. and Sunday noon to 5:00 p.m.; for information call (816) 471-4030 or visit www.1856.com. The museum is at 400 Grand, Kansas City.

Wearin' o' the Green—Italian-style

The North End is where I grew up. We lived with my grandmother, "Nana" Randazzo, until I was about twelve years old. I went to the Catholic school a couple of blocks from our home—Holy Rosary School—and rarely left the neighborhood. My grandma spoke Sicilian, my parents were bilingual, and I grew up knowing just enough Sicilian to stay out of trouble with my Nana. Everyone in the neighborhood was Italian. There was a penny candy store on one corner, an Italian bakery on the other, and a park with a bocce court and a swimming pool a half block away. A good restaurant served the area, and we could open fire hydrants on hot summer days and play kick-the-can in the streets. Yelling "first light!" when the street lights came on was a nightly contest. We even had lightning bugs. Why would anyone want to leave a neighborhood so wonderful? It was safe. It was home.

But one of my earliest childhood memories, kindergarten or first grade, was of walking to school on March 17—a day that meant absolutely nothing to my family— and finding everyone else dressed in green. Now remember, this was an Italian neighborhood. There was not a drop of Irish blood anywhere for miles. Suddenly everyone was Irish, and I was the one who got pinched dozens of times—for not wearing green—before the bell rang to begin classes. I was terrified, and when the lunch bell rang, I took off for home with my lunch tucked under my arm like a football. (We wrapped our lunch in newspaper; sacks didn't exist for us.) When I arrived home unexpectedly, crying, my Nana couldn't understand what the problem was. I refused to go back to school until she found me something green to wear. When she saw that I was adamant, she began to rummage in the closets muttering "manacia l'America!" under her breath. (That is phonetically spelled and is some sort of Sicilian-American *slanguage*. It means "blame it on America" and was used whenever things American got to be too much for her.) I returned to school wearing green but not understanding why. I noticed that nobody pinched Sister Mary Margaret. Although she was wearing black, she had a green shamrock pinned to her habit.

Across from the Fifth Street market building is **Cascone's Grill,** 17 East Fifth Street, where the market crowd eats. The Cascone family cooks up the most amazing early morning Italian breakfasts (Italian-breaded steak, Italian sausage, fried eggs, hash browns, and Italian-bread toast) and late-in-the-day lunches featuring Vita Cascone's own spaghetti sauce. They open and close seasonally with the rhythm of the market crowd. But Tuesday through Saturday 6:00 a.m. to 2:00 p.m. will usually find them open. Call (816) 471-1018.

Catty-corner from the market, across the street at 513 Walnut, is **Planters' Seed and Spice Co.** Step inside this old building and inhale the wonderful odors of fresh bulk herbs and spices, the scent of old wood, the aroma of exotic teas and coffees, and the clean smell of seeds. Need a watering can? They've got 'em. Want to buy a pound of dried bay leaves? Look no further. It's a delightful place. Call (816) 842-3651.

Just down the street from the City Market at 400 East Fifth Street is a French bistro—admittedly a most unlikely spot to find such a place—but it is as authentic as it can be, with an outdoor cafe in the alley just as they are in Paris. **Le Fou Frog** isn't really faux at all (it means "the crazy frog"), as owner and chef Mano Rafael will tell you. He is from Marseilles and made his reputation as head chef in some New York hot spots (Petrossian and Casanis). He met and married Barbara Bayer from Kansas City, and the rest is history.

The real test of a French bistro is the *soupe a l'oignon gratinee* with a bubbly top of Gruyère cheese. This one passes with gold stars. Of course, it is impossible to taste everything on the menu, but give it a good try. The *poulet aux olives et herbes de provences* (whole baby chicken roasted in a fragrant sauce of olives and fresh herbs and served with garlic mashed potatoes) is a personal favorite. Seasonal menu changes daily. Entrees range from $19 to $42—and are worth every franc. Le Frog is open for dinner only Tuesday through Thursday 5:30 to 10:00 p.m., Friday and Saturday 5:30 to 11:00 p.m., and Sunday 5:00 to 9:00 p.m. Sunday nights feature live music. Call (816) 474-6060. There is an excellent wine list with some very good and inexpensive wines available, just as there should be in a bistro. You can visit their Web site at www.lefoufrog.com; call (816) 474-6060 for reservations.

Keep going east on Fifth Street to Harrison, and on the corner is a restaurant that has changed hands a few times but has always been Italian, because this is a neighborhood simply known as "The North End." It is the Little Italy that many big cities have. Here Mass was said in Italian at nearby Holy Rosary Catholic Church in the old days. Now the neighborhood had blended into a more Vietnamese/Italian mix, but it still has the feel of the streets we played on as children—where opening a fire hydrant was the coolest thing that happened

The Ghost of St. Mary's

The ghost of St. Mary's is believed to be that of Father Henry Jardine, who was rector of St. Mary's in 1879. A crypt was built under the altar for Father Jardine's body before his death. Because he suffered from a painful facial nerve disorder, he took laudanum (tincture of opium) and used chloroform to help him sleep. One night he died from the combination. The bishop declared it a suicide, and therefore Father Jardine's body was buried in unconsecrated ground rather than in his beloved church. There have been several ghostly incidents. When one acolyte arrived at the church, he saw a priest, in vestments, who stood facing the altar. He hurried to the sacristy thinking he must be late, only to find the rector waiting for him there. When they went back to the sanctuary, no one was there. Several people have sensed a presence in the gallery where his restless ghost hovers. St. Mary's rector, The Reverend Dr. Bruce Rahtjen, is attempting to have Father Jardine's remains moved from the cemetery to the church's columbarium, perhaps allowing his spirit to rest in peace at last.

on a hot summer day—and that ambience is still there. *Garozzo's Ristorante,* 526 Harrison, Kansas City, has soft music by Frank Sinatra, a lively bar, and really, really huge servings of pasta. Do not, repeat, do not order spaghetti and meatballs unless you want to eat it for a week or can share it with several other people. The other dishes are more moderately proportioned but excellent. If you like, no, love garlic, order some olive oil to dip your Italian bread into and you will get a bowl of oil smothered in garlic and Parmesan cheese. Hours are Monday through Thursday 11:00 a.m. to 11:00 p.m. and Saturday 4:00 to 11:00 p.m. Call (816) 221-2455 or visit www.garozzos.com.

As long as you are in the River Market area, visit *Cheep Antiques River Market Emporium,* 500 West Fifth Street. The store carries furniture in every price range and features antiques from Belgium, France, Germany, England, and Holland. A specialty is making entertainment centers from old armoires. Hours are 9:00 a.m. until 3:00 p.m. Tuesday through Friday and until 5:00 p.m. on Saturday and Sunday. Call (816) 471-0092.

St. Mary's Episcopal Church is a grand old church at 1307 Holmes in downtown Kansas City. The redbrick church has been there forever (since 1888) and as with many old churches, it has some interesting history and a good ghost story. Amazingly, the building was spared when the neighborhood around it was razed during urban renewal in the 1960s. It is a wonderful Sunday morning experience to follow the sound of the carillon and to hear the organist make the huge pipe organ sing for the Solemn High Mass celebrated every Sunday at 10:00 a.m., complete with incense and bells. The congregation is an interesting and varied collection of people from the urban area as well as suburban people who make the drive into the city every Sunday. Call (816) 842-0975 for the times of other services.

K.C. Power and Light District downtown opened recently with nightlife and more (800-767-7700; www.visitkc.com). People from Kansas City remember when downtown was the go-to place. There was jazz, there were parties, it was alive with rhythm and blues, and one of the places remembered fondly is still tucked away in the historic Hilton President Kansas City hotel, within walking distance from the Power and Light District. *The Drum Room,* 1335 Baltimore, has been open since 1941 and still has the flavor of old K.C. You can feel the presence of Frank Sinatra, Benny Goodman, Sammy Davis Jr., Tommy Dorsey, Glenn Miller, The Marx Brothers, and Pasty Cline, who have all played this venue. There is live entertainment still on Friday and Saturday nights from 9:00 p.m. until 1:00 a.m. Happy Hour is 4:30 to 6:30 p.m. and the perfect time to try one of their infamous nine-ounce martinis. Lunch is served from 11:00 a.m. to 4:00 p.m. (try the sweet potato fries) when dinner begins (go for the Paellas named after Sinatra and his Rat Pack) and is served until 10:00 p.m. Call (816) 303-1686 or visit www.drumroomkc.com.

Then party on at *Seven,* 613 Walnut—K.C.'s newest nightclub—which doesn't come alive until 10 o'clock at night. Dance to a D.J. and before closing time at 1:00 a.m., you can try all "Seven Deadly Sins Cocktails" or get VIP bottle service by reserving a table in the loft. It's right in the heart of downtown, so you can walk to your hotel. Seven is known for its Northern Italian cuisine, too. Call (816) 777-1107 or visit www.seven-kc.com.

Along Southwest Boulevard the scent of chili peppers fills the air. This is Kansas City's Hispanic neighborhood, and the restaurants here are very popular, especially at lunchtime.

If you are looking for homemade tamales wrapped in corn husks, go to *La Posada Grocery* at 722 Southwest Boulevard, Kansas City. They sell about any Mexican ingredient you could want—chilies, spices, corn husks, even Mexican coffee. Speaking Spanish will ease the shopping queries here. Hours are Monday, Tuesday, Thursday, Friday, and Saturday 8:00 a.m. to 6:00 p.m. and Sunday 8:00 a.m. to 3:00 p.m. Call (816) 842-1891.

There is always some discussion about which, exactly, is the best Mexican restaurant in the Southwest Boulevard area. It just depends on who you ask. One favorite of people who work downtown and eat there often is *Mannie's* at 207 Southwest Boulevard (816-474-7696; www.mannyskc.com). Mannie's is open for lunch and dinner from Tuesday through Saturday and makes a mean margarita. Another favorite is *Ponak's Mexican Kitchen* at 2856 Southwest Boulevard (816-753-4886). Everything at Ponak's is good. You decide.

The Hallmark Crown Center, 2450 Grand Avenue, is a little city of its own with luxury residences and hotels and several levels of shopping. It even has an outdoor ice-skating rink. This is not off the beaten path, though, it is one of the cities most popular areas. Across the street—or over the skywalk if the weather is bad—is the old Union Station. You *can* buy the **Best of Kansas City** at the shop of the same name here at Crown Center. Everything from apple butter (Stephenson's) to Zarda barbecue sauce is sold here. Call (816) 842-0200. Order gift baskets at (800) 366-8780. Hours are 10:00 a.m. to 9:00 p.m. (Sunday until 5:00 p.m.)

There is a little-known museum under a well-known tower standing sentry on a hill across from Crown Center. *The National World War I Museum at Liberty Memorial,* 100 West 26th Street, is in a new complex and uses inter-active technology to bring the history of this "war to end all wars" alive. Then ride the elevator to the top of the tower for a breathtaking view of Kansas City. Visit www.nww1.org for more information.

This is an old industrial area with some pretty good eating places hid-den away in it. One of them, **Lidia's,** at 101 West Twenty Second Street, is located in a converted warehouse. Lidia's is very well known around town—there are three in New York—and beautifully done. The food, of course, is quite good, as is the wine list. Call (816) 221-3722 for reservations; www .lidiasitaly.com. Hours are 11:00 a.m. to 2:00 p.m. weekdays for lunch and 5:00 to 9:30 p.m. for dinner. Saturday dinner hours are from 4:30 to 10:30 p.m. This area is the up and coming art district of K.C. The **Crossroads Art District** is situated between Crown Center and downtown. It's just behind the old Union Station. A hundred-year-old railroad trestle bridge was recently moved from the river, through downtown K.C. and placed at Union Station. It will be used as a walkway from the station to the nearby art district. The amazing move was filmed and shown on the History Channel. For a really fun evening, join the 6,000 other people who flock to First Fridays, the city's monthly art walk from 7:00 to 9:00 p.m. Shops and galleries stay open late and the restaurants tease you with scents of wonderful food to nibble as you walk.

trivia

The Crossroads Art District began in the 1980s when a professor from the Kansas City Art Institute bought an old building in the warehouse district and turned it into lofts where young artists could afford to live. Their rent then subsidized the gallery downstairs, where their work was displayed. Today that building is the Voulkos Art Center, and many other galleries and lofts have made this a popular urban art community.

Some of the many places in this old district are **Creative Candles** (816-474-9711) at 2101 Broadway, Kansas City, at the corner of Southwest Boulevard and Broadway. Creative they are indeed. Then there is the every popular **Christopher Elbow Artisanal Chocolate** (816-842-1300), where every piece of chocolate is a work of art. Christopher's signature Stiletto vodka chocolates compete with strawberry balsamic caramel (from Modena), rosemary caramel (locally grown rosemary), caramel with *fleur de sel* (a soft ganache infused with French sea salt) or a personal fav the bourbon pecan (with dark chocolate making it very healthy). This famous chocolatier is at 1819 McGee Street Tuesday through Saturday from 10:00 a.m. to 6:00 p.m. It's all on the Web site, www.elbowchocolates.com. **Black Bamboo** at 1815 Wyandotte Street (816-283-3000; www.black-bamboo.com) and **Aesthetica** 1801 Wyandotte, (816-421-5455) both filled with accessories and gifts. **Lula Mac,** at 110 Southwest Boulevard (816-474-4966; www.lulamac.com) is the place to go for an incredible collection of European antiques and Persian rugs. One of the most interesting to visit is **Webster House,** 1644 Wyandotte (816-221-4713; www.websterhousekc.com), a circa 1885 schoolhouse restored and filled with antiques, gifts, and home goodies. It is also a favorite place for lunch.. Another good spot to eat in the district is **1924 Main** (816-472-1924; www.1924main.com). The menu changes every day according to what is in season. It doesn't get any better than that when you are eating out.

Nearby at 2 east 20th Street (corner of East 20th and Main Street) is the ever popular **Hereford House** (816-584-9000; www.herefordhouse.com), which has been a local tradition for more than fifty years. Probably the first restaurant K.C. natives remember (from Prom Night, say) and still one of the best places to have a K.C. steak cooked just right.

The perfect place to cool off on a sweltering summer day used to be the corner drugstore in any small town. It was a perfect spot to meet your favorite sweetie and the only place to get a fizzy chocolate phosphate, an ice-cold cherry Coke, or a tall ice-cream soda. The Kansas City Museum, at 3218 Gladstone Boulevard, is in the process of renovation. Only hard-hat tours are available for Corinthian Hall (originally the carriage house) in the foreseeable future although a drive-by to see this magnificent home is worth it if you are in the area. Meanwhile the museum is situated in the Union Station (30 West Pershing Road). The museum has re-created that spot for the children of the city. What the heck's a phosphate? A combination of flavored carbonated water and ice. Why is that chocolate-covered dip of vanilla called a sundae? Old "blue laws" made it illegal to sell soda water on Sunday, so it had everything an ice-cream soda had except carbonated water. Most soda pops were originally hawked as health tonics. In fact, Coca-Cola was invented by a pharmacist. The cherry-wood pharmacy dates from 1886, the marble-topped soda-fountain counter and stained-glass lamps with spigots from about 1910. All came from the Kirby Drugstore in Modena. The museum hours are 9:30 a.m. to 4:30 p.m. Tuesday through Saturday, and noon to 4:30 p.m. on Sunday. Regular museum admission is $2.50 for adults and $2.00 for kids and seniors. Call (816) 460-2020 or visit the Web site at www.kcmuseum.com.

Just south of the busy interstates that ring downtown Kansas City proper is **Central Park Gallery,** 110 East Missouri, Kansas City (816-471-7711); Peter McCoy has a showcase of Midwestern fine art, highlighting lithographs, raku-ware, and original paintings. Hours are 10:00 a.m. to 6:00 p.m. Tuesday through Friday and 10:00 a.m. to 4:00 p.m. Saturday.

The Thirty-ninth Street area of Kansas City is a wonderful old area in which to stroll. There are antiques shops, crystal shops, and just a lot of interesting places. There are also some of the city's best restaurants.

Around the corner at 3906 Bell Street is the **Genghis Khan Mongolian Barbecue,** an eat-all-you-can meat, seafood, and vegetable grill that is well worth its modest prices. Don't be misled by the name. It is not a barbecue in the KC sense of smoked ribs. This is fresh raw meat cooked before your eyes on a huge griddle-type cooking area. You choose your shrimp, calamari, meat, veggies, whatever and they throw it on the grill and stir fry it while you watch. Hours are Monday through Friday 11:00 a.m. to 9:30 p.m., Saturday noon to 10:00 p.m. Closed Sunday. Call owner Ling Chang for more information at (816) 753-3600 or visit www.gkbbq.com.

Drive on toward Main on Thirty-ninth Street and you will dead-end at an old art deco building, and the only clue you will have that you have found the right place is the occasional neon beer sign in the second-floor windows. You have found **Harling's Upstairs** at 3941-A Main Street (816-531-0303). The best time to search out Harling's is between 1:00 and 6:00 p.m. on any Saturday, when Diane "Mama" Ray and her blues band pour their heart into a jam session that packs the house every week. A long list of Kansas City jazz and blues musicians join her to jam on any given Saturday. Stay put once you are there, if you give up your seat, you will never get it back. There are other things going on at Harling's at night, including Irish music on Thursdays. But Mama Ray is worth the trip on a Saturday afternoon, and if you love the blues, you will get there early and stay through the entire session.

There is more good jazz and blues in Kansas City than anywhere in the country. Pick up a copy of Jam (Jazz Ambassador magazine), with listings of all the jazz clubs in town and who is playing where. Then you can search out nightlife at such places as the **Levee** at 16 West Forty-third Street (816-561-2821; www.thelevee.net), with wonderfully loud rock 'n' roll to dance to on Saturday afternoons until 8:00 p.m.

Mediterranean food with a Greek flavor is presented in the tiny **Sun Ray Cafe** at 813 West Seventeenth Street by Yannis Vantoz, who brought his native Greek dishes to the Kansas City area not long ago. The appetizer menu offers a selection of ten typical Greek choices, including hummus, calamari, tzatziki, spanakopita, feta cheese, and an absolutely wonderful marinated octopus.

Main courses include lamb chops, salmon, and different fresh fish daily. Yannis does not have a liquor license, so bring a favorite bottle of wine and he'll provide the wineglasses. With no corkage charge, you'll get a dinner as good as any in the best restaurants of Kansas City, at very reasonable prices. The appetizers are about $3.00 each, and entrees range from $14.50 to $17.50.

The cafe is open for lunch Tuesday through Saturday from 11:00 a.m. to 2:00 p.m. and for dinner from 6:00 to 10:00 p.m. on Friday and Saturday. Yannis will also serve small private parties on other nights. Call (816) 221-5757.

In case you are cruisin' on your Harley (or even if you're not) and want to experience an upscale "biker-bar atmosphere," check out Frank Hick's **F.O.G. Cycles & Knucklehead's Saloon** (816-483-1456). It's a honky tonk blues bar next to FOG bike shop at 2715 Rochester in the East Bottoms just off Interstate 435 and Front Street. Live bands play that cool Kansas City blues music. When weather permits, you might find yourself at an outdoor street party. Wear your leathers if you want to fit right in. Knucklehead's is open Thursday from 4:00 to 11:00 p.m., Friday and Saturday until 1:00 a.m. Check the web at www .knuckleheadskc.com for upcoming shows and show times.

The saloon took some top honors for blues clubs and is the primer club for that venue in K.C., awarded Best of K.C. 2005 by *Pitch,* a Kansas City newspaper, and the "Keepin' the Blues Alive" award in 2008.

You can have the usual hamburgers, tacos, or sausage, of course, but you gotta try the Knucklehead Sandwich. Don't ask what's in it, just order it. (Okay, if you must know, it's Fried Bologna.)

The club is open Tuesday through Saturday. It is an over-21 club, so minors must be with their parents.

From downtown Independence Avenue (east of Prospect) go north on Chestnut. Go to the stoplight at Nicholson Avenue and turn left. Turn left onto Montgall. Turn left one more time onto Rochester and you are there. Call the club at (816) 483-1456 or the office at (816) 483-6407 to order tickets to upcoming shows.

At the corner of the block at 1700 Summit, the **Bluebird Bistro** serves lunch Monday through Saturday—great homemade soups and interesting sandwiches on crunchy sunflower-seed bread. This corner cafe is much larger than it looks from the outside, but it fills up quickly at lunchtime. The tin ceilings and antique cabinets make the high-ceilinged rooms cozy. A long bar along one wall is a fine spot to wait for a table. Lunch is available from 11:00 a.m. to 2:00 p.m. Monday through Saturday. Dinner is served Wednesday through Sunday from 5:00 to 10:00 p.m. Call (816) 221-7559 or visit www.blue birdbistro.blogspot.com.

Historic Westport, some 40 blocks south of downtown, was the whole city at one time. Some of us think it still is. **The Broadway Café** (816-531-2431) and the **Broadway Roasting Co.** (816-931-9955) are just two neighborhood coffeehouses in Westport, one at 301 Westport Road and the other at 4106 Broadway. There is a blackboard where colorful chalk lists today's beverages and baked-today scones, biscotti, and cakes (their famous apple cake, for example). Sara Honan and Jon Cates invite you to taste samples of that day's baked goods and have a cup of one of the more than 20 types of coffee they roast every day (Ethiopian Harrar for example). The coffee is roasted at the roastery on Westport Road, but you can still smell the coffee roasting "when the wind's right" at the other address, too. Why two cafes so close together? They like the Westport area. And so will you. Visit their Web site at www.broadway cafeandroastery.com. The cafe is open daily 7:00 a.m. until 9:00 p.m. and the Roasting Company is open Monday through Friday 7:00 a.m. until 5:00 p.m.

The **Classic Cup,** owned by John Meyer, has moved to Forty-seventh and Central (816-756-0771; www.classiccup.com). The all-time favorite entree here is the raspberry–Dijon mustard sauce on grilled pork tenderloin (sometimes it's blueberry, blackberry, or tart cherry–Dijon sauce). Hours are Monday through Friday from 8:00 a.m. to 10:00 p.m., Saturday from 8:00 a.m. to 11:00 p.m., and Sunday from 9:30 a.m. to 10:00 p.m.

Three Dog Bakery at 612 West Forty-eighth Street, Kansas City, has tasty-looking cookies arranged in a bakery case. You might be tempted to buy a bagful to munch on as you walk. What you need, however, is a doggie bag, because owners Mark Beckloff and Dan Dye are serving freshly baked treats for your pooch. You can buy your canine a pupcake or a cheese pizza. For the vegetable course there is "collie-flower," and for dessert there are "snicker-

hasanyoneseen dan'snephew?

Kelly's in historic Westport (500 Westport Road; 816-561-0635) is a good place to sip a brew. This has been a very popular Kansas City nightspot for more than thirty years. In fact, Daniel Boone's nephew used to hang out here. Well, he once ran a trading post in the building, which is the oldest in Kansas City. He hasn't come in lately.

poodles," always a favorite. A portion of the price goes to help abused dogs. The treats have no salt or chemicals and are low-fat (your dog will thank you). You can also order your loving pet its own specially decorated birthday cake to share with other dogs on the block. Three Dog Bakery has grown from it origins here in KC to a franchise that has tongues hanging out around the world. They use only human-grade ingredients, so you can join your pup for a snack if you are so inclined. You can order treats online not only for your dog but for your cat as well. But there is only one feline product, a freeze-dried salmon treat called We Pity the Kitties. Hours are 10:00 a.m. to 7:00 p.m. Monday through Saturday (Thursday until 9:00 p.m.) and 11:00 a.m. to 5:00 p.m. on Sunday. Call (816) 753-3647 to order that special pal a special cake. Visit their Web site at www.threedogbakery.com.

Let's get small. If you love tiny things (or if you haven't quite grown up), don't miss Kansas City's *Toys and Miniatures Museum* at 5235 Oak Street (816-333-2055). Childhood friends Mary Harris Francis and Barbara Marshall started the museum in a Mediterranean-style mansion built in 1906. It has been expanded to 21,500 square feet. The mansion and the surrounding property are owned by the University of Missouri–Kansas City, but the toys and miniatures belong to a private nonprofit foundation. Miniatures are not toys; scale is important in a miniature—everything in a miniature room must look exactly like a full-size room. Toys are a separate collection.

Tucked upstairs is a Victorian nursery with a brass cradle made in Paris in 1850. It has been in Mary's family for several generations. Barbara's father, Hallmark Cards founder Joyce C. Hall, had a dollhouse built for his daughter at a local high school. When it was time to pick it up for Christmas, it was too big to take out of the school, so she did not get her dollhouse. Now they have a museum recognized as one of the largest miniatures museums in the world. There are more than eighty-five antique furnished dollhouses at least one hundred years old, scale-model miniature rooms, and toys. The museum is open Wednesday through Saturday 10:00 a.m. to 4:00 p.m. and Sunday 1:00 to 4:00 p.m. It is closed for two weeks following Labor Day. Admission is $6 for adults, $5 for seniors and students, and $4 for children. Every Saturday at 1:00 p.m. you can enjoy storytellers, and at 2:30 p.m. on the first Saturday of the month there's a magician to entertain you.

The Crestwood Shops around 55th and Oak Streets lure antiquers. There's Charlecote (816-444-4622; www.charlecoteantiques.com), *Pear Tree* at 303 East 55th Street (816-333-2100), and even an antique-book store, *Bloomsday Books,* where you can find used and rare books. Rest and eat at *Europa Market & Bakery* at 323 East 55th Street (816-523-1212). Their lemon cake will get you going again.

South of Country Club Plaza, in an old Texaco station in **Brookside,** is a small wine bar and cafe called **Joe D's Winebar-Cafe & Patio** (6227 Brookside Plaza, Kansas City). It was the first wine bar in the country. Owner Shawn Braken has the largest by-the-glass wine list in Kansas City, and the house wines are excellent. The menu changes each day, depending on what seasonal fresh produce and meat the chef has discovered. Unusual entrees such as breast of chicken with strawberry-peppercorn sauce, orange cream fettuccine, or fresh marlin with coconut-banana-curry sauce are written on a chalkboard. The pizza du jour on fresh Italian Boboli bread (artichoke and crab pizza? Yes!) changes with the chef's mood. Joe D's (816-333-6116; www .joeds.com) opens weekdays at 11:00 a.m. and serves lunch until 3:00 p.m. Between 3:00 and 5:00 p.m., only appetizers and salads are served; dinner is served after 5:00 p.m. Joe D's closes at 11:00 p.m. on Monday and Tuesday, midnight on Wednesday and Thursday, and 1:00 a.m. on Friday and Saturday. After dinner be sure to try the bread pudding with hot caramel sauce, just like grandma used to make.

There is a **Maggie's Cellar and Loft** here in Brookside, downstairs next to the post office at 112 West 63rd Street. It is like the original in Kearney with gift items and flowers, jams, jellies and preserves, and a wine cellar. But this one has a rathskeller as well. It's actually a wine and coffeehouse with Internet service. Jay LaRue is the manager and can be reached at (816) 444-2444. Hours are Monday through Saturday from 10:00 a.m. until 6:00 p.m.

If you have children along you might want to swing by **Brookside Toy & Science** at 330 West 63rd Street (816-523-4501; www.brooksidetoyandscience .com), where a fine display of bugs under glass and an array of toys not to be believed will keep the kids busy for a while. Nearby is the **Reading Reptile** (816-753-0441), a well-loved kids' bookstore. For the grown-ups, a well-named place called **Stuff** (816-361-8222; www.pursuegoodstuff.com) is packed with the same: stuff such as antiques, collectibles, fine art, and gifts.

The piano bar seems to be a dying breed of nightclub, which is what makes **Piano Room Lounge** at 8410 Wornall Road, Kansas City, such a great find. This is a comfortable neighborhood bar in a strip mall. But don't be fooled by its quiet storefront: They invite people to pick up the mike and sing. This is not a karaoke bar, however, and the people who come up to stand by the mike are regulars and, for the most part, have the voice and style of professionals. Open Monday through Saturday from 10:00 a.m. to 1:30 a.m. Call (816) 363-8722.

The city of **Independence,** just east of downtown Kansas City on Interstate 70, could be a day trip in itself: There's Harry S Truman's home, now a national park, and the **Truman Presidential Library,** at U.S. Highway 24 and Delaware

(816-268-8200 or 800-833-1225), is open 9:00 a.m. to 5:00 p.m. Monday through Saturday and noon to 5:00 p.m. Sunday (closed Thanksgiving, Christmas, and New Year's Day). There's a special program night on Thursdays, when the museum is open until 9:00 p.m. Admission is $7 adults, $5 seniors, $3 children ages six to eighteen, children younger than age six admitted free. Self-guided tours. For information visit www.truman library.org.

In Independence you'll also find the world center for the Reorganized Church of Latter-Day Saints and the RLDS Auditorium. There are also Civil War battlefields, as well as the beginnings of the Santa Fe Trail, still visible in the worn earth. (Sometimes it seems as if half the towns on this side of the state claim the trail, but in Independence they still celebrate the Santa-Cali-Gon, where the Santa Fe, California, and Oregon Trails jumped off into the wilderness.) The National Frontier Trails Center is a fine place to learn more about the hardships and adventures of those who dared to leave civilization behind and strike out across the wilderness to a new life. It's in the historic Waggoner-Gates Milling Company building. Call (816) 325-7575 or (800) 810-3900 or visit www.visitindependence.com for further information about the city.

The **Rheinland Restaurant** at 208 North Main, Independence, serves a scrumptious *Zigeunerschnitzel* (Gypsy Schnitzel), a pork cutlet with a spicy pepper sauce and a side of *späetzle* (tiny dumpling or noodles). A large dark beer will help the digestion. Heinz and Rosie Heinzelmann are the owners, and they suggest the *Jaegerschnitzel* (hunter-style), which is less spicy and covered with a creamy burgundy-mushroom sauce. These and the *Rouladen* with *Rotkoiil* (beef filled with bacon, pickles, and onions, served with red cabbage and späetzle) are available for dinner only; however, the lunch crowd can try the *Schnitzel à la Holstein* or many kinds of sandwiches (the Strammer Max is a favorite—thin-sliced Black Forest ham on rye topped with a fried egg). The Rheinland is open Tuesday through Saturday from 11:00 a.m. to 9:00 p.m. and on Sunday from 11:30 a.m. to 2:30 p.m. Friday and Saturday nights there is live music—on Friday nights it's sing-along accordion music and from a hammer dulcimer and guitar on Saturday nights. Call (816) 461-5383 or visit the Web site www.rheinlandrestaurant.com.

There are antiques stores, bed-and-breakfasts, and dandy places to eat in Independence—in short, there's entirely too much to include in a single volume. We've narrowed it down to these few, which are off the beaten path by virtue of location, arcane historical significance, or ambience. Of course, the best tenderloin in town is at the ***Courthouse Exchange,*** 113 West Lexington. The portion is huge. Call (816) 252-0344. Hours are 11:00 a.m. to 9:00 p.m. Monday through Thursday, and until 10:00 p.m. on Friday and Saturday.

Don't miss ***Clinton's*** on the square, at 100 West Maple. When he was on the campaign train in Independence, President Bill Clinton visited here; they have photos and a thank-you letter to prove it! (He's wearing a Clinton's sweatshirt.) Just how long has it been since you've had a real chocolate soda or cherry phosphate? While you're there, ask them to make a chocolate-cherry cola; it's like a liquid, chocolate-covered cherry with a twist. This is a real old-time soda fountain, complete with uniformed soda jerks and a marble counter with a mirrored back; the malts still whir in those tall, frosty metal containers as they did when we were kids. Call (816) 833-2046 for more information. Clinton's is open Monday through Saturday 8:30 a.m. to 5:00 p.m.

And if all this hedonistic revelry doesn't get you, maybe the historical angle will: Truman's very first job was at Clinton's. You don't have to be a soda jerk first to be president, but maybe it helps. Harry was one of our most popular commanders in chief.

Visitors to the historic Independence Square can now experience the excitement and charm of Scandinavia. Just a few steps from the Harry S Truman Home ticket office, ***Scandinavia Place*** at 209 North Main in downtown Independence features a smorgasbord of traditional Scandinavian gifts complemented by a splash of the unique and the unexpected. In addition to the wide selection of items from Denmark, Sweden, Norway, Finland, and Iceland, a shopper can also find an assortment of gifts from other European countries, especially packaged gourmet foods. Gift wrapping and shipping are available. Come and browse the many fine foods and gifts and visit with Nina, the Icelandic owner. Hours are 10:00 a.m. until 6:00 p.m. Monday through Saturday and from noon to 4:00 p.m. on Sunday. Call (816) 461-6633.

You think celebrity prisoners in our jails are pampered now. When Frank James was held at the jail in Independence, his cell sported an Oriental carpet; he had guests in for dinner and served them fine wines. For that matter, so did William Quantrill when he was incarcerated here.

Although the dank cells with their monolithic stone walls were decorated when company called, they were still jail. More than 135 years after the fact, the cells are still dark, forbidding holes that look impossible to escape. The 1869 ***Jail Marshall's Home and Museum*** (816-252-1892) are at 217 North Main, Independence 64050. The museum is open April through October, 10:00 a.m. to 5:00 p.m. Monday through Saturday, 1:00 p.m. to 4:00 p.m. Sunday; November,

December, and March, 10:00 a.m. to 4:00 p.m. Tuesday through Saturday, 1:00 to 4:00 p.m. Sunday; closed January and February. Admission is $4 adults, $1 ages six to seventeen, and free for children younger than age six.

Several interesting B&Bs are in Independence. *Serendipity Bed & Breakfast* at 116 South Pleasant Street is a step back in time. This three-story 1887 brick house is full of Victorian details. An authentic-looking iron stove hides an electric range, and tall glass-door cabinets are full of antique food containers and plates. Even the brick-edged flower beds in the garden are alive with color from spring through fall. The most modern item is the 1926 Studebaker in the carriage house, which is driven to take guests on a tour of Independence. Rates are around $95, which includes a full breakfast in the dining room. Longer-stay discounts and economy rates without breakfast are available. If there are six or more in your party, you can arrange for a Victorian Tour and Tea for $15 a person. Contact Susan for more information (816-833-4719 or 800-203-4299; www.bbhost.com/serendipitybb).

Perhaps you remember the nineteenth-century painting of two trappers in a long wooden canoe. A big black animal—perhaps a bear—sits in the bow gazing enigmatically at the viewer. Or maybe The Jolly Boatmen is more your style, with the rivermen dancing at the dock, playing instruments, and generally raising a ruckus. Artist George Caleb Bingham painted both, along with many others depicting life along the Western Frontier.

Bingham made his home in Independence for a time at the elegant *Bingham-Waggoner Estate* at 313 West Pacific, Independence, where he watched two Civil War battles rage across his front lawn (not conducive to painting a decent picture. Think what that would do to your concentration!).

Visit from April to October, Monday through Saturday from 10:00 a.m. to 4:30 p.m. and Sunday 1:00 to 4:00 p.m., to find out how "the other half" lived in the last century—or rent the mansion for a festive event and make the past your own. The mansion is also open from late November through December for the Christmas season; they decorate all twenty-six rooms. Admission is $5.00 for adults, $4.50 for senior citizens, $2.00 for children ages six to sixteen, and free for children younger than age six, with slightly higher winter fees to defray the cost of all those decorations. Call (816) 461-3491 for more information or go to www.bwestate.org.

Another beautiful visit is to the *Vaile Mansion* at 1500 North Liberty in Independence. It is open from April 1 to October 31, Monday through Saturday from 10:00 a.m. to 4:00 p.m. and from 1:00 to 4:00 p.m. on Sunday. Admission is $5 for adults and $2 for children ages six to sixteen. Call (816) 325-7430.

There is great antiques shopping in this region. Independence was the jumping-off point for pioneers heading west, so this is as far as a lot of their furniture got. Shlepping across the country with a wagon full of sideboards and armoires didn't seem practical, so Independence is where many pioneers began jettisoning large pieces of furniture. (Rocking chairs often made it as far as the Platte River.)

National Frontiers Trails Center exhibits commemorate the Santa Fe, California, and Oregon Trails, all of which passed through or began in Independence. The Trails Center doesn't feel like a museum, because it presents the trails through the words of the pioneers who traveled them. The layout of the center is patterned after the trails. At one point, a fork in the path forces visitors to choose between taking the Santa Fe or the Oregon-California routes. One route dead-ends, so if you choose that route, you have to go back and try again. Voice-activated boxes tell stories of how the West was settled, and the murals by Charles Goslin show how it was accomplished. There are many pioneers' journals, which make fascinating reading, and there is a theater with a trails film. The center is located at 318 West Pacific Street, Independence. Call (816) 325-7575. Hours are 9:00 a.m. to 4:30 p.m. Monday through Saturday, 12:30 to 4:30 p.m. Sunday. Closed Thanksgiving, Christmas, and New Year's Day. Admission is $3.50 for adults, $3.00 for seniors, $2.00 for children ages six to seventeen, and free for those age five and younger.

whatgoesaround comesaround

William Clark returned from the historic expedition with Meriwether Lewis to become Administrator of the Missouri Territory. Respectful and frail, Clark was accorded similar courtesies by the tribal chiefs, sparing the state some of the woes brought upon other areas by mismanaged dealing with the Native Americans.

The *Woodstock Inn Bed & Breakfast* at 1212 West Lexington, Independence, was originally a doll and quilt factory. It features eleven uniquely and beautifully appointed guest rooms. Innkeepers Todd and Patricia Justice have completely refurbished the place, which now features a fenced-in courtyard and garden area, thermo-massage spa tubs, fireplaces, and a wealth of fine collectibles, rare antiques, and priceless artwork from around the world. Rooms range from $98 to $219 and all rooms have private baths. Call (816) 833-2233 for reservations or visit www.independence-missouri.com.

Every town tries to have the weirdest little museum, and Leila's Hair Museum, 1333 South Noland Road, gives Independence a lock on that title. (Ow! Sorry!) It is the only hair museum in the country. You can see a 14-inch-high tree made of human hair. The museum is inside Leila Cohoon's Independence School of Cosmetology. Her collection of more than 2,000 wreaths, brooches, watch fobs, bracelets, and buttons (all made from human hair) began in 1956 when she found a little square frame made of hair. She was a hairdresser then and it piqued her interest. Hair art was a reminder of a loved one before cameras were invented. You have to see the wreaths (she has more than 300 now), which are created by carefully weaving hair over fine wires to make tiny flowers. Her oldest piece is a finely detailed brooch from 1680, brought to this country from Sweden. Go to www.hairwork.com/leila for more information. The museum is open from 9:00 a.m. to 4:40 p.m. Tuesday through Saturday. Admission is $5.00 for adults $2.50 for seniors and children. Call (816) 833-2955.

Independence is the center of the Reorganized Church of Latter Day Saints, and the temple is something to behold. Inside the 1,600-seat sanctuary at 201 South River is a 102-rank, 5,685-pipe organ built by Casavant Frères Limitée in Quebec, Canada. That is only the beginning. The rest you have to see for yourself. It is truly magnificent. The building is open to the public for guided tours from 9:00 a.m. to 5:00 p.m. Monday through Saturday and from 1:00 to 5:00 p.m. on Sunday. You can attend free organ recitals at the auditorium from 3:00 to 3:30 p.m. daily from June to August, and on Sunday only during the remainder of the year. Also open to the public is a daily prayer for peace at 12:30 p.m. in the temple sanctuary.

At the old RLDS auditorium, the one with the green dome at 1001 West Walnut, Independence, you can take your children to the nondenominational **Children's Peace Pavilion.** There they will have a good time playing games that help them build self-esteem and learn cooperation and communication. The Peace Pavilion is on the fourth floor; admission is free. Call (816) 521-3030 for information. Hours are 9:00 a.m. to 5:00 p.m. daily; closed Christmas and New Year's Day. There are guided tours and free organ recitals on Sunday at 3:00 p.m. (daily in June, July, and August).

Just outside Independence is the town of **Sugar Creek,** where in 1914 a small girl named Caroline Rozgaj immigrated with her family from their native Croatia. She met and married Michael Kobe in 1927 and raised a family in a home filled with the delightful aroma of warm povitica bread. The children learned the art from their mother. Her philosophy, "If you put good things in it, it'll taste good," still works today at the **Kobe House Bakery** at 114 North Maple. Caroline's children also will indulge you with mama's strudel and other Croation favorites. (Great cabbage rolls locals say!) Hours are 7:30 a.m. to 6:00 p.m. Thursday and Friday, 7:30 a.m. to 4:00 p.m. Saturday. Call (816) 254-3334 or (888) 254-3334 if you are out of town and want to order *povitica* bread.

Oh, and don't leave town without having dinner at **Salvatore's,** 12801 East Highway 40, and trying some of the excellent spadini and a glass of chianti. Call (816) 737-2400.

Historic River Section

How about a day trip back in time? It's 1803, the year of the Louisiana Purchase: Imagine Missouri nearly empty of "civilization," as it was when it became part of the United States. Early fur trappers traded necessities—like tobacco, tomahawks, blankets, fabrics, and cookware. The Osage peoples were the most common Indians in this area, and they did business amicably with both French and American trading posts.

East of Independence you'll explore **Fort Osage,** a National Historic Landmark and the westernmost U.S. outpost in the Louisiana Purchase. Its site was chosen by Lewis and Clark; construction was originally supervised by William Clark himself. Strategically overlooking the Missouri River, the fort was reconstructed from detailed plans preserved by the U.S. War Department. The factory building stands today on its original foundation. Artifacts unearthed during the excavation are on display in the visitor center.

You may find a living-history reenactment in progress, complete with trappers and military men, Indians, explorers, storytellers, and musicians. Clothing displayed is authenticated down to the last bit of trim, and guides learn their alter egos' life and times so thoroughly that you forget you are only visiting the past. Sit inside the blockhouse looking out at the river, watch arrowheads being made from local flint, or visit the gift shop to purchase unique items with a sense of history (such as real bone buttons).

Rustle up a group to enjoy one of the after-hours programs offered by the Jackson County Heritage Program. You

Fort Osage, Sibley

can reserve a place at a hearthside supper in the factory's dining rooms, for example. Enjoy an authentic nineteenth-century meal by candlelight; then cozy up to the fireplace and savor the entertainment.

Several weekends a year, special events such as the Sheep Shearing (May) or Militia Muster and Candlelight Tour (October) are offered, or spend the Fourth of July as our forebears did—the fort's a great place for it.

To find Fort Osage (816-650-5737; www.jacksongov.org) take US 24 from Kansas City east to Buckner; turn north at Sibley Street (Highway BB) and follow the gray signs through the tiny town of Sibley. The fort is open year-round on weekends from 9:00 a.m. to 4:30 p.m. You can explore on your own Wednesday through Sunday April through November. Admission is $3 for adults and $2 for senior citizens and children ages five through thirteen. Children younger than age five are admitted free.

A more historic (and scenic) route between Fort Osage and Lexington will take you down the Highway 224 spur through Napoleon, Waterloo, and Wellington. This is Lafayette County—beginning to get the picture here? Must have been history buffs around this area since dirt was young. The road runs along the Missouri River, sometimes almost at water level, other times from a spectacular river-bluff view. Don't miss the turnoff to tiny downtown *Napoleon.*

A bit farther on is Waterloo, just between Napoleon and Wellington—the obvious place, don't you think? There's not much here but a sign and a few houses, but it would be perfect even if it were only the sign! A great photo op.

rideonby

The Pony Express house at 1704 South Street is not open to the public, but it is interesting that one of the founders of the Pony Express, William Bradford Waddell, built it, and family members have lived there ever since. The person who now occupies the house—Katherine Bradford Van Amburg—is his great-great-granddaughter. Members of the Waddell family have lived in the house since 1840.

On the way into *Lexington,* watch for colorful sights guaranteed to make you smile, like the A-frame wedding chapel overlooking the river, the old Peckerwood Club, and a grain silo painted to look like a lighthouse—and that glorious old river.

Once you enter historic Lexington, soak up the antebellum ambience. The homes along US 24 and on South Street are wonderful examples of Victorian charm—and, remember, we're not just talking 1890s gingerbread here. The Victorian era began in the 1840s. You'll itch to get inside some of these beauties; check with the chamber of commerce for dates and times of historic homes tours. Lexington has four national historic districts and 110 antebellum and Victorian homes and shops. There are several good B&Bs, too.

The *Victorianne,* at 1522 South Street (660-259-2868), is the labor of love of Mary Ault. This lovely Victorian was built in 1885 by the town banker. It has thirteen rooms and ten beautiful fireplaces. Mary has done a lot of renovation and added an enclosed gazebo and hot tub in the garden. There's a carriage house with one room and a private bath. It is almost like an apartment, with a refrigerator filled with soft drinks and a sitting area with a wicker couch and television. Two more rooms are in the main house. Rates are $85 and $100 with continental or full breakfast. The Web site is www.thevictorianne.com.

Owned by Shirley Childs, *Riley's Irish Pub and Grill,* at 913 Main Street in Lexington, is a pub tucked into a historic building, a pub in the real sense of the word—families gather there to eat and the bar is open until closing time. There is an Irish menu as well as food cooked on the grill, so it is an interesting place to stop. It is open Wednesday through Saturday from 11:00 a.m. until 10:00 p.m. Call (660) 259-4770 or visit the Web site at www.rileyspub.com.

The area around the courthouse has plenty of places to browse in. Probably the neatest place in town is the *Victorian Peddler Antiques Shop and Tea Room* at 900 Main Street, Lexington. Melissa and Mark Clark carry fine Victorian furniture, but you can also have lunch there. The tearoom has an eclectic assortment of antique tables and chairs. As Melissa says, "If you like your table, you can take it home with you." The menu changes each day, but there is always a quiche, a soup, and a gourmet sandwich available to eat before you order a piece of homemade pie. Everything is made from scratch, including ice cream in fruit flavors. The tearoom is open Monday from 11:00 a.m. to 2:00 p.m., Wednesday and Thursday from 11:30 a.m. to 9:00 p.m., and Friday and Saturday 11:00 a.m. to 10:00 p.m. Call (660) 259-4533 for more information.

The *Velvet Pumpkin Antiques* shop is at 920 Main Street, Lexington. Owner Georgia Brown keeps regular hours Monday through Saturday from 10:00 a.m. to 5:00 p.m. and Sunday from noon to 4:00 p.m. Call (660) 259-4545 or visit www.thevelvetpumpkin.com.

Be sure to stop by the restored *Log House Museum* at 307 Broadway in Lexington. This 1830s home was discov-

andthestate mottois

The state motto is a quotation from Cicero: "Salus popali suprema lex esto." (Let the welfare of the people be the supreme law.)

ered in a rundown condition and was moved and rebuilt log by log by the volunteer efforts of local citizens. It has been surrounded by wildflowers and paths as it might have been when it was new. It was a museum but the Lexington Historical Society put it up for sale due to the rising cost of maintenance. Just by chance, artist Maggie Bonanomi visited the town in 2002. She took one look at the town, fell in love, and decided to stay. In 2004, when the log house was put on the market, it became *Simply Butternut.* You have to ask about the name so you can hear a bit of history you probably didn't know if you are not from around here. The name butternut is derived from the butternut tree. Dye was extracted from the butternut to dye homespun textiles. Many of the local, down home, Confederate soldiers wore the brownish colored butternut uniforms and were called "Butternuts." Just so happens that Maggie is a textile artist and the log house was the perfect home for her studio. She teaches rug hooking and applique, and she also has primitive antiques and textiles for sale. She says the butternut trees are mostly gone, but the spirit of the Butternuts lives on. Her shop is open seasonally by chance or appointment, because there was no heat or air-conditioning in the 1830s—and there still isn't—so call Maggie at (660) 232-4406.

The Battle of Lexington was fought in September 1861 when General Sterling Price moved his Confederate troops north after the Battle of Wilson's Creek and the fall of Springfield. After fifty-two hours of fighting, Union troops surrendered to the invaders. General Price took 3,000 prisoners and broke the chain of Union-held posts along the Missouri River. Remnants of the battle endure; a cannonball remains lodged in a pillar of the courthouse. You can still find earthworks out behind The *Battle of Lexington State Historic Site* (660-259-4654) overlooking the Missouri River. This redbrick house served as headquarters and hospital for both sides and is now a Civil War museum. More information can be found at www.mostateparks.com.

Along US 24 toward *Waverly,* the land undergoes a change from fenced, row-cropped fields to orchards. The peach crop is always at risk in Missouri's unpredictable weather. Blossoms are often teased out early by a mild February to be punished by an April freeze. It is a dangerous business, but the area around Waverly perseveres. The best peaches from this area are huge and sweet and dripping with juice. A bad year for the peach business is when the fruit is too big, too juicy, and not nearly plentiful enough to make shipping profitable. This is bad for orchard owners but wonderful for anyone lucky enough to be driving through.

US 24 is the old Lewis and Clark Trail along the river. Now it is filled with markets where orchard owners sell their bounty to travelers. Pick up peaches and apples or honey, homemade sausages, cheese, and cider along this scenic drive.

The Santa Fe Trail ran through here at one time, and it is still a trail of sorts for people living in the area: It is Missouri's apple and peach country. The Santa Fe Trail Growers Association is made up of seventeen members in the area. On a drive along US 24 you will see a bountiful expanse of apples, peaches, nectarines, strawberries, raspberries, and blackberries—and all for sale if the season is right. Schreiman and Burkhart are just two of the orchards you will pass along the road. Greenhouses along the way are filled with vegetables, sweet corn, cider, and honey. In July, *Peters Market* is worth the drive from Kansas City for many people.

Pioneers stopped at historic **Arrow Rock** on their way west; it was a Santa Fe Trail town, a river port, and a meeting place for those who shaped history. More than forty original buildings remain. Arrow Rock is still a real town, with permanent residents, a grocery store, a gas station, and a post office, but it is also a state park and historic site. The population numbers only seventy (and the historic district is so tightly controlled that someone has to die before someone new can move in, they say) but the place is packed in the summertime when the Lyceum Theatre is active. The state leases out the **Old Tavern Inn,** and it draws people from across the state. Fried chicken, ham, blueberry cobbler, and wonderful bread pudding make people come back again and again. There is more, too. The 170-year-old tavern (that word was synonymous with *hotel* then) was home to travelers on the Santa Fe Trail or people bound for Independence and the Oregon Trail. Some died here of the cholera and typhus that stopped the westward trek of many. And so, the place is haunted. Beds used in exhibits on the second floor have been found mussed, quiet voices have been heard as well as the cries of a child whose mother died here, photos show strange images that are not really there, and once, a mysterious cloud of smoke appeared in the manager's upstairs bedroom. They seem to be friendly spirits, though. Dinners are bounteous and amazingly inexpensive ($10.95 will buy a huge meal, from salad to dessert). The museum is upstairs.

Arrow Rock looks like a normal town, but normal for a hundred years ago. Streets and gutters are made from huge blocks of limestone; board sidewalks clatter with footsteps. The old bank acts as ticket office for the Lyceum, and the tiny stone jail still waits for an inmate. You may camp at Arrow Rock State Park; sites are available for groups or individuals. Visit the Web site at www .arrowrock.org.

Today, the **Lyceum Repertory Theatre** (660-837-3311) offers performances throughout the summer in an old church building; it's Missouri's oldest repertory company. Call ahead for a list of plays and their rotating dates, or visit www.lyceumtheatre.org.

Borgman's Bed and Breakfast, at 706 Van Buren (660-837-3350), is a nineteenth-century inn with five bedrooms and a common game room. Play a quick round of Scrabble, or enjoy a fireside chat with owner Kathy Borgman, who did much of the restoration work herself; take a look at the fascinating "house book," which shows step-by-step what's been done. After a generous breakfast, Kathy will give you a tour of the town—she's an official Arrow Rock guide. Additional meals are available if you make prior arrangements. A cat and bird are in residence, so no other pets are welcomed. Rates are $60 to $65 for a double.

aglimpseof southamerica

Eleven miles south of Arrow Rock you may see some beautiful animals grazing in a field. Jim and Marcia Atkinson breed show-quality llamas on their farm. If you have never seen a llama close up, it is well worth the short drive. These animals are strong and intelligent as well as quiet and gentle. They have expressive faces and long, lovely wool. Their gentle temperament makes them good companions. They are bred as pack animals in South America, and the Atkinsons' llama Kong is one of the largest herd sires in this country.

Artist George Caleb Bingham's home is here (remember him from Independence?), as is the home of Dr. John Sappington, one of the first to use quinine to treat malaria. Kathy Borgman will tell you all about it.

Historic **Arrow Rock Tavern** at 302 Main was known for years as the John Huston Tavern. The tavern dates from 1834, when Arrow Rock was a thriving river port. Proprietors Mary and Mike Duncan say the most ordered item on the menu is the specialty of the tavern, fried chicken. And why not? This recipe, like many others here, has been handed down for generations. Ole-time hominy salad, bread pudding, and fudge pie are included in those hand-me-downs. Hours are June through September Tuesday through Saturday 11:00 a.m. to 3:00 p.m. and 5:00 to 8:00 p.m. Just lunch is served on Sunday. During the winter, the tavern is open on weekends only and serves lunch and dinner on Saturday and lunch only on Sunday. Call (660) 837-3200.

Arrow Rock Bed and Breakfast is an elegant home built in 1853. At 633 Main Street, Arrow Rock, it is within walking distance from everything. Innkeeper Linda Hoffman knows her way around the town and will set you on your way exploring. The home has two rooms for guests, one with a fireplace. The rooms are spacious and have sitting areas. One is on the first floor with semiprivate bath, the other is upstairs, where there are two full shared baths. A Steinway grand piano is in the parlor, and the home is furnished with period antiques. A continental breakfast is served in the formal dining room each morning. The home has a large wraparound porch with a swing and wicker furniture. Rooms are $75. Call (800) 795-2797, or visit www.arrowrock.org.

There are seven B&Bs in Arrow Rock. It is quite a draw for Missourians in the summertime when the theater is going.

At **Boonville,** following the river east, the western prairie meets the Ozarks. The town was settled in 1810 by the widow Hannah Cole, who, with her nine children, built cabins on the bluffs overlooking the Missouri River. During the War of 1812 the settlement was palisaded and named Cole's Fort. It became the main river port for all of southwestern Missouri.

The older residential section of Boonville has an unusually well-preserved collection of antebellum brick residences with wide halls and large rooms. Modest neoclassical homes are mixed with more flamboyant Victorian ones; many are on the National Register of Historic Places.

While in Boonville visit the *Old Cooper County Jail and Hanging Barn* at 614 East Morgan. The jail was built in 1848 and used until 1978 when public hanging was declared cruel and unusual punishment. Prisoners' quarters resemble dungeons, where the inmates were sometimes shackled to the wall with metal rings. Outside the jail is the hanging barn where nineteen-year-old Lawrence Mabry was executed in 1930, the state's last public hanging (as told in historian Bob Dyer's folk song, "The Last Man to Hang in Missouri").

Thespian Hall, 522 Main Street, is the oldest theater still in use west of the Alleghenies. Originally built in 1857, it has been used as an army barracks, Civil War hospital, and skating rink, among other things. It featured gymnastics, opera, and movies in its day and is now home to Boonville Community Theatre.

If you have come to town for one of Boonville's many bluegrass festivals—where musicians play everything from harmonicas to paper bags—Thespian Hall is the center of the activity. The folk-music tradition lives on here through the efforts of the Friends of Historic Boonville. If you can, try to coordinate your visit with one of these festivals. The Big Muddy Folk Festival is in April, and the Missouri River Festival of the Arts is in August.

If you are out walking around, search out *Harley Park,* where Lookout Point sits atop a bluff over the Missouri River, and get a feel for what early townsfolk saw along the long bend of the river. An Indian burial mound surmounts this high point; imagine the prospect of immortality with such a view.

In nearby *New Franklin* on County Road 463, the *Rivercene Bed and Breakfast* will take you back in time to the 1869 home of a riverboat captain, Joseph B. Kinney, who ran a line of twenty-one stern-wheelers up and down the Missouri River. The three-story brick Second Empire, or Baroque, revival home has survived flood after flood because of Kinney's understanding of the river and its architect's foresight in building it upon a pyramidal, floating foun-

cupid's arrow indian-style

Legend has it that the town of Arrow Rock was named after a bow and arrow competition between Indian warriors vying for the hand of a chief's daughter. One arrow—the winner's, no doubt—shot from a sandbar in the river flew so far that it lodged in a distant bluff above the river.

dation that kept water away from the first floor. Marble fireplaces warm the rooms, and hosts Jody and Ron Lenz wake the guests in the seven rooms each morning with the aroma of breakfast. You can spend the day on one of several porches watching the birds and wildlife or take off on the KATY Trail. If you do, one of the rooms has a Jacuzzi, which feels fine after a day on the trail. Rooms are $95 to $259. Call (660) 848-2497 or (800) 531-0862, fax (816) 848-2142. Visit the Web site at www.rivercene.com and see the rooms online.

The mid-Missouri area was the site of many of the key battles of the Civil War. The first land battle of the war was fought 4 miles below Boonville on June 17, 1861. State troops under the command of Confederate colonel John S. Marmaduke were defeated by federal forces led by Capt. Nathaniel Lyon. Military historians consider this victory important in preserving the Union.

Jefferson City, Missouri's capital, is smack in the center of the state on U.S. Highway 50, handy to legislators and lobbyists. Built on the steep southern bluffs of the Missouri River, the city and the surrounding rural landscape offer considerable scenic variety. Large streams are bordered with steeply sloping and heavily forested hills. Bottomland here is rich with alluvial and yellow loess soils that don't look the way you expect fertile topsoil to look but support more wheat and corn than any other section of the Ozarks.

Here also is Jefferson Landing, one of the busiest centers of the nineteenth century. It's still busy; the Amtrak station is at the landing, as are the Lohman Building, the Union Hotel, and the Maus House.

The state capitol is certainly on the beaten path; however, once inside the House Lounge, you will find a mural painted in 1935 by Thomas Hart Benton. This mural stirred controversy in 1936 because some of the legislators said it lacked refinement. Always quick with an answer, Benton retorted that he portrayed "people involved in their natural, daily activities that did not require being polite."

Central Dairy at 610 Madison Street, Jefferson City, still has old-fashioned ice cream and old-fashioned ice-cream prices. This is a must-stop place for people on the KATY Trail on a hot summer's day and for everyone else, for that matter. Hours are Monday through Saturday from 8:00 a.m. to 6:00 p.m. and Sunday from 10:00 a.m. to 6:00 p.m. One of the specialties is called the Rock and Roll. It's like a banana split but with four, count 'em, four flavors of ice cream and toppings. Betcha can't eat one! Call (573) 635-6148.

Arri's Pizza at 117 West High Street, Jefferson City, is a favorite with the members of congress in the capital city. Hours are 11:00 a.m. to 10:00 p.m. Monday through Thursday, until 11:00 p.m. Friday and Saturday, and 4:00 to 10:00 p.m. on Sunday. Call (573) 635-9225 or visit online at www.arrispizza online.com.

Missouri's Melting Pot

Head west to **California** (that's California, Missouri) on US 50, and go south on Highway 87, 2½ miles to **Burgers' Smokehouse,** 32819 Highway 87, if you fancy a ham to carry home. It is open from 7:30 a.m. to 5:00 p.m. This family-owned smokehouse has been in business for more than twenty-five years and is one of the largest country meat-processing plants in the United States, producing 200,000 hams annually. You can take a tour of the plant any day but Sunday between 7:30 a.m. and 4:00 p.m. There is a toll-free number for ordering a ham: (800) 345-5185. Call (573) 796-4111 for information if you are in the area. Visit the Web site at www.smokehouse.com.

What you wouldn't expect to find here are the seasonal dioramas, which show the beauty of the Ozarks with great care for botanical and zoological detail. These scenes by artist Terry Chase depict the influence of Ozark geography and changing seasons on the process of curing meat.

Leave California on Highway 87 and travel about 12 miles to **Jamestown** and, if it's between June and fall, pick some berries at **Missouri Highland Farms** at 17071 Garrett Road. Growers Dan and Mary Brauch begin the year with asparagus and follow it up with berries of about any color you might be craving: blackberries, blueberries, and raspberries in three colors (black, red, and yellow). Hours are from 8:00 a.m. until about 5:00 p.m. in the summer and from 10:00 a.m. in the fall when the raspberries are ripe. Call (660) 849-2544 for more information. To find the farm, turn right off Highway 87 in Jamestown and follow "Y" Road (the one next to the post office) to the end.

US 50 will take you to the town of **Tipton.** Follow the signs to the **Dutch Bakery and Bulk Food Store** (660-433-2865). Located on Highways 5 and US 50 at the west end of Tipton, the shop is owned by Leonard and Suetta Hoover. Suetta does all the baking right here in the house while minding their six children and seems unruffled by it all. Old Order Mennonites, they came here from Pennsylvania and speak Pennsylvania Dutch when alone in the shop or talking to the children. Her pies are baked from homegrown berries and fruit; fresh vegetables from their garden are available in season. Homemade breads (a favorite is a wonderful oatmeal bread) and rolls fill the shelves along with bulk foods. But the primary reason for stopping here is the "Dutch letters"—crisp, thick pastry

trivia

The cemetery in the little town of Belton on U.S. Highways 71 and 58 might be worth a stop if you want to see the graves of Carry Nation and Dale Carnegie. The museum in the old city hall is fraught with memorabilia of the two leaders.

rolled and filled with almond paste and shaped into letters. They are cheaper if you buy five, and you might as well so you won't have to turn around and come back in an hour. Open 6:00 a.m. to 6:00 p.m. Monday through Saturday.

While in Tipton try to visit the **McClay House** on Howard Street and Highway B, which is open on the second or fourth Sunday of each month. This beautiful old three-story house has been restored and contains the original furniture. It is the site of the annual Fourth of July ice-cream social and features dinner and entertainment in September. The first Saturday in July is called Super Saturday around here and draws a thousand visitors for the barbecue contest, volleyball, and three-on-three basketball contests. Call the Tipton Chamber of Commerce (660-433-6377) for more information about the McClay House and Super Saturday. Be sure to notice the "Eight-Ball" water tower.

There's a Fischer's Pool Table manufacturing plant in town. You can find the Web site for the town of Tipton at www .tiptonmo.com.

If you're in the mood for some really good barbecue, turn south on U.S. Highway 65 where it intersects with US 50 and drive to 1915 South Limit to **Kehde's Barbecue, Sedalia** (660-826-2267), where John and Chelsea Kehde (pronounced K.D.) serve the best barbecue in the area. But that's not all.

In memory of The Wheel Inn, Sedalia

Kehde's also has jalapeño fries (french fries dipped in some kind of spicy coating) and a grilled tenderloin sandwich that is as good as the fried kind but without all the fat. Kehde's is a regular stop for folks headed to or from the Lake of the Ozarks and Kansas City. Kehde's added a railroad dining car to the building to handle the extra crowds from the state fair and the summertime Lake of the Ozarks crowd. It's fun to sit up in the old dining car and watch the traffic go by while enjoying the best barbecued ribs in the area. Take home a bottle of the sauce. In fact, take a couple or you will have to send for more when you get home. To find out more about Sedalia go to www.mysedalia.com.

If you drive into Sedalia on US 65, you will probably pass (off to your left and way up) a beautiful stone mansion overlooking the highway. It is

Stonyridge Farm in **Bothwell State Park,** 19350 Bothwell State Park Road. Bothwell chose limestone as his primary building material for the lodge and cliff house. There are more angles to this place than a Chinese puzzle—it must have driven the roofers crazy. The original carriage road rises almost 100 feet but in a gentle ascent, with the lay of the land; hand-laid stone culverts allow water passage under the road. Take the first left after you pass the house on US 65 going toward Sedalia (or, driving north, watch very carefully for the small sign marking the turn or you will have to turn around and go back when you finally see it). It is worth the trouble to find; there are spectacular views and wonderful walking trails near the house.

There are several antiques malls in Sedalia, but remember that in August this is the home of the **Missouri State Fair,** which attracts more than 300,000 people. The path gets beaten smooth, but it leads to midway rides, big-name entertainment, livestock shows, and car races—good, clean, all-American fun.

In the little community of **Georgetown,** just outside of Sedalia on Highway H, stands a three-story girls' school built in 1842 by Gen. George R. Smith, who founded the town of Sedalia. He built the girls' school for his own two daughters. The ten-room, white-brick beauty now houses Lorene Downing's **Georgetown Bed and Breakfast.** Three (or four) guest rooms, two with private baths, come with a big "farmer's breakfast" and are priced from $65 to $75. You can call Lorene at (660) 826-3941.

The KATY Trail snakes along the river for 83 miles from Sedalia east to Jefferson City, burrowing through its only tunnel at Recuperate. The trail also treats you to the only Missouri River railroad bridge near

Bothwell State Park, Sedalia

Franklin, and then it goes past glittering Burlington limestone bluffs containing millions of fossils from the sea. The Mighty Mo has been out of banks twice since the trail was begun, once in the Great Flood of '93 and again in the almost-great flood of '95, but work is progressing to connect the trail here with its other end in St. Charles. When the river is behaving, you can look "across the wide Missouri" and have a magnificent view of the river traffic of barges and boats.

Western Missouri waited a long time for a botanical garden; St. Louis, in the east, has one of the finest in the country. Finally, after much hemming and hawing among folks in the Greater Kansas City area and those just over the Kansas border, the people of *Powell Gardens* couldn't wait any longer and began their own. Hurrah for private initiative! This almost 25-year-old garden is a beautiful 915-acres of blooms and a natural resource center where you can wander among the flowers and indigenous plants, learn about "S-s-s-s-snakes!," make an all-natural wreath, or learn how to plant, prune, and harvest your own backyard botanical garden—you get the idea. The size sounds a bit overwhelming, but this oasis has free trolleys to help you cover the ground. Notice the hen and chicks, and the sedum and other plants peeking out from the crevices of a 600-foot-long stone wall in the Island Garden. Take time to visit the secret sunken garden where floating lotus blossoms glisten in the dappled sunlight. The Hummingbird Garden calls these little creatures in droves and although pockets of blooms pop up around every corner, find the Perennial Garden, which has 1,200 kinds of flowers covering 3½ acres. The stunning redwood and glass Marjorie Powell Allen Chapel at the gardens was designed by E. Fay Jones, a nationally honored and recognized architect who built Thorncrown Chapel in Arkansas. Plans are in the works for a Missouri Star quilt pattern planted in vegetables, a demonstration kitchen, and a kitchen garden. Hours are from 9:00 a.m. to 6:00 p.m. daily. Workshops and seminars are scheduled year-round. There are also a cafe and a gift shop, which opens at 10:00 a.m. Admission is $8 adults, $7 seniors, and $3 for children five to twelve years old. Powell Gardens (816-566-2600) is just south of US 50 at Kingsville.

Watch for signs from I-70 (or Highway 291) for *Fleming Park* and *Lake Jacomo.* You'll find the usual sailing, swimming, and fishing as well as the *Burroughs Audubon Society Library* (816-795-8177). Learn about the birds, take a hike, browse through the books, and discover how to turn your backyard into a wildlife sanctuary. The library is open from 12:30 to 4:30 p.m. Tuesday through Saturday.

Stop in your tracks. The world is moving altogether too quickly, but there's an antidote: *Missouri Town 1855* in Fleming Park. Managed by the Jackson

County Parks Department, one of the two largest county parks departments in the United States, it is a collection of original mid-nineteenth-century buildings moved on-site. They now make up a brand-new old town founded in 1960.

A wide variety of architectural styles add to the historical significance of the town. It's just that sort of progression from rugged log cabins to fine homes that would have taken place in the last century as settlers arrived and commerce thrived. You'll find antebellum homes, a tavern, a schoolhouse, a church, a lawyer's tiny office (apparently the law was not quite so lucrative then), and the mercantile, where settlers would have bought outright or bartered for their goods. It has even been the setting for several movies, including the television version of *Friendly Persuasion* and the more recent movie *Across Five Aprils,* a story of a family split by the Civil War.

thekatytrail

The KATY Trail is named for the MKT (Missouri-Kansas-Texas) Railroad tracks laid down more than a century ago. The MKT came out of Fort Riley, Kansas, in the mid-1890s and shot into Indian Territory. It was the heart of the area, rumbling in and bringing the lifeblood of freight, newspapers, and passengers needed to make the Midwest part of the Industrial Revolution. By 1892 the KATY had a direct route to St. Louis and connections to the eastern seaboard. Many of the small towns along the trail were born—and died—with the railroad.

If the buildings alone aren't enough to pique your interest, this is a living-history experience. You're liable to see the blacksmith at work, watch oxen tilling the soil, or be followed by the resident flock of geese. You can wander around a real herb garden and discover how many herbs were used as medicinals in the past century—hospitals were rare in those days, and medical insurance was unheard of.

Missouri Town 1855 is at 8010 East Park Road in **Lee's Summit.** It is on the east side of Fleming Park. Take Colbern Road east to Cyclone School Road. Turn north (left) and follow the signs 2 miles to the entrance. Admission for adults is $3 and $1 for youths, and children younger than age four get in for free. The town is open Wednesday through Sunday from 9:00 a.m. until 5:00 p.m. from April 15 through November 15 and on weekends only from November until April.

Ray Julo's place is always full of ice-cream connoisseurs, people who know how special frozen custard is. **Custard's Last Stand** at 308 Southeast 291 Highway in Lee's Summit, has been in town since 1989, and business is fine even with the competition. Frozen custard is a super-premium ice cream with one-third less air than regular ice cream and is served at 28 degrees Fahrenheit instead of 10 degrees Fahrenheit like regular ice cream. It doesn't freeze your taste buds. And, Ray points out, it has eggs in it, which makes it creamier and very thick—so thick it is handed to you upside down.

Custard's Last Stand was voted best ice cream in the Kansas City area two years in a row by a local magazine. There are forty-five flavors to choose from, including peanut butter, bubble gum, and the ever-popular "Berry, Berry, Berry" (a combination of strawberry, blueberry, and raspberry). Call a member of the Julo family (there are three generations working there) at (816) 347-9922. Hours are from 11:00 a.m. to 10:00 p.m. (10:30 p.m. on Friday and Saturday) and from noon to 10:00 p.m. on Sunday. Visit the Web site at www.custardslast stand.com.

what'sinaname

In 1868 when fifty-one pioneer families settled in the area, they applied for a post office and name for their town. Excelsior was suggested, but it was already taken. More names were sent, and more had already been assigned. Finally, the frustrated citizens of this settlement on the east branch of the Grand River sent one last request: "We don't care what name you give us, so long as it is sort of 'peculiar.'" Well, that's exactly what they got: Peculiar, Missouri.

Across the street stands a 108-year-old church at 509 West Main. It is no longer a place of worship unless you worship the God-of-Good-Things-to-Eat. It is now the *Cafe Petit Four,* a deli and bakery where Lynn Phelps creates some wonderful meals. But the atmosphere is unique because of the 14-foot ceilings with the original brass chandelier lighting the room and seating for about ten in the choir loft. Lunchtime people find all manner of home-cooked soups, quiches, and sandwiches on fresh bread. There is a vegetarian menu, too, and the veggie burger is quite good. Dinnertime brings out the big appetites, and they are satisfied with items such as steaks or shrimp Creole. The desserts are handmade delicacies, the favorite being peanut butter pie, which will tempt you right off that diet. Not only can you go there for lunch or dinner, but there is also a grand Sunday brunch. Hours are Tuesday through Friday 9:30 a.m. to 3:00 p.m. and Saturday 8:00 a.m. to 4:00 p.m. That Sunday brunch is served from 9:30 a.m. to 2:00 p.m. Call (816) 537-5983 or visit www .petitfourbakery.com.

Ciao! Bella Ristorante at 235 Southeast Main (816-554-2442) is open for lunch Tuesday through Saturday from 11:00 a.m. until 3:00 p.m. and Sunday from 10:00 a.m. until 3:00 p.m., Dinner is served Tuesday through Thursday from 5:00 to 9:00 p.m. and until 10:00 p.m. on Friday and Saturday.

Once upon a time there was a little village named Cockrell on Old US 50, and in that little village was an old mercantile general store. But that was more than 115 years ago. Today the vintage village is known as *Cockrell Mercantile Company* at 30003 East Old US 50 Highway between Lee's Summit and Lone Jack. Proprietors Chris and Becky Glaze have made the five cottages and barns home to five unique shops. The Mercantile carries gadgets galore—aprons, tea towels, glassware, pots and pans—and treats you to a free cup of coffee or tea while you shop. The Fiesta Cottage has the largest selection of Fiestaware in this part of the country. The Morton House features bakeware and most anything a baker could need, including King Authur Flour products. Cockrell Cottage is filled with home decor items, barbecue supplies, gift books, candles, and the line of Aromatique products. There are butcher blocks, pot racks, and gourmet foods throughout the village and gift wrapping is complimentary. Then last—but certainly not least if you are a gardener—is the Cockrell Annex, an outdoorsy shop full of surprising garden accessories. To find the village, travel east on US 50 through Lee's Summit and go ¾ mile past the Highway 7 exit. Turn right at the Cockrell sign and follow the road for ½ mile. The store is on the right. Hours are Monday through Saturday 10:00 a.m. to 6:00 p.m. and Sunday noon to 5:00 p.m. Call (816) 697-1923.

Lake Lotawana is a fine place to be on a warm summer night. If you are out in a boat it's even better. Float up to the docks at *Marina Grog and Galley,* 22 A Street, and enjoy great food and a view to match. The circa 1934 building has been renovated. There are four dining options, and all are elegant. The Main Dining Room overlooks the lake on one side and a 1,500-gallon saltwater aquarium on the other. The Upper Deck, features two fireplaces and provides a cozy atmosphere for dining. On a warm summer night you can sit on the Outer Deck, right at water's edge. The Marina has an extensive wine list consisting of 160 varieties from all over the world. Only USDA prime dry-aged steaks are offered, as well as Alaskan King Crab legs. The house specialty is Deep Fried Lobster. From the intersection of Colbern Road and Highway 7, drive east 1½ miles to Gate 1 (#1 is on the sail on both stone pillars). Take a right, travel ¼ mile down the lake road, and the lake is before you. The Marina is on your right before the dam. Call (816) 578-5511 to get directions by car or check the Web at www.marinagrogandgalley.com for detailed directions from other places.

Take Highway 7 from the Lake Lotawana area to East Colbern Road and then south to 9515 South Buckner Tarsney Road, in Grain Valley, and pig out, so to speak at *Porky's Blazin' BBQ.* This barbecue comes highly recommended by weekend bikers—businessmen, lawyers, doctors, etc. disguised in leathers—who really know how to find good food on straight roads. Hours are from 11:00 a.m. until 8:00 p.m. Friday and Saturday and until 5:00 p.m. on Sunday. Call (816) 566-0203.

Unity Village, on US 50 just west of Lee's Summit, is an incorporated town with its own post office and government. It's a peaceful setting with an old-world feel; spacious grounds contain a natural rock bridge, Spanish Mediterranean-style buildings, and a formal rose garden with reflecting pools and fountains. In the last few years the fountains have been stilled and the pools empty waiting repairs but people of all faiths still use the resources for holistic healing at Unity. The restaurant, bookstore, and chapel are open to the public, and you can arrange an overnight stay at the "spiritual life center" by calling (816) 524-3550 or going to www.unityonline.org.

Little *Greenwood* is just south of Lee's Summit on Highway 291, then east on Highway 150. This was once a bustling place with not one but two train stations. It was a major shipping center for cattle and lumber. It still has two explosives factories and a rock quarry nearby, accounting for the heavy trucks rumbling through this sleepy town.

An old wooden bridge marks the end of downtown proper; watch for signs to find any number of little antiques stores and factory outlets. *Greenwood Antiques and Country Tea Room* at 502 Main Street is a mall-type operation by the railroad bridge and just full of small booths. More than seventy shops occupy 15,000 square feet of space. The food is excellent; add your name to the waiting list when you go in the door, and they'll find you. Hours are 11:30 a.m. to 2:30 p.m. Tuesday through Saturday, Sunday noon to 5:00 p.m. Call (816) 537-7172 for more information.

Then there is *Perazzelli's Italian Ristorante* at 509 West Main Street (816-537-9997; www.perazellis.com). Hours are Tuesday through Thursday 11:00 a.m. to 9:00 p.m., Friday and Saturday until 10:00 p.m., Sunday brunch from noon to 2:00 p.m., and Sunday dinner from 3:00 to 8:00 p.m.

Lone Jack is another unlikely spot for a winery. *Bynum Winery* at 13520 South Sam Moore Road in Lone Jack, (816) 566-2240, is 3 miles east of Lone Jack at the intersection of US 50 and Sam Moore Road. The Bynum family was among the earliest settlers here in 1836. Mr. Bynum's great, great-uncle George Shawhan was a well-known whiskey maker before Prohibition. Carrying on the family tradition, Floyd Bynum opened the winery in 1989. Bynum Winery is a six-acre vineyard, tucked in Missouri's rolling hills, with plans to develop over thirty acres in time. Both red and white wines, along with fruit wines, are made here. The winery is open seven days a week. Hours are Monday and Wednesday noon to 4:00 p.m. and Tuesday, Thursday, Friday, Saturday, and Sunday noon to 5:30 p.m. Visit www.missouriwine.org/wineries/bynum/htm.

If you still haven't gotten enough of the War between the States, head south and east of *Warrensburg* to *Cedarcroft Farm* at 431 Southeast County Road, Warrensburg, a farm getaway bed-and-breakfast where Bill and Sandra

Wayne have an 1867 farmhouse on eighty scenic acres. The house was built by Sandra's great-grandfather, who was a Union soldier. Bill is a Civil War reenactor and historian who can tell you a lot about the history of this area. He even has a uniform you can try on and a musket he will teach you to shoot. Bill and Sandra have added a secluded romantic cottage with spa, fireplace, and king-size bed; it costs from $195 to $245 a night. They will even pick you up at the Amtrak station. Horseback riding is available nearby, too.

The farmstead is on the Historic Register and dates from the 1860s. The basement barns for the horses are unique because the horses sleep downstairs and the loft is at ground level. This prominent farmstead has what Sandra calls "a little Garden of Eden on the back 40," so consenting adults can walk in the woods, play in the creek, and "do some smooching." It's a good place to get away from the kids for the weekend. As you might suspect, this cottage goes quickly, so call early. Sandra can direct you to the nearby Amish community in Windsor and lots of other interesting places in the area. E-mail them at bwayne@cedarcroft.com or visit their Web site at www.cedarcroft.com. For information call (660) 747-5728 or (888) 655-9830.

Warrensburg is the home of Central Missouri State University. It is a fair-to-middlin'-size city now as it grows with the university.

The **Camel Crossing Bed and Breakfast,** 210 East Gay in Warrensburg (660-429-2973), belongs to Joyce and Ed Barnes. It is a lovely turn-of-the-last-century home in the residential area near the university. Tastefully decorated with Middle Eastern and Oriental accents gathered while the couple lived in Saudi Arabia, the place has a unique flavor, including a collection of several hundred camel figures. A camel-crossing sign is used as their logo. Rates are $60 to $90 with private bath. Visit their Web site at www.bbonline.com/mo/camelcrossing.

If you are headed north on Highway 13, there is a little surprise waiting for you about 4 miles north of Warrensburg near Fayetteville. Standing patiently near the highway are Ogbid and his wife, Ishtar, watching traffic roll by day after day. Ogbid and Ishtar are made of old oil drums, engine pistons, metal buckets, and assorted springs and reflectors, giving them a nightlife of sorts. Their son, Nimrod, joined them a few years ago. Nimrod resembles his parents, although he is unique because his head is an old metal chamber pot. Then cousin It joined the family. He is made from an old water heater with a Freon canister for a head, and he's covered with thousands of yards of baling wire, each strand individually

trivia

Warren Goodall invented the power rotary mower in Warrensburg and sold them for $100 a piece.

attached. Cousin It, with 150 pounds of hair, looks more like a furry family pet than a relative.

The creator, J.C. Carter, lives up the hill. He's had fun with his hobby of creating "assembled metal sculptures," sort of recycling-gone-bonkers. He has visions when he sees industrial junk—Freon canisters and chamber pots take on a life of their own. But he pulls the whole community into the fun. When locals complained that Ishtar and Ogbid looked lonely standing out there, he threw a wedding, complete with preacher, cake, reception, and birdseed to throw (instead of rice) there at the corner, then carted the 1,400- pound wedding couple off for their honeymoon. A couple of weeks later they returned with Nimrod. (Gestation period of robots is sort of undetermined at this time.) It wasn't long (how long is a mystery) until little Offazzie joined the family, and a cute little thing she is, too. Cousin It was then joined by "The Reaper," and the happy family spent its days watching the road. But this is the real world, and there are bad people in it. One dark and stormy night, little Nimrod was kidnapped. J.C. and his wife, Karen, offered a reward for his return, but to no avail. Then a neighbor called. He had found Nimrod in a field beaten to a fare-thee-well. J.C. took the pickup out there and brought him home. He was in intensive care for a long time as J.C. worked to bring him back to life. Since the street isn't safe anymore, Carter brought little Offazzie and the cousins home, leaving Ishtar and Ogbid lonely sentinels by the road, their sheer weight making them safe from kidnappers, or so they thought. Bad guys came again and vandalized the brave twosome. This time they were nearly killed off, but J.C. managed to unscramble them once again. The Carters' insurance paid off once again, but then they said "nevermore." Now the recovered family lives its life in **Carter's Gallery,** just up the road from where the two stood. But they are very lonely, so please, if you plan to drive by, call J.C. at (660) 747-5506 and see these wonderful, gentle creatures. A visit to the gallery would make both J.C. and his "family" very happy. There is no charge.

The Web site for Warrensburg is www.warrensburg.org.

Bristle Ridge Winery, between Warrensburg and **Knob Noster,** is ½ mile south of US 50 at Montserrat and produces high-quality wines that range from subtle, dry whites to bright, sweet reds. It sits on a hill with a panoramic view, the perfect spot to picnic with a bottle of wine, bread, cheese, and summer sausage—all sold at Bristle Ridge. Open Monday through Saturday 10:00 a.m. to dusk and Sunday 11:00 a.m. to dusk. Winter hours vary. Call (660) 422-5656 or visit www.brvwine.com.

Look up while driving through Knob Noster, because there are interesting things in the air above Whiteman Air Force Base. The previously very, very, top-secret Stealth Bomber calls this base home, and its eerie Batmanlike silhouette can be seen low in the sky on approach to the base's runway. If you see it, you might as well pull off to the side of the road—as everyone else is doing—to watch it land.

North of Knob Noster on Highway 23 is the town of *Concordia,* where they take their German heritage very, very seriously. The *Plattdutsch Hadn Tohopa* (Low German Club) of Concordia has an annual Low German Theater at the Concordia Community Center at 802 Gordon Street. This lavish fall production is compiled and written by people of the town. Saturday night offers a dinner theater serving German

delights such as peppered beef and bratwurst. Sunday is usually matinee theater only. Lavona Larimore will know the dates for this year. She can be reached at (660) 463-2454, the chamber of commerce office.

Concordia's rich German heritage draws thousands of visitors each year for the annual Concordia Fall Festival in September. There are exhibits, carnival rides, and German food and beer at the "Heidelberg Gardens" in one of the two beautiful parks in town. Across the street from one park is *Mrs. G's B&B* at One South East Fourteen Street, patterned after British bed-and-breakfasts. The Cotswold Village Room on the main floor, Welsh Garden Room, and Scottish Highlands Room have claw-foot tubs, decorative fireplaces, and coffee- and tea-making facilities. This ranch-style home with a loft is decorated with antiques in a charming eclectic style that proprietor Nancy Gilbertson (Mrs. G) calls "stocking-feet cozy." Rooms are $70 to $75. Call (660) 463-2160.

The Ozarks

Cole Camp is a tiny town that would be easy to miss, but don't. The first place to stop, if you have planned this right and it is lunchtime, is *Gartenfest Tea Room* at the four-way stop in the heart of town (660-668-9952)—you can't miss it, the town is small This European bistro cafe has a fireplace to keep you warm, in the fall and winter and a trickling fountain to keep you cool in the spring and summer.

Pick up a copy of the *Antiques and Shop Guide* and stroll through town. You will find many, many places to poke around.

While you are in Cole Camp, stop by *Maxwell's Woodcarving,* 113 Main

Hier Snackt wi Plattdüütsch (Here We Speak Low German)

In 1835 a wave of immigrants from northern Germany began to move in to the farming areas near Cole Camp, bringing with them their Low German language, strong work ethic, and Lutheran religion. This German heritage is evident in the many annual festivals, plays, and heritage events. In fact, many residents still speak the Low German brought over by their ancestors. Being off the beaten path, it has changed little over the years. But the Civil War brought turmoil into the community. Relations between the Anglo-American settlers and Germans had been good, but that changed with the coming of the Civil War. The area became bitterly divided. The Germans hated slavery and were fervently loyal Unionists, while many of the Anglo-Americans retained their sympathies for their own Southern heritage.

Street, and take a look at Jim Maxwell's caricature wood carvings. The finely detailed carvings feature Missouri coal miners, gangsters, artillery men from the Civil War, and doughboys of World War I. The limited-edition carvings are original pieces of art sought after by collectors. Maxwell is the author of two wood-carving books and creates a variety of subjects from casually styled Ozark Hill people to very accurately detailed caricatures of other bygone eras. Jim and his wife, Margie, are there Monday through Saturday from 10:00 a.m. to 5:00 p.m. unless the weather is cold (heating the historic old building is difficult). Call (660) 668-2466 for more information or visit Jim's Web site at http://woodcarver.colecampmissouri.com/.

Nearby (everything is nearby) in the historic Bellview Hotel is the **Maple Street Café and Bakery** at 124 South Maple Street. Chef Michael Decker turns out breads and pastries ranging from focaccia to fruit turnovers and cinnamon rolls. Every dish he creates is special. Breakfast and lunch are served Monday through Saturday, dinner is available on Friday nights. Call (660) 668-2273.

For more places to visit, check www.colecampmissouri.com.

Highway 52 runs into Highway 5 at the city of **Versailles** (pronounced just as it looks, not the French way). Versailles is the gateway to the Lake of the Ozarks area. Here you make the decision to go east on Highway 52 to the St. Louis side of the lake or southwest on Highway 5 to the Kansas City side. Start at the Web site www.funlake.com or call (800) FUN-LAKE before you begin the trip.

Just ½ block southeast of the square in Versailles, a brick walkway leads to a two-story white Victorian home that has now become the **Hilty Inn Bed and Breakfast,** 206 Jasper. This elegant home built in 1877 has four rooms with private baths. Owner Doris Hilty knows her way around the area and can guide you in your shopping or lake fun. If a quiet afternoon is what you want, though, there is a sitting room. The East bedroom has a private front porch, and there is a screened side porch with swings for the other guests. A good breakfast with gourmet coffee and tea is part of the package. Doris also serves dinner in the dining room of her home—lovely, candlelight gourmet dinners. Simply call her twenty-four hours in advance to reserve a seat any night of the week. She can accommodate parties as large as twenty people or as small as two. Rates are $75 to $125. Call (573) 378-2020 or (800) 667-8093. The Web site is www.bbonline.com/mo/hilty.

World Craft and Thrift Shop at 123 East Newton Street, Versailles, is owned by the Mennonite Church. Crafts are imported from throughout the world, and you can browse in the thrift shop in the back room for great used stuff as well. Profits from this shop support Mennonite missions all over the world. Call (573) 378–5900.

In recent years, Versailles has become home to a number of gift and coffee shops, a group of rug weavers, and other arts-oriented businesses. The Shop at Shady Gables, 300 East Newton Street, is a favorite place for women to fine peace and serenity in a fine cup of tea. This quaint little tearoom is in a Victorian farmhouse in Versailles. Reba Starling-Silvey purchased the big white house a decade ago, and because she loved all things related to tea (her most cherished possession was a white china teapot painted with yellow roses) opening a tearoom came most naturally. It is a favorite spot in town because the menu includes cream teas (tea, scones, clotted cream, and lemon curd before lunch), light afternoon tea (finger sandwiches, sweets, fresh fruit, scones, clotted cream, and lemon curd), and a luncheon tea, which includes a croissant chicken sandwich and miniature quiche in addition to the items in the light afternoon tea. Food is presented on a traditional three-tiered tea server with scones on top, sandwiches on the middle shelf, and sweets on the bottom. The scones and sandwiches are all

trivia

Cole Camp was at the hub of four major roads at the time of the Civil War. It became the site of one of the first battles of the Civil War on June 19, 1861. A force of around 700 Home Guards was mobilized on June 13 and had its "baptism by fire" that same week. The pro-Confederate Missouri governor, Jackson, was retreating from his defeat at Boonville, but the Union Home Guards were blocking his escape route, which would have brought him through Cole Camp. A force of Confederate sympathizers was organized at Warsaw and on June 19 launched an early morning attack on the Home Guard encampment. The Home Guard was routed and the way cleared for Governor Jackson to escape, adding another bloody footnote to Missouri's Civil War history.

made in the Shady Gables kitchen every morning. Some forty different types of tea are available, but you cannot get so much as a cup of coffee or a soft drink at Shady Gables because they would overwhelm the delicate scent of tea. Reservations are required; call (573) 378-2740. Many of the Shady Gables recipes are available in Reba's cookbook, *Made in the Shade: Simple Recipes for an Elegant Tea Time,* available there or at the Web site www.shadygables.com.

Winter Solace

The Missouri Ozarks are a quiet labyrinth of rugged hills and deep valleys, as famous for its folk culture as its beauty. Our home was perched high above a lake looking down at the very tops of the old oak trees with dozens of dogwoods sprinkled among them. The glass front let us watch the summer people on the lake; the screened porch was a perfect spot for breakfast. A telescope allowed us a view of the other side of the lake, a toll call away by road.

The chimney of the stone fireplace rose to the second-story ceiling, a loft above the one-room living area held our bed. The change of the seasons moved like a kaleidoscope across north window glass, the spring dogwoods and wild pear trees splashed white and pink across the barely budded trees. Bright daffodils popped up in the woods where earlier settlers must have planted them. Summers were intensely green, with ivy taking over the woods around the house. Deer and almost-tame raccoons and fox shared the woods around the cottage with us. The roar of the boats and shouts of the skiers began early and continued until after sunset.

When the leaves changed in the fall, the quiet made the woods a private place. The color, not so garishly bright as New Hampshire's maples, but a rustic red and gold of Missouri oak, gave the hills a new texture, a different feel. The leaves fell—some years slowly, one by one; other years it seemed, all at once—leaving the view unobstructed and breathtaking when the cool, early-morning lake fog hung over the still-warm water.

The most beautiful spectacle I remember took place deep in winter. One special day, the sun was warm, the air crisp and cold. We built a huge fire in the fireplace and grilled steaks and baked potatoes there that evening. In the morning, the whisper of snowflakes woke us. The sleeping loft was bathed in the reflected light of a deep snow. The quiet was almost tangible; I could feel it, taste it, touch it. We threw more logs on the smoldering fire and curled up on the couch with the down comforter and a cup of hot coffee. We were treated to the sight of a bald eagle perched on a tree limb outside the window. We watched him dive for fish twice and carry them off to a nearby nest.

Putting the FOR SALE sign by the roadside of our little wooded acreage was a sad day. But like the seasons, the times of our lives change, and with those changes come new colors and new sights. Our lives move in new directions, just as the winds change from south to north and back again. The memories, though, will be mine forever.

The **Lake of the Ozarks** area is called the "Land of the Magic Dragon." If you look at the lake on a map and go snake-eyed, it has a dragon shape; hence the name. The Ozark heritage stems from the first immigrants here, who were from Tennessee, Kentucky, and nearby parts of the southern Appalachians. The Upper-South hill-country folks were descended from Scottish-Irish stock.

For many years the Ozark Mountains sheltered these folks, and few outsiders entered the area; you may have heard of the Irish Wilderness. Because of the rough topography, the railroads avoided the area, and this extreme isolation until a little more than fifty years ago created the "Ozark Hillbilly." The values, lifestyle, and beliefs of those first settlers are still much in evidence.

The building of Bagnell Dam to form the Lake of the Ozarks eroded that isolation and turned the area into the Midwest's summer playground. Because it is not a Corps of Engineers lake, homes can be built right on the water's edge; the 1,300 miles of serpentine shore has more shoreline than the state of California!

Miles of lake coves, wooded hills, and steep dusty roads are still unsettled. Most undeveloped areas have no roads at all leading to them. The east side of the lake, which houses the dam, has become the drop-in tourist side. The track is beaten slick over here. There are restaurants, shopping malls, and water slides galore.

Some of the unique places on the east side deserve a mention before you head to the west side of the lake, where the more fascinating spots hide. If you go to Bagnell Dam from Eldon, watch for wintering eagles—here and at most of the lake crossings. They retreat from the Arctic chill up north, following flocks of migrating geese.

You may not have thought of Missouri as a state for bald eagle watching—and spring through early fall, it's not, though a captive breeding program of the Missouri Department of Conservation has been in effect since 1981 to reestablish a wild breeding population. But come winter, these big birds take up residence wherever they can find open water and plentiful feeding. One recent year, more than 1,400 bald eagles were counted, making this state second only to Washington in the lower forty-eight states for eagle sightings. At most Missouri lakes, their main diet consists of fish—they have far better luck with fishing than most humans.

Charley's Buffet is a unique spot on this side of the lake, and well worth the drive if you can find it. People come from all around to eat there (and get lost in the process), and because it's only open on Friday and Saturday evenings, folks line up for the delicious Mennonite-cooked and -served food. This restaurant has taken third place in the *Rural Missourian*'s "Best of Missouri" polls the last two years—in the "Places Worth the Drive" category. They don't advertise and apparently don't need to, based on the size of the crowds there on weekends. Their mailing address is in Lincoln, but begin on Highway 52 between Cole Camp and Versailles and take either Highway B or Highway W. The restaurant is just east on Highway B off of Highway W (in Benton County). There's no Web site and you are lucky to have a number to call, because many Mennonite businesses have neither. Call (660) 668-3806 if you get lost. When you find it, bon appétit!

Taking the back way around the lake along Highway 52 to Eldon and then U.S. Highway 54 to Bagnell Dam is more interesting than the much-traveled and very crowded Highway 5/US 54 route.

A left turn (north) on Highway 5 puts you in the middle of the Mennonite community. On the roads around Versailles, horse-drawn buggies carry Mennonite citizens on their daily tasks. They are less strict than the Jamesport Amish—the somber black attire is uncommon—and most of the homes have telephones and electricity, though many don't. Old Order Mennonite women wear prayer bonnets but dress in printed fabrics. Some families have cars, but many of the cars are painted black—chrome and all. To get a good tour of the area, begin where Highway 5 splits into Highway 52. Follow 52 to Highway C on the left.

Mennonite Barbara Lehman used to serve people wonderful dinners in her parents' home on Highway C near Versailles. The place was so popular with locals and tourists alike, she outgrew it and moved to a new building on Highway 5 just north of Highway 52 in Versailles, at 15830 Highway 5.

The food is still fabulous, with the same wonderful family-style service, home cooked with farm-fresh everything from the garden and barn, prepared daily by Barbara.

The vegetables are fresh by season, this morning's eggs are just in from the barn, and the jam, of course, is homemade. In the winter the vegetables come from the Lehman farm by way of the freezer. Barbara serves two kinds of pie with the meal, and when the season is right, fresh strawberry and peach pie or cobbler. Smoked turkey, ham, beef, or chicken are part of the three-course meal, which includes six salads, two veggies, homemade rolls, and desserts. Call (573) 378-4010 for more information about *Lehman's.* Open Tuesday through Saturday from 6:30 a.m. to 8:30 p.m. They also sell baked goods and homemade jams and jellies.

Follow Highway C about 6 miles to *Pleasant Valley Quilts.* There is a sign by the road where you can turn and drive about three quarters of a mile on gravel. The Brubaker family gathers a fine selection of quilts and crafts from Mennonite families in the area. Their daughters, Lydia and Lucille, handle the quilt shop, where quilts of all sizes and colors are hung for display. In fact, quilts will be made to order for you if you have a particular color or style in mind. Quilts made by local Mennonite ladies join aprons, dolls, and other hand-crafted items for sale here. The store is open from 8:00 a.m. to 5:00 p.m. every day but Sunday. Call (573) 378-6151.

Follow the sign off Highway C down a gravel road to the **Dutch Country Store,** which carries bulk foods as well as a huge selection of freight-damaged groceries and toiletries. There are usually buggies parked out front along with the automobiles. The store always has a good selection of name-brand cereals and canned goods, shampoo, and dog food—just about anything. The selection is different every week.

Turn north on Highway E, then follow E to Highway K (this sounds harder than it really is), but watch closely for horse-drawn buggies and bicycles on these hilly back roads. Highway K leads east to the tiny, tiny town of **Excelsior** and **Weavers' Market,** serving this community of about 250 Mennonite families. Weavers' carries fresh-frozen farm produce, frozen homemade pies ready to pop into your oven, an enormous assortment of teas and spices, and other bulk foods, including homemade noodles. Nearby (follow the signs) is **Excelsior Fabric,** where Anna and Sam Shirk and their family carry an extensive collection of quilting fabrics.

Going along Hopewell Road is an adventure all by itself. You will find the **Excelsior Book Store,** and the **Excelsior Harness Shop** along there, too, although even though you are off the beaten path, you probably won't need harness repair if you are a visitor to the area.

If you decide to turn left back at Highway E on some pretty Sunday morning about 10:00 a.m., you will come to the Clearview Mennonite Church and see dozens of horse-drawn buggies tied up in stables and at hitching posts around the church. It's quite a sight.

Now find your way back to Highway 52 and go east past the Highway C Junction, 3 miles after the Save-a-Lot store at 16151 Old Marvin Road in **Barnett** to Leah Zimmerman's bake shop (a sign on the highway says FARMER'S MARKET. Leah's is the first house on the left; a large sign in her yard reads LEAH'S BAKE SHOP.

Her buggy is near the barn, where her horse, Major, waits for excursions to the grocery store, Weavers' Market, or church on Sunday. Leah has produce from her own wonderful garden, but she also is the source for eggs from free-range chickens, fresh fruit from family orchards, and a whole range of baked goods she turns out daily. Cinnamon bread, pies made with whatever fresh fruit is in season, cookies, jams, and canned goods deck her shelves in the pantry just off the front porch. The sign says COME IN, and that's just what it means. Leah's usually in the kitchen baking something tasty—she does custom bak-

Leah's Bake Shop

ing for regulars—and comes out when she hears the door slam. And say "hi" to Cody Bear, her loveable sweetheart of a Welsh Corgi, and Patches, the cat. Call (573) 378-6401 to order something special (in the fall her apple dumplings are wonderful).

The difference between the east and west sides of the lake has been described as like "flipping channels between *Hee Haw* and *Lifestyles of the Rich and Famous.*" Welcome to the St. Louis side, a road more traveled but still lots of fun. The Ozark Web site has plenty of information about the area: www .ozark-missouri.com.

US 54 through *Osage Beach* is, in a word, touristy. The path here is not only beaten, it's three lanes wide and heavy with traffic in the summer—the bumper-to-bumper gridlock type you came here to get away from. The road is filled to overflowing with craft shops, flea markets, bumper cars, and water slides. There are plenty of good eating places, from fast-food chains to little places tucked in corners. You are on your own here. If you stay at *Cliff House Bed & Breakfast* in Osage Beach on State Road KK (at the 25-mile marker by water) it will be more peaceful; it's a truly unforgettable and romantic spot. Each of the four suites has fabulous lake views, and all have private entrances and baths, a Jacuzzi, fireplace, television, and stereo. Cascading decks lead to the water's edge, where a gazebo and hot tub await, as well as a dock for fishing, swimming, and boating. Not only do you get a 180-degree view of the lake from your private deck, you can also charter a wonderful 37-foot teak-and-mahogany trawler, complete with captain, to cruise the lake. Innkeepers Gary and Cindy Brooks can tell you the good places to visit and how to avoid the rat race on the highway. They will also fix a complete breakfast served in your room in the morning. This romantic spot is not just another Lake of the

Ozarks experience! Rates are $150 to $160 on weekends (two-night minimum). Off-season rates are $125 to $150. Call (573) 348-9726 or (866) 943-LAKE. Cliff House is on Osage Beach. Visit it on the Web at www.lakecliffhouse.com.

The **Potted Steer Restaurant** (573-348-5053) is in a comfortable-looking wooden building tucked in at the west end of the Grand Glaize Bridge on US 54 in Osage Beach. Owner Joseph Boer, a native of Holland who came to this country on refugee status on Christmas Day in 1956, opened the restaurant in 1971. It is a very laid-back place where casual clothes are the rule and long waits are expected. But the crowd is vacation-loose and fun. The specialty here is deep-fried lobster tail (which sounds like heresy to a seafood lover). Boer says he has never tasted the creation that made the restaurant famous. You see, he hates seafood. To tide you over until dinner arrives, order the massive onion rings. Boer also has one of the finest wine lists in the state. The restaurant is closed from the middle of November until the third Friday in March.

If you have taken the route along the west side of the lake, you will begin to see the real Ozarks now. Missouri has surprisingly diverse wildlife, from the blind cave fish to the black bear, which still forages in the heavy woods. The pileated woodpecker (the size of a chicken, no kidding!) will certainly wake you up in the morning if he decides to peck on your shake shingles. The west side of the lake is still undiscovered except by Kansas City people, who have tried to keep it quiet. Here, great eating places abound and small shops hide off the beaten path.

Highway 5 cuts like a razor slash through the hills between **Gravois Mills** and Laurie. There are some quiet, low-key places not to be missed. Locals recommend a couple of places to eat in Gravois: the **Cactus Rose** at 113 North Main (573-374-4900) and the **Boardwalk Grill** at 401 North Main (573-374-2002).

The Olive Branch in Gravois Mills is in an old church at 26955 Highway 5. The philosophy here is: "Many a new beginning got its start over a good meal, and many a person has felt at peace and in harmony with the world after a time of fellowship and dining. It was for this purpose that the Olive Branch came in being. It is more than a restaurant; it is a gathering place once again just as it was when it was a church." You will be enjoying not only great Italian food, but salmon, grouper, frog legs, shrimp, and fried chicken. There is a full-service bar and, of course, wine—surely something for every taste. Open at 5:00 p.m. for dinner Thursday through Monday. Call (573) 372-2090, and take a look at the pictures at www.olivebranchatthelake.com.

Rachel Featherston has come up with a unique idea to change the menu with the season—thus the name **Season's Café & Bakery,** at 248 South Main in *Laurie.* During winter a heartier menu is served with one specialty being the meat loaf sundae (mashed potatoes take the place of whipped cream on this sundae). The bakery carries all homemade goodies from melt-in-your-mouth scones to the all-American chocolate chip cookie. Winter hours are Tuesday through Thursday from 7:00 a.m. until 2:00 p.m., Friday until 4:00 p.m., Saturday from 8:00 a.m. until 2:00 p.m., and Sunday from 10:00 a.m. until 2:00 p.m. Summer hours extend to 7:00 p.m. on Friday and Saturday to give everyone more time on the water.

Just outside of Laurie on Highway 5 is *St. Patrick's Catholic Church.* Father Fred Barnett is the pastor here. This unique church sits on acres of outdoor gardens that feature waterfalls, fountains, and a shrine dedicated to mothers, the *Shrine of Mary Mother of the Church.* You may add your mother's name to the list to be remembered in ongoing prayers. On summer Sundays, Mass is at 8:30 a.m. at the shrine, and casual dress is in the spirit of a Lake of the Ozarks vacation. The outdoor candlelight procession and Mass on Saturday nights at 8:30 p.m. at the shrine are beautiful and open to anyone. Times change in winter, so call (573) 374-MARY for a current schedule.

In the town of Laurie you can turn right onto Highway 135, which wanders back to *Stover* and Highway 52, over some genuine roller-coaster dips and beautiful, unpopulated Ozark country.

The *Buffalo Creek Vineyards and Winery,* 2888 Riverview Road, Stover, is a bit of a surprise in the lake area. Owner Jim Stephens has five acres of vines growing near Stover. His tasting room is accessible by water at the 70-mile marker between Little Buffalo Cove and Big Buffalo Cove. (Watch for the signs.) The Concord grape wine is light and not too sweet. He also bottles a Foch, Seyval, Vignoles, and a ruby Cabernet that is aged in oak. The most popular wines are the fruit wines: pear (also aged in oak) and persimmon. Another favorite is the Show-me Red, a blend of Foch and Concord grapes, aged in Missouri oak. It is a semidry wine with a pungent finish.

The tasting room is located above the water in a remodeled old barn and offers a panoramic view of the lake. Boat visitors can dock in the five-well dock and call the winery to be picked up and transported up the hill. The atmosphere is relaxed and comfortable. A large lounging deck sits right on the crest of the hill overlooking the water.

Overnight accommodations are available, too. The snug guest cottage with panoramic views of the lake can accommodate up to six people. The winery also sponsors live music, special dinners, and other "happenings" throughout the summer. It is open year-round 11:00 a.m. to 6:00 p.m. April through October and until 5:00 p.m. November through March. For reservations call (573) 377-4535 or (888) 247-1192. Visit the Web site at www.buffalocreekwinery.com.

Marschall and David Fansler moved to the Ozarks from Colorado and bought a vineyard in Stover. Trained and licensed in wine making, it wasn't long until the **Grey Bear Vineyards and Winery,** 25992 Highway T, opened for public enjoyment. Fansler began growing grapes in 1990 and has been what he calls a "mad scientist" of wines ever since. His wines are, well, creative. They have funny names, too. For example, there is the Bushwacker, a Riesling/Gerwurz blend, with a raspberry finish, or one called McWine, a sweet blend of Vignoles and merlot. A personal favorite is Bear claw, a dry chocolate cab. If sweeter is more your taste, try Pride of Osage, a semisweet chocolate cherry Cabernet. The Web site has a more complete list of what is available this year at www.grey bearvineyards.com. The tasting room is open mid-March through December Monday through Saturday from 10:00 a.m. until 6:00 p.m. and in the winter by appointment. On the first floor of the winery is the **Black Canyon Ale House Microbrewery and Bistro,** which is open from 4:00 p.m. until midnight. On Friday and Saturday you can order glorified appetizers (deep-fried portabella mushrooms), a special chili, or Black Cuban sandwiches. Lighter fare? How about a spinach and grilled salmon salad? Call (573) 377-4313 for more details.

To find the winery by car, take Highway 135 (6 miles east of Stover, or 16 miles west on Highway 135 from Laurie). Turn southwest on T Road and continue 9 miles to the winery.

If you are looking for a bed-and-breakfast instead of a resort on the Lake of the Ozarks, check with Kay Cameron at Ozark Mountain Country Bed & Breakfast Service at (417) 334-4720 or (800) 933-8529 or e-mail at mgcameron@aol.com. Kay has listings for cottages on the water in Camdenton, Osage Beach, Sunrise Beach, and other small towns around the lake. For more lake information visit www.funlake.com on the Web.

Either way you circle the lake, east or west, you will end up in **Camdenton** at the intersection of Highway 5 and US 54. Continue west on US 54 and turn onto Highway D to **Ha Ha Tonka State Park.** High on a bluff overlooking an arm of the Lake of the Ozarks, poised over a

Ha Ha Tonka State Park

cold, aqua blue spring that bubbles out from under a limestone bluff, are the ruins of a stone "castle" with a story to tell. There is a European feel to the ruins; it's as if you have stumbled on a Scottish stronghold here in the Missouri woods. The place was conceived in 1900 as a sixty-room retreat for prominent Kansas City businessman Robert Snyder. But tragedy struck; Snyder was killed in an automobile accident in 1906 and construction halted. Later, the castlelike mansion was completed by Snyder's son, but in 1942 a fire set by a spark from one of the many stone fireplaces gutted the buildings. All that was left were the stone walls thrust up against the sky. Ha Ha Tonka is now a state park, although the mansion is still a ghostly ruins half hidden in the trees.

The park is a classic example of karst topography, with caves and sinkholes, springs, natural bridges, and underground streams. (This typical southern Missouri geology is responsible for the many caves in the state.) There are nine nature trails here; explore on your own or check in with the park office (573-751-2479) for a naturalist-guided tour; programs are available year-round.

Missouri places second nationwide for the largest number of caves, but the state beats number one Tennessee in the number of "show caves" that are developed for touring. The state records more than 5,000 caves. The southern half of Missouri—in the Ozarks region—is where most of the caves are because of the limestone deposits there. The complex of caves, underground streams, large springs, sinkholes, and natural bridges at Ha Ha Tonka State Park makes it one of the country's most important geologic sites.

About halfway between Warsaw and Clinton on Highway 7 is the town of **Tightwad** (population 56). There's a UMB Bank in Tightwad, and the branch manager says that people from as far away as Florida have accounts there just to get the checks with "Tightwad" on them.

The city of **Clinton** is every chamber of commerce's dream come true. It has one of the most active squares in the country, filled with more than 150 shops and services, and there is lots of parking. You can't miss the wonderful old courthouse and outdoor pavilion in the center of the square. The town has changed little since 1836, when it began as an outpost in the heart of the Golden Valley.

History buffs will find plenty of research material at the **Henry County Museum** at 203 West Franklin Street, just off the northwest corner of the square in Clinton. The building itself was owned by Anheuser-Busch from 1886 until Prohibition. Huge blocks of ice (often cut from the nearby lake) were used to chill the kegs in the cooling room. The second room contains a skylight and double doors leading to the old loading dock and courtyard. Quick dashes in horse-drawn wagons were necessary to transport the beer while still cool to the depot, where there was access to three railroads. The building houses the Courtenay Thomas room, commemorating the Clinton native, who became an international operatic soprano.

Find Commercial Street in **Harrisonville** and hit the antiques jackpot. There are too many antiques and flea markets to mention, but it looks like three cherries on the antiques slot machine for flea-market gamblers.

In case you are hungry after all the antiquing and strolling around the historic square, stop in at **Pearl Street Grill,** 101 South Lexington (it used to be on Pearl Street), Harrisonville (816-380-1121). The grill is decorated with many antiques and whimsical things, some even suspended from the ceiling. You will find a one-man helicopter and 1920s bikes with huge wheels. There are also bronze sculptures, including some Remingtons. There is a separate Elvis room that continually plays Elvis music. The booths are family style and can fit up to two families, so it is a gathering place for good times. The food is excellent and there are daily specials. The dessert case, filled with homemade pies and other temptations, greets you as you walk in the door. Visiting the grill is a great eating and relaxing experience. **Younger's Livery,** 107 East Pearl, Harrisonville (816-380- 2311), is another unusual restaurant, especially for horse lovers. It is a bar/restaurant with a jillion horse things, including a Well's Fargo Stagecoach, wagons suspended from the ceiling, and more antique Western saddles than you can count. The food and service are excellent.

Another don't-miss town is **Pleasant Hill,** at the intersection of Highway 7 and US 58. Way back in 1828 David Creek settled a piece of land and became the first recorded non-native settler in Cass County. A town grew here until the Civil War. The "border war" between Kansas and Missouri, which was waged long after the Civil War officially ended, decimated the population. The next big event was the coming of the railroad, when the town began to resurrect itself. Each year the town celebrates Pleasant Hill Railroad Days in September. The town has a cupola-design caboose on display here that was part of the Missouri Pacific Railroad Line. This captivating little town has much to offer. **Neighbor's Café,** 117 First Street (816-987-3723), serves home-cooked meals that will fill you up and make you smile. Their hours are Sunday 7:00 a.m. to 3:00 p.m., Monday 6:00 a.m. to 3:00 p.m., and Tuesday through Saturday 6:00 a.m. to 8:00 p.m. Their interesting and informative menu will give you a "history lesson" about many interesting events in the history of Pleasant Hill. *Mulberry Hill B&B,* 226 North Armstrong (816-540-3457), is a beautifully restored 1900s colonial home lovingly renovated. Innkeepers Roy and Pat Keck will welcome you into their lovely home, which has five spacious suites. A full breakfast is served with Belgian waffles and all the trimmings. Rates are from $75 to $125 for two. You can just kick back and enjoy the amenities of Mulberry Hill or stroll downtown to hunt antiques. Visit www.mulberryhillbandb.com. There is also the Pleasant Hill Golf Course and a year-round pool in the town. You might also want to take advantage of the *Big Creek Country Music Show,* 110 South Lake. Every Saturday night since 1982 Emcee Dennis Dittmore and his wife, Cindy, along with the rest of the cast, have entertained thousands of people. Showtime is 7:30 p.m. Call (816) 524-6856 or (816) 987–3919 (on Saturday) for tickets and show details, or visit www.bigcreekcountry.com.

While taking your stroll around Pleasant Hill, stop in at *Flat Bottles* in the historic Railroad Depot (816-739-4663) and visit with Warren Angell. He says he "turns bottles into keepsakes." It's an interesting twist on recycling, as he turns bottles into items that can be used as a candy dish or a relish tray. He has an array of bottles that can be hung on the wall.

Cheese Country

Go west on US 54 to *El Dorado Springs* (*Da-RAY-do,* this being a very non–Spanish speaking part of the country) as a shortcut to the Osceola area.

Large dairy barns and silos built around the turn of the last century are still in use, and dairy cattle—Holsteins and Guernseys—graze alongside beef cattle.

El Dorado Springs, just east of Nevada (pronounced Ne-VAY-da) off US 54, is a pretty little town complete with a nostalgic bandstand in the tree-shaded park at the center of town. It looks like something straight out of *The Music Man.* There's a band here every Friday and Saturday night and Sunday afternoon; a local band has played in the park for more than a hundred years. The old spa town was crowded with bathhouses and hotels, but the spa business ended long ago for most towns like this one. El Dorado Springs has done a great job of preserving itself anyway.

While in El Dorado, you can see the free museum above *Carl's Gun Shop,* 100 North Main Street. Owner Carl McCallister and his son, Terry, have more than 1,000 guns in glass showcases and a fine collection of trophy-size taxidermied animal mounts, including two full-body bears—one a Giant Kodiak—in a gymnasium-size room. The gun shop takes up ½ block and has one of the most complete private collections of firearms in the state. You won't find any assault rifles for sale here, and there's no survivalist gear on display. The well-lighted display rooms have a staff of people who know guns. Carl even has toy guns for sale for customers' children. The family environment makes women and children feel comfortable. Terry's wife, Terri, also works at the store. Carl's is open Saturday from 9:00 a.m. to 5:00 p.m. (in hunting season until 6:00 p.m.) and year-round Tuesday through Friday until 6:00 p.m. Call (417) 876-4167 for more information.

Hammons Emporium, at 210 Town Square on the northeast corner in Stockton, is the world's largest processor of black walnuts and its retail store has been moved, enlarged, and improved ("like Starbucks, only better"). Not only can you get the walnut brittle or chocolate-covered walnuts for your sweet tooth or a nutty breakfast with black walnut pancake and waffle mix and a bottle of walnut syrup, but you can also have gourmet ice cream, pastries, espresso, a latte, and buy coffee beans (maybe a walnut-flavored coffee?) as well. The Emporium is open Monday through Thursday from 7:00 a.m. to 7:00 p.m., Friday and Saturday until 9:00 p.m., and Sunday from 8:00 a.m. to 6:00 p.m. Call (800) 872-6879. Visit the Web site www.black-walnuts.com for recipes using black walnuts in not only cookies, fudge, and muffins, but everything from fish to, well, nuts.

If you don't take the shortcut, you will continue down Interstate 71 to *Lamar;* history fans will find *Harry S Truman's Birthplace* here. (No, there is no period after the S, because the president didn't have a middle name—his folks just put an S in there.) It's a long way from this little house at 1009 Truman Street in Lamar to the big white one on Pennsylvania Avenue in our nation's capital. Hours are Monday through Saturday 10:00 a.m. to 4:00 p.m. and Sunday noon to 4:00 p.m. Call (417) 682-2279 or visit www.mostateparks .com/trumansite.htm.

In *Golden City* bicyclists know a place called *Cooky's* at 529 Main, at the junction of Highways 126 and 37 south and east of Lamar. Out of season it's a small-town cafe on the south side of the main drag. During bike-riding season, though, Cooky's is the place to dream about when you are 300 miles out on the trail. Bikecentennial, Inc., of Missoula, Montana, put Cooky's on the map—the TransAmerica Trail map, that is—and riders have flocked here ever since for some serious carbohydrate loading. It's not uncommon to watch a rider from Australia chow down on three or four pieces of Jim and Carol Elred's terrific pies; you can be more moderate, if you like. You can get an affordable steak dinner here too; the home-raised beef will keep you going down the trail whether you come by car or bike. Hours are 6:00 a.m. until 8:00 p.m. Tuesday through Thursday and Sunday. On Friday and Saturday it is open until 9:00 p.m. Call (417) 537-4741 for information.

trivia

Ground black walnut shell is a hard, chemically inert, nontoxic, and biodegradable abrasive. It makes up a large percentage of the nut and is a very useful product with a wide range of applications. Hammons began marketing this product more than fifty years ago and is now the world's leading supplier of black walnut soft grit abrasives.

Jerry Overton, president of the Missouri Prairie Foundation, puts in a good word for **Golden Prairie,** designated a National Natural Landmark by the federal Department of the Interior. It's not reclaimed prairie or replanted prairie—this is a virgin remnant of the thousands of acres of grassland that once covered the Midwest, important not only for the historic plants it contains, but also for the varieties of wildlife that inhabit it. Here you can still hear the sound of the prairie chicken. Listen for them exactly 3 miles west of Golden City on Highway 126 and exactly 2 miles south of Highway 26 on the first gravel road.

A roadside park just outside **Osceola** on Highway 82 West will show you what attracted Indians and settlers to the area: the breathtaking view of the white bluffs where the Sac and Osage Rivers meet. Highway 82 also has a Sac River access point and boat ramp if you are hauling a boat to the Truman Reservoir.

Highway 13 bypasses the town square but is home to **Osceola Cheese Shop** and **Ewe's in the Country** (417-646-8131; www.osceolacheese.com). Mike and Marcia Bloom own both shops, which share the building. The Blooms buy the cheese in bulk and smoke and flavor it in the former cheese factory; they have been at this same location for more than fifty years. They now offer more than sixty-nine varieties of cheese, mostly from Missouri, with each type cut for sampling. Try jalapeño (extra hot), instant pizza, or chocolate (yes!) cheese. Pick up a catalog; they ship cheese anywhere in the world—except from April to September, when it might arrive as hot cheese sauce. Hours are variable depending on the season.

Take a right at the sign on Highway 13 and wander into Osceola. On the southwest corner of the square is the more-than-110-year-old Commercial Hotel, recently renovated and opened as a craft shop.

Places to Stay in Central Missouri

KANSAS CITY

Hotel Phillips (downtown KC)
106 West 12th Street
(816) 221-7000
Moderate

International Hotel (on the Country Club Plaza)
401 Ward Parkway
(816) 756-1500
Expensive

Quarterage Hotel at Westport
508 Westport Road
(816) 931-0001
Moderate

Raphael Hotel and Restaurant
Country Club Plaza
325 Ward Parkway
(816) 756-3800 or
(800) 821-5343
www.raphaelkc.com
Moderate

INDEPENDENCE

Sports Stadium Inn
9803 East 40 Highway
(near the sports complex)
(816) 353-0005
Inexpensive

BOONVILLE

Days Inn
2401 Pioneer
(660) 882-8624
Inexpensive

Holiday Inn
2419 Mid America
Industrial Drive
(660) 882-6882
Inexpensive

JEFFERSON CITY

Capitol Plaza Hotel
415 West McCarty Street
(573) 635-1234
www.jqhhotels.com
Inexpensive

Holiday Inn
1716 Jefferson Street
(573) 634-4040
Inexpensive

KNOB NOSTER

Whiteman Inn
2340 West Irish Lane
(660) 563-3000
Inexpensive

SEDALIA

Best Western State Fair Motor Inn
3120 South 65 Highway
(660) 826-6100 or
(800) 528-1234
Inexpensive

BOTHWELL KENSINGTON
103 East Fourth Street
(660) 826-5588
Inexpensive

WARRENSBURG

Days Inn
204 East Cleveland Street
(660) 429-2400
Inexpensive

Holiday Inn
626 East Russell Avenue
(660) 747-3000
Inexpensive

OSAGE BEACH

Tan–Tar–A Resort and Golf Course
P.O. Box 188TT
(800) 826-8272
Moderate

LAKE OZARK

Lodge of the Four Seasons (spa and golf course)
(888) 265-5500
Moderate

WHEATLAND

Sunflower Resort
Route 2, Box 2681
(800) 258-5260
Inexpensive

CLINTON

Best Western
106 South Baird Street
(660) 885-2206
Inexpensive

HELPFUL WEB SITE FOR THE OZARKS

www.funlake.com

SELECTED CHAMBERS OF COMMERCE

Arrow Rock,
(816) 837-3443

Independence,
(800) 748-7328
www.independencechamber.org

Jefferson City,
www.jcchamber.org

Kansas City,
Kansas City Convention & Visitors
Association
1100 Main Street, Suite 2200
(816) 221-5242
www.visitkc.com

Ozarks,
(800) 769-1004

Places to Eat in Central Missouri

KANSAS CITY

Blue Stem
900 Westport Road
(816) 561-1101
Expensive

1924 Main
1924 Main Street
(816) 472-1924
Prix fixe dinner $30

Savoy Grill (seafood)
219 West Ninth Street
(816) 842-3890
Moderate to Expensive

BOONVILLE

Stein House
421 Main Street
(660) 882-6822
Inexpensive

LAURIE

Big E Smalls Pizza
(inside Osage River Bar & Grill)
2475 South Main Street
(573) 374-2443
Inexpensive

JEFFERSON CITY

Das Stein Haus
1436 South Ridge Drive
(573) 634-3869
(behind the Ramada Inn)
Inexpensive

Madison's Cafe
216 Madison Street
(across from parking garage)
(573) 634-2988
Inexpensive

BELTON

Oden's Family Barbecue
1302 North Scott
(816) 322-3072
Inexpensive

GRAVOIS MILLS

Vinny's Cafe and Lounge
751 North Main (5 Highway)
(573) 374-9982
Inexpensive

LAURIE

Val's
610 North Main (5 Highway)
(573) 374-0922
Inexpensive

OSAGE BEACH

Lucky Duck Cafe
HH to Point of Cherokee Road
(closed winter)
(4-mile marker)
(573) 365-9973
Inexpensive

SUNRISE BEACH

Sunrise Cantina
Highway 5 (.25 miles north of Lake Road 5-35)
(573) 374-8185
Inexpensive

LAMAR

Lamarti's
54 Southeast 1 Lane
(417) 682-6034
Inexpensive

Northwest Missouri

It does get cold in northwest Missouri—make no mistake—especially near the northernmost border, where the plains are chilled by every stiff wind howling down from the frigid north. Alberta Clipper, Siberian Express, whatever you call it, Missouri catches hell in the winter, bringing to mind that old joke: "There's nothing between here and the North Pole but two bobwire (barbed wire) fences, and one o' them's down." In 1989 all records were broken—along with that fence—when the nighttime temperature bottomed out at -23 degrees Fahrenheit (wind chill made that -60 degrees Fahrenheit). It also gets hot in Missouri; August days can soar over the 100 degrees Fahrenheit mark.

But at its temperate best, Jesse James country is a great place to visit that's filled with great hideouts. (James knew them all. It seems that, like George Washington, Jesse James slept almost everywhere—in northwest Missouri, anyway.)

Not that that's all there is to this section of the state; we'd hate to say we're living in the past on the rather unsavory reputation of our own "Robbing" Hood. There is a national wildlife refuge on the central flyway that is absolutely essential to migrating waterfowl. There is Excelsior Springs, where folks once came to take the waters and where Harry S Truman heard he had lost the presidential election to Thomas Dewey—at least according to the *Chicago Tribune*.

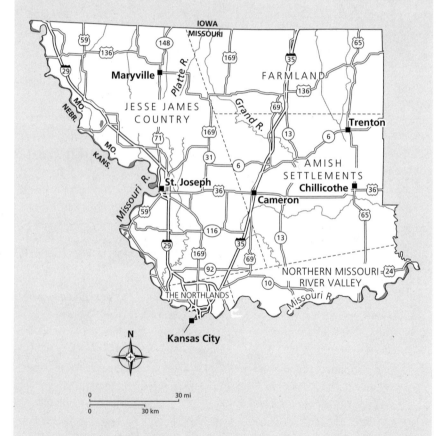

The Northlands

Just across the Missouri River from the town with a similar name is **North Kansas City.** This is a separate city, with a healthy industrial tax base and a coordinated downtown shopping area complete with plazas, fountains, and wide streets. "Northtown" has its own mayor, its own police department, and its own quirky charm. There are cafes and delis and bakeries; North Kansas Citians know how to eat. Northtown has a Web site at www.nkc.org.

Tiny **Avondale** is slightly off Highway 210 as you leave North Kansas City. Here you'll discover **Nichols Pottery Shop and Studio** at 2615 Bell (816-452-0880). Deanna Nichols handcrafts stoneware that is both beautiful and functional. "You can hang it on a wall, or take it down and serve from it," she says. The studio is filled with examples of her work, and not only mugs and platters, but also intricate, earthy fountains some 32 inches high. She does custom work, lamps, and dinnerware. Browse through the shop Tuesday through Friday from 10:00 a.m. to 5:00 p.m., until 4:00 p.m. Saturday. A garden full of shrubs and trees interesting in all four seasons has been added to the side of the building.

As long as you are here, check out **Avondale Furniture and Antiques** at 2600 North Highway 10. Hours are catch-as-catch-can; call (816) 452-2690 for an appointment if you prefer. Owner Lillian Waskovsky has an auction service and warehouse and likes to move pieces quickly. This place may not be glitzy, but the prices are very right.

AUTHOR'S FAVORITE ANNUAL EVENTS IN NORTHWEST MISSOURI

MAY

Excelsior Springs
The Gatsby Festival,
always the weekend after Mother's Day,
(816) 630-0750,
www.epsi.net/gatsby/welcome.htm

Richmond
Morel Mushroom Festival,
parade, food and craft booths, model
train show, carnival,
(816) 776-5304 or (816) 776-5306,
http://cofcommerce.home.mchsi.com/
festival.html

SEPTEMBER

Excelsior Springs
Waterfest, second Saturday of
September, arts, crafts, and food
booths; games, music, and rides,
(816) 630-6161,
escoc@epsi.net

DECEMBER

Lee Summit
Christmas in the Park,
(816) 524-2424

Hayes Hamburgers at 2502 Northeast Vivion Road in suburban Kansas City North (at Antioch Road) serves the kind of hamburgers that you could order before "fast food" was invented. This is the place to go for a hamburger after a football game or late at night on a date you don't want to end. The hamburgers are small and made of fresh chopped meat rolled into a ball and mashed onto the grill with a handful of onions. The aroma of onions and hamburger grilling together sparks an appetite. People buy them by the bag and have been known to eat a dozen. The chili is all-American good, too. The diner is open all the time—twenty-four hours a day.

Take the Interstate 435 exit north off Interstate 35 and keep an eye out for Highway 152. A right turn will take you to *Hodge Park,* a fine place to get away from the "two Ps": progress and people.

Those big, hairy critters you spot as you enter the park are American bison; the Kansas City Zoo maintains a small herd here, where once there were thousands. Elk and deer share the enclosure; you may be able to get "up close and personal" with some of the Midwest's largest indigenous animals.

If human history is more your thing, park your car in the lot and keep walking. *Shoal Creek* is a restored frontier town at Hodge Park, full of historic buildings moved here by the Kansas City Parks and Recreation Department. The tiny, two-story jail built of monolithic limestone blocks (how did they lift those things?) came from nearby Missouri City. What a place for a lockup! Local ne'er-do-wells slept off Saturday night festivities here some one hundred-plus years ago. Other buildings include square-hewn log cabins, a one-room schoolhouse, a barn, a replica of an old mill complete with mill wheel and race, and some pretty fine houses for the gentry. Stop by during one of their living-history weekends for a re-creation of frontier life; you'll feel as if you've stepped back a century. Fine nature trails lead into the woods from Shoal Creek.

If you are interested in archaeology and the peoples that inhabited this land before Europeans moved in, get yourself to *Line Creek Park* at 5940 Northwest Waukomis. This is a Hopewell Culture site, where Native Americans lived and worked from approximately 50 B.C. to A.D. 200. The museum houses artifacts found on the spot and in the surrounding areas.

The Kansas City Parks and Recreation Department operates the site, and schoolchildren from grade four up come for mock "digs" (artifacts are salted back into the ground so that the kids have the excitement of discovery). You can take your chances; the museum is usually open Saturdays and Sundays from 11:00 a.m. to 4:00 p.m. There's no charge for the museum, but for reservations for group programs, call the above number; there is a small fee for groups.

AUTHOR'S FAVORITES IN NORTHWEST MISSOURI

Hayes Hamburgers

Martha Lafite Thompson Nature Sanctuary

Jamesport

The Hall of Waters

The Elms Hotel

Church of St. Luke, the Beloved Physician

The Inn on Crescent Lake Bed and Breakfast

Weston

Candyman's Mule Barn

Do you want to have some real fun now? Well, there is a most unusual place in Kansas City North to do just that if you are up to trying something different. *Jaegers Subsurface Paintball,* deep in the caves at 9300 Northeast Underground Drive, is the place to find. For $35, manager J. J. Johnson will give you a safety briefing, helmet and goggles, and a semiautomatic weapon with 130 rounds of ammunition—i.e., paintballs.

The caves are spooky—dark stone walls and dirt floors—littered with washing machines, wire spools, and a beat-up delivery van to hide behind or trip over. Old paintball pellets and shards of exploded ones are debris on the floor. Fluorescent lights illuminate parts of the cave; other parts are dark. The color of your helmet designates the team you belong to. You are the hunter— and the hunted—on a field that consists of the cave's labyrinthine stone passages and lots of sand.

"Paintball . . . may be an inherently dangerous activity that can result in loss of life, eyesight, or hearing," says the waiver you sign before entering the field, and, although harmless, those little pellets *hurt* when you are hit. So it is easy to follow the next rule: When hit, you raise your gun above your head and yell "I'm hit!" and run off the field while the referee counts to ten. Aficionados of the game find the rapid-fire shooting under pressure and the thrill of catching the enemy unaware exciting and exhilarating (along with the satisfaction of hitting a moving target). You can spend a lot of money on more advanced equipment (ear-mouth pieces to communicate with your partner or teammates, or an RT Automag semiautomatic airgun for $700) in places such as the Irish Brigade Paintball Proshop and Supplies of Kansas City, or just drop in at Jaegers. Hours are Monday through Friday 5:00 to 10:00 p.m., Saturday 9:00

a.m. to 11:00 p.m., and Sunday noon to 8:00 p.m. Jaegers is just off of I-435 near Worlds of Fun. Take I-435 to the Highway 210 exit. Turn right at Randolph Road and go south to Underground Drive. Call (816) 452-6600 for more information, or e-mail jaegersp@earthlink.net. Check it out at www.jaegers.com.

Northern Missouri River Valley

Head east back on Highway 152 and you'll come to historic **Liberty.** The downtown square has been restored to Civil War–era glory, with authentic paint colors and fancy trim—most of it original.

The restored **Corbin Mill Place,** at 131 South Water, is now a compendium of six specialty shops housed in an old brick mill, among them the **Liberty Quilt Shoppe.** Hours at the quilt shop vary each day: Monday and Thursday from 10:00 a.m. until 7:00 p.m., Tuesday, Wednesday, Friday, and Saturday until 5:00 p.m. You can also shop **With a French Accent,** a shop full of gifts and French antiques (816-792-8320). Also there is the **Old Mill Stitchery** (816-792-3670). Behind the mill is **Bratcher Cooperage,** where you can watch the cooper turn out kegs and churns. It is open Monday through Saturday from 10:00 a.m. until 5:30 p.m.

Under the same roof is a cozy little restaurant called **Martinali's.** Owner Martha Bond serves great food to the lunchtime crowd in Liberty. Their grouper with rice pilaf is a favorite dish, and where else in town can you find high tea at 4:00? Only here at Martinali's. Call (816) 781-3313.

Sandy and Tom Williams opened the mill in 1986 as an outgrowth of their original antiques store a few blocks away, and now they offer a great place to spend an afternoon—it just keeps growing. The mill, with its 24-inch-thick limestone foundation and 18-inch brick walls, is built on an original land grant from President James Monroe for relief from the 1811 New Madrid earthquake (that event had far-reaching consequences!). Corbin Mill Place is open from 10:00 a.m. to 5:00 p.m. Monday through Saturday.

There are three museums in downtown Liberty, either on the square or within easy walking distance, among them the **Jesse James Bank Museum Historic Site** (816-781-4458) and the **Historic Liberty Jail** at 216 North Main Street (816-781-3188). The museum provides exhibits, audiovisual presentations, and art to help visitors understand the significant events that took place in the jail. It is sponsored by the Church of Jesus Christ of Latter-day Saints. Hours are daily from 9:00 a.m. to 9:00 p.m.

The town is chock-full of antiques and craft shops, so plan on browsing. You can pick up a map at Corbin Mill or check out the Web site at www.ci .liberty.mo.us.

William Jewell College is alma mater of nationally known writer Patti DeLano (brother in California, cousins in New York) and the location of one of the most interesting little cemeteries around. The college was founded before the Civil War and used as a military hospital during the war. The cemetery has tombstones dating from the 1800s. Walking around there you can see the dates of flu epidemics and wars and discover husbands with several wives and those wives buried with their newborns. It is a lesson in history for a sunny afternoon.

The *Martha Lafite Thompson Nature Sanctuary* (816-781-8598; www .naturesanctuary.com) offers a wonderful place to watch the wildlife, take a naturalist-guided walk, or enjoy special programs—from making your own bird feeder to learning about the constellations on a night hike. More than 600 species of plants and many fish, reptiles, amphibians, and mammals make their homes here, and more than 160 species of birds have been sighted. Worn out? Take in the lovely new sanctuary building with its displays of indigenous plants, or watch snapping turtles and catfish in the creek-habitat aquarium. Enjoy one of the sanctuary's many programs. Relax on the spacious deck in redwood Adirondack chairs, or buy a book, a bird feeder, or bird call to take home. Watch for the sanctuary sign at 407 North La Frenz Road.

howmanytonsof siltayear?

As the Missouri River cut through mountains and prairie, it gathered huge quantities of silt and sand. It earned its nicknames—"the Muddy Mo" and "the Big Muddy"—because it used to dump about 200,000,000 tons of silt a year into the Mississippi River.

North Water Street is in the Lightburne Historic District and contains a diverse collection of structures built during the late-nineteenth century, such as Lightburne Hall, an elaborate 1852 mansion, and the 1898 Simmons house. These are all private homes.

I-35 South from Liberty will take you to the little town of *Claycomo* known mostly for the giant Ford Motor Plant that resides there. Of course, if there is a Ford plant in town, then there must be somewhere that serves home cookin' to the people going to or coming off the 24/7 shifts there. That place would be *Nelle Belle's Diner* at 150 Northeast 69 Highway (816-452-9786). Owner Dixie Edwards knows what to cook for hungry people. Her specials are on the wall, and you can get a really early start there because her hours are from 4:00 a.m. (Yes, you read that right!) to 2:00 p.m. Monday through Friday and until 1:00 p.m. on Saturday. This is a personal favorite because 4:00 a.m. isn't early if you have been up all night. It's just very, very late.

heatherlywar

The "Heatherly War" of 1836 made it into the history books. Some sources list this as an Indian war; in fact, it was a family of white outlaws who killed their neighbors and laid the blame at the feet of the Iowa Indians. Several companies from Clay and Ray Counties were dispatched to investigate and/or quell a supposed uprising. Ma Heatherly instigated the murders that were carried out by her brood of mixed-blood offspring.

Take Highway 210 through the tiny towns of Missouri City, Orrick, Fleming, and Camden, which are dotted along the Missouri River. The views are spectacular, especially from the observation stop just this side of Missouri City. At your back is Nebo Hill, an important site for prehistoric Indians who found this a perfect place for ceremonies and camps; the site was in use for hundreds of years. After a good spring rain, you're liable to see artifact hunters out in the fields nearby.

Highway 210 will take you to **Richmond.** Here the **Ray County Museum** occupies a beautiful old brick home on West Royale Street (816-776-2305). The Y-shaped building is unusual in itself, and the contents will tell you much about this area, from pre–Civil War days to the present. A special natural-history section highlights indigenous wildlife.

To find the museum, go past the four-way stop at the edge of town on Highway 210 to Royale Street, and west to the large brick building atop the hill on the left. The library is open Wednesday through Sunday from noon until 4:00 p.m., but call for the museum hours, which changed after its remodeling. If you are here the first weekend in October, you'll find mountain men, trappers, and traders as well as old-time arts and crafts at the Old Trails Festival on the grounds of the museum.

Just 5 miles north of Richmond on Highway 13 is **Die Brok Pann Bakery,** at 14711 Highway 13, where you can buy high-quality baked goods as well as bulk foods and cheese. This friendly Mennonite shop is run by Paul and Delores King. It has homemade cookies, pies, and wonderful cinnamon rolls. Doughnuts are fresh every morning. It is open every day but Sunday 7:30 a.m. to 5:00 p.m. Call (816) 776-3275.

Amish Settlements

For a visit to a very special small town, spend some time in **Chillicothe;** don't pass it by. (It has a Web site at www.chillicothemo.com.)

For sheer indulgence, Francine Davenport can bake some triple chocolate muffins—something so sinful you will repent for days—or you can indulge without the guilt with her low-fat peaches 'n' cream muffins. Whatever you choose, *Francine's Pastry Parlor,* tucked away inside a plain white store-front at 1007 Bryan, is the place to go if you are looking for some warm, fresh-from-the-oven treats. Hours are 6:30 a.m. to 2:30 p.m. Tuesday through Friday. The just-like-mama-made apple and cherry pies are the favorites of the lunch crowd.

It's not just pastries here, though; her homemade chili and sandwiches make it a perfect spot for lunch. Call Francine at (660) 646-3333.

The *Grand River Historical Society Museum* is also in town at Forrest Drive and McNally. Hours are 1:00 to 4:00 p.m. Tuesday through Sunday (April through October).

North on U.S. Highway 65 is the town of *Trenton.* Don't mistake Trenton Cemetery Prairie for a neglected eyesore, with its rough grasses obscuring some of the old tombstones. Established in 1830, its protected status as a cemetery happily resulted in one of the few precious parcels of native prairie remaining in the state. Today it is maintained by the Missouri Conservation Department. Preservation is especially crucial; prairie north of the Missouri River is scarce. These patchwork remnants produce the seeds adapted to the northern Missouri climate that are essential to reestablishing prairie ecosystems.

This is an area of oddities; what you see may not be what you get. *Riverside Country Club* (660-359-6004), Trenton's golf course, has tree stumps carved into life-size animals around the fairways. (If you hit a birdie or an eagle around here, it may be a wooden one.) Former greenskeeper Don McNabb was an artist with a chainsaw and has salted the nine-hole course with bears and other critters. The club is open for golf to anyone for the cost of a greens fee (and cart rental, if you wish), but nongolfers are welcome to check out the carvings.

What's it like to live like a governor? You can find out for yourself. Hosts Robert and Carolyn Brown offer lodging in former Gov. Arthur Hyde's mansion at 418 East Seventh Street, Trenton (660-359-5631). The 1950s *Hyde Mansion Bed and Breakfast* was completely renovated by the Browns. The large dining room contains several small tables for more intimate breakfasts. Carolyn serves a very nice breakfast. There are five bedrooms; the living room and its baby grand piano are all yours. In fact, they added a 9-foot-long pool table. Rooms, all with private baths, are $65 to $110. Hyde's is near enough to Jamesport to fill up on festival weekends, so make your reservations early. Go to the Web site www.travelguides.com or www.bbgetaways.com.

Drive north on US 65 about as far as you can go in the state, and Glen and Connie Mock will welcome you to *Mockville Land & Cattle Company,* Corn Place, 3 miles outside *Mercer.* Glen has an 1880s bed-and-breakfast. Actually,

"Real World" Experience

It was a warm and wet November day, the color gray and dismal. Yellow leaves had begun to stick to the raindrops and fall with them, cluttering the streets with mats of browning vegetation. We were looking for a day trip from Kansas City and chose Jamesport. Saturday is a busy day in this Amish community. Local residents were hurrying by in their horse-drawn carriages—wooden boxes with tiny windows in the back—headed for the nearby bulk food stores.

Books give only the minimum information about the Amish, the strictest branch of the Mennonite Church. The founder, Jacob Amman, was a Swiss religious reformer who laid the foundation for the difficult lives the Amish lead. It is strange to see the farmhouses sitting unattached to the life-giving power poles we are so accustomed to seeing in neat rows down the roadway. Forbidden modern conveniences, the Amish live in a sunrise-to-sunset world. The absence of television antennae or satellite dishes transports the little farms' appearances back to simpler times. The people shun vanity. Their clothes are black and fastened with straight pins—they are forbidden the vainglory of buttons—and their hair is hidden under bonnets and hats. They will not allow themselves to be photographed.

We bought handmade quilts and hand-loomed rugs. We drove away in our fast car, back to our modern lives, stocked with every possible convenience, from zippers to microwave ovens. So why do the women of the Amish community have the time to quilt by the light of a kerosene lamp while we are so busy we barely have time to sew on a lost button? Ah, vanity. It is such a time-consuming sin.

it's more like a bread-and-staples. You are taken to this rustic cabin in the rolling hills by horse and wagon to begin your 1880 adventurous stay as the old settlers did years ago. Seven cabins wait for you where a fireplace provides warmth. There is a fine outhouse and an outdoor shower with water that you pump yourself. Glen breeds horses—paints to be exact—so there is unlimited horseback riding included in the price. He has 250 acres, and the neighbors will let you ride their land, too. So, if you really want to get away from it all (including telephones and electricity) and ride in a beautiful hardwood forest, this is the place for you. You can bring friends because the cabins will accommodate four people. The price for four is $500. There's not another place like this, and it is sometimes booked a year in advance for the colorful fall season. It is now open for turkey season, and you will soon be able to hunt buffalo here. Call (660) 382-5862 for reservations and directions. There is one other amenity: For a little extra, Glen will cook dinner for you. Ask about menu selection when you call or visit the Web site at www.mockville.com. A new lodge has been opened for large gatherings—weddings, reunions, or business meetings—with more modern and indoor facilities.

Jamesport is a different world. It is the largest Mennonite settlement in Missouri and home to the most orthodox "horse-and-buggy" Mennonites. Here the Amish wear black, fasten clothes with pins, and allow no electricity in their homes. Don't ask the Amish to pose for pictures, though; it's against their beliefs.

Before spending a day wandering around Jamesport's Amish community, you might want to stay at the **Marigold Inn** on Highway F in Jamesport and browse through **Marigold's,** a pretty marigold-colored home-cum-shop just 3 blocks west of downtown. Nancy Tracy will be at the shop and will show you quilts, folk art, and collectibles galore. She knows her way around the community and can give you a map to get you started. She and her husband, Larry, are the innkeepers at the inn next door, which has twelve delightful rooms with hand-stenciled walls and handmade quilts. The rooms have either a king-size bed ($59) or two queen-size beds ($69). Call (660) 684-6122.

Now, with map in hand, let's tour Jamesport. Remember, just about everything in town is closed on Thursday and Sunday. You can begin and end where Highway 6 meets Highway F and leads into the western part of downtown. **Anna's Bake Shop** off of Highway F in Jamesport would be a good place to start, with fresh-baked doughnuts, pies, breads, or cinnamon rolls. It opens at 8:00 a.m. so you can get an early start. It stays open until 6:00 p.m. (closed from Christmas until February).

Jamesport Amish horse and buggy

Fern Rosenbaum manages *It's a Hoot* on South Street (second block west of the four-way stop), and she knows more about the Amish people than just about anyone. Tell her what you are looking for and she will tell you how to find it. Her shop is full of fun stuff, too; call (660) 684-6569. Need a broom? *Colonial Rug and Broom Shop* is just 2½ blocks west of the four-way and has handwoven rugs and brooms made daily. You can purchase them already made or have them created to your own needs by artisans Larry and Jane Martin; call (660) 684-6211.

Still in the city square just past the four-way on South Street is *Downhome Oak & Spice,* specializing in oak furniture, woodcraft, teas, and spices. But the real reason for finding it is the hand-dipped ice cream. It's open 9:00 a.m. until 5:00 p.m. Monday through Saturday. Call (660) 684-6526 or visit www .jamesportmo.com.

The Mennonite-owned *Gingerich Dutch Pantry and Bakery* is right at the four-way in Jamesport and has real, Amish-style meals with lots of wonderful homemade food and baked goods. It is open Monday through Saturday from 6:00 a.m. until 9:00 p.m. For more information, call (660) 684–6212 or go to www.gingerichdutchpantry.com.

Now let's get out of town a bit. The roads here are described as "gravel roads," but gravel would be a big improvement. You won't need an all-terrain vehicle to find them, but driving slowly is definitely in order unless you want to disappear into a pothole, never to be seen again. The horse-and-buggies pack down a couple of very strong little paths in the center of the roads, but the rest of the road is pretty much shot. It makes passing another car going the other way a bit of an adventure, and the buggies, understandably, won't leave the path under any circumstances. But aside from a bit of horse poop on your tires, you will emerge undamaged if you go slowly. Remember most of these shops are closed on Thursday and Sunday and have no telephones or electric lights.

Kerosene lamps light the *H & M Country Store* just south of Jamesport. It's a good place to stock your kitchen. You'll find bulk groceries at great prices (wonderful high-gluten flour for your bread machine), dried fruit, beans, homemade mixes for just about anything you want (biscuits, pancakes, muffins), and spices and herbs by the wall-full. You want noodles? Every kind you can imagine is here. You can buy fresh produce and brown eggs here, too.

To find a nice selection of hand-quilted pieces, venture out of town east on Highway F and 1 mile south on Highway U for *Sherwood Quilts and Crafts,* which has a large selection of handmade quilts, rugs, and baskets. It has a bed piled high with beautiful quilts; dig through until you find the one you can't live without. It is open from 8:00 a.m. until 5:00 p.m.

South of town on Highway 190 is the **Rolling Hills Store,** offering sturdy dry goods at excellent prices and lots of natural-fiber fabrics, plus boots and shoes.

You can stay at the **Country Colonial Bed and Breakfast,** 106 East Main, and allow hosts Myrick and Janet den Hartog to tell you a little bit about the area. After shopping, you can return to this early 1900s home and enjoy playing the baby grand piano, and when night falls again snuggle back into the feather-bed. You will awake to the aroma of a large country breakfast being prepared, and if the weather is fine, it will be served in the flower garden. Rooms are $75 to $95. Call (660) 684-6711 or (800) 579-9248.

So many places to see, so little time! If you leave town the way you came in, you can stop at the **Country Cupboard Restaurant,** in downtown Jamesport, open Tuesday through Sunday from 6:30 a.m. until 9:00 p.m. They always have a daily special and homemade pies and breads (660-684-6597).

The Mormons settled in western Daviess County in the 1830s. Just north and west of Gallatin (take Highway 13 north and turn west onto Highway P) is the historic **Adam-Ondi-Ahman Shrine,** believed by Mormons to be the place where Christ will return. Northwest Missouri is important historically to the Mormon people; there were once thousands of them here. The majority were forced out during the Mormon Wars, when the state militia was ordered to drive them out of Missouri. The town of **Far West,** now no more than a historical marker, comprised 5,000 souls, all exterminated or driven from their homes. Many died during a forced march in this land of religious freedom. The marker is off Highway 13, west on Highway HH and north on Highway D, near Shoal Creek (just northwest of Kingston).

Ever wonder where retail giant J.C. Penney got his start? No, not New York, or even Chicago. It was right here in **Hamilton** in 1895 that he got his first job at Hale's Department Store. By the time he returned to Hamilton to buy his old employer's place of business in 1924, it was number 500 in his chain of stores. His company motto was: "Honor, confidence, service, and cooperation"—no wonder he did so well.

The **J.C. Penney Memorial Library and Museum** (816-583-2168), uptown on Davis Street in Hamilton, is open Tuesday through Saturday from 10:00 a.m. to 5:00 p.m. You'll love the displays of early merchandise—makes you wonder who wore the stuff. The Penney farm cottage has also been restored.

Even cattlemen like this area's history. J.C. Penney once raised great herds of Angus, and at the Penney farm there is a monument—a big monument—to Penney's prize bull.

Jesse James Country

Take the Business 69 exit to ***Excelsior Springs.*** Once a magnet for people who wished to "take the waters," this old spa has enough moxie to try for a comeback. The health-spa ship was scuttled in the 1950s when an article in the *Saturday Evening Post* declared mineral waters an ineffective form of treatment; the demise was clinched when Missouri passed a bill prohibiting advertising by doctors. So now we enjoy the waters—and the baths and massages—for the lovely, hedonistic fun of it. The town was founded in 1880 for the waters. Even the Native Americans living here valued its healing properties.

Visit the ***Hall of Waters*** (816-630-0750; www.exsmo.com) at 201 East Broadway, Excelsior Springs, the world's longest mineral-water bar, and sample some of the waters that attracted thousands near the turn of the last century. There are more naturally occurring types of mineral waters here than anyplace else on earth except the German city of Baden-Baden, which ties Excelsior Springs.

Hall of Waters

Taking the Waters

Excelsior Springs has long been famous for its waters. Native Americans were aware of the benefits of the springs, but the settlers called them poison (or "PIE-zen", as they pronounced it). The medicinal uses of the waters were responsible for the founding of the town in 1880. There are five categories of mineral water, and each has a medicinal purpose. Excelsior Springs is one of only six cities in the world to have all of them—one of two in the United States—and you can still experience most of them at the Hall of Waters there. They are: iron manganese, which as the name suggests, is a source of iron; sulfo-saline, which is a very, very strong laxative (given a two-ounce cup, people were told not to drink it in the elevator but to wait until they got to their rooms. This was no joke!). The next is soda bicarbonate, which was naturally carbonated and was used to settle a queasy stomach. The fourth category used to be the last—the neutral waters, which could be drunk in unlimited amounts—until it was discovered that they had very different compositions and served different purposes. These were calcium and lithium waters. The lithium water had properties that soothed depression (the most famous and best-tasting water in the world was Blue Rock Lithia) and of course, the calcium water, which is the only water still bottled today in Excelsior Springs is an excellent no-calorie source of calcium.

For a truly sybaritic experience, check the schedule for baths and massage, also at the Hall of Waters. You can once again "take the waters," as they used to say. The bathhouse is open by appointment from 9:00 a.m. to 5:00 p.m. Monday through Friday (the spa is closed on Tuesday) and from 10:00 a.m. to 5:00 p.m. Saturday and Sunday. A sampling of the available treatments includes: *light vapor bath:* with forty-four sixty-five-watt light bulbs to warm joints and muscles and open pores to the steam; *mineral water bubble tub:* soak in a deep bath of mineral water aerated by powerful bubbles; *salt rub:* a scrub-down with sea salt, Epsom salts, and a loofah sponge to exfoliate and stimulate; *massage:* a classic deep-tissue Swedish massage with reflexology acupressure by a licensed massage therapist (a water-based cream is used while you lie on a padded table, and eucalyptus candles and soft music relax you); *steam bath:* opens your pores at 115 degrees while you rest on a bed; and last, and best, the *Fango mud bath:* black mud painted on the body is left to dry, followed by a thorough rinsing. There are all kinds of special packages of these services ranging in price from $20 to $399, with plenty of options in between.

The lovely art deco-style building, built in 1937 as "the finest and most complete health resort structure in the U.S.," is a fine example of a WPA project begun during the Great Depression. Moreover, how many towns have city offices that are shared with mineral baths and massage rooms—not to mention a 25-meter indoor pool?

The **Paradise Playhouse** is a dinner theater done in Hawaiian theme. It's right across from the Hall of Waters at 101 Spring Street. The buffet is cooked right there in the shiny, cutting-edge kitchen. Tables are tiered for best view of the stage, and the plays are very well done. Call (816) 630-3333 for show times.

If you like old-fashioned burgers, don't miss **Ray's Lunch,** at 231 East Broadway. The hash browns are killer good, and the secret chili recipe is a favorite with locals. Call (816) 637-3432.

The wonderful **Olde English Garden Shoppe** at 115 East Broadway, Excelsior Springs, cultivated by Jim and Ginger Nelson, overlooks the river and has waterfalls and garden delights. It is stocked with all kinds of garden ornaments and gifts for gardeners, from large engraved paving stones to little seed-row markers. The Nelsons carry some books as well. The shop is open Tuesday through Sunday from 10:00 a.m. to 6:00 p.m. Call (816) 630-5060 or visit www.englishgardenshop.com.

Scandinavian Shop is next door at 109 East Broadway. Susan and Jytte offer *hygge* (the Danish word for "friendship," pronounced hooy-ga), in this unique shop. The Tivoli Tea Room hides in the balcony, near the beautiful old tin ceiling. Glass French doors open into the quiet garden in warm weather. You can find unusual Scandinavian art and items for your home. Hygee also implies a cozy place or feeling, and the real fireplace burning in the winter months certainly imparts that. Hours are Tuesday through Saturday 10:00 a.m. to 6:00 p.m., Sunday 10:00 a.m. to 5:00 p.m.; lunch is served from 11:30 a.m. until 2:30 p.m. Call (816) 630-6400 or visit the Web site at www.scandinavian country.com to see what is offered for lunch.

The **Old Bank Museum** at 101 East Broadway, Excelsior Springs (816-630-3712; www.ci.excelsior-springs.mo.us), in a former Bank Building, circa 1906 and itself an interesting architectural achievement, preserves spa-town history. (Check out the dentist's office, and thank your lucky stars this is the present.) Look up to find a pair of murals; they're wonderful copies of Jean-François Millet's *The Gleaners* and *The Angelus,* painted by an itinerant artist with more talent than fame. You can buy postcards, homemade lye soap, or a museum membership (for $1); you may find the Women's Auxiliary of the museum quilting or weaving rag rugs when you visit on a Wednesday. The chamber of commerce is here; Pat Wilson will fill you in on local happenings.

The **Olde Towne Mall** has antiques galore at 1225 North Jesse James Road, Excelsior Springs, where Leonard Jones, Pat Fish, and Phil Broadbent have opened a huge space and filled it with lots of stuff. This "Olde Towne" area is bursting with new shops since the Elms Hotel has reopened, and it is a fine place to walk on a Saturday afternoon.

An old-fashioned hardware store has withstood the test of time—the newest generation of **Brunke's Supply** at 423 Thompson is exactly like the old one—row upon row, deep into the bowels of the store, lined up in some kind of order only John Brunke knows, are thousands and thousands of things. Stuff. Gadgets. Cast-iron pots. Aluminum pans. Screws. Bolts. Signs. Anything. Everything. A real if-we-don't-have-it-you-probably-don't-need-it kind of place. You're gonna love it. Call (816) 637-3155.

What do Harry S Truman, Al Capone, and Franklin D. Roosevelt have in common? They all stayed at the **Elms Hotel** at Elms Boulevard and Regent Street in Excelsior Springs. You can, too. The elegant old hotel—built originally in 1888—and the beautiful grounds around it underwent a complete ($8 million) renovation in 1998. The hotel has been a resting place for the famous and the infamous, from Presidents Franklin Roosevelt and Harry Truman to Al Capone, who hosted all-night drinking and gambling parties here during

Attractions in and around Excelsior Springs

Prohibition. The new look celebrates the time of that bygone era. In fact, the workers in the renovation process claim to have seen the ghost of someone who looks a lot like Al Capone drifting down the hall of the fourth floor.

Look for the 1948 Chevrolet Stylemaster out front of the hotel. President Truman arrived in just such a car on election night in 1948. He came to avoid the press on a night when everyone thought he would be defeated by Thomas Dewey. He went to bed thinking he had lost the election and was awakened at 3:00 a.m. to learn that he had been reelected. The famous photo of him glee-fully holding an early copy of the *Chicago Daily Tribune* carrying the blatant headline DEWEY DEFEATS TRUMAN was taken in front of the Elms Hotel.

The original tile floor and the huge "walk-in" fireplace in the lobby, as well as the art deco designs and stained glass in the Monarch Room, make this magnificent hotel worth a visit. It is, of course, on the National Register of Historic Places.

The Elms offers 153 guest rooms and suites, and the feeling of Truman's genteel time is augmented with such modern amenities as a communications system with voice mail, dataport, and cordless phones. There is twenty-four-hour room service and concierge service. A gourmet shop features coffees, espresso, cappuccino, entrees, and homemade ice creams. A beauty salon for hair and scalp treatments, facials, manicures, pedicures, and makeup is also available.

Boxer Jack Dempsey used the hotel as a training center. Now a new and complete fitness center on the grounds has tennis courts, riding stables, jog-ging trail, mountain biking, and, of course, an outdoor pool. Indoors there is a European swim track and banked jogging track. This indoor pool is shaped like a paper clip, with two sides extending the length of the room, and then curling back through two short rounded ends so that you can swim laps without having to turn around. The small islands in the middle of the pool are set with brightly painted giant flowers and playing-card symbols—hearts, spades, clubs, and dia-monds—and bright bursts of color hang above the pool. Classes in yoga and t'ai chi, and nutrition and health programs including wellness cooking, are featured.

The new spa is the real center of this elegant hotel. Look at this list of pos-sibilities: body treatment rooms for mud, aloe, and seaweed-algae wraps, salt glow and body-polish exfoliation, and hydrotherapy; Swiss and Vichy showers; massage rooms for reflexology, sports, signature, and couples massage; and relaxation facilities with sauna, steam, mineral baths, and whirlpools. Rooms and suites are $99 (rooms Sunday through Thursday) to $299 (Friday and Saturday), and all include breakfast and dinner. Various golf, spa, and honey-moon packages are also offered. Visit www.elmsresort.com for current package options, or call (800) 843-3567.

The beautiful little stone church across the street from the Elms, at the corner of Regent and Kansas City Avenues, is the **Church of St. Luke, the Beloved Physician.** The Episcopal congregation began having services in Excelsior Springs as far back as 1905, but it was 1933 when the church was built on property donated by Major W.A.J. Bell of Blechingly, England. The church is built in the English style, similar to The Church of St. Mary the Virgin A.D. 1090 in Bell's home parish. It

strangeasitsounds

Mormon travelers on the old trails left legends and stories. There is still a site inside the Excelsior Springs city limits that is visited by pilgrims. Mormons were being chased from the country and took refuge in an old church; such a storm came up that it spooked their pursuers' horses, the river rose, and the pursuers gave up and went home, leading the Mormons to believe they had been delivered by a miracle.

is built of stones quarried on Major Bell's property nearby. The inside of this remarkable church is so lovely that it is often requested for weddings. Guests at the Elms are frequently visitors on Sunday mornings. You will be most welcome, so sign the guest book and plan to stay for coffee and refreshments in the undercroft.

Right down Kansas City Avenue at Chillicothe Street—beside the Elms Hotel—is an old depot where trains brought guests from Chicago and Kansas City to the hotel. Now it is the **Wabash Barbecue,** 646 South Kansas City Avenue. The meats smoked in the old brick garage out back are very good and so is the secret barbecue sauce. Jim McCullough and his wife, Cheri, have restored the building to its 1925 charm. After its days as a depot, which ended in 1933, new owners converted it into a dairy, delivering milk to the residents of Excelsior Springs. The dairy sold milk shakes and burgers, too, and Jim—whose family goes back six generations in town—remembers hanging out here in the 1960s. He and Cheri looked at the walk-in coolers that once held cans of fresh milk and knew they would be perfect for slabs of meat, the big garage fine for smoking. On summer weekends you can enjoy music out on the patio. Call (816) 630-7700 for carryout, too. Visit their Web site at www.wabashbbq.com.

Excelsior Springs Fine Art Gallery at 520 Kansas City Avenue was built in 1909 as a boardinghouse. Later it became a convent for the nuns who taught at the Catholic school across the street. Then it stood empty for years and years.

Now it has found rebirth as a home and art gallery. Keith Bowman and his wife, Jeri—who are both art teachers in the local school district—bought the old building and with hard work and a little money have begun to restore it to its original beauty. Inches of tar and tiles were removed from the hardwood floors; staircases and sliding doors were painstakingly rebuilt. Beautiful stained-glass windows grace the entryway. Now the gallery and studio show the works of local artists Tuesday and Friday 4:00 to 7:00 p.m. and Saturday 10:00 a.m. to 4:00 p.m. You're also welcome to call for an appointment. There's even more: The Armchair Film Society shows old movies on the second or third Friday of each month. Call (816) 630-5671 for information about the movies and art shows held at the gallery.

Downtown the old **Mill Inn Restaurant** at 415 St. Louis Avenue looks vaguely south-of-the-border. Inside you'll find wonderful cinnamon rolls (if you can beat the local farmers to them!), peanut butter pie, and, on Wednesday and Saturday only, homemade bread pudding. Call (816) 637-8008.

Edward and Irene Heege are the innkeepers at the **Inn on Crescent Lake.** It is a three-story Georgia colonial mansion on twenty-two acres at 1261 St. Louis Avenue, Excelsior Springs. The home was built in 1915 and still has the crescent-shaped moat for which it was named encircling the estate.

The guest rooms all have private baths (some have whirlpool tubs) and individual temperature control and cable television. Edward and Irene shared a dream of having the perfect country inn where people could unwind. This is a good place to do it. The swimming pool is a fine spot for cooling off, and the ponds are great for fishing. Paddleboats are available for tooling around the little lakes. There is even a fishing boat to use.

Breakfast may be served in the dining room, living room, or in the sun-filled solarium. Rooms are $115 to $250. Call (816) 630-6745 for reservations, e-mail info@crescentlake.com, or visit the Web site at www.crescentlake.com.

Excelsior Springs also has one of the most beautiful old golf courses in the Kansas City area, and it's a municipal course, so it's affordable. Rolling hills, big trees, and surrounding woodlands make it challenging; watered fairways and paved cart paths make it pleasant year-round. It is an "English-type" course, unique because it has no sand traps or bunkers, which keeps play moving smoothly (so leave your sand wedge in the car). If you go into the snack bar for a cold drink, don't miss the tiny log cabin tucked inside the clubhouse. It's one of the original structures in this old town and lets you see how Missouri settlers once lived. The Battle of Fredericksburg, a Civil War skirmish, was fought along the southwest sector of the course, and a monument commemorating the event stands near the fifteenth tee. At the bottom of Golf Hill Drive in East Valley Park, you can stop and take a walk along the Fishing River path to see a new view of this old town—here you'll find one of the original mineral-water wells towering over the park. Visit the Web site at www.exsmo.com.

Hometown Notes

I call Excelsior Springs home. I have always been very active in the community, beginning with a few years as PTA president when my children were young, and moving on to become the Honorable Patti DeLano, Mayor of Excelsior Springs. I was elected to two terms on the City Council and served on the Planning and Zoning Commission and the Road and Bridge Commission. I have also served on the Board of Directors of the Missouri Municipal League and the Board of Directors of the Good Samaritan Society, a local charitable organization. For three years I wrote a weekly column for the *Daily Standard,* the local newspaper. I then went back to school at William Jewell College in Liberty and earned my B.A. in communication.

Just south of Excelsior Springs about 10 miles is the little town of ***Orrick,*** and there, in my humble opinion, you can find Missouri's greatest tenderloin sandwich. This sleepy little town used to raise lots of potatoes. That business has moved on, but this is delta land from the Big Muddy Missouri. The place to find that tenderloin is ***Feebler's Cove,*** at 109 Front Street, Orrick (816-770-3878). Owners Tim and Cheri Heady work hard to make you a memorable meal in this old storefront. They feature walleye dinner on Friday. Top off your meal with homemade blackberry or peach cobbler. Their breakfast menu features the "Farmer's Special"—enough food to keep any farmer going all day for the reasonable price of $5.45.

Follow the signs to the ***Watkins Woolen Mill State Historic Site*** west off U.S. Highway 69 onto Highway 92 near Lawson and get ready to walk back in time. The visitor center is open from April 15 through October 15. The decades fall away like leaves as you wander down the footpath from the parking area. You pass deep Missouri woods, then a tiny stone-walled cemetery where the gravestones are encrusted with lichen. Farther along the path a brick giant rises to your right, and a graceful mansion crowns the hill to your left. A young belle could make quite an entrance down the lovely, curved walnut staircase in the entryway—and probably did, more than once.

Waltus Watkins built his empire here around 1850, in the years before the Civil War. Quite an empire it was: The three-story brick mill employed dozens, providing woolen fabrics to the area. The milling machinery, from washing vats to looms, is still intact, providing pristine examples of early industrial ingenuity. The house and its outbuildings reflect a gracious life—the reward for hard work and hard-headed business sense.

Before it became a state park, the mill seemed destined for destruction. The family was selling it after more than a century of occupancy, and the place was on the auction block. Representatives from the Smithsonian were on hand to bid on rare equipment—but the day was saved, along with the integrity of the mill complex, when private individuals bought the site lock, stock, and barrel (and there were a few of those about). Eventually they were able to pass the mill complex along to the state of Missouri, and now you can tour the mill and the elegant home on the hill, participate in living-history weekends (try not to miss the Victorian Christmas), or watch an ongoing archaeological dig intended to discover still more about day-to-day life one hundred years ago and more. Tours are given Monday through Saturday from 10:00 a.m. to 4:00 p.m. and Sunday from 11:00 a.m. to 4:00 p.m. Winter hours are from 11:00 a.m. to 4:00 p.m. Admission is $1.25 for adults and 75 cents for children younger than age twelve. Special events are usually free. An interpretive center acts as museum and buffer between now and the nineteenth century. Call (816) 580-3387 for more information.

A brick church and an octagonal schoolhouse are nearby, both restored to their original condition. The Watkins children and those of mill workers and local farmers attended to their readin', 'ritin', and 'rithmetic here. See the schoolhouse when it's open, if you can; call (816) 296-3357. The ventilation system of windows high in the octagonal clerestory turret is ingenious. Sunlight reflects softly around the white-painted walls inside; not much artificial light would have been necessary, with the tall windows on every side.

The park also has a 5-mile-long bike path through the woods as well as a sandy beach for swimming in the lake. Riding trails for horses are also a feature of the park. There are ninety-eight campsites with hookups. Check their Web site at www.mostateparks.com/wwmill/camp.htm for special events held during the spring, summer, and fall months.

History buffs should look for the *Jesse James Farm Historic Site* (816-628-6065) just off Highway 92 on Jesse James Drive, between Excelsior Springs and *Kearney* (watch for signs). The white house with its gingerbread trim and cedar roof sits just over a rise, a little way back from the road; the new asphalt drive and path make the place wheelchair accessible. The original part of the house is a log cabin, which was recently rescued from a precarious slide into decay. The cabin contains, among other things, the remains of Jesse's original coffin, which was exhumed when the body was moved to nearby Kearney (pronounce CAR-ney); the family originally buried him in the yard to keep the body from being disturbed by those bent on revenge or looking for souvenirs. The

trivia

The "Jesse James Farm Club" was a three-hole golf course operated at the Jesse James Farm in the 1920s by Frank's son.

coffin is odd by today's standards; there was a glass window at face level—presumably for viewing the body, not for providing a window on eternity for the deceased!

The newer section of the house was a Sears & Roebuck mail order. Mrs. James decided that the old place was getting too run-down—not to mention crowded—and she sent for the two-room addition, assembled on the spot. It still sports the original wallpaper.

This is the famous outlaw's birthplace, the place where his father was hanged and his mother's arm was lost to a Pinkerton's bomb. Enjoy the on-site museum, which includes a gift shop full of James memorabilia, books, and local crafts, or stick around in August and September for the play *The Life and Times of Jesse James*. Brother Frank was there, too. Oh, you want to know about the DNA test, do you? It was Jesse, all right.

Admission to the museum and home is $7.50 for adults, $6.50 for seniors, and $4.00 for children ages eight to fifteen. The hours are from 9:00 a.m. to 4:00 p.m. six days a week, Sundays from noon to 4:00 p.m. Call (816) 628-6065, or visit the Web site www.jessejames.org.

July 17, 1995, was a big day in Kearney. The body buried in Jesse's grave was exhumed for DNA testing to finally settle the debate about who, exactly, was buried in the James family plot. Jesse's ancestors offered DNA samples, and another man who claims that his grandfather is buried in Jesse's grave also offered his DNA for testing. People who believe that James died in 1950 at a very old age as well as people who believe it is Jesse's body in Mt. Olivet Cemetery brought folding chairs that morning to watch. "You goin' to the digging?" was the question asked at the local cafe when it opened early that morning. By clos-

trivia

Frank and Jesse James's dad was a preacher at the Pisgah Baptist Church in Excelsior Springs. They moved to the farm in 1843.

ing time, lots of people were wearing "We Dig Jesse" T-shirts that were being sold at Maggie's Attic across the street from the cemetery at the intersection of Highways 92 and 33. Maggie's, at 190 West Sixth Street, carries the usual gift items—candles, dishes, and such—but owner Jay LaRue has even more going on here. There is reproduction furniture made of plantation mahogany, and manager Anita Hemmerling runs a complete Teleflora and FTD flower shop. And the first thing you see when you walk in is an entire room full of jams, jellies, and preserves. But Maggie's also has a wine room and wine club with more than a thousand members and an amazing selection of good wines and imported beers. The club has beer and wine tastings monthly. Guess that's why it's called *Maggie's Attic . . . to Cellar* now. Hours are Monday through Saturday from 10:00 a.m. until 5:00 p.m., and on Saturday from 10:00 a.m. until 4:00 p.m. Call (816) 628-6355.

A couple doors down from Maggie's in the Kearney Commercial Plaza is *Slivinskis' Bakery,* where Doug Slivinski bakes scrumptious muffins and other decadent delights. Get there very early if you want to try the white chocolate raspberry muffin and a cup of great coffee. Early means 5:00 a.m. Tuesday through Friday. You can sleep in on Saturday and Sunday, when Doug doesn't open until 6:00 a.m. Everything is gone by 1:00 p.m. all week, which is when he closes. You can call manager Terry Kinney and have a few saved for you, (816) 903-2245.

And if you've ever wanted to lay a flower on the outlaw's grave, it's located in *Mt. Olivet Cemetery* on Highway 92, ½ mile east of I-35 in Kearney. Look for it near the cedar trees at the west end of the cemetery, which is open during daylight hours year-round.

Legend has it that Jesse, Frank James, and/or Cole Younger visited darn near every fallen-down log cabin in this part of Missouri—not to mention the surrounding states. The James gang would have had to be in three places at once, the way their exploits were reported, but no matter. That's the fun thing about legends; they're much more elastic than the truth.

At *International Beanery* at the Old Church Plaza, 105 South Jefferson Street, Suite B-7 (816-903-BEAN), owner Jennifer Downer provides a quiet place to sit a spell and enjoy comfy chairs and a fireplace or small tables where you can have a bite to eat—muffins or the quiche of the day and various sandwiches and wraps (a killer coney for those with a real appetite)—and an excellent espresso. Hours are Monday and Tuesday from 6:00 a.m. to 8:00 p.m., Wednesday until 10:00 p.m., Thursday until 8:00 p.m., Friday until 10:00 p.m., Saturday from 8:00 a.m. until 6:00 p.m., and Sunday 8:00 a.m. until 2:00 p.m.

If small-town treasure hunting is your thing, then be sure to visit *The Dirty Hippo,* also at the Old Church Plaza, where the latest styles are resold at great prices. Hours are Tuesday through Friday from 10:00 a.m. until 8:00 p.m. and on Saturday from 10:00 a.m. until 6:00 p.m. Sandy and Heather Simmons are the owners.

On the same path, but in the historic downtown area, is *Trash & Treasure* at 109 East Washington (816-628-6119), where new and used clothing, toys, office supplies, tools, whatever! can be found. You can also visit Jeanette Montgomery's shop online at www.stores.ebay.com/trashandtreasure, too. Store hours are Tuesday through Thursday from 10:00 a.m. to 6:00 p.m., Friday from noon to 6:00 p.m., and Saturday from 10:00 a.m. until 3:00 p.m.

Whimsy Hollow, 100 East 6th Street, is rightly named. It is pure whimsy to design your own perfume and lotion that say "me, me, me. It's all about me." Go ahead and indulge. Owner Liza Crawford will help you with this indulgence. How about a bath fizzie with almond skin oil? You can sit in the tub and relax while it fizzes for more than four minutes and step out with skin that feels like the finest silk. Hours are Monday through Saturday from 9:00 a.m. until 6:00 p.m. Call (816) 903-2284.

Speaking of indulgence! Take your now-silky skin right over to *Gracie's Chocolate* (816-903-9001) at 101 West Washington Street from 11:00 a.m. until 5:30 p.m. Tuesday through Saturday. Locals in Kearney keep this specialty shop so busy the owner doesn't even have time to brag about all the yummy things she has in the shop. But as an outside observer, the strawberries dipped in chocolate are at the top of the healthy list as chocolate goes. The pecan and peanut nut clusters would bring in a tight second to a grown-up eye, but the chocolate chip cookies fly off the shelves, so there must be some youngsters voting, too.

Now your silky self and your chocolates can slip into *Mojo's to Go* (816-902-6656) at 100 East 6th Street, which is, according to locals, the best little coffee shop in town. Great coffee, and great people who, a recent visitor said, make you feel so welcome you feel like a native—a silky, chocolate-filled native, at that. It's open Monday through Friday from 6:00 a.m. to 6:00 p.m.

Gino's Italian Cuisine, 123 East Washington (816-903-4466), has the old-world charm and ambience of Italy. It is located in downtown Kearney in an old storefront building that has been beautifully restored. They feature authentic Sicilian and Northern Italian cuisine. Gino's is family owned by George (Gino) and Julie Disciacca. Gino has more than thirty years of restaurant experience, and his entrees are influenced by his mother's Sicilian recipes and the tutelage of one of the premier Italian chefs in the area, Sam Gianini, who specialized in Northern Italian cuisine. You can start with homemade mozzarella sticks and one of Gino's signature entrees, Pasta Gino (penne pasta, meat sauce, one meatball, and one Italian sausage topped off with mozzarella cheese and then baked in the oven). Their steaks are superb and can be cut with a fork. One of my favorites is the Steak Mediterranean—a five-ounce filet topped with a red cream sauce, shrimp, and crab meat. The luncheon menu features daily specials and is very reasonable. Gino's also specializes in Italian desserts. They range from tiramisu, Italian almond cream cake, spumoni amaretto cheese cake, and Gino's premier dessert, which he calls Xanadu: a flour tortilla with cream cheese filling, fried and topped with cherry, chocolate, and amaretto, and covered with whipped cream and fresh bananas. Your meal will be accompanied by lovely romantic music, and you can enjoy their full wine list. If you are really lucky, Gino will serenade you himself. Hours are Monday through Thursday 11:00 a.m. to 9:00 p.m. and Friday and Saturday 11:00 a.m. to 10:00 p.m.; closed Sunday.

Are you ready for breakfast? Fast-growing Kearney still hangs on to small-town charm. In any small town there is always a place that is "the heartbeat of the community." Here in Jesse James's hometown is an old restored farmhouse called *At Sarah's Table.* At the intersection of Highways 92 and 33, go north 1 block to 405 South Jefferson (816-903-6627). Owners Carl and Sarah Moore, together with Tammy Grosserode, serve up the best breakfast in town. The parking lot begins to fill up at about 5:30 a.m. with the locals, as well as travelers on I-35 who are lucky enough to take the Highway 92 exit east through town. There is always a daily breakfast and luncheon special, with prices starting at $5.49. Fresh tenderloins and chicken-fried steak are specialties, and the home-cooked meals will fill you right up. Dinner selections range from walleye to steaks. The Sunday lunch special is fried chicken with all the trimmings. One of the restaurant's philosophies is "Life is short, eat dessert first." Good advice when you see the array of homemade pies and cobblers. The waitresses are great here and always greet you with a smile and a hot cup of coffee. Hours are Monday through Wednesday and Saturday 5:30 a.m. to 4:00 p.m., Thursday and Friday 5:30 a.m. to 8:00 p.m., and Sunday 7:00 a.m. to 1:00 p.m.

Kearney may be a small town but it does not lack in diversity. If really good Mexican food is what you desire, *laFuente Mexican Restaurant,* 105 South Jefferson (located in the Old Church Plaza Shopping Center; 816-903-9922), serves authentic specialties. Try chilaquiles Mexicanos with green tomatillo sauce or the chile rellanos with a cold Dos Equis. The service and food are both excellent, and they are open seven days a week for lunch and dinner. Hours are Sunday through Thursday 11:00 a.m. to 10:00 p.m. and Friday and Saturday until 10:30 p.m.

Bob and Fern Buhlig have opened their circa-1907 home to guests passing through Kearney. The *Hospitality Inn* is a bed-and-breakfast at 400 South Jefferson. This is a B&B the way they were meant to be. You will feel right at home here because guests are invited to use the living room for relaxation. The home is decorated with antiques, and the breakfast is a crowd pleaser. The rooms are $65, but the "Sweetheart Room" is $95. It has a private entrance, whirlpool tub, fireplace, and a king-size bed and lives up to its name. Call (816) 628-3922 for reservations, or visit the Web site at http://home.kc.rr.com/selnsplace/index.htm.

Western Way Bed & Breakfast, 13606 Henson Road, Holt, is a unique B&B. Over the Hill Ranch, 4½ miles north and west of Kearney, has been Connie and Bill Green's home for more than thirty years. Not only do they take care of people in a wonderful way, but they will also board horses overnight. That is one reason their first year in the B&B business was such a raging success. The production company filming the movie *Ride with the Devil* in the Kansas City area spent time here with their steeds, and Connie and Bill make appearances in the movie as wagon drivers. Country singer Shania Twain is one of the bed-and-breakfast's most famous guests. The singer spent three days at the ranch with her horse while appearing in Kansas City. The Greens have a draft horse now, too, so carriage rides are available for guests. The guesthouse offers all the privacy you could want. A suite with a king-size bed and double Jacuzzi goes for $125 a night. The other room has a smaller Jacuzzi tub and rents for $110. A room in the main house is $120. Horses stay for $25 a night per stall (two or more for $20). Call (816) 628-5686 for information and directions (the driveway is ½ mile long and in the woods) or visit www.westernwaybedandbreakfast.com.

Highway 9 will lead you to the charming little college town of *Parkville,* just twenty minutes from Kansas City. This is a bustling yet pedestrian-friendly crafts and antiques center that moves at a leisurely pace with longtime shops interwoven with new establishments. Wear comfy shoes and a warm coat in cool weather and enjoy the brisk walk between shops. Stop to rest at the *Cafe Cedar* at 2 East 2nd Street, next to the Post Office; it serves Mediterranean cuisine. It is not only luscious food but healthy as well. Owners Osama Aburas and Jahad Saleh are rightly proud of their creations. They offer plenty of vegetarian dishes and any kind of kabob—lamb, chicken, shrimp, beef—you could want. The entrees cover a range from rack of lamb to baked salmon or stuffed Cornish hen. Nothing is fried; everything is baked or broiled. There are six different kinds of salads, lots of sandwiches, and appetizers. Hours are Monday through Saturday 11:00 a.m. to 10:00 p.m. and Sunday noon to 9:00 p.m. Call (816) 505-2233 or visit www.cafecedar.com for more information. *The Skillet* is in the same place and owned and operated by the same people. It serves good old-fashioned American comfort food, like fried chicken and mashed potatoes.

Just past the shopping complex is quiet English Landing Park on the banks of the Missouri. Look for the historic 101-year-old Waddell "A" truss bridge, one of only two of this type left in the country. It was salvaged and moved to its present location. Now it's the focal point of the park, providing a walkway across a small feeder creek leading to the big river.

Peddler's Wagon, a quilt shop at 115 Main in downtown Parkville (816-741-0225), sells anything a quilter may need as well as some country gifts.

There are also classes in quilting and silk embroidery. Hours are Tuesday through Saturday from 10:00 a.m. until 5:00 p.m., year-round, and Sundays October 1 through December 3 from 12:30 to 4:00 p.m.

Of course there is a magnetic attraction when chocolate is mentioned, so you will be irresistibly drawn to **Constant Cravings** at 113 Main Street, Parkville. (Their specialties, fudge toffee and espresso, come highly recommended by a sincere chocoholic.) Owners Jim Scarpino and Ralph Lebedreau added even more to tempt you, especially if you can resist the siren call of chocolate, with speciality gifts to browse among. Winter hours are Tuesday through Saturday 10:00 a.m. to 5:00 p.m. and Sunday 1:00 to 5:00 p.m. Call (816) 587-4200 for more information on hours of operation.

You can't miss **Home Embellishments** at 102 Main in Parkville (816-505-1022). Just look for the yellow building with the purple awning and a funky metal chicken made from found parts out front. Inside you can find brass hardware, furniture, and art from nearly fifty local craftspeople. There is jewelry, metal sculptures, handmade kaleidoscopes, hand-blown lights, fused lights, and lamps made of truck parts (talk about one-of-a-kind gifts!). Alicia deSlon, the new owner, knows her way around Parkville too. She can direct you to **River's Bend Gallery** at 201 Main Street (816-587-8070). Kathryn Buckley and Catherine Forbes will show you a collection of fine arts and crafts, delicate mobiles, and other beautiful things. This gallery is more normal, less funky, than Home Embellishments. Hours at both galleries are Tuesday through Thursday 10:00 a.m. to 5:00 p.m., Friday and Saturday until 6:00 p.m., and Sunday from noon to 5:00 p.m.

Downtown Parkville is loaded with places to shop, so it is a fine day trip from Kansas City. You can find "unconventional" clothing at **Bohéme,** 105 Main Street (816-505-2181), taste wine at **Wines by Jennifer,** 405 Main Street (816-505-9463), scout out new kitchen gadgets at **Now You're Cookin',** 109 Main Street (816-505-2338), or indulge in chocolate, chocolate, chocolate at **The Sweet Guy,** 10 Main Street (816-505-2788). Just pick up a little map of downtown at any shop and spend the day.

When lunchtime comes you have multinational choices. **J. Yoshiko,** 160 English Landing Drive (816-741-9966), a Japanese steak house and sushi bar; **Piropos,** 4141 North Mulberry Drive (816-741-3600), an Argentinean restaurant; **Blue Agave,** 100 South Main Street (816-587-0060), for Mexican food; **Café des Amis,** 112 Main Street (816-741-5387), for a French bistro; and **The Power Plant Brewery,** 2 Main Street (816-746-5051), for a beer and a burger are all downtown. But let's head for **Stone Canyon Pizza** at 15 Main Street (816-746-8686; www.stonecanyonpizza.com). A personal favorite here is the Verdura pizza: fresh mushrooms, artichoke hearts, sun-dried tomato, sweet roasted red peppers, mozzarella, and fresh basil. This is not just a pizzeria, though; it has plenty of other choices as well. The tequila-lime chicken comes to mind. It is a cozy, rustic place with lots of small-town friendliness. Hours are Monday through Friday 11:00 a.m. to 2:00 p.m.

Here's an interesting place to stop just for the heck of it: *H.M.S. Beagle,* 180 English Landing Drive (816-587-9998; www.hms-beagle.com), a shop that makes science fun for both kids and grown-ups. There is a real live scientist on duty every day to help you conjure up your own perfume recipe of essential oils and all other kinds of fun scientific stuff.

The Porch Swing Inn, a bed-and-breakfast at 702 East Street (Highway 9) in Parkville, is the place to bed down for the night. This is the renovated Victorian home of Rhonda Weimer and Ellen Underkoffler. Four bedrooms with private attached baths (and a two-person whirlpool tub in one suite) and a hearty breakfast make this a place to meet new friends and learn about historic downtown Parkville a few blocks away. Rooms are from $90 to $140 a night. Call (816) 587-6282 or go to the Web site at www.theporchswinginn.com.

A former millionaire's estate on seventy-three acres is now the *Basswood Country Inn* Resort at 15880 Interurban Road, *Platte City.* This 1935 lakeside home has six suites—each with two bedrooms and a mini or full kitchen, some with fireplaces, and all in country French decor. There is television, VCR, and a phone in each room. Host Gary Ferguson can direct you to nearby golf courses and antiques malls. Rates are $45 to $379. Call (816) 858-5556 or (800) 242-2775. The Web site is http://basswoodresort.com.

Just off Highway 45, *Weston* is a beautiful town tucked between rounded hills, its past shaped as much by the nearby Missouri River and its thread of commerce as by the orchards, vineyards, distilleries, and good tobacco-growing soils here. After the signing of the 1837 Platte Purchase, it attracted settlers who recognized its rich soil—and appreciated the low prices.

Historic preservation in Weston has been a high priority for many years; the place exudes charm as a flower exudes scent. A beautiful old Catholic church overlooks the town, and tobacco and apple barns stand tall on many of the surrounding hills. It has a foursquare flavor that just feels historic—and in fact, Weston bills itself as the Midwest's most historic town. There are more than one hundred historically significant homes and businesses from before the Civil War alone. Book a tour of the homes (advance reservations are required for the tour; call (816) 640-2650 and ask to arrange a minitour for groups of fifteen or more of two of the homes), or visit the *Weston Historical Museum* at 601 Main Street. Hollywood has discovered Weston, and it's not unknown for movie cameras to roll on Main Street. Life in Platte County goes way back, long before these neat homes were built or the first still was cranked up; the museum will take you from prehistoric times through World War II. Hours are Tuesday through Saturday from 1:00 to 4:00 p.m., and Sunday from 1:30 to 5:00 p.m. (closed January and February). This one is a bargain; admission is free, and it's a day trip all by itself. Call (816) 386-2977 or visit www.weston historicalmuseum.org/.

Weston's **McCormick Distilling Company** (816-640-2276) is a rare treat, 1¼ miles south of town on Highway JJ. They say this is the oldest continually active distillery in the country—or at least west of the Hudson River. It was founded in 1856 by stagecoach and Pony Express king Ben Holladay.

You can't tour the distillery anymore, but be sure to visit the **McCormick Country Store** at 420 Main Street in Weston, where Terri French handles all McCormick goods. You can find mugs, T-shirts, and other gift items as well as a fine line of cigars. There's a tasting room in which you can taste the products of the distillery for 25 cents. Call (816) 640-3149 for more information, or visit www.mccormickdistilling.com on the Web.

Pirtle's Weston Vineyards Winery (816-640-5728) is one of Missouri's most interesting wineries, located in the former German Lutheran Evangelical Church at 502 Spring Street, Weston. Jesus made wine, why not Pirtle's? Owner Elbert Pirtle's striking stained-glass windows depict the winery's logo and a wild rose—the math professor from the University of Missouri at Kansas City is quite the Renaissance man.

Northern Platte County soil is conducive to some fine viticulture; taste the products of these rolling hills Monday through Saturday from 10:00 a.m. to 6:00 p.m. and Sunday from 11:00 a.m. to 6:00 p.m. The Pirtles love to talk wine and vines. Schedule a wine-tasting party here, and don't forget to try the mead, a honey-based beverage once thought to be a "love potion." (So what have you got to lose?) It's sweet and smoky—and so it should be, because it's aged in McCormick Distillery oak barrels. Newest in the mead line are sparkling and raspberry mead. Great stuff and just as romantic as the original. They say that originally the church was upstairs and a cooperage was in the basement, where barrels were made to serve northwest Missouri. The winery now has a wine garden where you can take a basket of cheese, sausage, and bread to enjoy with your wine. Visit their Web site at www.pirtlewinery.com.

Across the street at 505 Spring you'll find **The Vineyards** (816-640-5588; www.thevineyardsrestaurant.com). The restaurant features country Continental cuisine and is considered one of the finest places to eat in the Kansas City area. With that reputation, you'd best call for reservations; the place is charming but small, seating only thirty-six . . . well, forty-two in a pinch, if they push the tables together. The kitchen is tucked into every nook and cranny in the basement. Duck, lamb, salmon, and white perch are just some of the featured items on the menu. Appetizers of baked Brie with roasted garlic and fresh fruit give you some idea of the restaurant's Continental style. Patio dining during fine weather is a treat. There's a nice mix of art and music in the tiny 1845 Rumpel House. Lunch is served Wednesday through Saturday from 11:00 a.m. until 2:00 p.m. Dinner is from 6:00 until 8:30 p.m. Owner Cheryl Hartell says reservations are a must on weekends. There is a Sunday dinner, too, from 4:00 to 7:00 p.m.

Just around the corner northwest from The Vineyards is the ***American Bowman Restaurant*** ("where the Past is Present"), the oldest continually operating pub in Weston at 150-plus rollicking years old. Owners Mike Caokley and Corey Weinfurt offer Irish-style food and entertainment, pewter mugs, and kerosene lamps on the tables. There's O'Malley's 1842 Pub, the Post Ordinary, the Heritage Theater, and malt and hops cellars in the same building. There's an actual brewery here!

At Christmas try the Dickens Dinner; during other seasons, 1837 Dinners, Civil War Dinners, and Nineteenth-Century Irish Banquets are yours for the ordering. For reservations call (816) 640-5235. Hours are from 11:30 a.m. until 3:00 p.m. every day but Monday. On Friday, Saturday, and Sunday dinner is served until 9:00 p.m. Visit their Web site at www.westonirish.com.

Steamboat Gothic describes Sheri and Mitchell Gutherie's place, the ***Benner House Bed and Breakfast*** (816-640-2616) at 645 Main Street in Weston (Sebastion the dog lives here, too). With its double-deck, wraparound porch and gingerbread trim, the jaunty, turn-of-the-century mansion looks as if it could steam away like the nearby riverboats. Brass beds, and baths with pull-chain water closets are mixed with Jacuzzi tubs to add to the interior decor and to your mood. There is a private bath for each room. The view from the second-floor rooms is spectacular. You can see the wide Missouri across the floodplain. Sheri's candlelit breakfasts star her delightful little pastries and secret-recipe muffins. A double room ranges from $120 to $145. A new hot tub has been added that guests may use. Visit www.bennerhouse.com to see pictures of everything.

The ***Missouri Bluffs Boutique*** is full of quirky, unique clothes, jewelry, and handmade purses at 512 Main Street, Weston (816-640-2770; www.missouri bluffs.com). It's like a maze, with rooms opening off rooms, but the clothing is delightful and the art is worth the search. Owner Ann Bollin obviously enjoys shopping to stock the boutique. Hours are Monday through Saturday 10:00 a.m. to 5:00 p.m. and on Sunday noon to 5:00 p.m.

If you're in the mood for something a bit more upscale, the ***Avalon,*** across the street from the museum, offers an excellent beef tenderloin with a bourbon sauce. Kind of a salute to Weston's distillery history, but as tender and flavorful as it's possible to be. A little bar area opens onto a charming outdoor courtyard. Owners/chefs Kelly Cogan and David Scott grill a fine salmon and offer an entire wild game section on the menu. There are pasta dishes and salads and sandwiches for the lunchtime crowd, too. Hours are Tuesday through Thursday from 11:00 a.m. until 2:00 p.m. and then dinner from 5:30 to 8:00 p.m. Dinner hours are to 9:00 p.m. on Friday and Saturday. Call (816) 640-2835 or visit www.avaloncafeweston.com.

Take a short jaunt west of Weston back on Highway 45 to see a view worth going way out of your way for. **Weston Bend State Park** is one of Missouri's newest, and the scenic overlook that spreads a panorama of the Missouri River and rolling fields, wooded loess hills, and Leavenworth clear across the river in Kansas is simply not to be missed. There's also camping, picnicking, hiking, and bicycling, if that's your pleasure. Call (816) 640-5443 for more information.

A bit farther west at the junction of Highways 45 and 92 and almost to the bridge to Kansas is the **Beverly Hills Antiques Mall**—in **Beverly,** definitely not in California. Sure, there are plenty of antiques malls across the state, some better than others. This one's one of the best, with high-quality goods and plenty of variety from fifty-five dealers. No garage-sale stuff here, thank you. The mall is open every day from 10:00 a.m. to 5:00 p.m. You can't miss it; it's in the old two-story Beverly Lumber Company building at 24630 Highway 92, and there's virtually nothing else there—but if you get lost, call (816) 330-3432, and they'll send out the Mounties.

Snow Creek Ski Area (816-640-2200), just north of Weston, is open seven days a week through the cold months. There's plenty of man-made snow (up to 4 feet), lifts, a ski rental, and a cozy lodge for après-ski. Normal costs include a Snow Pass (a lift ticket), plus rental equipment if needed. (Yes, there is down-hill skiing in Missouri; the big hills near the Missouri River are satisfyingly steep, if not long. You can still break a leg if you're so inclined.) Snow Passes are sold thirty minutes before each session, which are Monday through Friday noon to 9:00 p.m., Saturday 9:00 a.m. to 9:00 p.m., and Sunday 9:00 a.m. to 8:00 p.m. Beginning in early January every year, there is a special midnight-madness ski on Friday and Saturday from 10:00 p.m. to 3:00 a.m at the bargain price of $60, including rental. The regular rates vary so much that calling (816) 640-2200 and listening to the recording is a good idea. Snowboards are available, too. To reach Snow Creek from the north, take Interstate 29 south to exit 20 (Weston), then go to Highway 273 and drive about 5 miles. When you reach a flashing red light at Highways 273 and 45, turn right onto Highway 45 and go 8 miles north. Snow Creek is on the right. There is a restaurant and bar, so you can stay for dinner. Lessons are available, too. Check out the Web site at www .skipeaks.com for prices and more information.

Iatan Marsh near the water treatment plant is the place to be in winter if you're a birder. The warmer waters here attract flocks of migrant waterfowl; who knows what you might spot. Nearby Bean Lake and Little Bean Marsh catch the birds—and birders—year-round. You may see rails and bitterns, yellow-headed blackbirds, green herons, and egrets along with the ducks and geese. An observation tower makes sighting easier; Little Bean Marsh is the largest remaining natural marsh in Missouri, a remnant of our wetlands heritage.

If you've read Lewis and Clark's journals, you'll remember the description of an oxbow they dubbed "Gosling Lake." This is now thought to be Sugar Lake in *Lewis and Clark State Park* (816-579-5564; www.mostateparks.com), just off U.S. Highway 59. There's a huge fish hatchery here; you can see anything from fry to fingerlings to lunkers.

St. Joseph ("Where the West Officially Started Getting Wild") is a river town that lost the race to Kansas City when KC was first to bridge the Muddy Mo with the Hannibal Bridge. Still a big and bustling town, it has plenty for the day-tripper to do and see. Consider this: St. Joe has eight (count 'em!) museums. The *Albrecht-Kemper Art Museum* (816-233-7003 or 888-254-2787) has a collection of some of the finest American art in the country, including works by Mary Cassatt, William Merritt Chase, George Catlin, and Missouri's own Thomas Hart Benton. Traveling shows are often exhibited at the Albrecht, including an excellent George Catlin exhibit. Remember Catlin? He's the artist who gave up virtually everything to record the Indian tribes in the early 1800s. It's the best record we have. Housed in an old Georgian manse at 2818 Frederick, the museum has been in operation since 1966. Hours are Tuesday through Friday from 10:00 a.m. to 4:00 p.m., Saturday and Sunday from 1:00 to 4:00 p.m. Entry fees are $5 for adults, $2 for seniors, and $1 for students with any type of ID. Children younger than age six get in free. Go to the museum's Web site at www.albrecht-kemper.org or e-mail akma@sleepy.ponyexpress.net.

Then of course there's the *1858 Patee House* at 12th and Penn, St. Joseph's only National Historic Landmark. The magnificent old hotel was the original headquarters for the Pony Express. It houses a tiny village inside a downstairs room, plus a steam engine that almost pulls into the rebuilt "station." Admission is $5. Also at 12th and Penn is the *Jesse James Museum* (816-232-8206), and the *Robidoux Row Museum* is at 3rd and Poulin. Admission to each is $2. The *Pony Express Museum* at 914 Penn Street chronicles the history of these early mail runs. Admission is $3, and it is open April through October from 9:00 a.m. to 5:00 p.m.

There's a morbid fascination to this next one, the ***Glore Psychiatric Museum,*** at 3408 Frederick Avenue, 1 mile west of I-29 exit 47. The museum is housed in an old, rather forbidding wing on the hospital grounds. If you get a little shaky mentally, consider yourself fortunate; the museum features twenty display rooms of arcane treatments for psychiatric disorders, from prehistoric times to the recent past. (What did cavemen do, you ask? Knocked a hole in your skull to let out the evil spirits. Some patients even lived!) The museum is wheelchair accessible, and admission is free. Call (816) 364-1209 or (800) 530-8866) or visit www.gloremuseum.org.

Missing a museum? It's the ***Sally Rand Museum*** at 1716 Francis Street in St. Joe. Now for you young'uns who don't remember Miss Sally Rand, well, what can I say? She had a career in, um, the performing arts that spanned fifty years. She starred in silent films, but she was most celebrated for her creation called the Fan Dance. (Ah, now you remember hearing of her.) The museum is located inside the historic Barnard House (1877) and is open May through September Tuesday, Wednesday, and Thursday and the first Saturday and Sunday of those months (except holiday weekends). Call (816) 671-0670 or visit their Web site at www.missouribeautiful.com.

As long as we are on the subject of museums, here's a bizarre one that might interest you: The ***Heaton-Bowman-Smith & Sidenfaden Funeral Museum*** at 3609 Frederick Boulevard in St. Joseph displays the state's oldest funeral home, circa 1842, belonging to the state's first licensed funeral director. It is free, but you have to call first (816-232-3355 or 816-232-4428). Find more information at www.heatonbowmansmithchapel.com.

Did we neglect dinner? Oh dear! Find ***Boudreaux's Louisiana Seafood & Steaks*** (816-387-9911; www.heyboudreaux.com) for some good Cajun cuisine in a historic brick building downtown at 224 North 4th Street. *Laissez les bon temps roulez!*

Stay at ***Whiskey Mansion,*** 1723 Francis Street (816-676-1529; www.whiskey mansion1885.com/index.html). This historic 1885 mansion has been restored in Saint Joseph's historic center. The rooms are quiet and full of antiques, and they are reasonably priced between $69 (for the maid's room) to $99. Or move from whiskey to beer and step into the wealthy world of the ***Nunning House Bed and Breakfast,*** 1401 Jules Street, built in 1887 for August Nunning, owner of the Nunning Brewery. This is a grand Queen Anne Victorian like no other in St. Joseph or perhaps the state of Missouri. No expense was spared when this home was built. There are thirty-four original stained-glass windows, including the spectacular one of Romeo & Juliet at the landing of the staircase that measures 8 feet tall and 5.5 feet wide. The front parlor is bird's-eye maple with 10-foot pocket doors. There are seven beautiful fireplaces, a cherry wood

Squaw Creek National Wildlife Refuge, Mound City

dining room with built-in china cabinet, a walnut gentlemen's parlor with a beer cooler built into the floor, and an oak foyer, truly the most luxurious home in St. Joe in 1887. There is even a secret tunnel 30 feet below the basement floor. Rooms are $150. Call (816) 364-1500 for more information.

Visit www.stjomo.com for a complete listing of everything going on in town.

Jerre Anne Cafeteria and Bakery (816-232-6585; www.jerreanne.com) has whipped up home-style cooking since 1930. Everything is made fresh here. Try the gooseberry pie or the fruit salad pie, originated in the 1930s and still sold today to an enthusiastic clientele. The chicken and dumplings are better than Grandma's, and the pork tenderloin is breaded and fried to perfection. They also do a brisk carryout business; the banana nut bread is wonderful. Jerre Anne's is open Tuesday through Saturday from 11:00 a.m. to 7:00 p.m. at 2640 Mitchell Avenue in St. Joseph.

For sheer spectacle visit *Squaw Creek National Wildlife Refuge, Mound City* (660-442-3187), during the fall migration. You may see up to 350,000 snow geese fill the air like clouds. These clouds, though, are full of thunder; the sound of that many wings is deafening. Snow, blue, and Canada geese, migrating ducks, and attendant bald eagles (as many as 150 representatives of our national symbol), plus coyote, beaver, muskrat, and deer make this a wildlife lover's paradise. At least 268 species of birds have been recorded on the refuge. It's an essential stop on the flyway for migratory waterfowl, and it has been for centuries; this area was described in the journals of Lewis and Clark.

There are now 7,193 acres on the refuge just off Highway 159; watch for signs. Unusual loess hills that look like great dunes, reddish and fantastically eroded, are threaded with hiking trails. For more about this area go to www.fws.gov/midwest/squawcreek.

Maryville is home to *Five Mile Corner Antique Mall* at 30622 U.S. Highway 71 South (660-562-2294). Hours are 10:00 a.m. to 5:00 p.m. Monday through Saturday. Gailen and Twilla Hager have 5,000 square feet of antiques for you to peruse. There's more to do here than just shop, of course. For instance, you can visit the Mary Linn Performing Arts Theater to hear a concert or watch a play performed by the Missouri Repertory Company.

If all this antiques hunting has you ready for a bit of quiet, retreat from the world at *Conception Abbey* at the junction of U.S. Highway 136 and Highway VV in *Conception Junction.* Benedictine monks run The Printery House (660-944-2218), where they make greeting cards and colorful notes (ask for their catalog) when they are not going about their real work. Benedictines consider their true work to be prayer—but the work of their hands is prayer, too. Stay over at the 1,000-acre retreat, 900 of which is productive farmland; visit with "the weather monk," or learn along with the seminarians. The Romanesque Basilica of the Immaculate Conception (1891) adjoining the monastery has examples of Beuronese art. Tours can be arranged by calling the guest master at (660) 944-2211 to make a reservation. Visit the Web site at www.conception abbey.org or e-mail communications@conception.edu.

As you near *Lathrop,* your sweet tooth will begin to ache. It's *Candyman's Mule Barn,* 7950 East Highway 116 (816-528-4263; www.candymancorp.com), 600 feet off I-35 at the Lathrop exit. An odd name for a candy place, you say? Owner Alma Collins bought the shop because it resembles one of the mule barns that put Lathrop on the map; the town was once the mule capital of America, selling hundreds of these sturdy animals at the turn of the last century. Foreign buyers flocked to Lathrop, and nearly all the pack animals used in the Boer War were from this little Missouri town. All the barns are gone now, and there's no trace of the busy hotels that housed the buyers; so the original builders decided to re-create a bit of history. The candy factory began more than twenty-five years ago, making the best hand-dipped chocolates to come down the pike. Alma does the same; you can watch the kitchen-fresh candy being made Monday, Wednesday, and Friday from 10:00 a.m. to 1:00 p.m. Retail shop hours are the same. The gift shop also handles other "Best of Missouri Hands" products, including hillbilly bean soup. Lunch is served at the *Hungry Mule Cafe* on Highway 116 (816-528-6294); hours are from 6:00 a.m. to 9:00 p.m. Monday through Saturday.

In *Plattsburg, Tiques & Stuff* (816-539-3232) is Charles and Michele Spease's place on the west side of the courthouse at 108 Maple. It is open Monday through Saturday from 10:00 a.m. to 5:00 p.m.

If antiques—really nice antiques—excite you, visit *Spease Antiques* at 205 Northeast Street in Plattsburg (816-539-3170), which specializes in Victorian walnut furniture. They sold a walnut bedroom set for $15,000. This is no junque shoppe. Hours are 9:30 a.m. to 4:30 p.m. Monday through Saturday.

There are several good places to eat in Plattsburg, depending on what you are looking for, and all of these have been recommended. *Bert and Ernie's* at 108 Broadway (816-539-3484), has the best food, they tell me. *Bo'Bann Beads* at 202 North Main is a good spot to pop in and buy a pretty bead necklace, or a pair of dangling earrings for the girls in your life. Beads galore are there for the do-it-yourselfer. It is not just about beads, though. There are semiprecious stones, cut glass, pearls, and Swarovski crystals. Owner Ann Varnes has classes and ready-made jewelry as well. Hours are Monday, Tuesday, Wednesday, and Friday from 10:00 a.m. until 6:00 p.m., Thursday until 8:00 p.m., and Saturday until 4:00 p.m. You can do a lookie-look or order online at www.bobann beads.com. Or call (816) 539-0065 or (966) 669-8854 toll free.

A little southwest of Plattsburg on U.S. Highway 169 and Highway Z is the town of *Edgerton.* Here *Harmer's Cafe,* 501 Frank Street, has long specialized in old-fashioned favorites such as pan-fried chicken, mashed potatoes, and cobbler. Karen Belt, who took over the restaurant from her mother, hasn't changed it much. You don't mess with success. The green beans are done in the traditional Midwestern way with bacon, brown sugar, and onions and slow cooked for hours. They alone are worth the trip. Call (816) 790-3621

President for (Less than) a Day

The Greenlawn Cemetery in Plattsburg is the final resting place of a man who served as president of the United States for one day—Sunday, March 4, 1849. Outgoing vice-president George M. Dallas had already resigned from office the Friday before. The term of President James K. Polk expired at noon on the fourth. The incoming Zachary Taylor refused to take his oath on the Sabbath, waiting until 11:30 Monday morning. For that 23½-hour period, the nation had no elected chief executive. The Succession Law of 1792 stated that the head of the senate automatically became president should the top two offices be vacant. David Rice Atchison was that man. They say the president slept through much of his term of office. There is no presidential library here, but there is a statue of Atchison at the entrance of the Clinton County courthouse in Plattsburg.

for more information. Hours are Monday 6:30 a.m. to 2:00 p.m., Tuesday and Wednesday to 7:30 p.m., Thursday through Saturday to 8:00 p.m., and Sunday 8:00 a.m. to 2:00 p.m.

Gower is north of Plattsburg on US 169. Every Friday night people from the surrounding region flock here to hear old-time music at a place called *Gower Goodtimes Hall.* They come dressed in overalls or jeans; some carry pillows or chairs. Some carry musical instruments. There is no charge to get in, and none of the musicians will be paid. If it were jazz music, it would be called a jam session. What it is is a regular old-fashioned hootenanny, because only bluegrass music is allowed. No electrical instruments or drums are used, and anyone who wants to participate is welcome.

On an average Friday night, 300 people may show up. Everyone joins in the free potluck dinner while the musicians warm up. The music always starts at 7:00 p.m., when Jim Snyder rings an old cow bell that hangs over center stage. Jim is the power behind this get-together. In 1986 he started to call everyone in the area who played an instrument and invited them all to his house to play. He wanted to re-create on his farm the family get-togethers he remembered as a child. His dad, his uncle, and many of their friends would sit around with their guitars, fiddles, mandolins, and harmonicas to play until it was time to do evening chores. Within a year they had to rent the American Legion Hall. When that became too small, they raised some money and built their own place. Now it has a full stage, sound equipment, and a kitchen. But the generous applause is still there to encourage even the youngest or rankest beginner. Applause and good food and it's all free—what more could you want?

Smithville is near the intersection of US 169 and Highway 92, and if all you know about the place is that it used to flood, you're in for a nice surprise. The town is close by the new *Smithville Lake* for summer fun, and there are plenty of shops to browse in.

Smithville Lake is a fairly recent addition to Missouri's array of man-made lakes. Constructed by the U.S. Army Corps of Engineers to control the flooding that Smithville residents have lived with since there was a Smithville, the lake is also a magnet for water-lovers. Turn north off Highway 92 (between Kearney and the town of Smithville) for sailing, fishing, boating, or just messing around.

Also at the lake is Missouri's own *Woodhenge,* a re-creation of a Woodland Indian site that may have been used as an astronomical observatory around 5,000 years ago. The original location of Woodhenge was uncovered during the building of the lake, and dredging was halted until archaeologists could study the area. It was important enough that the present site was reconstructed as an aid to further study; scientists from Woods Hole, Massachusetts, have come here to observe the solstice and equinox.

Near the new dam at Smithville Lake, one of the largest glacial erratics in the area squats like a patient dinosaur under an accretion of graffiti. A large, pink Sioux-quartzite stone, this elephant-size monster was brought here by the last glacier some 15,000 years ago. It may have been an important landmark for the Paleo-Indians who lived in the area.

At the *Jerry Litton Visitors' Center* (816-532-0174), also near the dam, you can find out about these earliest inhabitants, about visits by Lewis and Clark as they came through on the nearby Missouri River, about the pioneer settlers, and about the birds and animals that make this area home. Admission is free. Visit the Web site at www.nwk.usace.army.mil. Stop for lunch at the *Brick House Cafe and Pub,* 111 North Bridge (816-532-8865).

Places to Stay in Northwest Missouri

KANSAS CITY

Holiday Inn
11130 Ambassador Drive
(airport)
(816) 891-9111
Inexpensive

NORTH KANSAS CITY

Inn Towne Lodge
I-35 North and Antioch
(816) 453-6550
Inexpensive

Marriott at the Airport
775 Brasallia Avenue
(816) 464-2200
Moderate

LIBERTY

Days Inn
209 North 291 Highway
(816) 781-8770
Inexpensive

Fairfield Inn
8101 North Church
(816) 792-4000
Inexpensive

GALLATIN

Sandman Motel
512 South Main
(660) 663-2191
Inexpensive

EXCELSIOR SPRINGS

Monterey Motel
217 Concourse Avenue
(816) 637-3171
Inexpensive

HELPFUL WEB SITE FOR KANSAS CITY

www.kansascity.com

SELECTED CHAMBERS OF COMMERCE

Excelsior Springs,
(816) 630-6161
www.exspgschamber.com

Kansas City (Visitors and
Convention Bureau),
(816) 221-2424

Places to Eat in Northwest Missouri

KANSAS CITY

Cascone's Italian
Restaurant and Lounge
3733 North Oak Trafficway
(816) 454-7977
Moderate

George Brett's
Restaurant & Bar
210 East Forty-seventh
Street
(816) 561-6565
Moderate

Majestic Steakhouse
(Downtown)
931 Broadway
(816) 471-8484
Expensive

Stroud's
5410 Northeast Oak Ridge
Drive
(816) 454-9600
Moderate

AVONDALE

The Depot Saloon & BBQ
2706 Bell
(816) 452-2100
Inexpensive

PARKVILLE

Café des Amis
112½ Main Street
(816) 587-6767
Inexpensive

The Skillet
across from the
Post Office
(816) 587-7272
Inexpensive

LAWSON

Catrick's Café
410 North Pennsylvania
Avenue
(816) 580-4177
Inexpensive

RIVERSIDE

Corner Cafe
4541 Northwest Gateway
Drive
(816) 741-2570
Inexpensive

WESTON

Weston Red Barn Farm
16300 Wilkerson Road
(816) 386-5437
Inexpensive

Northeast Missouri

North of St. Louis the land changes. Hills are gentler; they are the legacy of a wall of glacial ice that smoothed rough edges and brought with it tons of rich, deep soil some 15,000 years ago. Thanks to that gift, quintessentially Mid-American towns are dotted with the docile shapes of cows; barns are large and prosperous-looking; fence rows blossom with wildflowers; and bluebirds and meadowlarks sing.

Northeast Missouri is rich in history as well. That consummate storyteller Mark Twain was born here; he has endowed us with more colorful quotations than any writer before or since. You've heard of Mark Twain Cave and his boyhood home in Hannibal, but did you know that near Florida, Missouri, you can explore Samuel Clemens's birthplace? General Omar Bradley's birthplace is in this area, too, along with General John J. Pershing's boyhood home and a monument to General Sterling Price. (Generally speaking, it seems to be a great place for great men.)

The Civil War raged from St. Louis to the Iowa border, where the Battle of Athens took place. Tiny Palmyra was the site of an atrocity that presidents Abraham Lincoln and Jefferson Davis called the worst of war crimes.

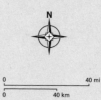

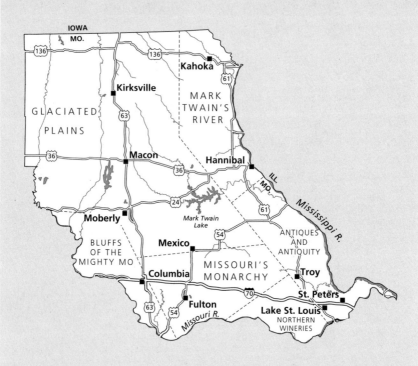

All along the Missouri River valley are tiny, picturesque towns, many with a German heritage, and many with wineries where you can taste the best the United States has to offer. (Mount Pleasant's port won the gold in international competition.) Lewis and Clark passed by these town sites on their way to the Northwest Passage and remarked on them in their journals.

missouriborders

Missouri borders eight states. Only Tennessee touches as many neighbors.

The mighty Mississippi is busy with commerce, as it has been for more than 200 years. Barges churn by, and the power of that mile-wide channel vibrates under you as you stand on a riverboat's deck. The Great River Road, which runs along the Mississippi from New Orleans to its source, is so picturesque that plans are afoot to make it a National Scenic Byway.

Bald eagles feed along both rivers in winter, drawn by open water and good fishing below the locks and dams. Amish communities, college towns, museums, eateries, petroglyphs, wildlife refuges—whatever your interest, you'll find it satisfied in northeast Missouri, where literally everything is off the beaten path.

Antiques and Antiquity

Just north of St. Louis is **St. Charles.** The first capitol of Missouri is located at 208–216 South Main Street (636-940-3320); legislators met here until October 1826, when the abandoned buildings began to settle slowly into decay. In 1961 the state of Missouri began a ten-year restoration project that sparked the revitalization of St. Charles. Shops, restaurants, and delightful little surprises abound. Take a walking tour of history; the St. Charles Convention and Visitors' Bureau (636-946-7776) can get you started. Their Web site is www .historicstcharles.com.

Boone's Lick Trail Inn, 1000 South Main Street (636-947-7000), is an 1840 Federal-style home on the Boone's Lick Trail, right where the trail has crossed Main Street for more than 155 years. Seven guest rooms are decorated in regional antiques, and there are two gathering rooms for the use of innkeepers V'Ann and Paul Mydler's guests. The rooms range from $125 to $160 weekdays, $145 to $285 on weekends. (On festival or other special weekends, there is a two-night minimum stay.) It is close to the airport, the **KATY Trail,** and the casino. Fax (636) 946-2637 or visit the Web site at www.booneslick.com.

The city is the state's largest National Register Historic District, with 10 blocks of mid-1800s buildings authentically restored. Stroll along cobblestone streets, watch the river flow by, and enjoy fine dining, antiquing, and history.

trivia

The Missouri River flows north—the wrong way and against all natural order—along St. Charles County. It flows north for several miles, then turns east to join the Mississippi River. This is one of the few places in the Western Hemisphere where a major river flows north.

Both of our big rivers claimed more than their share of casualties. Steamboats sank with dismal regularity, and to this day—locks and dams not withstanding—riverboat captains watch their charts and take their soundings much as Samuel Clemens did when he sang out, "Mark Twain." The channels of both the Missouri and the Mississippi are graveyards for boats, from tugs to stern-wheelers; the rivers are not to be taken lightly. Our Lady of the Rivers Shrine, a lighthouse-like monument at Portage de Sioux, is a reminder that brave travelers needed all the help they could get. That said, it's time to board at the *Ameristar Casino St. Charles,* 1260 South Main, St. Charles (636-940-4300; www.ameristar.com). The station is off Interstate 70 just ten minutes west of Lambert Airport and gives you two action-packed casinos. The casino on the boat is open from 8:00 a.m. until 5:00 a.m. during the week and twenty-four hours Friday, Saturday, and holidays. Take the Sixth Street exit (229a) just across the bridge.

If you enjoy a little wine tasting, try the *Winery of the Little Hills* at 427 South Main Street, St. Charles. Call (636) 946-9339. If beer is more to your liking, head over to *Trailhead Brewing Company,* at the corner of Main Street and Boonslick in historic downtown St. Charles. Trailhead crafts its own beer and carries a variety of other brands. It's a good place to find a sandwich, salad, or burger, too. Hours are 11:00 a.m. to 10:00 p.m. Sunday through Thursday; Friday and Saturday until 11:00 p.m. Call (636) 946–2739 or visit www.trail headbrewing.com.

People who like to have just a salad or soup for lunch so that they can justify indulging in dessert will love *Miss Aimee B's Tea Room,* 837 First Capitol Drive. Hours are 8:00 a.m. to 3:00 p.m. Tuesday through Saturday. If you're there in the spring or summer, be sure to try a seasonal dessert, such as the chocolate-strawberry pie. Call (636) 946-4202 or go to www.missaimeeb .com for more information.

The *Mother-in-Law House* at 500 South Main Street must first have its name explained. In 1866 a French bride so missed her mother that her understanding husband built her a home with a dividing wall down the center so his mother-in-law could come to America and move in with them. Donna Hafer found the redbrick beauty on Main Street in the historic district of St. Charles and gave it the TLC it needed to become the gracious, antiques-filled restaurant

AUTHOR'S FAVORITE ANNUAL EVENTS IN
NORTHEAST MISSOURI

JULY

Hannibal
National Tom Sawyer Days (and
National Fence Painting Contest),
(573) 221-2477

Macon
Annual Demolition Derby,
(660) 385-2811

SEPTEMBER

Macon
Annual Buzzard Run, car show,
(660) 226-5286

Kirksville
Annual NEMO Tri-Fed Midwest
Regional Triathlon,
(660) 626-2213

NOVEMBER

Columbia
Fall Craft Show, Missouri's largest
indoor craft show,
(573) 874-1132

---

it is today. The dining room has the original oil lamps. Glittering prisms pour a soft glow on the antique furnishings. Fresh flowers adorn each table and the staff wears dainty pinafores. The recipes have been in Donna's family for more than a century and make the salad bar a delight. Her coconut cream pie is renowned in the area.

The restaurant is open for lunch Monday through Saturday and for dinner Tuesday through Saturday. Hours are Tuesday through Saturday with lunch from 11:00 a.m. to 2:30 p.m. and dinner from 5:30 to 9:30 p.m. Reservations are recommended; call (636) 946-9444. Their Web site is at www.motherinlawhouse.com.

This is an area with more than one hundred quaint shops and restaurants plus many art, crafts, and historical festivals offered throughout the year. Be prepared to spend at least a day here. St. Charles is also right on the KATY Trail. If you didn't bring your bike, you can rent one at the *Touring Cyclist* at 104 South Main. The cost is $12.50 for the first two hours with a maximum of $25.00 per day. Call (636) 949-9630.

trivia

The north service road in Wright City was the home of the Elvis Museum. (It was moved to Hattisburg, Mississippi, if you are an Elvis follower.) It was a shrine to The King, with his Cadillac and a reproduction of his tomb. Well, Elvis has left the building. The building is now a Baptist Mission. But it is mentioned here because they do help stranded travelers. Call (636) 745-3154.

AUTHOR'S FAVORITES IN NORTHEAST MISSOURI

St. Charles Historic District	Poppy
KATY Trail	The 63 Diner
Hannibal	Les Bourgeois Vineyards
Mount Pleasant Wine Company	Rocheport
Buck's Ice Cream	

Winfield, Clarksville, Louisiana—the names are strung like beads along the Great River Road (now scenic Highway 79) between St. Louis and Hannibal. These little towns harbor more antiques shops than you know what to do with. There are so many, in fact, that we have room to include only those towns that have additional attractions. Don't let that stop you, though; Missouri is a mecca for affordable goodies. If you can't find what you're looking for, you just haven't found the magic spot yet, and isn't the search as much fun as the finding?

Age-old traditions of quilting, stained glass, blacksmithing, and furniture making are found in Clarksville. Much of the town is on the National Register of Historic Places, and it has a good museum.

Little *Eolia* has *St. John's Episcopal Church* and cemetery, the oldest Episcopal church west of the Mississippi.

Bowling Green features antiques shops along Business U.S. Highway 61. *Honeyshuck* is the restored home of House Speaker Champ Clark. Several miles outside Bowling Green on Highways Y and M is a thriving Amish community. It is filled with talented craftspeople who carry on the traditions passed down to them by their parents. Several families make and sell handmade crafts and bakery goods. A woodworking shop creates beautiful handmade furniture and cabinets. You can arrange for a tour of the area by calling the Bowling Green Chamber of Commerce at (573) 324-6800.

If your sweet tooth needs satisfying while you're in Bowling Green, be sure to visit *Bankhead Chocolates.* They've been making candy since 1919, and experience does make a difference! Owner Laura Portwood says most people tell her that candy is an impulse item, not a destination—"Not with us!" she says with a laugh. But that's not all! This is also the home of an old fashioned ice-cream soda fountain and a bistro, as well. Ah, the bistro—home of the Bistro Salad with candied pecans, strawberries, and bacon. Perfect with a hot smoked-turkey melt or the daily-changing quiche. The bistro is open for lunch Wednesday, Thursday, and Friday from 11:00 a.m. till 2:00 p.m. Bankhead Chocolates is open 9:00 a.m. to 5:00 p.m. Monday through Friday and 9:00 a.m. to 5:00 p.m. Saturday. You can find it at 810 North Business US 61 in Bowling Green. Call (573) 324-2312 or visit online at www.bankheadchocolate .com. Oh yes, order a bag of the white-chocolate-covered popcorn to take with you. It's addictive.

Lock and Dam No. 25 on the Mississippi is a fine place to watch the eagles feed in the winter. Or take the old Winfield Ferry across the river to Calhoon County, Illinois. (Don't worry, you can come right back if you're not through antiques hunting.)

snakingfrolics

Clarksville was called Appletown by river men because of the huge quantity of apples it shipped on the river each fall. But "snakeville" would have been more accurate, because the really big feature of the town was its rattlesnake population. During its early years Clarksville was a choice place for a popular sport called "snaking frolics." The record was set by the town constable, who, along with others in town, killed 9,000 rattlers on one of the town's annual spring hunts.

If you fancy a bit of wilderness about now, a short detour west on Highway 47 will take you to spectacular Cuivre River State Park (636-528-7247; www .mostateparks.com). More than 31 miles of trails will let you discover one of the state's most rustic parks. The rough terrain is more like the Ozarks than the rest of glacier-smoothed northern Missouri, and like the Ozarks, it encourages many plants found only farther south, such as flowering dogwood, Missouri orange coneflower, and dittany. Frenchman's Bluff overlooks the Cuivre River Valley. The Lincoln Hills region, where Cuivre River State Park is found, formed millions of years ago when intense pressures caused the earth to buckle. Erosion cut even deeper; the resulting springs, sinkholes, and rocky cliffs make this an outdoors-lover's paradise. Archaeologists speculate that the region was home to prehistoric humans as early as 12,000 years ago; a 1937 dig unearthed a stone chamber containing a skeleton and pieces of a clay pot.

Clarksville is finding its way back—but back toward the past. With about the same population that it had in 1860, this spic-and-span town has new life in its old veins. A historic preservation effort mounted in 1987 has saved many of the delightful buildings in record time. There are also some new antiques and gift shops open to explore.

The **Clifford Wirick Centennial House** at 105 South Second Street in Clarksville (573-242-3376) is on the National Register of Historic Places. Owner/ historian Vernon Hughes is here to answer your questions about Clarksville or provide you with fine examples of American dinnerware, glass, china, pottery, and prints. There is a fine collection of antique furniture, too.

The house is open Monday through Saturday from 10:00 a.m. to 5:00 p.m. (open a little later on Sunday). It is closed July, August, and September. Vernon says the community is growing, and many skilled artisans, glassblowers, and artists are forming quite a creative enclave. He can direct you to **Harlequin Antiques** (106 South 2nd Street), which is also worth a visit. Vernon operates the shop, which shares the Wirick Centennial House's phone number, (573) 242-3376.

The town commands an 800-square-mile view of the valley of the Big Muddy from an aerie on the highest point overlooking the Mississippi. Surprisingly, barge traffic on the river below is constant—you don't expect to see so much action. See ice-formed drumlins (those are hills) in this panoramic view.

Clarksville is a great place to observe wintering eagles; the Missouri Department of Conservation's Eagle Days, held here the last weekend of January, can swell the town's normal population of 500 to more than 5,000. Is it worth it? You bet it is. Even the *New York Times* visited to check out the bald eagles, which can number from the hundreds to the thousands, depending on the weather. (The colder the winter has been, the more eagles gather here.) The **Clarksville Eagle Center** offers information, a museum, and spanking-clean restrooms. Call (573) 242-3132 or check out www.seatriverroad.com/hannibal/hanevents/eagledays.htm.

Erin Garrison and her husband Bud retired to Clarksville a few years ago and now spend their time at the potter's wheel. This quaint Mississippi River town is dedicated to preserving the past while offering artists the opportunity to work in the restored buildings. They are at the highest point on the Little Dixie Highway (dubbed that when it was the only road heading south) along the river's banks. Recently, she and her husband established the **Great River Road Pottery Shop** at 107 South First Street, where Erin creates unique stoneware pottery. Her signature pieces have original wildflower design brushwork on an eggshell-colored clay body. There is oven- and tableware, oil lamps, and many things for the garden, including flowerpots, planters, and bird feeders. Each piece is wheel-thrown or hand-built by Erin. This high-fire stoneware is oven, microwave, and dishwasher safe, and the glazes are lead free. Erin's working studio and gallery overlook the river in downtown Clarksville. Shop hours are 10:00 a.m. to 5:00 p.m. Wednesday through Saturday, 11:00 a.m. to 5:00 p.m. on Sunday, and by appointment Monday and Tuesday. Call (573) 242-3000. Plan to visit the many artists' studios and antiques shops while in historic Clarksville. Ask Erin about her friend, jewelry artist Gale Bez, who has a shop just down the street.

The entire business district of downtown **Louisiana** is on the National Register of Historic Places and is well known for its antiques shops along

Georgia and Main Streets. There are two museums—the **Louisiana Historical Museum** and the **Phillips Museum.** But most interesting is the fact that it has the most intact Victorian streetscape in the state. Dozens of historic homes line Georgia and Main Streets and it still, of course, has a town square. Also worth a visit, perhaps, is the old **Gates of Peace Jewish Cemetery** off U.S. Highway 54.

There are many antebellum homes in this old river town. The **Louisiana Guest House Bed and Breakfast** at 1311 Georgia Street is a more-than-100-year-old Cape Cod on the Mississippi River that offers spacious rooms, private baths, cable television, and a queen-size bed. You are welcomed by your hosts, Mett and Betty Jo Bryant, with a cheese tray and something to drink, and a full breakfast will be ready for you in the morning. Betty Jo will be happy to give you a map and some good directions to find the nearby Amish community and its many places to shop. Rates are from $85 to $95. Call (573) 754-6366 or (888) 753-6366. Their Web site is www.theinnkeeper.com/bnb/102530.

There is some good antiquing in Louisiana. Right down the street at 515 Georgia Street is **Kate's Attic Antiques and Mini Mall,** with forty booths to browse through. Hours are 10:00 a.m. to 4:30 p.m. every day except Sunday, when hours are 11:00 a.m. to 4:00 p.m. Call (573) 754-4544.

There's a new place to stay in town, too. **Eagle Nest Winery, Inn, and Bistro** has it all at 221 Georgia Street. The bistro can begin your day with omelets made to order, waffles, homemade biscuits and sausage gravy, or jumbo cinnamon rolls. Special breakfasts like the Eggs Ranchero (English muffin topped with shaved ham, Pico de Gallo, poached eggs, and hollandaise) are served from 7:00 a.m. to 10:30 a.m. Monday through Friday and 8:00 a.m. to 10:30 a.m. Saturday and Sunday, and brunch is from 9:30 a.m. to 2:00 p.m.

From 11:00 a.m. to 4:00 p.m. Tuesday through Saturday and from 11:00 a.m. to 2:00 p.m. Monday, you can try the Eagle (hickory-smoked turkey breast, smoked bacon, baby Swiss cheese, red leaf lettuce, tomato, and basil mayo on foccacia bread) or the Chicken Caesar Wrap (grilled chicken in a herb and garlic wrap with Caesar dressing, grated Parmesan, romaine, and red onion) or the daily Pizza Specials, which are different every day.

Dinner is prepared between 3:30 and 5:00 p.m., but coffee and other beverages, soup and house salad, and items from the bakery are available in the bistro during that time, so all is not lost. The bakery prepares all the baked goods at the Eagle's Nest. Jumbo cinnamon rolls, apple strudel, cherry turnovers, muffins, cookies, elephant ears, orange golden raisin scones, breads, cranberry walnut bread pudding, and specialty cakes and pies are warm from the oven.

The winery is a destination by itself. The wines are very Missouri: Pikers Blush is made from Catawba grape; Mississippi River Rouge is Chambourcin grape with some Cabernet and other red grapes; Red Bud is Catauba and various French and American hybrid red and white grapes; Rivera de Sel is made with Seyval, Vidal, and Vignoles grapes; and the Sweet Louisiana Basye is from the Vida and Muscat grapes. Buffalo Fort Norton is made from Missouri's own Norton grape and then aged in oak barrels. If wine is an important part of your dinner, you will enjoy the Thursday Nights After Glow from 4:00 to 7:00 p.m. to taste some of these unusual wines with snacks of the specialty foods from the bistro. The Patio is open April through October. The garden is tucked in by the four Eagle's Nest buildings and a hundred-year-old 10-foot stone wall, providing protection from brisk winds on cool days and a cooler environment on hot days.

If you want to take a bit of Missouri home, The Winery Shop has gifts—a custom gift basket can be filled with gourmet foods, wine accessories, little gift items for the home, coffees, teas, and, of course, any of the wines.

Rooms at the inn begin at $95 and go up to $125 for the suite, and the room rates include full breakfast in the Bistro.

Due to the historical nature and furnishings, children younger than fifteen years of age are not accepted. Everything except the wine garden is nonsmoking. To make reservations or learn more, visit their Web site at www.theeagles nest-louisiana.com. (573) 754-9888.

Mark Twain's River

For tourists, **Hannibal** is not exactly "off the beaten path." Half a million people annually come through this picturesque little town. Everybody knows about the Mark Twain Boyhood Home. Everybody's seen that fence—or at least pictures of it—where Tom Sawyer tricked his buddies into doing his work for him. (The original fence was 9 feet tall and a lot longer than the one that stands here now—no wonder the kid didn't want to paint it by himself.) You may even know about Margaret Tobin Brown's home (remember the Unsinkable Molly Brown?) and the fine dinner cruise on the Mississippi riverboat the *Mark Twain*. So we'll let you find them on your own—it's easy.

But did you know that right across the street, at 211 Hill Street, is the **"Becky Thatcher" House**? Actually Becky was Laura Hawkins, who lived here in the 1840s and attended school with young Sam Clemens. She was his childhood sweetheart, immortalized in print as Tom Sawyer's Becky Thatcher. The upstairs parlor and bedroom of the home are restored and are open to the public at no charge. The main floor features a bookshop carrying the largest selection anywhere of books by or about Mark Twain. First editions and out-of-print books are sometimes available. This is owned by the Mark Twain Museum (573-221-9010; www.marktwainmuseum.org).

Stop at **Becky's Old Fashioned Ice Cream Parlor & Emporium** at 318 North Main for a cool ice-cream treat. The back third of the shop has a collection of Mark Twain books and other children's classics as well. Call (573) 221-0822.

While you're in the historic district, look for **Ayers Pottery.** Steve Ayers does beautiful work, using primarily Missouri clays, and the shop is set up to encourage your involvement. There's a hall around three sides of the work-shop, so you can see every step in the process. He also stocks a selection of beautiful kites, porcelain jewelry, baskets, and hand-forged things—goodies he picks up while on the craft-show circuit.

Even when Steve's out of town, the shop is open at 308 North Third, 7:00 a.m. to 3:30 p.m. Monday through Friday (573-221-6960 or 800-227-6960; www .ayerspottery.com). It's only half a block from the Mark Twain Museum. Steve has opened another shop, aptly named **Java Jive Coffee House,** at 213 North Main Street in Hannibal (573-221-1017), where, along with pottery, Steve also carries coffee beans in many flavors. If you want to try some of them, there is a delightful cappuccino bar in the back of the store. Hours are Monday through Thursday 7:30 a.m. to 10:00 p.m., Friday and Saturday to 10:30 p.m., and Sunday 10:00 a.m. to 6:00 p.m. Steve is involved in a project to list all of the artists living along the river route. While you sip your espresso, he can give you directions to many other craftspeople to visit along the way. Steve also owns **Fresh Ayers, Too** at 209 North Main, where he has a fine collection of primitives and furniture.

One of the first places you will find is **Hammon Glass,** nearby at 115 Hill Street, Hannibal. It is the shop of John Miller, a third-generation glassblower who grew up tending the furnaces for his uncle and grandfather. His shop is in a former bottling plant, all concrete and perfect for his trade. John's grandfa-ther blew lamp chimneys, communion glasses, railroad globes, and functional glassware back when it wasn't so much an art as a functional craft. His father grew up working in a glass shop. Drop by the shop and look at the unique items he makes now. Marbles are his biggest sellers, believe it or not, but there is a wonderful collection of perfume bottles, paperweights, and oil lamps as well as striking free-form sculptures. Of course there are glasses and bowls, candy dishes, and all manner of beautiful glassware. Call (573) 221-3900 for more information. Hours are Monday through Saturday 10:00 a.m. to 5:00 p.m., Sunday noon to 4:00 p.m. (Closed in the winter until March).

If elegant Victoriana is your weakness, stay in gingerbread heaven at the **Garth Woodside Mansion.** This one's on the National Register, and it deserves to be. Mark Twain was often a guest of the Garths. Built in 1871, this stunning Victorian summer mansion is on thirty-nine acres of gardens and woodlands at 11069 New London Road in Hannibal.

You won't believe the three-story flying staircase with no visible means of support; you might not trust it, either, though they say it's quite safe. Enter the walnut-lined library through 9-foot doors, or check out the extra-wide hostess's seat in the dining room (no, the hostess wasn't that wide; it accommodated the voluminous petticoats of the era). The eight bedrooms still have the discreet opulence of Twain's era. The aroma of freshly baked pastries and muffins draws you to the dining room, where the eight-leaf walnut table is just as it was then. You can spend the day rocking on the veranda or watching deer or fox from the library window, and spend the evenings leisurely near a fire. Christmas is an especially fine time to visit, when the mansion becomes a fairyland of authentic Victorian decorations. Rates are from $139 to $395. Call (573) 221-2789 or (888) 427-8409 for more information or visit the Web site at www.garthmansion.com.

Innkeepers Julie and John Rolsen say that the new feather beds make people sleep later. Julie serves hot chocolate-chip cookies every day at 4 o'clock. Not only do the guests congregate for this, even the UPS delivery person and the mail carrier show up. The mansion is in a beautiful setting—thirty-nine acres of meadows and woodlands that retain the feel of early Hannibal countryside. Visit the upscale **Woodside Restaurant** any day from 5:00 to 8:00 p.m. for prime Missouri cuisine.

Garth Woodside Mansion

Don't miss the mansion where Mr. Clemens addressed the cream of Hannibal society on his last visit here in 1902. It's ***Rockcliffe Mansion*** (573-221-4140; www.rockcliffemansion.com), at 1000 Bird Street, Hannibal, a wonderfully quirky place full of art nouveau decor, which was a breakaway style from the established Victorian. It, too, is on the National Register of Historic Places. There are guided tours daily year-round, 10:00 a.m. to 4:00 p.m., and from December through February, noon to 3:00 p.m. There's a small admission charge.

Mrs. Clemens Antique Mall is at 305 North Main Street, Hannibal, and is one of the largest antiques malls in the area. More than forty booths offer a great selection of glassware, dolls, primitives, and all manner of collectibles. Call (573) 221-6427.

If you're at all Irish (and who isn't, at least one day of the year?), don't miss ***St. Patrick,*** the only town in the world (with a post office) named for everybody's patron saint. If you like, send a package of mail containing stamped, addressed envelopes to Postmaster, St. Patrick, MO 63466, to get the special St. Paddy's Day cancellation.

It's more fun to visit the post office, though. The letter boxes are antique, and the hospitality is the old-fashioned kind you'd expect in a town of fourteen souls. Hours are 9:30 a.m. to 5:00 p.m. every day of summer but Tuesday through Saturday 10:00 a.m. to 4:00 p.m. the rest of the year.

The ***Shrine of St. Patrick*** is fashioned after the Church of Four Masters in Donegal, Ireland; the style is ancient Celtic. There's a round bell tower with a circular staircase of the kind used on the Auld Sod. Dublin-made stained-glass windows are patterned after the famous illuminated manuscript, the Book of Kells; the most unusual has St. Patrick surrounded by the symbols of Ireland's four provinces: Ulster, Leinster, Munster, and Connaught. Perhaps you are beginning to catch the flavor of the place.

Oh, yes, there's another unusual attraction: geodes. What's a geode, you may ask? You must not be a rock hound, if you are wondering. A geode is a rather undistinguished blob that looks like a rounded river rock. But inside—ah, inside—there is magic. Beautiful crystal formations fill the hollow center of a geode like a Fabergé egg; they're considered gemstones.

Some of the world's finest geodes are found in this small area. You can buy one at Buschling Place, 3 miles north of Dempsey; the Buschlings specialize in country crafts, turquoise, and, of course, geodes. Or you can find your own at ***Sheffler Rock Shop and Geode Mine*** (660-754-6443), located 2 miles south of Wayland on the U.S. Highway 136 Spur. This is the only geode mine in the United States that is registered with the Federal Bureau of Mines. Watch for the round rock building made entirely of sixty tons of mineral specimens. This shop is open year-round and has been selling minerals, agates, and jewelry-making supplies for more than thirty years. If you come to dig your own geode, bring a rock hammer and a bit of muscle; these treasures don't come without sweat equity. The mine is open in the winter from 9:00 a.m. to 5:00 p.m. and in the summer from 8:00 a.m. to 5:00 p.m. Tim Sheffler will be there to help you. He has expanded the shop and added a huge collection of fossils. There are plans to move part of the facility, so call before visiting.

Bethel is the kind of place you dream about when you're feeling nostalgic for "the good old days," when things were simpler and the world was more easily understood, when people could meet one another's eyes directly and a handshake meant everything. Bethel old-timers say, "When you get it right, why change?" And here, they've pulled it off.

It's not all old-time ambience and down-home goodies. Bethel has a thriving art colony. The town plays host to frequent festivals, workshops, and seminars celebrating its agricultural, cultural, and social heritage throughout the year. Thousands of people flock here for the World Sheep and Wool Festival (ouch! a pun!). Other festivals throughout the year draw folks for antiques, fiddlers, music, and Christmas in Bethel. If you see a line on the sidewalk downtown, likely it's for the family storefront bakery that opens only during festivals. Breads, cinnamon rolls—they've got it. Get in line!

Founded as a utopian religious colony in 1844, the whole town is listed on the National Register of Historic Places. The museum can fill you in on the details; it's open daily.

Bethel is friendly; you're family as soon as you arrive. And it's best to arrive hungry. The **Fest Hall Restaurant** on Highway 15 in Bethel (660-284-6493) serves "good food and plenty of it," the folks say, at reasonable family prices. They also serve homemade pies seven days a week that make it worth jettisoning a diet. Hours are from 6:00 a.m. until about 9:00 p.m.

If you want to stay overnight, the **Bethel German Colony Bed and Breakfast** (same telephone number as Fest Hall) welcomes visitors to four rooms furnished in a simple country style above the Colony Restaurant. Incredibly affordable rates of $15 per person include a country breakfast blessed with home-baked bread and the Fest Hall's own apple butter. (Close your eyes. Imagine the rich, sweet aroma of bubbling apples and spices in an old copper kettle. That's what goes on your breakfast muffins.) Check out their Web site at www.bethelcolony.missouri.org.

Northern Wineries

Take a different loop to see the Missouri River and the little wineries that sprout like vines along its banks. There's a lot of history along the Missouri; whatever your interest, you'll find plenty to see and do.

Take Highway 94, for example. It's for people who don't like their roads straight and flat: mile after mile of two-lane blacktop that curves and winds from St. Charles to Jefferson City. It is one of the most beautiful and exhilarating drives in the state and is a practical route to mid-Missouri for those of us who don't enjoy the mind-numbing 65 mph of the interstate. Since you have this book with you, the assumption can be made that you like to drive, so Highway 94 is a "must-do" trip. Cross U.S. Highway 40 outside St. Charles, go a mile, and turn into the **August A. Busch Memorial Wildlife Area.** This 7,000-acre preserve has nature trails, hunting areas, shooting ranges, and thirty-two lakes for fishing. It features a self-guided tour of native prairie, pine plantation, and farming practices that benefit wildlife. In the spring and fall, thousands of migrating birds can be seen at the shorebird and waterfowl preserve.

Missouri River State Trail, Missouri's part of the KATY Trail following the old MKT Railroad right-of-way, meanders through here, and on weekends large crowds of bikers and hikers wander along the 26 miles of trail from US 40 at Weldon Springs to Marthasville. If you have a bike on the roof, there is convenient parking all along the trail. There are plenty of places to get a meal or rent bikes if you didn't bring your own. There's even a bed-and-breakfast and a winery for a picnic lunch along the trail.

There's a spectacular view of the river beyond the outskirts of St. Louis on I-70. There are so many good destinations along this route that you don't have to tell anyone that you are on it because you like to hug the corners and push the federally mandated speed limit to its max. This road will challenge the best Grand Prix wannabe with its collection of diamond-shaped signs warning of another set of sharp curves. But slow down and watch for wild turkey and deer. Enjoy the tidy farmhouses and pretty churches as you aim for towns such as Augusta, Dutzow, and Hermann that wait along the route.

trivia

Defiance is so named because the local townsfolk were so defiant in gaining a stop for their community when the railroad was being built through the area.

You will enjoy **Defiance**'s little shops and taverns and be amazed to learn that this whole town was under water during the Great Flood of 1993. History buffs will want to take a 6-mile detour from Highway 94 down Highway F to the Daniel Boone home. You could also stop in for a visit to the **Sugar Creek Winery** at 125 Boone Country Lane to taste some of Missouri's wine. Call (636) 987-2400. Becky and Ken Miller will show you around. The Web site is www .sugarcreekwines.com.

Somehow you would imagine a log cabin—or a sod hut, maybe. This beautiful stone house with ivy clinging to its double chimneys, crisply painted shutters, and ample back porch is not what you'd expect at all. Built in 1803, **Daniel Boone's Home,** 1868 Highway F, Defiance, is ruggedly elegant and comfortable. Add a VCR and a microwave, and you could move in tomorrow. Boone lived to a ripe old age. The naturalist John James Audubon described him as a "stout, hale, hearty man." He died here in 1820 at age eighty-six.

Here are Daniel's powder horn and his long rifles, his writing desk, and the very bed where his long career on the American frontier ended. It's a small bedchamber; the four-poster bed looks as if it were just made up with fresh sheets and a clean white counterpane, ready for the man himself to come in from a hard day of hunting, settling the frontier, and making history. Daniel kept a coffin he had made for himself under the bed and periodically tried it out. Alas, he grew too big for it and had to give it away!

The kitchen is cozy, with low beams and a huge fireplace. Mrs. Boone's butter churn sits nearby, and you can almost see the family gathered here, waiting expectantly for that rich, yellow butter to spread on hearth-baked bread. Your tour guide will point out where the whole foundation of the house moved thanks to an earthquake. A chapel, summer kitchen, and spool house have been added on the grounds, and down in a little valley are a number of historic structures that have been moved to the property. A small chapel done in blue and white still hosts weddings set to its 1860 organ music.

Tours are given daily during the winter from 9:00 a.m. to 4:00 p.m. Call Monday through Saturday and Sunday from noon to 4:00 p.m. Spring/summer hours are Monday through Saturday 9:00 a.m. to 6:00 p.m. and Sunday noon to 6:00 p.m. Call (636) 798-2005 or go to www.lindenwood.edu/boone for more information.

Leaving Defiance, you'll enter the Missouri River Valley wine region. There are more wineries along Highway 94 than anywhere else in the state. You can visit **Montelle Winery** at Osage Ridge (201 Montelle Drive, Augusta; 636-228-4464; www.montelle.com), **Augusta Winery** (636-228-4301; www .augustawinery.com), and Mount Pleasant Wine Company in Augusta, and Blumenhof Vineyards in Dutzow. All offer wine tasting and sales as well as great spots to enjoy a bottle of wine with a picnic lunch.

Just down the road apiece from Dan'l's house you'll find the little German wine-producing town of **Augusta.** More than a hundred and fifty years ago it was a self-sufficient town with a cooperage works, stores, and a German school. Before Prohibition, when Missouri was the second-largest wine-producing state in the nation, there were thirteen wineries located in Augusta's valley, beyond the bluffs above the southernmost bend of the river. Deep, well-drained soil and freedom from spring frosts were perfect for viticulture. This is recognized as America's first official wine district and the first in the New World to bear an official "Appellation Control" designation.

Augusta still deserves its reputation. **Mount Pleasant Winery,** 5634 High Street, at Interstate 44 at the Highway UU exit, 2 miles east of Cuba, was purchased in 1966 by Lucian and Eva Dressel (it's now owned by MPW, Inc.). A short twenty years later, the Dressels' 1986 Vintage Port took top port honors in the International Wine and Spirit Competition in London, England, making theirs the first Missouri winery since Prohibition to win an international gold medal, from a field of 1,175 wines and more than twenty countries.

Mount Pleasant's 1987 Jour de la Victoire Ice Wine also won a silver medal, the highest award given to an American ice wine. The **Cheese Wedge,** on-site at the winery, features products made in Missouri. You can buy cheese from Emma (that's a town), sausage from Washington, and mustard from Wolf Island, Missouri. There is cider and grape juice and fresh area fruits in season,

Mount Pleasant Winery

Missouri Vintners—1800s and Beyond

Wine making isn't new to the state. The first designated wine district in the country was actually here in Missouri—not California! In the 1800s the wine business thrived here and the wines were internationally acclaimed. By the late nineteenth century, the entire nation's wine manufacturing and distribution was centered in St. Louis, and Missouri was producing two million gallons a year. It was second only to California in wine production. Then Prohibition shut down the wineries, and the state's wine industry all but disappeared for more than four decades. Only one winery continued to operate during the 1920s: St. Stanislaus Winery, located at a seminary, made sacramental wine for religious orders.

along with the Missouri cheeses and sausage for a picnic in the grape-entwined patio. Hours are noon to 5:00 p.m. Mount Pleasant even delivers! Call (800) 467-WINE for more information. Visit the Web site at www.mountpleasant.com or e-mail mailto@mountpleasantwinery.com.

If you appreciate lovely wooden sculpture and vessels with an elegant, contemporary feel, you'd hardly expect to find them in the backcountry. But at *Michael Bauermeister Studio,* craftsman Michael Bauermeister is full of surprises. He works with Missouri woods to create delicate, finely designed pieces that would grace the best of homes.

Michael's shop is in an old-fashioned store building in the town of Nona, which isn't a town anymore. It's just Michael's house and shop and a few other buildings. Follow High Street west, which turns into Augusta Bottom Road, 3 miles to the shop on the left side of the road. Shop hours are unpredictable because special orders and commissions keep the craftsman hopping. Call (636) 228-4663 to make sure your trip won't be for nothing. Visit the Web site at www.michaelbauermeister.com.

Augusta is a town worth the visit. Click on www.augusta-missouri.com in order to get the grand tour. There you will find a link to *Augusta Wood Ltd.* at 5558 Walnut, which was established in 1979. Works by Thomas Kinkade are on display—beautifully hand-carved early American furniture—as well as art by Jesse Barnes. You can reach them at (636) 228-4406 or (800) 748-7638, or visit www.augustawoodltd.com. Hours are 10:00 a.m. to 5:00 p.m. Monday through Saturday.

There are several bed-and-breakfasts in Augusta. The most luxurious is the *H.S. Clay House* at 219 Public Street. Leigh and Alan Buehre give 100 percent to making guests feel like royalty, including a gourmet breakfast. They serve not just homemade cookies but appetizers and wine at 5:00 p.m., and a glass of port appears in your room with the turndown service. Visit the Web site for more about the Buehres and their beautiful home surrounded with 1,600 feet of deck at www.hsclayhouse.com. You can e-mail hsclayhouse@msn.com or call toll-free (888) 309-7334. Rooms range from $150 to $235.

A one-lane bridge followed by a ninety-degree turn leads you to **Dutzow.** (If you found Augusta charming, Dutzow is downright quaint.) This historic Dutch town, founded in 1832 by Baron Von Bock, was the first German settlement in the Missouri River Valley. In the mid-nineteenth century "Missouri's Rhineland" attracted immigrants who were inspired by enthusiastic accounts of natural beauty and bounty; among the most convincing was Gottfried Duden's *Report on a Journey to the Western States of North America,* published in 1829, which contributed to the settlement of these lovely little enclaves all up and down the Missouri River. The town offers several antiques shops.

The severe floods of 1993 and 1995 were setbacks for **KATY Trail State Park,** which runs along the river for more than 200 miles. This long, skinny state park snakes along connecting towns from St. Louis to Sedalia. Completed portions are at each end, and work is continuing between them. The finely crushed gravel trail allows biking or hiking for 45 miles, from St. Charles west to Treloar. You cross bottomland forests filled with migratory birds, wetlands, fields of wildflowers, and dolomite bluffs. The small towns along the way welcome trail users. You can stop for wine tastings at Defiance and Marthasville and lunch at Augusta.

Blumenhof Vineyards and Winery in Dutzow (636-433-2245; www .blumenhof.com) takes its name from the Blumenberg family's ancestral farm in the Harz Mountains of Germany; *blumenhof* translates as "court of flowers."

Enjoy the winery's Teutonic decor and the welcome invitation to stop and smell the flowers—along with the bouquet of the wine. Blumenhof produces wines from the finest American and European varietal grapes. There's a full range of wines, but dry table wines are a tour de force. (The Vidal Blanc won a gold medal in international competition.) Visit any day except Easter, Thanksgiving, Christmas, or New Year's, 10:30 a.m. to 5:30 p.m. Monday through Saturday and noon to 5:30 p.m. on Sunday.

Marthasville celebrates Deutsch Country Days every October—rain or shine—a German living-history festival on the Luxenhaus Farm, 3 miles northeast of town on Highway O. Everything from homemade jellies and apple butter to crafts and lace is there. There's a covered bridge that takes you to a time when life was simpler. The sweet aromas of sorghum and grilled wurst and *aptel nachtisch* (apple cake) fill the air. Crafters in nineteenth-century costumes make the weekend educational and fun. Watch a lantern being made in a tin shop or see gourd crafters at work. Drink ice-cold homemade root beer while you watch gunsmithing and listen to period music, whistling steam engines, and the ring of the blacksmith's anvil. Tickets are higher at the gate so call ahead, $12 for adults, $10 for seniors, and $6 for children ages six to sixteen. There is no charge for children younger than age six. For more information call (636) 433-5669 or visit the Web site at www.deutschcountrydays.org.

The **Concord Hill Bed and Breakfast,** 473 Concord Hill Road, Marthasville (636-782-2042), offers city-weary guests two large bedrooms and a huge loft that comfortably sleeps five adults. Add a hot tub and full kitchen, and it's an ideal weekend retreat for groups of up to eleven. Try the Carriage House Room, complete with an antique claw-foot bath, an antique iron bed, and a lovely view. A full breakfast is provided, and anything from elegant candlelight dinners to lunches can be prearranged; now that's a getaway. This nineteenth-century farmhouse is in the tiny agricultural town of Concord Hill, population forty; this is definitely off the beaten path! Rooms cost $90 for two guests. Call hosts Maggie Fendelman & George McVicker for more information. The Web site is www.concord-hill.com.

When you are ready for dinner, find **The Gables** at 101 West Highway 47, Marthasville, and let owner and cook Linda Murphy fix you some real down-home food. You are especially lucky if you happen to be there on a Friday or Saturday night, when she's out back fixing her famous barbecued pork. Your nose will lead you to the building with the four gables. It is a "family tavern," as locals describe it, a very casual place with a full bar ("John the Bartender" handles orders here), where children are welcome. Hours are 11:00 a.m. to 1:30 a.m. Monday through Saturday. Call (636) 433-5048 for more information.

Bluffs of the Mighty Mo

Highway 94 winds over steep hills set with ponds and quiet, picturesque farms. Small and almost picture-postcard pretty buildings nestled in the trees are clearly visible in winter and half-hidden in summer; you'll have to look sharp. The highway follows the river through a series of tiny towns that give you a taste of Missouri past. Rhineland, Bluffton, Steedman, Mokane—each is as inviting as the last. Heads up: You may find a great little cafe here or a hidden mine of antiques.

Plan to stay awhile in **Columbia.** It's a great base camp for some far-flung exploring—that is, once you can tear yourself away from the town itself.

Columbia is home to the **University of Missouri,** which has a beautiful campus that houses a number of disciplines. If you have an interest in antiquities, don't miss the **Museum of Art and Archaeology,** boasting a collection from six continents and five millennia. The museum, in Pickard Hall at the corner of

University Avenue and Ninth Street, is on the historic Francis Quadrangle. Built in 1894, it's on the National Register of Historic Places. You'll find artworks by Lyonel Feininger, Lakshmi, Francken the Younger, and many well-known classical and contemporary American artists. The museum is open 9:00 a.m. to 5:00 p.m. Tuesday through Friday and noon to 5:00 p.m. on weekends.

Archaeology has long been a strong field of study at the university, which offers B.A., M.A., and Ph.D. degrees as well as courses in museum studies. The museum's collections reflect almost a century of work by students and faculty in places as diverse as Africa, Egypt, South Asia, Greece, and the American Southwest. Pre-Columbian and Oceanic works round out the collection.

The museum is wheelchair accessible; there are tours for the visually impaired available without prior notice. Other guided tours can be arranged by calling (573) 882-3591 (at least two weeks in advance for groups). See the Web site at http://maa.missouri.edu/ for more information.

The *Museum of Anthropology* reopened after extensive renovations and now has displays of Native America that are most interesting. Included in the displays are an Arctic fishing village and a pre-pioneer Midwest settlement—a one-room prairie cabin and a fur trader's canoe filled with beaver pelts and ropes of tobacco. Call (573) 882-3764 or (573) 882-3573 for more information.

While the museums are easy to find, a well-guarded secret on the university campus is *Bucks Ice Cream,* in Eckles Hall, at the corner of Rollins and College Streets, part of the food and nutrition service. Ice cream and frozen yogurt are made here daily, and it is wonderful stuff. Try their own special Tiger Stripe ice cream. (Just because the nutrition service makes this wonderfully sinful treat doesn't mean it isn't high in butterfat. It is. But what the heck, it is sooooo good.) Hours are noon to 5:00 p.m. Monday through Friday and on Saturday during warm weather (Bucks is closed between semesters). Call (573) 882-1088 or visit http://bucks.missouri.edu/.

The *Flat Branch Pub and Brewery,* downtown at 115 South Fifth Street, needless to say, is very popular with students here. (Students love the homemade root beer and ginger ale.) You can tour the brewing area or have lunch in the pub. Call (573) 499-0400. Hours are 11:00 a.m. to 1:00 p.m. Monday through Saturday and 11:00 a.m. to midnight Sunday. Visit the Web site at www.flatbranch.com.

Columbia has an active and varied crafts community. ***Bluestem Missouri Crafts*** (573-442-0211; www.bluestemcrafts.com) showcases the work of more than eighty Missouri artists and craftspeople. Whatever your particular weakness, from wrought iron to weaving, from folk-art whirligigs to fine jewelry, you'll find it at Bluestem (named after the native prairie grass); the shop is located at 13 South Ninth Street. Shop 10:00 a.m. until 6:00 p.m. Monday through Saturday, until 8:30 p.m. Thursday, and noon until 5:00 p.m. on Sunday. ***Gail Shen's Chinatown*** is a toy store that is art in itself. You have to look for Gail's place because it is upstairs and doesn't even have a window display. But inside the shop is a bright, magical place filled with art and toys. The studio is so very colorful and lively that one little five-year-old boy stopped on the threshold and said, "Oh, this looks like fun!"

Much of Gail's fine art is on the walls, too. She carries her own handmade postcards and greeting cards. It is a festive spot where children can touch things and shop for themselves. Many of the toys are priced from 10 cents to 50 cents. Gail even keeps a tax fund in a little jar for kids who buy four 25-cent items and don't realize a dollar won't cover it.

As the name of the studio implies, she has a Chinese theme with posters, joss paper, New Year's creatures, and lithographs. There are hats and some clothing, too. The shop is at 1013 East Walnut (next door to Ernie's Steakhouse). Hours are somewhat eccentric because of her other job in the theater department of the university, where she makes costumes. Stop by Wednesday through Friday from 3:00 to 6:00 p.m. and on Saturday from 10:00 a.m. to 6:00 p.m. She is there full-time in the summer. Call her at (573) 499-3940 after 6:30 p.m. as there's no phone in the shop.

Another source for handmade and unusual items in Columbia is ***Poppy*** at 920 East Broadway. Whether you are looking for a gift or just browsing around, this is a place with personality, upbeat and colorful. Barbara McCormic and Jennifer Perlow work directly with the artisans who do what they do for a living—professionals—as you can tell from the high quality of their work. The store features hand-blown glass, pieces shaped in clay or created from fiber, and a line of exquisite—and expensive—jewelry. Although there is some two-dimensional art, it is mostly a gallery of fine crafts. The shop is open seven days a week: Monday through Saturday from 10:00 a.m. to 6:00 p.m., Thursday evening to 8:00 p.m., and Sunday from noon to 5:00 p.m. Call (573) 442-3223, or visit the Web site www.poppyarts.com.

One more gustatory note—okay, two: truffles and chocolate pizza. You'll find these and too many other rich temptations to mention at the ***Candy Factory,*** 701 Cherry Street. These folks call themselves "your hometown candy makers," but the good news is that even if Columbia isn't your hometown, they'll be glad to ship anything you want, nationwide. Use the special order number: (573) 443-8222. You can even buy sugar-free chocolates for those people on restricted diets who still need a treat. Prices seem moderate enough; a holiday gift basket ranges from $12 to $52. Hours are 9:30 a.m. to 5:30 p.m. weekdays

and 10:00 a.m. to 5:00 p.m. on Saturday with extended hours in December. Their Web site is at www.thecandyfactory.biz.

Carol Leigh Brack-Kaiser is the talent behind two businesses: *Carol Leigh's Specialties* and *Hillcreek Fiber Studio.* Carol Leigh's Specialties was created to market products made by Carol's own hands: handspun yarns and fabrics colored with natural dyes, woven shawls, blankets, and wall hangings. Hillcreek Fiber Studio is for teaching. It all began with a spinning class at the nearby university. Spinning led to weaving and then to dyeing, which led to advanced studies in fiber arts. Carol began to take her work to living-history events and rendezvous, where people appreciated the labor and old-world methods of her handmade textiles. Now she sits by her adjustable, triangular-shape loom, which she and her son, Carl Spriggs, patented and now manufacture at her home at 7001 Hillcreek Road, just outside Columbia. Today she has several classes in spinning special fibers, floor loom, and in the ancient methods of inkle and tablet weaving. She also conducts classes in Navajo-style weaving and a designer's yarn class. Standing over a simmering vat of wool dye, she produces vibrant colors from indigo; Osage orange (also called hedge apple), which gives vibrant yellows and golds; brazilwood for red, purple, plum, maroon, and burgundy; logwood for lavender and black; cochineal, a bug from Central and South America, for bright reds; madder root for orange-red, and other natural dyes. Carol Leigh asks that you call before you visit (573-874-2233 or 800-874-9328). The shop is open Tuesday through Saturday from 9:00 a.m. to 5:00 p.m. The Web site is www.HillcreekFiberStudio.com.

Formosa Restaurant is upstairs over 913 East Broadway, Columbia (573-449-3339) and serves seven styles of Chinese cooking. While this little spot is sort of hidden away, plenty of people know about it. Lunch is served from 11:00 a.m. to 2:00 p.m. Monday though Saturday; dinner is from 4:30 to 9:00 p.m. Monday through Thursday and until 10:00 p.m. on Friday and Saturday nights. There is full bar service.

Missouri's answer to the Hard Rock Cafe—63 Diner—is just outside Columbia at 5801 North New Highway (573-443-2331; www.the63diner.com).

Bright black, white, and chrome decor, dozens of photos of rock 'n' roll favorites and old movie stars, waitresses in saddle shoes and circle skirts, and the end of that big red '59 Cadillac sticking out of the front wall make the place loaded with atmosphere. The food's every bit as good as you remember, too. Hours are 11:00 a.m. to 9:00 p.m. Tuesday through Friday and 6:30 to 9:00 a.m. Saturday for breakfast

Swing by **Artichoke Annie's** (573-474-2056; http://nnama.tripod.com/dealer/) at 1781 Lindberg Drive in Columbia to prowl around about ninety antiques dealers with furniture and *tchotchkes* from the 1800s to the 1960s. Owner Louann Riggs says it feels like the hours are 8 to 8, 8 days a week. She got the hours right.

Rocheport is a good spot to sample the KATY Trail through Missouri's middle; it is among the longest of the nation's growing network of rail-trails and eventually will stretch 200 miles from Machens just north of St. Louis to Sedalia 90 miles east of Kansas City. The KATY Trail follows the old Missouri-Kansas-Texas Railroad bed that curves along the north bank of the Missouri River, and one of the most scenic parts of the trail rolls from Rocheport southeast to Jefferson City along a wooded band between the river and the cliffs—sheer limestone walls rising 100 feet above the Muddy Mo. The compacted rock pathway is easy riding even for thin racing tires, the canopy of oak and sycamore trees offers brilliant color in the fall, and the trail is flowered with dogwood and redbud in the spring. Summertime rides lead through kaleidoscopic colors of wildflowers and trumpet vine blossoms fluttering with hummingbirds.

Rocheport and many other small mid-Missouri river towns invite modern-day explorers to follow in the footsteps of Lewis and Clark. In the middle of Rocheport is a popular trailhead for the KATY Trail State Park, so whether you choose to follow Lewis and Clark's journey by river, by bike, by foot, or by car, Rocheport is a good place to begin. Missouri's **KATY Trail State Park** is the longest nonmotorized public portion of the entire Lewis and Clark Trail. The KATY Trail travels along the Missouri River for much of its 225-mile distance across the state. The scenery is beautiful, and it is the perfect place to find solitude with Mother Nature along the Mighty Mo. For more information about the KATY Trail, contact the Department of Natural Resources at (800) 334-6946 and order your free color brochure. For general trip planning call the Missouri Division of Tourism at (800) 877-1234 or visit their Web site at www.visitmo.com.

Rocheport is an interesting hamlet; it is so historic that the whole town was placed on the National Register of Historic Places. Its Web site is www.rocheport.com. It basks in the sun on the banks of the wide Missouri River and still has dirt streets, which is fine with the bicyclists who flock there to ride the KATY Trail. But there are outstanding antiques shops, such as ***Richard Saunders Antiques*** at 201 Columbia Street (573-698-3765).

You can rent bikes from the ***Trailside Cafe & Bike Rental*** ($10 a day) at First Street and Pike (closed in winter, November to April; 573-698-2702).

When you've biked up an appetite, stop for pasta at ***Abigail's,*** a family-owned restaurant located in an old church at 206 Central Street. Open Wednesday through Sunday for lunch, 11:00 a.m. to 2:00 p.m., and dinner starting at 5:00 p.m. The menu changes daily. Call (573) 698-3000.

More unusual than just your average antiques shop is ***Art & Antiques & Blacksmith Shop*** at Third and Pike Streets. Here, along with fine art and antiques (estate jewelry, silver, Oriental carpets, and china) is a working blacksmith shop where you can watch demonstrations on weekends. Hours are 11:00 a.m. to 4:00 p.m. Wednesday through Sunday or by appointment. Call (573) 698-3111.

If you are on the KATY Trail then you must be a cyclist or hiker. Look for ***KATY Trail Bed & Bikefest*** at 101 Lewis Street in Rocheport. This historic Adirondack-style carriage house is on the KATY Trail and has four guest rooms. It would be fine for a group doing the trail. There is even an outdoor hot tub, and you will be sent off with a fine breakfast. Call (573) 698-BIKE or visit www .katytrailbb.com.

Cycling works up an appetite, no question, so now you are ready for ***Grumpy's Bar-B-Q,*** 1.5 miles from Rocheport at 4624 Highway 240 (the US 40/Highway 240 junction). Enjoy down-home cooking and atmosphere Wednesday through Saturday from 6:30 a.m. to 8:30 p.m. and Sunday from noon to 8:30 p.m. Feast on barbecue ribs, giant breaded tenderloins, and hand-dipped ice-cream cones. Enjoy indoor and outdoor dining, homemade sides, and pies. There are always Friday and Saturday specials. Call (573) 698-2025.

Okay, you want to get totally off the beaten path? Hit the water. Find ***Mighty Mo Canoe Rentals*** at 205 Central Street and paddle the Mighty Mo with a local naturalist and river historian as your guide. Saturday excursions of up to ten canoes and kayaks depart from the Pebble Publishing Bookstore. Ride a shuttle or bike back from Huntsdale on the KATY Trail. Reservations required. Go to www.mightymo.com or call (573) 698-3903.

If it's not telling tales out of school, you may want to enroll for a term at the ***School House Bed and Breakfast*** at 504 Third Street, Rocheport (573-698-2022). Innkeepers Mike and Lisa Friedemann run this big foursquare edifice at Third and Clark Streets and made it more inviting than any school we've seen. The three-story school was built in 1914 and served as the area's cultural center for more than sixty years.

There are now ten guest rooms, each with its own style; there are antique bathtubs, sinks, and toilets. The Teacher's Pet Suite contains a two-person Jacuzzi. The garden courtyard invites relaxation. Room rates are from $115 to $260 per night and include a hearty country breakfast. Visit online at www .schoolhouseBB.com.

The family-owned winery ***Les Bourgeois Vineyards*** (573-698-3401) welcomes visitors. It is located south of Rocheport on Highway BB, 1 mile north of I-70. Admire a spectacular view of the Missouri River and watch the barges float by as you sample Bordeaux-style wines—plus a generous basket of Missouri sausage, cheese, and fresh fruit. Wine garden hours are noon to sunset, Monday through Saturday; Sunday noon to 6:00 p.m. from March through November, but the winery and sales room are open every day of the year from 11:00 a.m. to 6:00 p.m. Now lunch is served daily except Wednesday, and ethnic or regional theme dinners are served from 5:30 to 8:30 p.m. on Friday and Saturday.

All this driving makes a body thirsty, but by now you've had enough wine; how about an old-fashioned cherry phosphate? Or maybe a thick, rich malt made with hand-dipped ice cream? Stop by tiny ***Glasgow,*** where you'll find ***Henderson's,*** at 523 First Street, a fifth-generation drugstore on the main drag. They'll fix you the fantasy float of your dreams. Hours are Monday through Friday from 7:00 a.m. until 5:30 p.m., Saturday until 2:00 p.m. Call (660) 338-2125.

Glasgow's narrow, two-story city hall has a surprised expression; the round-topped windows look like raised eyebrows. But there's nothing too shocking in this historic little town unless you discover that the old bridge on Highway 240 is the world's first all-steel bridge, built in 1878. Eight hundred tons of steel were used in construction at a cost of $500,000; it costs more than that to salt the wintry streets of a small city today.

Near Fayette is the only spot in the entire Western Hemisphere—that's hemisphere, folks—where you'll find inland salt grass. ***Moniteau Lick,*** near the more familiar Boone's Lick, is the place. This area was once important for naturally occurring salt; there are more than eighty place names in Missouri containing the words "salt" or "saline."

Glaciated Plains

Civil War buffs will discover the General Sterling Price Monument by the highway at ***Keytesville.*** This is the heart of Little Dixie, the part of the state with its roots firmly in the South. The original courthouse, circa 1834, was burned by Bushwackers—bands of Confederate renegades who spent their time burning farms and killing Union sympathizers—in 1864. George Todd and John

Thralkill, with 130 men, surrounded a Union garrison of 35 men stationed in the fortified courthouse. When they surrendered, it was torched.

Sterling Price came to Missouri from his native Virginia in 1831. His father, mother, sisters, and brothers, who were all adults, came by ox wagon with their household goods. Slaves drove the livestock. He married and raised seven children at Val Verde, his family home. He became Missouri's eleventh governor in 1853 and served two terms. But with the threat of war he felt compelled to cast his lot with the Confederacy, although he favored the Union. He became a Confederate general in April 1862 and participated in several battles for the state—at Lexington, Pea Ridge, Poison Springs, Helena, Wilsons Creek, and West Port—but was forced to retreat south.

At the close of the war, General Price went to Cordova, Mexico, where he was granted a tract of land by Emperor Maxmillian to establish a colony for ex-Confederate soldiers. That failed with the fall of Maxmillian's government. Price returned to Missouri in 1867 and died in St. Louis that year. The **General Sterling Price Museum** (412 Bridge Street, Keytesville; 660-288-3204) is at 303 West Bridge Street, Keytesville, in the Masonic Lodge Building.

The magnificent, three-story **Hill Homestead,** also in Keytesville, is open for tours during the summer months. It was built by William Redding in 1832. He was killed there by Union soldiers.

Farther north you'll pass through a real Mickey Mouse town (**Marceline** is where Walt Disney grew up) on your way to Brookfield. Every Labor Day, hot-air balloon races are held nearby. There's a sustained *swooooosh* as the balloons lift off; it sounds like the sharp intake of the watching crowd's breath, but it's the hot breath of the craft themselves, rising in the morning air. More than fifty balloons join in the fun, filling the sky with crayon-box colors.

From here, a short jaunt north and west will take you to **Laclede** and the **General John J. Pershing Boyhood Home.** The rural gothic building is a National Historic Landmark and is as ramrod straight as the old man himself, softened with just a bit of gingerbread. The museum highlights Pershing's long career. Only 3 miles away is **Pershing State Park** (www.mostateparks .com/pershingsite.htm), with the largest remaining wet prairie in Missouri, Late Woodland Indian mounds, and the War Mothers Statue. Also, Locust Creek Covered Bridge State Historic Site is just north of Pershing's home.

You are now in what is known as the Glaciated Plains. A good example of the huge Laurentide ice-sheet movement is the **Bairdstown Church Erratic,** a huge, pink, lichen-covered granite boulder that stands 10 feet high, 20 feet wide, and 24 feet long and is estimated to weigh the same as a Boeing 747 (768,000 pounds). It sits in the middle of a pasture on the Dunlop family farm near Milan. Over the years these huge gifts from the north have been cut by pioneers for millstones or converted to monuments. This one remains untouched. It came to the state when the glacier pushed its way from Canada 175,000 years ago. It is obviously a very strange visitor to this flatland.

Open farmland dominates Highway 5 North; the rolling hills recall the prairie that covered much of presettlement Missouri. East of Milan on Highway 6 discover busy *Kirksville* and environs. There's a lot happening in Kirksville, as always in a college town. This is the home of Truman University and the *Kirksville College of Osteopathic Medicine*—lots of lively young things running around here, having fun, eating out, and just generally being college kids.

Is your family doctor an M.D. or a D.O.? If he is a Doctor of Osteopathy (D.O.), his profession got its start right here in Kirksville when Andrew Taylor Still established the first school of the osteopathic profession in 1892, in a one-room schoolhouse. The college has grown; today there are fifteen buildings (including two hospitals) on a fifty-acre campus, and the student body numbers more than 500. Former United States Surgeon General C. Everett Koop delivered the 1988 commencement address.

Visit the *Andrew Taylor Still National Osteopathic Museum* at 311 South Fourth Street, Kirksville, weekdays from 10:00 a.m. to 4:00 p.m., Saturday from noon to 4:00 p.m. It's a three-building complex that includes the log cabin birthplace of Dr. Still, the tiny white clapboard cabin that served as the school, and the museum itself, with its impressive collection of osteopathic paraphernalia. Admission is free.

Buildings of many architectural styles, from Romanesque and Renaissance Revival to Italianate and Victorian, from Art Deco and Art Nouveau to Beaux Arts and Prairie, strut their stuff on the walking tour of Old Towne Kirksville. Begin the grand tour at Old Towne Park (Elson and Washington Streets) and follow the signs, or pick up a map at any of the businesses marked with a red flag. It's only 1½ miles by foot—but well more than one hundred years if you're traveling in time.

When the nightlife gets too much for you in hoppin' Kirksville, head out of town to *Thousand Hills State Park.* This part of Missouri was sculpted by glaciers; rich, glacial soil is the norm, not the exception, and the streams and rivers that cut through this deep soil formed the "thousand hills."

The park straddles the Grand Divide. Like the Continental Divide, this geologic landform is an area where high ground determines the direction of surface water drainage. It always seems as if you should feel the difference as you cross, but you don't. This mini-mountain ridge runs along U.S. Highway 63 from the Iowa-Missouri border to just south of Moberly; western streams and rivers flow into the Missouri River, eastern waters into the Mississippi.

Where to Winter If You're a Canada Goose

Swan Lake National Wildlife Refuge is the wintering grounds for one of the largest concentrations of Canada geese in North America. This 10,670-acre refuge also attracts more than one hundred bald eagles each winter. The main entrance is 1 mile south of Sumner on County Road RA. Photography and birdwatching are permitted, and there is a 3/4-mile habitat trail and observation tower.

Much of the park is remnant prairie—look for big bluestem, rattlesnake master, blazing star, and Indian grass, which are maintained by periodic burning. Because of the cooler climate here, you'll find plants not found in other parts of the state, such as the lovely interrupted fern in the deep ravines in the park. There is a natural grove of large-toothed aspen, a tree common to northern states but quite rare in Missouri. In Thousand Hills State Park, you can find our grand-champion aspen.

If prehistory interests you more than natural history, don't miss the petroglyphs near camping area no. 3. Archaeologists believe these crosses, thunderbirds, sunbursts, and arrows were scratched into the sandstone by peoples who inhabited the site between A.D. 1000 and 1600. They may have been reminders of the order of the ceremonial rituals passed along by the Middle Mississippi culture, which were in use for a long period of time. Many glyphs appear to have been carved by hunters of the Late Woodland culture between A.D. 400 and 900. The site is listed on the National Register of Historic Places; it's nice to know this list contains more than the usual antebellum mansions and federal-style courthouses we seem to expect.

Take the highway south to **Ethel**—that is, if you love hand-thrown pottery. This little town is the home of *Clay Images,* 23067 Highway 149 (660-486-3471). Jim and Melissa Hogenson are well-known artists who work in clay; you may have seen their whimsies—dragons and wizards—at Renaissance festivals around the country. Don't miss this little gold mine (all right, clay mine). Visit the Web site at www.clayimages.com or e-mail clayimages@cvalley .net. Visit in person by appointment only.

It seems that everyone in this town of barely a hundred people must own a little business of some kind. The *Ethel Museum* is now open at 211 West Main Street. The next stop for lunch is the *Santa Fe Restaurant* at 120 East Main Street (660-486-3334). Owners Ray and Velma Mager will tempt your palate with steaks, chicken, and pork chop specialties. Homemade breads and desserts will top off your meal. Hours are Thursday and Friday from 5:00 a.m.

to 8:30 p.m., Saturday from 7:00 a.m. to 8:30 p.m., and Sunday from 11:00 a.m. to 2:00 p.m. (closed in January).

Visit **Weathervane Antiques,** owned by Paul and Phyllis Tate, at 2214 US 63 in **Macon** (660-385-2941), for a walk down memory lane. It's open seven days a week from 10:00 a.m. to 5:00 p.m. If you are just in the mood for a sweet treat, there is a soda fountain in **Miller's Rexall Drug Store** at 115 Vine Street, where you can sip a cherry phosphate or have a vanilla coke. Call (660) 385-2147.

There are several B&Bs in Macon, too, so if you relax and enjoy the nearby golf course and antiques shops in town, and shop till you drop, you can choose where to drop. One of them is the **Phillips Place Bed & Breakfast,** at 705 Jackson Street, Macon, owned by Carol and Scott Phillips. It is a yellow-brick house surrounded by a black iron fence. Built in 1899, it boasts a big, comfortable front porch with a swing. There are four suites, a day spa, hot tub, sauna, and even a lap pool. There is also a massage room with a massage therapist to make this the most relaxing of stays. Rooms are $129 to $169. Call (660) 385-3535. You can visit their Web site at www.phillipsplacebandb.com.

Tiny **Ten Mile** just north of Macon doesn't even show on the map; it's an Amish community near Ethel. Watch for little yard signs; many of these places have tiny shops on the farmstead where baked goods, yard goods, homemade candy, and baskets or quilts are sold.

Moberly is made up of farms in the Amish countryside, which begins at the end of Urbandale Drive and goes all the way to the town of Clark. **C.C. Sawyer's,** at 104 West Wightman Street in Moberly, has great steaks and seafood cooked on a wood-fire grill. Open Tuesday through Saturday 5:00 to 9:00 p.m. Call (660) 263-7744.

Take the grand tour through **Paris** (no, not the long way around; this is Paris, Missouri). Tiny **Florida** is the closest town to the **Mark Twain Birthplace State Historic Site** (573-565-3449) and **Mark Twain State Park,** which offers camping, swimming, and river recreation. Visit www.mostateparks/twainpark.htm. The two-room cabin where Samuel Clemens came into the world reminds you of something; it could have come straight from one

strangeasitsounds

If you can, find Founder's Cemetery on the north edge of Paris. It is listed in *Ripley's Believe It or Not* because it is the home of possibly the only tombstone in the world to list three wives of one husband.

As long as you are searching out cemeteries, find the Walnut Grove Cemetery and take a good look at the caretaker's building. Its architecture is Little Dixie Victorian, and it was constructed around 1870. The round turret originally enclosed a water tower for water storage.

of his books. A bit of Twain was Tom Sawyer and Huck Finn (you remember Huck, that red-haired scamp who lived life to the hilt, devil-take-the-hindmost). If you've read *The Adventures of Huckleberry Finn,* this won't come as a big surprise.

What is a surprise is that the two-room cabin is totally enclosed in an ultra-modern museum, which houses first editions of Clemens's works, including the handwritten version of *Tom Sawyer* done for British publication. Sit in the public reading room to conduct personal research—or just to get in touch with the old wag. For example, Twain once wrote, "Recently someone in Missouri has sent me a picture of the house I was born in. Heretofore I always stated that it was a palace but I shall be more guarded now." There is an admission charge. Hours are 10:00 a.m. to 4:30 p.m. seven days a week; in winter (November to April), closed Monday and Tuesday.

On the second full weekend of August each year, the U.S. Army Corps of Engineers, the Missouri Department of Natural Resources, and the Friends of Florida sponsor the Salt River Folklife Festival in the tiny town of Florida.

Although this is not Madison County, 5 miles west of Paris and 3 miles south on County Road C, you'll find a different kind of nostalgic symbol, the **Union Covered Bridge.** It is the only Burr-arch covered bridge left in the state. Named for the Union Church, which once stood nearby, this 125-foot-long, 17½-foot-wide bridge was built in 1871.

You can almost hear the clatter of horses' hooves and the rumble of wagon wheels through the old wooden tunnel. (You'll have to use your imagination; the recently restored bridge is open to foot traffic only—it's blocked to vehicles.) A set of interpretive displays at the unmanned site fills you in on covered-bridge history in Missouri. Call the Mark Twain Birthplace at (573) 565-3449 for information and directions to the bridge.

After a picnic at the covered bridge, continue west on U.S. Highway 24 to Highway 151. (Pay attention, now.) Go south to Highway M. After a few miles you will come to Highway Y. A drive south on Y will take you through another Amish community. There are no retail shops along the route except Sam's Store, which has no sign out front—you have to ask for directions—but there are signs in the yards offering a variety of handmade goods, including homemade candy, quilts, and furniture. Fresh garden produce, eggs, and honey are also sold. You can get off the highway and take many small buggy roads to explore the community. Small schools, like the one named Plain View, dot the landscape, and buggies leave dust trails on the roads. This is Middle America in its simplest form.

There are some pretty exotic destinations around here, aren't there? Milan, Paris—and now *Mexico,* south of "gay Paree." Mexico is called "Little Dixie," because of its strong Southern sympathies during the Civil War; now you can visit the Little Dixie Wildlife Area nearby.

In Mexico is the *Graceland House Museum,* at 501 South Muldrow, a stately antebellum mansion housing the Audrain County Historical Society. It is located in the eleven-acre Robert

ancienttrees

If you are interested in antique trees, look at the bicentennial tree at 710 Cleveland. This oak tree is more than 300 years old. There is a California redwood tree at 406 West Monroe that was brought by covered wagon from California in 1832.

S. Green Park, which has a playground, picnic area, and gracious lawn. It is one of the oldest homes in the county, built in 1857. This Greek Revival home is listed in the National Register of Historic Places. You can experience the lifestyle of the era with wedding dresses, an extensive doll collection, china, silver, and antique furniture as well as antique tools. Hours are from 1:00 to 4:00 p.m. Tuesday through Saturday and from 2:00 to 5:00 p.m. Sunday. Admission is $3 for adults and $1 for children.

American Saddlebred Horse Museum is also at 501 South Muldrow. Here is a fine-art exhibit including works by artists George Ford Morris, Gladys Brown, and B. Beaumont, and Saddlebred primitives by Audrain McDonough from the 1920s. Many famous horses are featured in the photographs and paintings. Hours and admission are the same as Graceland.

The *Audrain Country School,* also part of this complex, was constructed in 1903 and is furnished with authentic items used in country schools—slate blackboards, desks, games, and other memorabilia saved from rural schools in the county. An outhouse behind the school adds to the authenticity of the setting. Call (573) 581–3910 for information on all three places. The complex is closed from December 22 to February 1. Visit their Web site at www.audrain .org.

Notice all the redbrick buildings in the Mexico/Vandalia area? The land is underlaid with a type of refractory clay that makes great bricks; there are still four brick plants in Audrain County.

A 14-mile jog back east from Mexico will take you to *Centralia.* Don't miss it if you enjoy "kinder, gentler" countryside. *Chance Gardens* includes a turn-of-the-last-century mansion, home of the late A. Bishop Chance. Built in 1904, its onion-domed turret, gracious porticoes, and ornate woodwork invite visitors with an eye for elegance. A gift to the public from the A. B. Chance Company (the town's largest industry), it's been Centralia's showplace for years.

The gardens that surround the home say something about the kind of luxury money can't buy. It takes time to plan those masses of color that bloom continu-

ously through the seasons and lead the eye from one brilliant display to another—
time to plan and time to maintain. That's a luxury most of us don't have.

While you are there, you will want to visit the ***Centralia Historical
Society Museum*** at 319 East Sneed Street, in a house built in 1904 and dedicated to preserving and exhibiting artifacts that document the history of the
area. In the fall the museum is host to a quilt show, and hundreds have been
showcased here. Hours are from 2:00 to 4:00 p.m. Wednesday and Sunday,
May through November. Call (573) 682-5711 or visit http://centralia.missouri
.org/history.shtml.

Tiny ***Clark,*** a hoot and a holler from Centralia, is the birthplace of Gen.
Omar Bradley. There's an active Amish community in the Clark area; watch for
those horses and buggies. Some sport bumper stickers, much easier to read at
this speed than on the interstates. I'M NOT DEAF, I'M IGNORING YOU AND I MAY BE SLOW,
BUT I'M AHEAD OF YOU seem to be local favorites. You'll want to slow down yourself to admire the clean, white homes and commodious barns of the Amish.

Missouri's Monarchy

Winston Churchill journeyed to ***Fulton*** to address Westminster College in
1946 just after he had been defeated for reelection as England's prime minis-
ter. Churchill delivered the most famous speech of his life, the "Iron Curtain"
speech. "From Stettin in the Baltic to Trieste in the Adriatic, an iron curtain
has descended across the Continent. Behind that line lie all the capitals of the
ancient states of Central and Eastern Europe. . . . "

The invitation to speak at Westminster College had a handwritten note at
the bottom in a familiar scrawl: "This is a wonderful school in my home state.
Hope you can do it. I'll introduce you. Best regards, Harry Truman." The president and his respected friend arrived in Fulton on March 5, 1946. The Cold
War is over now and the iron curtain lowered, but the ties between the college, the town, and Great Britain remain unbroken. In the 1960s Westminster
president R.L.D. Davidson wanted to honor those ties. The resulting plan
was bold and perfect—if not as well-publicized as the move of the London
Bridge to Arizona. The college acquired the centuries-old Church of St. Mary
the Virgin from Aldermanbury, England, and dismantled it stone by stone.
The edifice was shipped across the Atlantic and cross-country to Fulton,
where it was reconstructed on the Westminster campus (Harry Truman himself turned the first spade of earth in 1964), and re-dedicated in 1969. It now
houses the ***Winston Churchill Memorial and Library,*** at 501 Westminster
Avenue, Fulton (573-592-5369; www.churchillmemorial.org), currently the only
center in the United States dedicated to the study of the man and his works.

Churchill's original oil paintings (the very public man had a private side, and enjoyed relaxing with his paints), letters, manuscripts, family mementos, and other memorabilia are on display, in addition to the fire-scarred communion plate rescued from the ruins of the church after World War II.

The church itself is deeply historical; built in twelfth-century London, it was redesigned in 1677 by Sir Christopher Wren, one of the finest architects of the period. Damage caused by German bombs seemed to signal its end until Westminster College stepped in to rescue the building. It is open from 10:00 a.m. to 4:30 p.m. seven days a week. Tours are available.

The Berlin Wall fell in 1989, and a piece of it, marked with angry graffiti of the past, was made into a sculpture by Churchill's granddaughter, Edwina Sandys. She cut out simple but powerful shapes of a man and a woman as openings in the wall and called it *Breakthrough*. That piece now stands on campus. In 1992 Mikhail Gorbachev spoke at Westminster, further symbolizing the end of the Cold War.

thekingdomof callaway

Callaway County in effect seceded from both North and South and stood independent briefly as the Kingdom of Callaway, when federal troops deposed Governor Jackson and established a provisional government in Jefferson City during the Civil War.

The *Auto World Museum* at 200 Peacock Drive in Fulton (573-642-2080; www.autoworldmuseum.com) has rare cars (among them the shiny black 1931 Marmon, a sixteen-cylinder car gangsters made infamous), vintage fire trucks (including a 1922 Ahrens Fox Pumper), tractors, and buggies. Open April through November, it is the dream come true of Bill Backer. Bill has been collecting and restoring old cars for almost fifty years. When the local K-Mart left town, Bill had the opportunity to grab 37,000 square feet of work space. When he moved in he thought he would open a museum for a month or so to show off his cars. It became so popular that he decided to divide the area and use the front as a museum and the back as a workroom. The rare cars were a hit—cars such as a Stanley Steamer, a DeLorean, and a 1986 Pulse (not old, but only sixty of these motorcycles-become-cars were made). They are right there with the Edsel and Studebaker as unique collectibles. He also has an 1875 Haynes, the only one in the United States in private hands (there is one in the Smithsonian in Washington, D.C.). If you want to see a great collection of more than one hundred vehicles, from horseless carriages to solar cars, this is the place. There is also a gift shop with local artisans contributing military memorabilia, railroad collectibles, fine china and crystal, and a little bit of flea market. In addition there's a large display of Kennedy memorabilia. You can

Biscuits and Gravy—the Ultimate Test

I have been writing since 1985, and as I read my notes and journals, it seems that most of my memories revolve around food. So it doesn't surprise me that I gain weight with each book I write. I have photos to remind me of the Eiffel Tower, but when someone asks, "best meal of your life?" my memory of sweetbreads in champagne sauce take me back to Paris, the world's most beautiful city.

And so it is with Missouri. I remember strolling along Washington's Front Street and watching the river amble by, hearing the trains approaching along the track that parallels the river, but if someone asks, "best biscuits and gravy?" I remember a little diner in town. The waitress heard me say I had never had biscuits and gravy. So she gave me no breakfast option. I would have biscuits and gravy. They were wonderful: soft flaky biscuits covered with thick, sausage-filled gravy. Since that fateful day I have ordered B&G at hundreds of restaurants, and it has never been the same. Hockey pucks covered with Elmer's glue—bland, dry, tasteless attempts at a meal fit for the gods. It is my ultimate test of an eating establishment that claims to serve breakfast.

Fried chicken—now there's another test. The best pan-fried chicken in the state is at Stroud's in Kansas City. Served family style on big platters with green beans and mashed potatoes covered with pan gravy, it is an all-you-can-eat-and-take-the-rest-home heaven. Oh my, is it any wonder you have to get there before they open to line up for a seat?

When I wrote about Arkansas, it was fried catfish and hamburgers (in honor of President William Jefferson Clinton) I searched out, but none of the hamburgers matched the tiny burgers at Hayes Hamburgers in suburban Kansas City.

In Kansas it was fried chicken and muffins (it seems that most of the B&Bs in Kansas make delightful muffins that are soft and warm and huge) that drew my attention. And while Missouri is famous for its steak and barbecue, there was a cold, smoked-trout dish at the Blue Heron in Osage Beach that has lingered in my memory for years.

Say what you will about scenic highways, back-road museums, and shopping, what is really important is the answer to the age-old question: "Where should we eat?"

---

make an appointment for a tour in the winter, too.

The *Loganberry Inn,* a turn-of-the-last-century Victorian home, offers guests bed-and-breakfast accommodations at 310 West Seventh Street, Fulton, only a block from Westminster College. This inviting 1899 Victorian home welcomed Margaret Thatcher in 1996. Hosts Carl and Cathy McGeorge bake fresh cookies for your arrival and serve a gourmet breakfast on fine china each morning. It is walking distance from the Churchill Memorial Museum and the Rare Car Museum downtown. The Loganberry Inn offers many creative packages to suit the traveler. One of the most popular is the Fireplace Dinner for two, for those weary travelers who arrive late on Friday and wish for a private, intimate repast in their room by the fire. Then there is the Pedal & Picnic package (in season), where a pair of bicycles are provided and a gourmet picnic lunch in a secluded park is found along a 6-mile loop. How about the KATY Trail for two? Bicycles and a bike rack are furnished in case you didn't bring your own. Other popular escapes are golf packages, Girl Friend Get-A-Ways, and a Wine Country Weekend. Rooms (and a suite) are $89 to $189. Call (573) 642-9229 or (888) 866-6661 for more information or visit their Web site at www.loganberry inn.com.

Beks Restaurant at 511 Court Street in Fulton (573-592-7117) offers upscale dining for medium prices. This charming eatery is housed in a circa 1880 building and serves imported beer, steaks (no, not just steaks, but filet with bleu cheese crumbles), and seafood. Try the salmon or shrimp Alfredo or some of the other specialities, such as Pepper Crusted Elk Rib Loin. See the complete menu at www.beksshop.com. There is live jazz music every Saturday night from 6:30 to 9:30 p.m. Restaurant hours are Monday through Wednesday 7:30 to 9:00 p.m., Thursday and Friday 7:30 to 10:00 p.m., and Saturday 8:30 to 10:00 p.m.

Fulton was also the home of Henry Bellamann, author of *King's Row.* Set in Fulton, the novel was made into a movie in the 1940s starring none other than Missourian Bob Cummings and a prepresidential Ronald Reagan. *Kingdom of Callaway Chamber of Commerce and Visitor's Center,* located at 409 Court Street (573-642-3055 or 800-257-3554; www.callaway chamber.com) displays memorabilia from the movie and offers a walking tour of the King's Row setting. Hours are Monday through Friday 8:00 a.m. to 5:00 p.m.

The *City of Fulton Walking Trail* is a 3-mile walking and biking trail that connects three parks. The trail runs along Stinson Creek, crosses a covered bridge, and passes below "Lover's Leap" cliff.

The *Fire Fighter's Memorial of Missouri,* 5548 Dunn Drive, Kingdom City (573-642-7692), features a bronze statue that is identical to the one donated to the city of New York after the terrorist attack of 9/11. Here tribute is paid to all the brave firefighters who have given their lives in the line of duty.

Summit Lake Winery, 1707 South Summit Drive, Holts Summit (573-896-9966), sits high on a bluff top overlooking US 54, the Missouri River, and Jefferson City. Try the distinctive Missouri wines on the bistro menu, and be sure to visit the tasting room. The winery is open year-round. In the summer enjoy the view in the outdoor garden terrace, or when the winds blow sit by the cozy fireplace. While *Crane's Country Store,* 10675 Old US 40, Williamsburg (573-254-3311), may look like an old-time General Store, once inside you find it is a real working store. Many antiques and memorabilia are on display. Have a sandwich and an ice-cold bottle of pop while you browse. Open 8:00 a.m. to 6:00 p.m. Monday through Saturday.

The tiny *Marlene's Restaurant & Antiques* (573-254-3356) at 10665 Old Highway 40, a few steps from the Country Store, has only six or seven tables. Marlene Crane is the co-owner of the Country Store with her husband Joe. This place is small but mighty. If you are traveling with a busload, just call ahead and they will make it happen.

From the Kingdom of Callaway, thence hie thyself back east along I-70 to *Graham Cave State Park* (573-564-3476) near *Danville.* (Oops, this royalty stuff gets to you!) Graham Cave is a huge arch of sandstone that dwarfs its human visitors. This rainbow-shaped cave is shallow, so the tour is a self-guided one. Spelunkers, don't let that put you off. Although this is not a deep-earth cave with spectacular formations, artifacts were found here dating from the area's earliest human habitation, some 10,000 years ago. Before the Native Americans formed themselves into tribes, Graham Cave was an important gathering place. Spear-type flints, made before the bow was invented, were found here, along with other signs of human use. The dig itself is fenced to prevent finds from being removed, but you can admire these fine examples of the earliest Show Me State inhabitants in the small museum in the park office. Take the Danville/Montgomery City exit off the interstate and follow Outer Road TT 2 miles west; it dead-ends at the park, so you can't go wrong. Check in at the park office to pick up a map to the cave. Check the park's Web site for the cave's seasonal hours at www.mostateparks.com/grahamcave.htm.

Places to Stay in Northeast Missouri

HANNIBAL

Comfort Inn
123 Huckleberry Drive
(573) 221-9988
Inexpensive

COLUMBIA

Best Western
Columbia Inn
3100 Interstate 70
Drive Southeast
(573) 474-6161
Inexpensive

Holiday Inn
2200 Interstate 70
Drive Southwest
(573) 445-8531
Inexpensive

LOUISIANA

River's Edge Motel
201 Mansion Street
(573) 754-4522
Inexpensive

ST. CHARLES

Red Roof Inn
I-70 and Zumbehl Road 3
(636) 947-7770
Inexpensive

MOBERLY

Best Western
Junction of US 63/US 24
(660) 263-6540
Inexpensive

KIRKSVILLE

Days Inn
US 63 South
(660) 665-8244
Inexpensive

Super 8 Motel
1101 Country Club Drive
(660) 665-8826
Inexpensive

MACON

Best Western Inn
28933 Sunset Drive
(660) 385-2125
Inexpensive

Super 8 Motel
1420 North Rutherford Street
(660) 385-5788
Inexpensive

MEXICO

Budget Inn
1010 Liberty
(573) 581-1440 or
(800) 528-1234
Inexpensive

FULTON

Westwood Motel
422 Gaylord Drive
(573) 642-5991
Inexpensive

KINGDOM CITY

Super 8 Motel
I-70 and US 54
(573) 642-2888
Inexpensive

KEARNEY

Super 8 Motel
210 Platte Clay Way
(816) 628-6800
Inexpensive

ST. JOSEPH

Best Western
Junction of Interstate 29
and U.S. Highway 169
(816) 232-2345
Inexpensive

BETHANY

Family Budget Inn
Exit 93, Highway 1351
(660) 425-7915
Inexpensive

MARYVILLE

Comfort Inn
2817 South Main
(660) 562-2002 or
(800) 528-1234
Inexpensive

CAMERON

Relax Inn
501 Northland Drive
(816) 632-6623
Inexpensive

SELECTED CHAMBERS OF COMMERCE

Kearney,
(816) 628-4229

Kirksville,
(816) 665-3766

Marceline,
(816) 376-3092

Paris,
(816) 327-4450

Plattsburg,
(816) 539-2649

Smithville,
(816) 532-0946

Places to Eat in Northeast Missouri

HANNIBAL

Lula Belle's
111 Bird
(573) 221-6662
Inexpensive

COLUMBIA

Booches Billiard Hall
110 South Ninth Street
(573) 874-9519
Inexpensive

Shakespeare's Pizza
Ninth and Elm Streets
(573) 449-2454
Inexpensive

KIRKSVILLE

Rosie's Northtown Cafe
2606 North Baltimore
(660) 665-8881
Inexpensive

KINGDOM CITY

Iron Skillet
I-70 and US 54
(573) 642-8684
Inexpensive

KEARNEY

Outlaw Barbecue
129 East Washington
(816) 628-6500
Inexpensive

MARYVILLE

A&G Restaurant
208 North Main Street
Business 71
(660) 582-4421
Inexpensive

Index

Abigail's, 225
Adam-Ondi-Ahman Shrine, 173
Aesthetica, 114
Akers, Tom, 67
Albrecht-Kemper Art Museum, 193
Allen's Back Yard Custom Stained
    Glass, 83
Alley Spring, 68
Alley Spring Mill, 68, 70
American Bounty Restaurant, 20
American Bowman Restaurant, 191
American Jazz Museum, 106
American Kennel Club Museum of
    the Dog, 15
American Saddlebred Horse
    Museum, 232
Americana Antique, Art, and
    Curio Shop, 24
Ameristar Casino St. Charles, 204
Amighetti's Bakery and Café, 13
Andrew Taylor Still National
    Osteopathic Museum, 228
Anna's Bake Shop, 171
Annapolis, 38
Annie Gunn's, 17
Anvil, The, 43
Arcadia Valley, 37
Arri's Pizza, 132
Arrow Rock, 129
Arrow Rock Bed and Breakfast, 130
Arrow Rock Tavern, 130
Art & Antiques & Blacksmith
    Shop, 225
Arthur Bryant Barbecue, 102
Artichoke Annie's, 224
Assumption Abbey, 74
At Sarah's Table, 186
Attic Treasures, 22
Audrain Country School, 232
August A. Busch Memorial
    Wildlife Area, 215

Augusta, 216
Augusta Winery, 216
Augusta Wood Ltd., 218
Auto World Museum, 234
Ava, 74
Avalon, 191
Avondale, 163
Avondale Furniture and
    Antiques, 163
Ayers Pottery, 211

B.B.'s Lawnside Bar-B-Que, 103
Bailey's Chocolate Bar, 8
Bairdstown Church Erratic, 227
Bankhead Chocolates, 206
Barn Again Bed and Breakfast
    Inn, 96
Barnett, 149
Bass Pro Shops Outdoor World, 60
Basswood Country Inn, 189
Battle of Lexington State
    Historic Site, 128
Becky's Old Fashioned Ice Cream
    Parlor & Emporium, 211
"Becky Thatcher" House, 210
Bek's Restaurant, 236
Bellevue Bed and Breakfast, 48
Benner House Bed and
    Breakfast, 191
Berger, 21
Bert & Ernie's, 197
Best of Kansas City, 113
Bethel, 214
Bethel German Colony Bed and
    Breakfast, 214
Beverly, 192
Beverly Hills Antiques Mall, 192
Bias Vineyards & Winery, 21
Big Bay Campgrounds, 83
Big Cedar Lodge, 91
Big Creek Country Music Show, 156

Big Oak Tree State Park, 51
Big Piney River National Scenic
    Trail Rides, 66
Big Spring, 70, 73
Big Spring Lodge, 73
Bingham-Waggoner Estate, 122
Birk's Gasthaus, 23
Bixby, 36
Black Archives of Mid-America, 108
Black Bamboo, 114
Black Canyon Ale House
    Microbrewery and Bistro, 153
Black River Cottage, 38
Bloomsday Books, 118
Blue Agave, 188
Blue Owl Restaurant and Bakery, 33
Blueberry Hill, 11
Bluebird Bistro, 116
Bluestem Missouri Crafts, 222
Bluff View Marina, 38
Blumenhof Vineyards and
    Winery, 219
Boathouse, 6
Bo'Bann Beads, 197
Bobby Powell's Jamboree, 38
Bohéme, 188
Boardwalk Grill, 151
Bolduc House Museum, 42
Bollinger Mill, 45
Bonne Terre, 34
Bonne Terre Mines, 34
Bonnots Mill, 23
Boone's Lick Trail Inn, 203
Boonville, 130
Bootheel region, 51–54
Borgman's Bed and Breakfast, 129
Bothwell State Park, 135
Boudreaux Louisiana Seafood &
    Steaks, 194
Bourbon, 30
Bowling Green, 206
Branson, 85
Branson Café, 87
Branson Scenic Railroad, 88
Bratcher Cooperage, 166

Bravo! Cucina Italiana, 105
Briar Patch, 71
Brick House Cafe and Pub, 199
Bristle Ridge Winery, 142
Broadway Café, 117
Broadway Roasting Co., 117
Brookside, 119
Brookside Toy & Science, 119
Broussard's Cajun Restaurant, 47
Brunke's Supply, 177
Bucks and Spurs Scenic River Guest
    Ranch, 74
Bucks Ice Cream, 221
Buffalo Creek Vineyards and
    Winery, 152
Bullwinkles Lounge, Rustic Lodge,
    & RV Park, 51
Burfordville, 45
Burfordville Covered Bridge, 45
Burgers' Smokehouse, 133
Burroughs Audubon Society
    Library, 136
Bynum Winery, 140

C.C. Sawyer's, 230
Cactus Rose, 151
Cafe Cedar, 187
Café des Amis, 188
Cafe Petit Four, 138
California, 133
Camdenton, 153
Camel Crossing Bed and
    Breakfast, 141
Cameron's Crag Bed &
    Breakfast, 86
Candlestick Inn, 89
Candy Factory, 222
Candyman's Mule Barn, 196
Cape Girardeau, 46
Carl's Gun Shop, 156
Carol Leigh's Specialties, 223
Carter's Gallery, 142
Carthage, 76
Cascone's Grill, 110
Cassville, 81

Castello's Ristorante, 51
Cathedral Church of the Prince of
    Peace, 92
Caveman BBQ, 66
Cedarcroft Farm, 140
Central Dairy, 132
Central Park Gallery, 115
Centralia, 232
Centralia Historical Society
    Museum, 233
Chance Gardens, 232
Charlecote, 118
Charley's Buffet, 147
Charlie Gitto's on The Hill, 12
Chateau on the Lake, 92
Cheep Antiques River Market
    Emporium, 111
Cheese Wedge, 217
Children's Peace Pavillion, 124
Chillicothe, 168
Christopher Elbow Artisanal
    Chocolates, 114
Church of St. Luke, the Beloved
    Physician, 179
Ciao! Bella Ristorante, 138
City Market, 108
City Museum, 13
City of Fulton Walking Trail, 236
Civil War Museum, 76
Clark, 233
Clarksville, 207
Clarksville Eagle Center, 208
Classic Cup, 117
Clay Images, 229
Claycomo, 167
Cliff House Bed & Breakfast, 150
Clifford Wirick Centennial
    House, 207
Clinton, 154
Clinton's, 121
Club 60, 76
Cockrell Mercantile Company, 139
Coldwater Ranch, 70
Colonial House Historic
    Reproductions, 78

Colonial Rug and Broom Shop, 172
Columbia, 220
Commerce, 48
Conception Abbey, 196
Conception Junction, 196
Concord Hill Bed and Breakfast, 220
Concordia, 143
Constant Cravings, 188
Cooky's, 157
Corbin Mill Place, 166
Country Club Plaza, 101
Country Colonial Bed and
    Breakfast, 173
Country Cottage 1840, 22
Country Cupboard Restaurant, 173
Courthouse Exchange, 121
Crane's Country Store, 236
Creative Candles, 114
Cross Country Trail Rides, 70
Crossroads Art District, 114
Crown Candy Kitchen, 8
Cuivre River State Park, 207
Cunetto House of Pasta, 12
Custard's Last Stand, 137–38

Daniel Boone State Park, 30
Daniel Boone's Home, 216
Danny Edwards Blvd BBQ, 103
Danville, 237
Dauphine Hotel, 23
Dawt Mill, 73
Dear's Rest Bed and Breakfast, 96
Defiance, 215
Depot, The, 35
Devil's Icebox, 223
Devil's Kitchen Trail, 82
Digiacinto's Italian Restaurant, 61
Dick's 5&10 Cent Store, 88
Die Brok Pann Bakery, 168
Dillard, 40
Dillard Mill State Historic Site, 40
Dirty Hippo, The, 184
Dixon, 25
Dobyns Restaurant, 90
Dogwood Canyon Nature Park, 95

Dorothea B. Hoover Historical
  Museum, 78
Downhome Oak & Spice, 172
Dr. Hertich's House, 44
Drum Room, 112
Dutch Bakery and Bulk Food
  Store, 133
Dutch Country Store, 149
Dutzow, 219

Eagle's Nest Winery, Inn, and Bistro,
  209
Eastlake Inn Bed and Breakfast, 11
Edgerton, 197
1858 Patee House, 193
El Acapulco, 51
El Dorado Springs, 156
Elephant Rocks State Park, 40
Elms Hotel, 177
Eminence, 68
Eminence Canoes, Cottages &
  Camp, 71
Eolia, 206
Ethel, 229
Ethel Museum, 229
Eureka, 17
Eureka Antique Mall, 17
Europa Market & Bakery, 118
Ewe's in the Country, 158
Excelsior, 149
Excelsior Book Store, 149
Excelsior Fabric, 149
Excelsior Harness Shop, 149
Excelsior Springs, 174
Excelsior Springs Fine Art
  Gallery, 179

Far West, 173
Feebler's Cove, 181
Ferrigno's Winery and B&B, 30
Fest Hall Restaurant, 214
Fiorella's Jack Stack Barbeque, 104
Fire Fighter's Memorial of
  Missouri, 236
Firehouse Gallery and Antiques, 17

Fisherman's Net, 50
Five Mile Corner Antique Mall, 196
Flat Bottles, 156
Flat Branch Pub and Brewery, 221
Fleming Park, 136
Float Stream Cafe, 72
Florida, 230
Florissant, 16
F.O.G.'s Cycles, 116
Forest Park, 6
Formosa Restaurant, 223
Fort Davidson State Historic Site, 36
Fort Leonard Wood, 67
Fort Osage, 125
4J Big Piney Horse Camp, 66
Francine's Pastry Parlor, 169
Fresh Ayers, Too, 211
Frisco Highline Trail, 60
Fulton, 233

Gables, The, 220
Gail Shen's Chinatown, 222
Gallery at the Spring, 84
Galloway, 64
Garozza's Ristorante, 111
Gartenfest Tea Room, 143
Garth Woodside Mansion, 211
Gary R. Lucy Gallery, 19
Gates and Sons Bar-B-Que, 102
Gates of Peace Jewish Cemetery, 209
Gateway Arch, 4
Gateway Riverboat Cruises, 6
Gem Theater Cultural and Performing
  Arts Center, 107
General John J. Pershing Boyhood
  Home, 227
General Sterling Price Museum, 227
General Sweeny's Museum of Civil
  War History, 64
Genghis Khan Mongolian Barbecue,
  115
George Washington Carver National
  Monument, 79
Georgetown, 135
Georgetown Bed and Breakfast, 135

Gingerich Dutch Pantry and
  Bakery, 172
Gino's Italian Cuisine, 185
Glasgow, 226
Glenn House, The, 47
Glore Psychiatric Museum, 194
Golden, 94
Golden City, 157
Golden Pioneer Museum, 94
Golden Prairie, 158
Golden Ox, 101
Good Ole Days Country Store, 36
Gower, 198
Gower Goodtimes Hall, 198
Graceland House Museum, 232
Gracie's Chocolate, 185
Graham Cave State Park, 237
Grain Valley, 139
Grand Avenue Bed and Breakfast, 78
Grand Divide, 228
Grand Gulf State Park, 73
Grand River Historical Society
  Museum, 169
Graniteville, 40
Gravois Mills, 151
Gray/Campbell Farmstead, 61
Great River Road Pottery Shop, 208
Greenwood, 140
Greenwood Antiques and Country
  Tea Room, 140
Grey Bear Winery and Vineyard, 153
Gruhlkes, 21
Grumpy's Bar-B-Q, 225

H & M Country Store, 172
H.M.S. Beagle, 189
H.S. Clay House, 218
Ha Ha Tonka State Park, 153
Hallmark Crown Center, The, 113
Hall of Waters, 174
Hamilton, 173
Hammon Glass, 211
Hammons Emporium, 157
Hannibal, 210

Hard Luck Diner, 87
Harlequin Antiques, 208
Harley Park, 131
Harling's Upstairs, 115
Harmer's Cafe, 197
Harrisonville, 155
Harry S Truman's Birthplace, 157
Hayes Hamburgers, 164, 235
Heaton-Bowman-Smith & Sidenfaden
  Funeral Museum, 194
Heinrichshaus Vineyards and
  Winery, 29
Henderson's, 226
Henry County Museum, 154
Hereford House, 114
Hermann, 22
Hermann Visitors' Information
  Center, 22
Hermannhoff Winery Festhalle, 23
Hess Pottery and Baskets, 84
Hidden Log Cabin Museum, 71
Highlandville, 92
Hill Homestead, 227
Hillcreek Fiber Studio, 223
Hilty Inn Bed and Breakfast, 144
Historic Liberty Jail, 166
Hodge Park, 164
Home Embellishments, 188
Honeyshuck, 206
Hornet Ghost Light, 80
Hospitality Inn, 186
Huber's Ferry Bed and Breakfast, 24
Hungry Mule Cafe, 196
Hunter-Dawson Home and
  Historic Site, 54
Hyde Mansion Bed and
  Breakfast, 169

I.B. Nuts & Fruit Too, 20
Independence, 119
Inn on Crescent Lake, 180
Inn St. Gemme Beauvais, 44
International Beanery, 184
International Bowling Museum, 5

Iron Mountain Railway, 45
Ironton, 34
It's a Hoot, 172

J.C. Penney Memorial Library and
  Museum, 173
Jackson, 44
Jaegers Subsurface Paintball, 165
Jail Marshall's Home and
  Museum, 121
Jamesport, 171
Jamestown, 133
Japanese Stroll Garden, 62
Java Jive Coffee House, 211
Jefferson City, 132
Jerre Anne Cafeteria and Bakery, 195
Jerry Litton Visitors' Center, 199
Jesse James Bank Museum Historic
  Site, 166
Jesse James Farm Historic Site, 182
Jesse James Museum, 193
Joe D's Winebar-Cafe & Patio, 119
Johnny Mack's Bar and Grill, 24
Johnny's Smoke Stak, 29
Johnson's Shut-ins, 38
Jolly Mill, 80
Joplin, 78

K.C. Power and Light District, 112
Kansas City, 101
Kansas City Museum, 114
Kate's Attic Antiques and Mini
  Mall, 209
KATY Trail, 133, 135, 137, 203,
  215, 224
KATY Trail Bed & Bikefest, 225
KATY Trail State Park, 219, 224
Kearney, 182
Kehde's Barbecue, 134
Kelly's, 117
Keytesville, 226
Kimmswick, 33
Kimmswick Bone Bed, 32
Kimmswick Korner Gift Shoppe, 34

Kimmswick Pottery, 34
King Jack Park, 81
Kingdom City, 236
Kingdom of Callaway Chamber of
  Commerce Visitor's Center, 236
Kirksville, 228
Kirksville College of Osteopathic
  Medicine, 228
Knob Noster, 142
Knucklehead's Saloon, 116
Kobe House Bakery, 124
Kroutman's Corner Café, 24

La Posada Grocery, 112
laFuente Mexican Restaurant, 186
Laclede, 227
Lake Jacomo, 136
Lake Lotawana, 139
Lake of the Ozarks, 147
Lake Wappapello, 50
Lake Wappapello Outdoor
  Theatre, 51
Lamar, 157
Lambert's Cafe, 49
Lampe, 95
Landers, 62
Lathrop, 196
Laumeier Sculpture Park, The, 11
Laura Ingalls Wilder–Rose Wilder
  Lane Museum and Home, 75
Laurie, 152
Le Fou Frog, 110
Leah's Bake Shop, 149
Leasburg, 30
Lebanon, 64
Lee's Summit, 137
Leggett House, 77
Lehman's, 148
Leila's Hair Museum, 123
Les Bourgeois Vineyards, 226
Lesterville, 37
Levee, 116
Lewis and Clark State Park, 193
Lexington, 126

Liberty, 166
Liberty Quilt Shoppe, 166
Lidia's, 113
Lillie's Cupboard, 34
Line Creek Park, 164
Lock and Dam No. 25, 207
Log House Museum, 127
Loganberry Inn, 235
Lone Jack, 140
Long Creek Herb Farm, 94
Loop, 8, 10
Louisiana, 208
Louisiana Guest House Bed and
  Breakfast, 209
Louisiana Historical Museum, 209
Lula Mac, 114
Lyceum Repertory Theatre, 129

Macon, 230
Maggie's Attic . . . to Cellar, 184
Maggie's Cellar and Loft, 119
Maggie Mae's Tea Room, 76
Magic House, 13
Maine Street Mall, 95
Malmaison, 19
Mama Toscano's, 12
Mannie's, 112
Mansfield, 75
Mansion Hill, 34
Maple Street Café and Bakery, 144
Marceline, 227
Margaret Harwell Art Museum, 50
Maries Hollow Herb Farm and
  Antiques, 26
Marigold Inn, 171
Marigold's, 171
Marina Grog and Galley, 139
Mark Twain Birthplace State Historic
  Site, 230
Mark Twain National Forest, 31, 40
Mark Twain State Park, 230
Marlene's Restaurant and
  Antiques, 237
Martha Lafite Thompson Nature
  Sanctuary, 167

Marthasville, 219
Martinali's, 166
Maryville, 196
Mastodon State Park, 32
Maxwell's Woodcarving, 143
McClay House, 134
McCormick Country Store, 190
McCormick Distilling Company, 190
Meramec Farm Cabins and Trail
  Riding Vacations, 30
Meramec State Park Lodge, 31
Mercer, 169
Mexico, 231
Michael Bauermeister Studio, 218
Mighty MO Canoe Rentals, 225
Mill Inn Restaurant, 180
Miller, 76
Miller's Rexall Drug Store, 230
Milo's Bocce Garden, 14
Mina Sauk Falls, 38, 39
Miner Indulgence Bed and
  Breakfast, 28
Mingo National Wildlife Refuge, 49
Miniature Museum of Greater St.
  Louis, The, 15
Miss Aimee B's Tea Room, 204
Missouri Bluffs Boutique, 191
Missouri Highland Farms, 133
Missouri Mines State Historic Site, 36
Missouri River State Trail, 215
Missouri State Fair, 135
Missouri Town 1855, 136
Missouri's Stonehenge, 28
Moberly, 230
Mockville Land & Cattle
  Company, 169
Mojo's to Go, 185
Molly's, 48
Moniteau Lick, 226
Montagues, 23
Montelle Winery, 216
Mother-in-Law House, 204
Mound City, 195
Mount Pleasant Winery, 217
Mountain Grove, 76

Mrs. Clemens Antique Mall, 213
Mrs. G's B&B, 143
Mt. Olivet Cemetery, 184
Mulberry Hill B&B, 156
Muny Theater, 6
Museum at the Old Courthouse, 29
Museum of Anthropology, 221
Museum of Art and Archaeology, 220
Museum of Westward Expansion, 5
Mutual Musicians' Foundation, 105
Myrtle's Place Backalley BBQ, 51

Nancy Ballhagen's Puzzles, 64
Napoleon, 126
National Frontiers Trails Center, 123
National WW I Museum at Liberty
   Memorial, 113
Nearly Famous Deli & Pasta
   House, 60
Negro League Baseball Museum, 106
Neighbor's Café, 155
Nelle Belle's Diner, 167
Nevada, 156
New Franklin, 131
New Madrid, 51
New Madrid Historical Museum, 51
Nichols Pottery Shop and Studio, 163
1924 Main, 114
Noel, 78
North Kansas City, 163
Not Just Cut and Dried, 20
Now You're Cookin', 188
Nunning House Bed and
   Breakfast, 194

Old Bank Museum, 176
Old Brick House, 42
Old Cathedral Museum, 6
Old Cooper County Jail and Hanging
   Barn, 131
Old Jail Museum Complex, 26
Old Mill Stitchery, 166
Old Red Mill, 68
Old St. Ferdinand's Shrine, 16
Old St. Vincent's Church, 46

Old Stagecoach Inn Museum, 66
Old Tavern Inn, 129
Olde English Garden Shoppe, 176
Olde Towne Mall, 176
Olive Branch, 151
Oliver House, 45
Omega Pottery Shop, 84
Onondaga Cave, 30
Orrick, 181
Osage Beach, 150
Osceola, 158
Osceola Cheese Shop, 158
Ozark, 95
Ozark Mountain Country Bed &
   Breakfast Service, 59, 89, 153
Ozark National Scenic Riverways, 69
Ozark Trail, 39
Ozarks, The, 143–56

Paradise Playhouse, 176
Paris, 230
Parkcliff Cabins, 83
Parkville, 187
Patricia's House, 88
Paxico, 49
Pearl Street Grill, 155
Pear Tree, 118
Peddler's Wagon, 187
Peola Valley Forge, 37
Perazzelli's Italian Ristorante, 140
Perryville, 44
Pershing State Park, 227
Peters Market, 128
Phillips Museum, 209
Phillips Place Bed & Breakfast, 230
Phil's Bar-B-Q, 16
Piedmont, 38
Piano Room Lounge, 119
Pierce City, 80
Pin-Up Bowl, 10
Piropos, 188
Pirtle's Weston Vineyards
   Winery, 190
Planters' Seed and Spice Co., 110
Plattdutsch Hadn Tohopa, 143

Platte City, 189
Plattsburg, 197
Pleasant Hill, 155
Pleasant Valley Quilts, 148
Point Lookout, 90
Ponak's Mexican Kitchen, 112
Pony Express Museum, 193
Poplar Bluff, 50
Poppy, 222
Porch Swing Inn, The, 189
Porky's Blazin' BBQ, 139
Potted Steer Restaurant, 151
Powell Gardens, 136
Power and Light District, K.C., 112
Power Plant Brewery, The, 188
"Praying Hands," 81
President Casino on the
    Admiral, The, 9

Rachel's Bed and Breakfast, 38
Rainey House, 28
Ranch House Restaurant, 77
Ray County Museum, 168
Ray's Lunch, 176
Reading Reptile, 119
Real Hatfield Smokehouse, 79
Reeds Spring, 83
Republic, 64
Rheinland Restaurant, 120
Rib, The, 81
Richard Saunders Antiques, 225
Richard's Puzzles, 65
Richland, 66
Richmond, 168
Ridgedale, 91
Riley's Irish Pub and Grill, 127
River Ridge Winery, 48
River's Bend Gallery, 188
River's Edge Resort, 71
River's Edge Restaurant, 23
Rivercene Bed and Breakfast, 131
Riverside Country Club, 169
Roaring River Inn, 82
Roaring River State Park, 82

Robidoux Row Museum, 193
Rocheport, 224
Rock Eddy Bluff Farm, 27
Rockcliffe Mansion, 213
Rolla, 28
Rolling Hills Store, 173
Rosebud, 16
Rosecliff on the River Lodge, 72
Route 66, 10

Sainte Genevieve Winery, 44
Sally Rand Museum, 194
Salt River Folklife Festival, 231
Salvatore's, 124
Santa Fe Restaurant, 229
Sara's Ice Cream and Antiques, 42
Scandinavia Place, 121
Scandinavian Shop, 176
School House Bed and Breakfast, 225
School of the Ozarks, 90
Science City, 107
Scotty's Trout Dock, 88
Season's Café & Bakery, 151
Sedalia, 134
Serendipity Bed and Breakfast, 122
Seven, 112
Sheffler Rock Shop and Geode
    Mine, 213
Shepherd of the Hills Fish
    Hatchery, 92
Shepherd of the Hills Inspiration
    Tower, 85
Sherwood Quilts and Crafts, 172
Shoal Creek, 164
Shop at Shady Gables, 145
Shrine of Mary Mother of the
    Church, 152
Shrine of St. Patrick, 213
Sikeston, 49
Silver Dollar City, 85, 88
Simply Butternut, 127
63 Diner, 223
Skif, 14
Skillet, The, 187

Slice of Pie, 29
Slivinskis' Bakery, 184
Smithville, 198
Smithville Lake, 198
Smoke House Market, 17
Sneathen Enterprises, 47
Snow Creek Ski Area, 192
Soulard, 14
Southern Hotel, 43
Spease Antiques, 197
Spiva Center for the Arts, 79
Springfield, 59
Springfield Art Museum, 62
Squaw Creek National Wildlife
    Refuge, 195
St. Albans, 18
St. Ambrose Church, 13
St. Charles, 203
St. Ferdinand's Shrine, Old, 16
St. James, 29
St. James Winery, 29
St. John's Episcopal Church, 206
St. Joseph, 193
St. Louis, 3
St. Louis Cardinals Hall of Fame, 5
St. Louis Cathedral, 8
St. Louis Mercantile Library
    Association, 8
St. Louis Walk of Fame, 10
St. Mary of the Barrens Church, 44
St. Mary's Episcopal Church, 111
St. Patrick, 213
St. Patrick's Catolic Church, 152
St. Roberts, 68
Stanton, 32
Ste. Genevieve, 41
Ste. Genevieve Museum, 42
Steamboat Arabia Museum, 108
Stone Canyon Pizza, 188
Stone Hill Wine Company, 90
Stone Hill Winery, 22
Stover, 152
Stroud's Restaurant, 104, 235
Stuff, 119

Sugar Creek, 124
Sugar Creek Winery, 216
Sullivan, 31
Summit Lake Winery, 236
Sun Ray Cafe, 116
Swan Lake National Wildlife
    Refuge, 229
Sweet Guy, The, 188
Sweet Things, 44

Table Rock State Park, 85
Taum Sauk Mountain, 39
Ted Drewes Frozen Custard, 9
Ten Mile, 230
Thespian Hall, 131
Thousand Hills State Park, 228
Three Dog Bakery, 117
Tightwad, 154
Tipton, 133
Tiques & Stuff, 197
Tivoli Theatre, 11
TLC Wellness Bed & Breakfast, 44
Top of the Rock golf course, 92
Touring Cyclist, 205
Tower Grove House, 3
Tower Rock, 44
Towosahgy State Historic Site, 52
Toys and Miniatures Museum, 118
Trailhead Brewing Company, 204
Trailside Cafe & Bike Rental, 225
Trash & Treasure, 184
Trenton, 169
Truman Presidential Library, 119

U.S. Army Engineer Museum, 67
Union, 16
Union Covered Bridge, 231
Union Italian Market, 16
Union Station, 4
Unity Village, 140
University of Missouri, 220

Vaile Mansion, 122
Van Buren, 71

Velvet Pumpkin Antiques, 127
Versailles, 144
Vichy, 28
Vichy Wye Restaurant, 28
Victorian Era Powers Museum, 76
Victorian Peddler Antiques Shop and
    Tea Room, 127
Victorian Veranda Bed and
    Breakfast, 36
Victorianne, The, 126
Vienna, 24
Vineyards, The, 190
Vintage Restaurant, 23
Virginia Rose Bed and Breakfast, 63

Wabash Barbecue, 179
Wallach House Antiques, 17
Walnut Street Inn Bed and
    Breakfast, 61
Warrensburg, 140
Washington, 19
Watkins Woolen Mill State Historic
    Site, 181
Waverly, 128
Waynesville, 66
Weathervane Antiques, 230
Weavers' Market, 149
Webb City, 81
Webster Groves, 12
Webster House, 114
West Plains, 73
Western Way Bed & Breakfast, 187
Westminster College, 233, 234

Weston, 189
Weston Bend State Park, 192
Weston Historical Museum, 189
Westphalia, 24
Westport, 117
Whimsy Hollow, 185
Whirlwind Ranch, 66
Whiskey Mansion B&B, 194
White Rose, 77
Wild Canid Survival and Research
    Center, 16
Wilderness Lodge, 37
William Jewell College, 167
Williamsburg, 237
Winery of the Little Hills, 204
Wines by Jennifer, 188
Winston Churchill Memorial and
    Library, 233
With a French Accent, 166
Woodhenge, 198
Woodland Carvings, 63
Woodside Restaurant, 212
Woodstock Inn Bed and
    Breakfast, 123
World Craft and Thrift Shop, 145

Yoshiko, J., 188
Younger's Livery, 155

Zanoni, 73
Ziggie's Café, 60
Zinnia, 12
Zona Rosa, 105

About the Author

Patti DeLano is a travel writer and photographer from the Kansas City area who has lived in the Ozarks of Missouri and vacationed across the borders in Arkansas and Kansas for more than forty years. She has also written *Arkansas Off the Beaten Path* and *Kansas Off the Beaten Path* for The Globe Pequot Press. She lives on the island of Venice, Florida, where she docks her sailing vessel, *Serafina*.

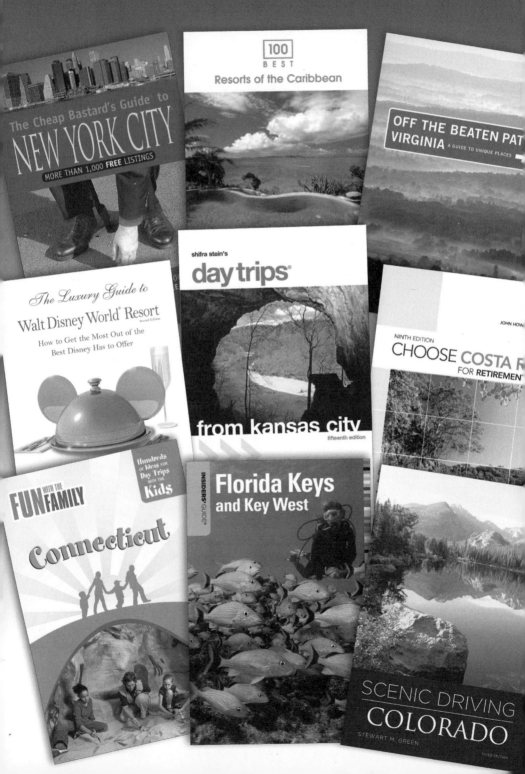